THE STUPIDITY OF WAR

It could be said that American foreign policy since 1945 has been one long miscue; most international threats—including during the Cold War—have been substantially exaggerated. The result has been agony and bloviation, unnecessary and costly military interventions that have mostly failed. A policy of complacency and appeasement likely would have worked better. In this highly readable book, John Mueller argues with wisdom and wit rather than ideology and hyperbole that aversion to international war has had considerable consequences. There has seldom been significant danger of major war. Nuclear weapons, international institutions, and America's role as a super power have been substantially irrelevant; post-Cold War policy has been animated more by vast proclamation and half-vast execution than by the appeals of liberal hegemony; and post-9/11 concerns about international terrorism and nuclear proliferation have been overwrought and often destructive. Meanwhile, threats from Russia, China, Iran, and North Korea, or from cyber technology are limited and manageable. Unlikely to charm Washington, Mueller explains how, when international war is in decline, complacency and appeasement become viable diplomatic devices and a large military is scarcely required.

JOHN MUELLER is a political scientist at Ohio State University, Senior Fellow at the Cato Institute, and member of the American Academy of Arts and Sciences.

The Stupidity of War

AMERICAN FOREIGN POLICY AND THE CASE FOR COMPLACENCY

JOHN MUELLER
Ohio State University and the Cato Institute

CAMBRIDGE
UNIVERSITY PRESS

University Printing House, Cambridge CB2 8BS, United Kingdom

One Liberty Plaza, 20th Floor, New York, NY 10006, USA

477 Williamstown Road, Port Melbourne, VIC 3207, Australia

314–321, 3rd Floor, Plot 3, Splendor Forum, Jasola District Centre,
New Delhi – 110025, India

79 Anson Road, #06–04/06, Singapore 079906

Cambridge University Press is part of the University of Cambridge.

It furthers the University's mission by disseminating knowledge in the pursuit of
education, learning, and research at the highest international levels of excellence.

www.cambridge.org
Information on this title: www.cambridge.org/9781108843836
DOI: 10.1017/9781108920278

© John Mueller 2021

First published 2021

Printed in the United Kingdom by TJ Books Limited, Padstow Cornwall

A catalogue record for this publication is available from the British Library.

Library of Congress Cataloging-in-Publication Data
NAMES: Mueller, John E., author.
TITLE: The stupidity of war : American foreign policy and the case for complacency /
John Mueller.
OTHER TITLES: American foreign policy and the case for complacency
DESCRIPTION: Cambridge, United Kingdom ; New York : Cambridge University Press,
2021. | Includes index.
IDENTIFIERS: LCCN 2020029064 (print) | LCCN 2020029065 (ebook) | ISBN
9781108843836 (hardback) | ISBN 9781108920278 (ebook)
SUBJECTS: LCSH: United States – Foreign relations – 20th century. | Cold War –
Influence. | United States – Military relations – 21st century. | United States – Military
policy – History – 20th century. | United States – Military policy – History – 21st century. |
War (Philosophy)
CLASSIFICATION: LCC E744 .M84 2021 (print) | LCC E744 (ebook) | DDC 327.73009/04–dc23
LC record available at https://lccn.loc.gov/2020029064
LC ebook record available at https://lccn.loc.gov/2020029065

ISBN 978-1-108-84383-6 Hardback

To Judy, again and always, and to Lois, Phyllis, Karl, Michelle, Karen, Erik, Susan, Kraig, Timothy, Sam, Cameron, Kara, Malcolm, Atticus, and, of course, Lida.

Contents

Figures

Acknowledgements

For help, comments, and advice along the way, I am grateful to Robert Jervis, John Glaser, Chris Preble, Chris Fettweis, Alex Thompson, Mark Stewart, and Karl Mueller. I would like to express particular gratitude to Steve Pinker for thoughtful advice, extended comments, and invaluable support. And thanks as well to Robert Dreesen and the gang at Cambridge University Press, including the anonymous reviewers, for putting this all together.

War is mankind's most tragic and stupid folly.

> General Dwight D. Eisenhower, Commencement speech at the United States Military Academy, West Point, June 3, 1947. Quoted by President Barack Obama at the same venue, May 28, 2014.

War is a profanity because, let's face it, you've got two opposing sides trying to settle their differences by killing as many of each other as they can.

> General Norman Schwarzkopf, 1991.

The Rise of War Aversion and the Decline
of International War

The idea that war is profoundly stupid has likely been evident pretty much for ever. One of the most famous wars in history (or mythology), after all, was fought over an errant wife, lasted for ten brutal years, and ended in the violent annihilation of an entire city-state. Later, Shakespeare had one of his characters rather ungraciously reflect on the essential stupidity of the much-storied enterprise in sentiments that had likely occurred to other people from time to time: "For every false drop in her bawdy veins a Grecian's life hath sunk; for every scruple of her contaminated carrion weight, a Trojan hath been slain: since she could speak, she hath not given so many good words breath as for her Greeks and Trojans suffer'd death."[1]

It took until recent decades, however, for substantial numbers of people effectively to act on and abide by the idea – and then only on one part of the planet (at least at first) and, for the most part, only for international war. By May 15, 1984, however, estimates historian Paul Schroeder, the countries in Europe had substantially managed to remain at peace with each other for the longest continuous stretch of time since the days of the Roman Empire. That rather amazing record has now been further extended, and in 2004, economist Bradford de Long proclaimed that by then we had gone through the longest period of peace on the Rhine since the second century BCE. The word, or term, "Europe" appears only to have been coined in the fourth century BCE, so that, by now, the continent may well have experienced (and, for the most part enjoyed) the longest period free from interstate war since the continent, itself, was invented as a concept.[2]

This is particularly impressive because Europe was once the most warlike of continents: Thomas Jefferson, for example, proclaimed it to be "an arena of gladiators." Commonly, as military and diplomatic historian Michael Howard puts it, war there "was an almost automatic activity, part of the natural order of things," and Charles Tilly observes, "It is hardly worth asking *when* states warred, since most states were warring most of the time." "Given the scale and frequency of war during the preceding centuries in Europe," notes Evan Luard, the decline of interstate war in Europe is "a change of spectacular proportions: perhaps the single most striking discontinuity that the history of warfare has anywhere provided."[3] Increasingly, that kind of war has come to seem not only futile, destructive, and barbaric, but profoundly stupid.

In reviewing *Retreat from Doomsday*, my 1989 book suggesting that major war – war among developed states – was obsolescent, Howard expressed a degree of skepticism, helpfully suggesting that "the prudent reader will check that his air raid shelter is in good repair."[4] However, by 1991 he was musing that it had become "quite possible that war in the sense of major, organized armed conflict between highly developed societies may not recur, and that a stable framework for international order will become firmly established." Two years later, the military historian and analyst John Keegan went somewhat further, concluding that the kind of war he was principally considering could well be in terminal demise: "War, it seems to me, after a lifetime of reading about the subject, mingling with men of war, visiting the sites of war and observing its effects, may well be ceasing to commend itself to human beings as a desirable or productive, let alone rational, means of reconciling their discontents." By the end of the century, Mary Kaldor was suggesting that "The barbarity of war between states may have become a thing of the past," and by the beginning of the new one, Robert Jervis had concluded that war among the leading states will not occur in the future, or, in the words of Jeffrey Record, "may have disappeared altogether." In 2005, historian John Gaddis labeled war among major states an anachronism.[5] Moreover, suggests Jervis, this "is the greatest change in international politics that we have ever seen." Notes Paul Johnson, "As a historian, I can confidently say that this is unique: There is no precedent in world history for war being ruled out of calculations at such a high level."[6]

Thus, reversing the course of several millennia, developed countries (whether in Europe or not) no longer really consider war among them to be a sensible method for resolving their disputes. In fact, however, not only have developed countries, including the Cold War superpowers, managed to stay out of war with each other since 1945, but there have been remarkably few international wars of any sort during the period, particularly in recent decades, as Figure 0.1 suggests.

Although armed contests between the Israeli government and Palestinian rebels have frequently erupted, no Arab or Muslim country has been willing since 1973 to escalate the contest to international war by sending its troops to participate directly. And after a series of international wars, India and Pakistan have not really waged one since 1971. The only truly notable exception between 1973 and the end of the Cold War in 1989 (and it is an important

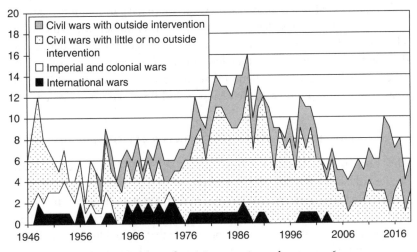

FIGURE 0.1 Number of ongoing wars in each year, 1946–2019

one) was the war between Iran and Iraq that lasted from 1980 to 1988.[7] Meanwhile, colonial wars, once an major preoccupation of many European countries, died out with the institution of colonialism.

After the Cold War, there have been some policing wars in the Middle East engendered by the United States – one in 1991 to eject invading Iraq from Kuwait, and two post-9/11 wars that succeeded in pushing out offending regimes in Afghanistan and Iraq but then degenerated into extended civil conflict waged by insurgent forces against the invaders. There have also been armed conflicts between Israel and substate groups on its borders. But of the international wars waged since the end of the Cold War, there has been only one that fits cleanly into the classic model in which two countries have it out over some issue of mutual dispute, in this case territory: the almost unnoticed, but quite costly, conflict between Ethiopia and Eritrea that transpired between 1998 and 2000. And, a fifth of the way through the twenty-first century, the brief regime-toppling invasions by the United States of Afghanistan and Iraq stand out as the only international wars of the period.

It should also be noted that there was a considerable expansion over the last half-century or more in the number of independent states. When these states were colonies, they could not, by definition, engage in international war with each other. It is particularly impressive that there have been so few international wars during a period in which the number of entities capable of conducting them has increased so greatly.

As Figure 0.1 also demonstrates, however, there have been quite a few civil wars – though perhaps declining somewhat in number since the 1980s. Moreover, although states may have been restrained from conducting wars directly between themselves, they have often intervened on one side or the other in civil wars, a phenomenon that has, if anything, increased in recent years – seen most prominently in civil wars in Libya, Syria, and Yemen.

THE RISE OF AVERSION TO INTERNATIONAL WAR

This book is something of a biography of the rise of the idea that war, particularly international war, is really very stupid, and it often draws on, updates, extends, and reconsiders my earlier writings. I argue that it was primarily the rise of an aversion to international war (not, for example, nuclear fears or American efforts at security provision) that has led to the remarkable, and expanding, condition of international peace that has arisen since 1945. More broadly, it really seems time to take into account the consequences of the fact that countries, particularly leading or developed ones, reversing the course of several millennia, have come to envision international war as a stupid method for resolving their disputes.[8] That is, the aversion to international war or the rise of something of a culture or society of international peace that has substantially enveloped the world has consequences: it should be seen as a causative or facilitating independent variable.

There may be some danger, however, in using the phrase "a culture of international peace" because this can conjure up images of grinning cherubs, cooing doves, and choirs of angels singing "peace on earth, goodwill to persons of all genders." In my view, it simply means a condition in which war has substantially been abandoned by states as a method for dealing with each other, not that perfect harmony or justice has been achieved.[9] There may well have been no essential improvement in the behavior or personalities of young men of the dueling class when that method of dispute resolution disappeared from their repertory. They likely remained as self-interested, grasping, petulant, small-minded, and disagreeable as ever. Indeed, in net, it is possible that civility may even have declined some. In the dueling age, to loudly and boorishly assert to a man in public that he is a bloody liar or (as happens in Tolstoy's novel *War and Peace*) that his wife has been sleeping around, might well lead to a dueling challenge with decidedly unpleasant results for the offending boor. That deterrent to incivility evaporated when dueling went out of fashion – when dueling came to be deemed stupid.[10] In like manner, a culture of international peace will not necessarily lead to the demise of war or of warlike behavior in total. Indeed, states may well feel freer to engage in behavior that might once have been taken to be *casus belli* such as tinkering in civil wars, seizing bits of territory, firing shots across bows, lobbing cyber balloons, exacting economic sanctions, or poaching fish.[11]

For my purposes, then, "peace" simply means agreement with the observation of American General Norman Schwartzkopf that "War is a profanity because, let's face it, you've got two opposing sides trying to settle their differences by killing as many of each other as they can."[12] That the process is less than fully cherubic, much less perfect, is suggested by the fact that Schwarzkopf uttered those words three months before ordering half a million troops into combat in the Gulf War of 1991.

However, whatever the flaws and whatever international incivility may remain, a pronounced, essentially Schwartzkopfian, shift in attitudes toward international war has taken place over the course of the twentieth century. This can perhaps be quantified in a rough sort of content analysis. Before World War I it was very – even amazingly – easy to find instances in which serious writers, analysts, and politicians in Europe and North America, far from regarding wars between states to be stupid, enthusiastically proclaimed them to be beautiful, honorable, holy, sublime, heroic, ennobling, natural, virtuous, glorious, cleansing, manly, necessary, and progressive. At the same time, they deemed peace to be debasing, trivial, and rotten, and characterized by crass materialism, artistic decline, repellant effeminacy, rampant selfishness, base immorality, petrifying stagnation, sordid frivolity, degrading cowardice, corrupting boredom, bovine content, and utter emptiness.[13] After World War I, such people become extremely rare, though the excitement of the combat experience continued (and continues) to have its fascination to some. Where international war had been accepted as a standard and permanent fixture, the idea suddenly gained substantial currency that it was actually quite stupid, that it should no longer be an inevitable or necessary fact of life, and that major efforts should be made to abandon it.

The change has often been noted by historians and political scientists. Arnold Toynbee points out that World War I marked the end of a "span of five thousand years during which war had been one of mankind's master institutions." In his study of wars since 1400, Luard observes that "the First World War transformed traditional attitudes toward war. For the first time there was an almost universal sense that the deliberate launching of a war could now no longer be justified." Bernard Brodie points out that "a basic historical change had taken place in the attitudes of the European (and American) peoples toward war." Eric Hobsbawm concludes, "In 1914 the peoples of Europe, for however brief a moment, went lightheartedly to slaughter and to be slaughtered. After the First World War they never did so again." And K. J. Holsti observes, "When it was all over, few remained to be convinced that such a war must never happen again."[14]

What was so special about World War I? There seem to be several possibilities.

The first is the most obvious: the war was massively destructive. But in broader historical perspective, the destructiveness of the war does not seem to be all that unique.[15] There had been hundreds, probably thousands, of wars previously in which far higher casualty rates were suffered – the "sack" of cities like Troy, for example, resulted in utter annihilation through massacre and enslavement (often sexual) and through the looting and incinerating of the city itself. Rape was also routine. Genghis Khan exultantly expressed the narcissistic sadism of the enterprise: "the greatest pleasure in life is to defeat your enemies, to chase them before you, to rob them of their wealth, to see those dear to them bathed in tears, to ride their horses, and to clasp to your breast their wives and daughters."[16] According to Frederick the Great, Prussia lost one-ninth of its population in the Seven Years War.[17] This was a proportion higher than almost any suffered by any combatant in the wars of the twentieth century.[18] Holsti calculates that, "if measured in terms of direct and indirect casualties as a proportion of population," the Thirty Years War was Europe's most destructive armed conflict.[19] In addition, there was a substantial belief that many of the wars had been even more horrible than they actually were. For example, a legend prevailed for centuries after the Thirty Years War holding that it had caused Germany to suffer a 75 percent decline in population.[20] Yet disastrous experiences and beliefs like this had never brought about a widespread revulsion with international war as an institution nor did they inspire effective, organized demands that it be banished. Instead, war continued to be accepted as a normal way of doing things.

Actually, in some respects World War I could be seen to be an *improvement* over many earlier wars. Civilian loss, in the West at least, was proportionately quite low, while earlier wars had often witnessed utter annihilation. And a wounded soldier was more likely to recover than in earlier wars where the nonambulatory wounded were characteristically abandoned on the battlefield to die in lingering agony from exposure and blood loss. Disease was also beginning to become less of a scourge than in most earlier wars.

Nor was World War I special in the economic devastation it caused. Many earlier European wars had been fought to the point of total economic exhaustion. For example, Richard Kaeuper's analysis of the economic effects of decades of war in the late Middle Ages catalogues the destruction of property, the collapse of banks, the severing of trade and normal commerce, the depopulation of entire areas, the loss of cultivated land, the decline of production, the reduction of incomes, the disruption of coinage and credit, the hoarding of gold, and the assessment (with attendant corruption) of confiscatory war taxes.[21] By contrast, within a few years after World War I, most of the combating nations had substantially recovered economically: by 1929 the German economy was fully back to prewar levels, while the French economy had surpassed prewar levels by 38 per cent.[22]

World War I toppled several political regimes – in Germany, Russia, Austria-Hungary, and Ottoman Turkey – but it was hardly unusual in this respect. And to suggest that the war was new in the annals of warfare in its tragic futility, sustained stupidity, and political pointlessness would be absurd – by most reasonable standards, huge numbers of previous wars would rival, and often surpass, it on those dimensions

World War I is often seen to be unusual because it was so unromantic. But if that is so, it is because people were ready to see, and to be repulsed by, the grimness of warfare. Mud, filth, leeches, lice, and dysentery were not invented in 1914, but are standard accompaniments of warfare as are terrible food; germ-ridden water; stale cigarettes; the absence of women; bone-deep fatigue; syphilitic prostitutes; watered or even poisonous liquor; sleep deprivation; family separation and homesickness; absence of privacy; constant and often brutal and pointless harassment or physical abuse by superiors and by the incoherent system; exposure to extremes of weather; masturbatory fantasies that become decreasingly stimulating; and boredom that can become cosmic, overwhelming, stupefying – an emotion, though only occasionally remarked upon, that is far more common in war than the rush that comes with combat.

For Europeans and North Americans, World War I was special in that it followed a century characterized by the beginnings of phenomenal economic growth, something that may have been in part facilitated by a century of decreased warfare in Europe.[23] However, the growth by itself did not change attitudes toward war. Even as they were enjoying the benefits of periods of comparative peace, people continued to assume war to be a normal fact of life and most continued to thrill at the thought of it.

In the end, the war seems to have been unique in one important respect: it was the first war in history to have been preceded by organized antiwar agitation. There had been some glimmerings earlier.[24] However, organized opposition to war substantially began only in 1889 with the publication of an antiwar novel *Lay Down Your Arms* by an Austrian noblewoman, Bertha von Suttner, that became a surprise international best seller. Suttner says the novel's remarkable success was "accidental," but it was an idea whose time had come, or, as she explained, "an idea that is in the air, that is slumbering as an idea in untold minds, as a longing in untold hearts." Applying a fanciful metaphor, she continued, "the stroke of lightning is only possible if the air is loaded with electricity."[25]

The novel tells the story of a woman, not unlike Suttner herself, who gradually comes to abhor war and its barbaric excesses, its consummate stupidity, and its absurd and often incoherent justifications. Like *Uncle Tom's Cabin*, to which the novel has often been compared, it is a brilliant piece of propaganda. When the woman's husband, an officer who has come to share her antiwar convictions, is missing in action in the two-month-long Austro-Prussian War of 1866, she goes to look for him and, late in the book, on page 249, she begins to describe the aftermath of battle:

> Before my feet, they laid a man who made, without cessation, a continuous gurgling sound. I bent down to speak a word of sympathy to him, but I started back in horror, and covered my face with both hands. The impression me had been too fearful. It was no longer human countenance – the lower jaw shot away, one eye welling out, and, added to that, a stifling reek of blood and corruption.[26]

Descriptions like that then continue for 40 pages, rather deftly supplying a counter to the popular image of war as beautiful, sublime, ennobling, glorious, and cleansing – although Suttner is too delicate to mention rape and dysentery, two of warfare's most common accompaniments.

Suttner thereafter was a major figure in a peace movement that rapidly grew, and in 1903 she was declared by a Berlin newspaper after a survey to be the most important woman of the time.[27] Peace societies proliferated; famous businessmen like Andrew Carnegie and Alfred Nobel (Suttner received the peace prize in 1906) joined the fray; various international peace congresses were held, and governments began to take notice and even sometimes to participate. Some joined the movement because, like Suttner, they had come to regard the institution as ridiculous and barbarous (her favorite descriptor), others, like the Quakers, because they considered it immoral, and others, like Norman Angell, another best-selling author, because they found it to be economically futile and stupid in that sense.[28] Meanwhile, political liberals and feminist leaders were accepting war opposition as part of their intellectual baggage. And many Socialists were making it central to their ideology.[29]

Although it was still very much a minority movement and largely drowned out by those who exalted war, its gadfly arguments were persistent and unavoidable. And the existence of this movement may well have helped Europeans and North Americans to look at the institution of war in a new way when the massive conflict of 1914–18 entered their experience. At any rate, within half a decade, war opponents, once a derided minority, became a decided majority: everyone now seemed to be a peace advocate, and international war of that sort came to be regarded as profoundly stupid.

Before the war, artists had been among the loudest lauding war. French novelist Émile Zola proclaimed that "war is life itself.... it is only warlike nations which have prospered"; English art critic John Ruskin animatedly designated war to be "the foundation of all the high virtues and faculties of men"; Russian composer Igor Stravinsky claimed that "war is necessary for human progress"; and, as he enlisted for combat in 1914 (where he was to perish from an infected mosquito bite in the war's eighth month), the English poet Rupert Brooke penned a poem ironically entitled "Peace" in which he deemed going to war to be like leaping "into cleanness."[30] In stark contrast, recalls Bernard Brodie, "one must have lived through that postwar period to appreciate fully how the antiwar and antimilitary attitudes engulfed all forms of literature and in time the movies."[31]

As something of an indicator of the change, one might look at Wikipedia's "List of plays with anti-war themes." As accessed on June 26, 2020, the anonymous compilers include three from the 5th century BCE: two by Aristophanes and one by Euripides. The next entry was staged in 1928, and it was followed by dozens more. The list-makers may have missed a few during the remarkable gap of two millennia such as Shakespeare's *Troilus and Cressida*. And, after that gap, they surely should have included the 1927 musical *Strike Up the Band*, the title song for which includes these irreverent lines: "We're in a bigger, better war/For your diplomatic pastime/We don't know what we're fighting for/But we didn't know the last time."[32] As for the movies, King Vidor's anti-war epic *The Big Parade* became the second highest grossing film of the silent era.

The real threat and the true enemy, then, had become *war itself*, and the preservation of international peace became a prime goal. Accordingly, the peacemakers of 1918 adapted many of the devices antiwar advocates had long been promoting, at least in part. A sort of world government, the League of Nations, was fabricated. Aggression – the expansion of international boundaries by military force – was ceremoniously outlawed. Legal codes and arbitration bodies that might be able to deal peacefully with international disputes were also set up, and quite a bit of thought went into the issue of arms control and disarmament.

World War I essentially served as a catalyst. It was not the first horrible or profoundly stupid international war in history, but, perhaps at least in part because of the exertions of the prewar antiwar movement, it was the first in which people were widely capable of recognizing and being thoroughly repulsed by those horrors and stupidities and in which they were substantially aware that viable alternatives existed.

It could be said that the war proved to be something of a "Black Swan," a concept invented by Nicholas Taleb to depict an event or episode that has "an extreme impact" and is characterized by being substantially unexpected and by grabbing the emotions and becoming popularly embraced as a major happening.[33]

However, one could also see the change as part of broader, longer-term developments. In particular, Steven Pinker has argued that "violence has declined over long stretches of time," and he documents declines, particularly in Europe, in chronic raiding and feuding, in homicide, and in such once socially sanctioned forms of violence as despotism, slavery, dueling, judicial torture, superstitious killing, sadistic punishment, cruelty to animals, capital punishment, and infanticide. He attributes the changes to declines in the appeals of dominance, revenge, and sadism, and to rises in empathy, self-control, moral progress, and reason, and he sees the mechanism of such changes in the rise in better governance, "gentle commerce," "feminization," and "the escalator of reason."[34] It is certainly possible to see some reverse trends, or as-yet inadequate developments, in the remarkable rise in the acceptance of a high-tech form of infanticide, abortion, which over the last decades has resulted in the extinguishment of more lives than World War II, and in the almost astonishing lack of empathy in the American public over the hundreds of thousands of lives that have been lost in the Middle East as a result of the American military interventions there.[35] But an aversion to international war, as Pinker discusses extensively, certainly fits into the trends in violence he documents.

In addition, there have been long-term developments in international affairs in Europe and North America that might have contributed to, or presaged, the change after World War I.[36] For example, in his survey of war since 1400, Luard notes an interesting change in the way war has been justified. In the first century or two of that period, no justification seemed necessary – war was seen as a "glorious undertaking" and a "normal feature of human existence, a favorite pastime for princes and great lords." By 1700 or so, however, attitudes had changed enough so that rulers found they were "expected to proclaim their own love of peace and their desire to avoid the tragedies of war."[37] They also gained a degree of control over war. Paul Schroeder suggests that "a fair generalization about international politics in the fifteenth, sixteenth, or seventeenth centuries is that most wars that could have started, did, and that most crises led within a relatively short time to war."

Later, particularly by the nineteenth century, "most wars that could have happened did not happen; most crises were managed more or less successfully."[38] And it should also be noted that some countries were altering their international life-style and seeking to avoid war entirely. These included the Netherlands, which came to concentrate on commercial and colonial ventures and sought to avoid all international war in Europe, a pattern Richard Rosecrance has examined more generally.[39] And Sweden, once a very warlike country, came eventually to regard war as stupid and has avoided it for centuries. However, although Europe did manage substantially to avoid international war from 1815 to 1854 and from 1871 to 1914, it still engaged in plenty of warfare elsewhere: fully 199 of the 244 wars that took place in the world between 1789 and 1917 were wars of colonization or decolonization – including by the Netherlands.[40] And, as noted, war remained, in general, an exalted and admired enterprise.

Finally, it is also possible that the antiwar movement, building on such trends and developments, was in the process of gathering an unstoppable momentum like the earlier antislavery movement.[41] For example, Norman Angell argues in his memoirs that if World War I could have been delayed a few years, "Western Europe might have acquired a mood" which would have enabled it to avoid it.[42] And some members of the prewar peace movement were in fact beginning to feel a not entirely unjustified sense of optimism. As the distinguished British historian G. P. Gooch concluded hopefully in 1911, "We can now look forward with something like confidence to the time when war between civilized nations will be considered as antiquated as the duel."[43]

The central problem with assigning a role to such gradual developments, however, is that before 1914 the institution of war still retained much of the glamor and the sense of inevitability it had acquired over the millennia. It still appealed not only to wooly militarists, but also to popular opinion and to romantic intellectuals as something that was sometimes desirable and ennobling, often useful and progressive, and always thrilling. Indeed, before 1914 the anti-war movement was still being ridiculed as a flaky fringe group. Bertha von Suttner was characterized as "a gentle perfume of absurdity" and the public image of her German Peace Society as "a comical sewing bee composed of sentimental aunts of both sexes." Angell reports that blunt friends advised him to "avoid that stuff or you will be classed with cranks and faddists, with devotees of Higher Thought who go about in sandals and long beards, live on nuts."[44] As Schroeder puts it, "the great majority of leaders and opinion-leaders everywhere believed ... that war was natural and more or less inevitable." Wrote the exasperated von Suttner in 1912, "War continues to exist not because there is evil in the world, but because people still hold war to be a good thing," while the pacifist William James lamented, "The plain truth is that people *want* war."[45] As Luard puts it, "what had not changed was the conviction that war remained an inevitable feature of human existence."[46]

Longer-term trends may have played a role, but in this case the change in attitudes toward war was sudden, not gradual. For the abolition of war to become an accepted commodity, it was probably necessary for there to be a black swan event: one more vivid example of how appallingly stupid the hoary, time-honored institution really was. As it happened, people in Europe and North America were at last ready to begin to accept the message.

Obviously, however, there were two key countries where, in different ways, that message failed to be delivered.

One was Japan, a distant, less developed state that had barely participated in World War I. Many people there could still enthuse over war in a manner that had largely vanished in Europe: it was, as Alfred Vagts points out, the only country where old-style militarism survived the Great War.[47] For example, a Japanese war ministry pamphlet of 1934 proclaimed war to be "the father of creation and the mother of culture."[48] It took a cataclysmic war for the Japanese to learn the lesson almost all Europeans had garnered from World War I. But the Japanese were to embrace it well. The war in the Pacific, then, while not inevitable, was clearly in the cards due to Japan's general willingness to risk all to achieve its extravagant imperial ambitions.

This was not the case in the second country, Germany. In contrast to Japan, it appears that only one person there continued to embrace war. He proved to be crucial, however. As military historian John Keegan puts it, "only one European really wanted war: Adolf Hitler."[49] In order to bring about another continental war it was necessary for Germany to desire to expand into areas that would inspire military resistance from other major countries and to be willing and able to pursue war when these desires were so opposed. There was simply no one else around who had these blends of desires and capacities. As Gerhard Weinberg concludes, Hitler was "the one man able, willing, and even eager to lead Germany and drag the world into war."[50]

That is to say, but for Hitler, the massive war there would likely never have come about – he was a necessary cause (if not, of course, a sufficient one).[51] As Jervis notes, few scholars believe that World War II would have occurred in Europe "had Adolf Hitler not been bent on expansion and conquest." And F. H. Hinsley says, "Historians are, rightly, nearly unanimous that . . . the causes of the Second World War were the personality and the aims of Adolf Hitler. . . . [I]t was Hitler's aggressiveness that caused the war." Similarly, William Manchester observes that the war Hitler started was one "which he alone wanted," while John Lukacs finds that World War II "was inconceivable and remains incomprehensible without him."[52]

Indeed, Hitler was successful in the 1930s in part because no one else on the continent could imagine that anyone could possibly be so stupid as to desire war. As Jeffrey Record notes, "few suspected that Hitler *wanted* war," while Paul Kennedy points out that "The long shadow cast by the memories and losses of the First World War, a self-inflicted disaster for Europe, [was] of such magnitude that it was impossible to imagine that governments would want to go to war again," and Ernest May notes that "Understanding of Hitler's aims and policies was clouded ... by a general unwillingness to believe that any national leader might actually *want* another Great War."[53]

World War I, then, shattered what some have called the "war-like spirit" in Europe and North America and made large majorities there into unapologetic peace-mongers. World War II, it appears, reinforced that lesson in those places (probably quite unnecessarily), and it converted the previously militaristic Japanese in Asia. As General Dwight Eisenhower said in a commencement speech at West Point in 1947, "War is mankind's most tragic and stupid folly." Moreover, the aversion to international war has gradually spread throughout the world in subsequent decades.

Thus, international war seems to be in pronounced decline because of the way attitudes toward it have changed, roughly following the pattern by which the ancient and once-formidable formal institution of slavery became discredited and then obsolete.[54] And the process of change suggests that international war is merely an idea, an institution or invention that has been grafted onto international society.[55] Its replacement in much of the world by a culture or society of international peace has come about, it seems, without the intervention or service of cherubs, doves, and choirs of angels; without changing human nature; without creating an effective world government or system of international law; without modifying the nature of the state or the nation-state; without fabricating an effective moral or practical equivalent; without enveloping the earth in democracy or prosperity; without devising ingenious agreements to restrict arms or the arms industry; without altering the international system; without improving the competence of political leaders; and without doing much of anything about nuclear weapons.

Steven Pinker understandably yearns for "a causal story with more explanatory muscle than 'Developed countries stopped warring because they got less warlike'" and, although he does hold that "new ideas" can sometimes have such an impact, he suggests that "the most satisfying explanation of a historical change is one that identifies an exogenous trigger."[56] Similarly, Azar Gat, allows that "attitude change has undoubtedly been involved in the modern decrease of war," but questions its historic importance and is decidedly uncomfortable with the notion that "the 'attitude change' toward war had no particular reason and was not different from a fashion or a fad that suddenly catches on."[57] And Jack Levy and William Thompson, while acknowledging that "ideas are not unimportant," contend that they do not "drop from the sky," but "emerge from and coevolve with more material changes."[58]

Yet, as Ernest Gellner observes, "A great deal can happen without being necessary and without being inscribed into any historic plan," and Francis Fukuyama has pointed to what he calls "the autonomous power of ideas."[59] The remarkable rise of aversion to international war seems to be a case in point. That is, as Luard stresses, "a general unwillingness for war" can be a quality that is very consequential.[60] It can be a cause with plenty of explanatory "muscle."

Robert Dahl argues that beliefs, ideas, ideologies, and attitudes are often "a major independent [or as Pinker would have it, exogenous] variable," and that they must remain in the consideration. He is uneasy, however: "one can hardly exaggerate how badly off we are as we move into this terrain" because "if it is difficult to account satisfactorily for the acquisition of individual beliefs, it is even more difficult to account for historical shifts of beliefs." Nonetheless, he recommends paying more attention to what he calls "the historical movement of ideas."[61] Indeed, contrary to the contention of Levy and Thompson, it is often difficult to come up with material reasons to explain important historical developments. For example, slavery declined over the nineteenth century even though the Atlantic slave trade was then entering what was probably the most dynamic and profitable period in its existence. The same can be said for the way formal dueling went out of style. And democracy began to take root in substantial countries only by the end of the eighteenth century even though it had been known as a form of government for millennia and even though there seem to have been no technological or economic advances at the time that impelled its acceptance.[62]

Yet, argues Dahl, "because of their concern with rigor and their dissatisfaction with the 'softness' of historical description, generalization, and explanation, most social scientists have turned away from the historical movement of ideas. As a result, their own theories, however 'rigorous' they may be, leave out an important explanatory variable and often lead to naive reductionism."[63]

THE CONSEQUENCES OF THE RISE OF AVERSION
TO INTERNATIONAL WAR

Over the twentieth century, then, something that might be called a culture or society of international peace or a widespread aversion to war (or a sensitivity to its essential stupidity) has been established with regard to how countries relate to each other, particularly within the developed world. And the chief consequence of this rise has been the remarkable decline – or, in the case of the developed world, the almost utter absence – of the venerable institution over the last several decades. Related is another development. "All historians agree," observed Leo Tolstoy in *War and Peace* in 1869, "that states express their conflicts in wars and that as a direct result of greater or lesser success in war the political strength of states and nations increases or decreases."[64] Whatever historians may currently think, this notion, it certainly appears, has become substantially passé. Prestige now comes not from prowess in armed conflict, but from economic progress, maintaining a stable and productive society, and, for many, putting on a good Olympics, sending a rocket to or toward the moon, or managing a pandemic.[65] That is, triumph in war is not required for countries to gain political strength or standing as can be seen in the cases of Germany and Japan, and the activity itself has increasingly come to seem futile, disgusting, and stupid.[66]

It is questionable, then, whether it is wise to place the concept of power at the center of any construct that tries to deal with international affairs. The concept has been important to a great deal of theorizing about international affairs particularly after realist Hans J. Morgenthau grandly declared in 1948 that "international politics, like all politics, is a struggle for power," defining "power" as "man's control over the minds and actions of others."[67] In that context, the word compellingly tends to imply military strength: as Samuel Huntington observed, "realist theorists have focused overwhelmingly on military power."[68] Indeed, declares Morgenthau without much elaboration, "The dependence of national power upon military preparedness ... is too obvious to need much elaboration."[69] As Robert Art and Kenneth Waltz conclude, "the seriousness of a state's fundamental intentions is conveyed fundamentally by its having a credible military posture. Without it, a state's diplomacy generally lacks effectiveness."[70] The notion that a disarmed country could possess great "power" is all but inconceivable under these patterns of thought. But it is not respect for these forces that makes the diplomacy of Japan or Germany effective. If "power" can be achieved with very little military capability or preparedness, the word, with its attendant and inevitable military implications, has become misleading or misdirecting at best.[71]

In this book, I survey and critique the foreign policy history of the post-World War II era during which an aversion to international war, or an acceptance of the idea that it is fundamentally stupid, has grown. Included is an assessment of the current threat environment. I also examine three additional and associated consequences of the rise of aversion to international war. First, under the circumstances, there is potential virtue in the tradition-ally maligned techniques of complacency and appeasement for dealing with international problems. Second, the phenomenon suggests that there is little justification for the continuing and popular tendency to inflate threats and dangers in the international arena – even to the point of deeming some of them to be "existential." And third, although problems certainly remain, none of these are of a kind and substantial enough to require the United States (or pretty much anybody) to maintain a large standing military force for dealing with them. I discuss an additional consequence of the rise of aversion to international war in this book's Afterword – the rather natural and substantially immutable establishment of something of a world order that has scarcely required the active machinations of the United States.

The Potential Application of Complacency and Appeasement

In a condition of international peace a certain degree of complacency is often justified, and it is frequently superior to the routine opposite: agitated con-frontation characterized by determined and often militarized alarmism.

Although troubles do exist, those inclined to alarm might from time to time bear in mind an observation of Calvin Coolidge, the president, suggests columnist George Will, with the "highest ratio of wisdom to words." In Will's rendering, Coolidge advised, "When you see 10 problems coming down the road at you, you can be pretty sure that nine of them will wind up in the ditch before they run over you."[72] As Coolidge suggests, complacency may not *always* be the wisest course, but it should surely be on the table for consideration. Indeed, as I will attempt to show, security threats once held to be dire – including the military one seemingly presented by the Soviet Union in the Cold War – did not simply drive into Coolidge's ditch, but actually, or effectively, did not exist at all.

Moreover, if Communist incursions in South Vietnam in the 1960s had been met with complacency rather than with militarized alarmism, some 55,000 young Americans and a million or more Vietnamese would not have been killed. Of course, the Communists might have won but, as it turned out, that happened anyway, and today the resultant regime is quite friendly with the United States as they jointly make glowering faces at dangers they fancy to loom in the area from China.

Complete complacency in the wake of the September 11, 2001, terrorist attack would not have been appropriate even to Coolidge. However, a more laid-back – and therefore Coolidge-like – approach would have been to go after the al-Qaeda perpetrators directly rather than to wage war against

Afghanistan's ruling Taliban group, which had nothing to do with the terrorist attack. Helping in the effort might have been Saudi Arabia and Pakistan, the chief (and almost only) supporters of the Taliban. In result, al-Qaeda might have been routed and a frustrating and disastrous 20-year war might well have been avoided.

And a complacent approach to Saddam Hussein's Iraq in 2003 would have stressed that the pathetic, if sometimes roguish, state was fully containable and deterrable with measures already pretty much in place. In the process, a war which has resulted in hundreds of thousands of deaths, including twice as many Americans as perished on 9/11, would have failed to come about.

As a diplomatic technique, appeasement has also frequently proved to be a useful approach. It worked like a charm in the Cuban missile crisis. When US President John F. Kennedy sternly suggested he would use his military to remove offending nuclear missiles in nearby Cuba, Soviet premier Nikita Khrushchev obliging appeased him, Kennedy pronounced himself satisfied, no attack took place, and all lived at least semi-happily thereafter.

However, appeasement has been given a bad name as a diplomatic technique by an experience in 1938 when Adolf Hitler insisted at an international conference in Munich that a German-filled area in neighboring Czechoslovakia be turned over to him, promising that this would be his last territorial demand in Europe. The British and French accepted this demand, but Hitler, contrary to his promise, was soon off invading other countries. The lesson often drawn is that Hitler's appetite for territory grew with the feeding, and therefore that the Munich appeasement led to a world war. However, Hitler had long had an ambition for future military expansion, and the experience at Munich was scarcely necessary or impelling. As historian Paul Kennedy puts it, "Hitler was fundamentally *unappeasable* and determined upon a future territorial order which small-scale adjustments alone could never satisfy."[73]

Moreover, it seems likely that peaceful dealmaking – appeasement – would have worked with any German other than Hitler. The Germans did have grievances, but most of these could not by themselves have led to another world war because the victors of World War I either assisted in removing the grievances or stood idly by as the Germans rectified the peace terms unilaterally.[74] In order to bring about another continental war it was necessary for Germany to desire to expand into areas that would inspire military resistance from other major countries and to be willing and able to pursue war when that desire was opposed. Only Hitler possessed that desire and war-willingness, and the capacity to carry it out. Most of the other top German leaders were toadies or sycophants, and certainly none could remotely arouse the blind adulation and worship Hitler inspired. As historian Matthew Cooper points out, "none of the military leaders of those critical years from 1933 to 1938 possessed any political ability."[75] Nor was there a drive for war among the German public: as William Manchester concludes, "the German people hated war as passionately as their once and future enemies."[76] "Had Hitler dropped dead the day after the Munich conference," notes Record, "that conference in all likelihood would be an historical footnote and 'appeasement' a nonpejorative word."[77]

Complacency and appeasement, then, have much to recommend themselves. After all, they are standard features of successful economic, or business, bargaining. In this, each bargainer more or less complacently assumes that, while both are acting out of self-interest, each has an interest as well in accommodating, or appeasing, the other and that the best bargain is one in which both leave happy with the deal struck. The same often holds for negotiations over legal disputes: as one experienced attorney has put it, "The worst settlement is better than the best judgement."[78] Hard bargaining in which only short-term advantage is the motivation is bad business in the long term. As P. T. Barnum put it, "Men who drive sharp bargains with their customers, acting as if they never expected to see them again, will not be mistaken." It actually took a long time for the wisdom of this approach to sink in among capitalists, but when it did, the massive, even miraculous, economic development of the last two centuries was launched.[79]

In international relations, theorists have for decades thundered that in that realm, all politics is motivated not by a quest for mutual benefit, but by a "lust for power" and that, due to the "anarchy" that prevails in the world, "there is little room for trust among states." Yet, eschewing such grim assessments, mutually-beneficial international bargaining, often relying on complacency and appeasement, has become commonplace in many areas. As will be discussed more fully in Chapter 6, China and Russia today seem not only to want to become rich, but to play a larger role on the world stage, overcoming what they view as past humiliations. However reprehensible some their internal policies may be, neither state seems to harbor Hitler-like dreams of extensive expansion by military means, and to a considerable degree it seems sensible for other countries, including the United States, to accept, and even service, such vaporous, cosmetic, and substantially meaningless goals. But that, of course, would smack not only of complacency, but appeasement. Instead, the two countries are frequently deemed to present a dire and gathering threat requiring perpetual and often militarized confrontation.

The Continued Quest to Identify and Inflate Threat

Rather than adopting a laid-back policy emphasizing complacency and appeasement, there has been a determined quest to identify, evaluate, and confront new threats – or to search for "monsters to destroy," as John Quincy Adams famously put it in a fourth of July speech in 1821. Massively extrapolating from limited evidence, determining to err decidedly on the safe side, dismissing contrary interpretations, and often striking a responsive chord with the public, decision-makers can become mesmerized by perceived threats that scarcely warrant the preoccupation and effort. Indeed, in *Overblown*, a book published in 2006, I argued that, with the benefit of hindsight, "every foreign policy threat in the last several decades that has come to be accepted as significant has then eventually been unwisely exaggerated."[80] That is, alarmism, usually based on what Brodie once called "worst case fantasies" perpetrated by a "cult of the ominous," has dominated thinking about security.[81]

Thus, historian John Lewis Gaddis observes that in 1950, at the time of the Korean War – quite possibly the most consequential event of the Cold War – *no one* at the summit of foreign policy (chief members of what was later rather irreverently labeled "the blob") imagined that "there would be no world wars" over the next half-century and that "the United States and the Soviet Union, soon to have tens of thousands of thermonuclear weapons pointed at one another, would agree tacitly never to use any of them."[82] To do so, of course, would have been to wallow in complacency.

However, that another world war, whether nuclear or not, might be avoided was compatible with facts and observations that were fairly obvious and fully available at the time. To begin with, those running world affairs after World War II were the same people or the intellectual heirs of the people who had tried desperately to prevent that cataclysm. It was entirely plausible that such people, despite their huge differences on many key issues, might well manage to keep themselves from plunging into a self-destructive repeat performance. Moreover, Communist ideology, while assertive and threateningly unsettling to the Western world, stressed class warfare, revolution, and civil war as methods for advancing its cause, not the direct military invasion of developed capitalist states.[83] Thus, it could have been reasonably argued at the time that major war was simply not in the cards and that the Korean War was essentially an opportunistic one-off – that is, an aberration rather than a harbinger. This less alarmist perspective was not, of course, the only one possible, but there was no definitive way to dismiss it. Thus, as a matter of simple, plain, rational decision-making, this comparatively complacent prospect – the one that proved to be true – should have been on the table. But, for the most part, it was not.

A similar phenomenon about threat took place in the wake of the terrorist attacks of September 11, 2001 – quite possibly the most consequential event of the post-Cold War period. At the time, Michael Morell was the CIA agent in charge of briefing the president, and he recalls the atmosphere vividly. "We were certain we were going to be attacked again." There was "an avalanche – literally thousands – of intelligence reports in the months following 9/11 that strongly indicated that al Qa'ida would hit us again," and some of these indicated that the terrorists might use chemical or biological weapons or "even crude nuclear devices."[84] Similarly, journalist Jane Mayer observes that "the only certainty shared by virtually the entire American intelligence community" in the months after September 11 "was that a second wave of even more devastating terrorist attacks on America was imminent," while, according to Steve Coll, CIA leaders "were thoroughly convinced that there would be another attack inside the United States soon and that it would be even more spectacular than September 11." And Rudy Giuliani, who was mayor of New York City at the time, recalls that "anybody, any one of these security experts, including myself, would have told you on September 11, 2001, we're looking at dozens and dozens and multiyears of attacks like this."[85]

Such fears and concerns about the threat presented by international terrorism were, of course, reasonable extrapolations from the facts then at hand. However, that *every* "security expert" should fervently embrace such alarmist – and, it turned out, erroneous – views, and that the intelligence community should be *certain* and *thoroughly convinced* about them, is fundamentally absurd. As with Korea, a less alarmist, even complacent, perspective was entirely possible even with the facts then in hand.

For example, immediately after 9/11, a reporter for the *Columbus Dispatch* queried several academics who, innocent of, or unencumbered by, any benefit that might derive from reading those thousands of dire intelligence reports, proposed a set of entirely plausible contrary observations: "There's a natural tendency to believe that because this is a big event, it's caused by big forces, when it's really somebody who just got lucky with two potshots," or "If we overreact, we're likely to generate a whole new group of opponents, which is exactly what these groups would like us to do." And we suggested that the problem could be handled as an international policing matter (as was done after a terrorist attack that had downed an American airliner over Lockerbie, Scotland, in 1988) or with methods previously used against pirates and slave traders.[86] It was also entirely plausible, if unconventional and of course complacent, to conclude from facts then at hand that, like the Korean War (and, for that matter, like the attack on Pearl Harbor to which 9/11 was often compared), 9/11 could well prove to be an aberration rather than a harbinger.[87]

Morell's recollections are included in a 2015 book about the fight against Islamist extremism that he extravagantly and portentously entitles *The Great War of Our Time*. Interestingly, even with 14 years of hindsight, at no point does he pause to reflect on why or how those "thousands" of alarming, hysteria-inducing intelligence reports that so "strongly indicated" that the terrorists were about to "hit us again" could have been so hopelessly and so spectacularly wrong. Not only has the al-Qaeda monster failed to "hit us again," but it hasn't even come close.[88] Indeed, contrary to the popular (or knee-jerk) post-9/11 perspective, the attack stands out a spectacular outlier: no other terrorist event before or after, in war zones or not, has visited even one-tenth as much total destruction. And al-Qaeda, the group responsible, has proved to resemble President John Kennedy's assassin, Lee Harvey Oswald – a fundamentally trivial entity that got horribly lucky once. Yet the event was taken to be some sort of new normal, the rise of a monster that had to be destroyed through a pair of destructive and unnecessary wars in the Middle East going after regimes that had nothing to do with the attacks.

Thus, *no one* in 1950 anticipated the distinct possibility that World War III might be avoided and *every* security expert was *certain* in 2001 that there would soon be a large repeat terrorist attack. In the process other plausible – and as it turned out correct – interpretations of the information available were simply ignored or dismissed as complacent.

Throughout, simplicity and spook, as political scientist Warner Schilling called it, have reigned.[89] In the process, American foreign and defense policy has very often inflated threat – routinely elevating the problematic to the dire – and urgently focused on problems, or monsters, that essentially didn't exist. This phenomenon is essentially farcical in its frequent misperception of information and avoidance of contrary explanations.

In a farce, a man might become suspicious that his wife and his best friend are having an affair. Various bits of evidence, including evasive statements by the presumed lovers, feed his suspicion. Although there are alternative explanations for the pair's behavior and for their statements, he increasingly excludes these from consideration and he emphasizes instead information that supports his suspicions. Eventually he animatedly, and in great anguish, denounces the couple at a gathering of friends and relatives. Someone then pulls back a screen and a well-stocked banquet table is revealed as balloons cascade from the ceiling. It turns out the pair had been indeed been meeting in secret, but that was because they were planning a surprise party for him.

That sort of process can be seen in operation when, throughout the Cold War, the major contestants engaged in what is often called a "security dilemma." Neither had the slightest interest or desire to go to war with the other, but each warily accumulated an impressive and hugely costly military arsenal to deter a threat of direct military aggression that, as it happened, didn't exist, and each took the other's buildup to be threatening, requiring them to amass ever more armaments in order to deter the non-existent threat. Robert Jervis characterizes the security dilemma as "tragic."[90] But surely, because it resulted primarily in massively unnecessary expenditure and planning and in frantic, if fundamentally insignificant, sound and fury, the theatrical form it most resembles is farce – or perhaps theater of the absurd.

It should be noted, however, that, although there are always people trying to espy monsters – sell fears and threats – their efforts are no guarantee that a promoted threat or fear will "take," that people and policymakers will be convinced it is notable and important, worth spending time and effort worrying about. If extensive promotion could guarantee acceptance, we would all be driving Edsels and drinking New Coke – legendary marketing failures in 1958 and 1985 by two of the (otherwise) most successful businesses in history: the Ford Motor Company and Coca-Cola.

Thus, the American public and its leaders have remained remarkably calm about the dangers of genetically modified food while becoming very wary of nuclear power. The French see it very differently. In the United States, illegal immigration is seen to be a threat in some years, but not in others. The country was "held hostage" when Americans were kidnapped in Iran in 1979 or in Lebanon in the 1980s but not when this repeatedly happened during the Iraq War or over the decades in Colombia. Slobodan Milošević in Serbia become a monster about whom we had to do something militarily, but not Robert Mugabe in Zimbabwe or thuggish militarists in Burma or Pol Pot in Cambodia or, until 9/11, the Taliban in Afghanistan. In the 1930s, Japan's ventures into distant China were seen to be more threatening than some of the actions of Hitler in Europe. Predicting what will arouse people's apprehensions in the future is difficult at best, and anyone who could accurately and persistently do so would likely quietly move to Wall Street and in very short order to become the richest person on earth.[91]

The Military Record: Are You Being Served?

It is also important to evaluate the accomplishments of the American military, which has often been put into service to deal with the threats that have been espied, sometimes with disastrous results, and to evaluate whether the money and effort spent has been worth it.

To do so, it would be worthwhile to apply a test proposed by Newt Gingrich. It is often said, even by many of his admirers, that at any one time Gingrich will have 100 ideas of which five are pretty *good*. Falling into the latter category was his remark when running for the Republican presidential nomination in 2012 that "defense budgets shouldn't be a matter of politics. They shouldn't be a matter of playing games. They should be directly related to the amount of threat we have."[92] As it happens, on his 95 percent side, Gingrich does imagine many threats and perils.[93] However, his test is a sensible one. It is determinedly bottom-up: instead of starting with defense spending as it is and looking for places to expand or to trim, it assesses the threat environment – problems that lurk, or appear to lurk, in current conditions and on (or even over) the horizon. Then, keeping both the risks and opportunities in mind, it considers which of these threats, if any, justify funding.

I apply that approach in this book. I evaluate the history of American foreign and particularly military policy since 1945 and conclude that, although there have been problems – or "challenges," as they are some- times called – the United States, despite fears and imaginings that have often been widely and fervently embraced, has never really been con- fronted by a truly significant security threat, a condition that persists to the present day.[94] At least since 1945, any imagined security threats vanished because the supposed threatener/challenger either lacked the capacity to carry the threat out or obligingly self-destructed or because the perceived threat pretty much failed, actually, to exist. There are policy implications of such an agreeable condition, and one might even be inclined to flirt unpleasantly with the notion that, just possibly, the United States would be better off if it followed the policy pursued by Costa Rica, which 70 years ago dismantled its military forces entirely – though perhaps postwar Japan and Germany provide more directly applicable models. But at any rate, an application of the Gingrich gospel/equation/wisdom leads to the conclusion that there is not now, nor ever has been, a good reason to maintain a huge military force-in- being.

In the last years, it has become common, even routine, in the United States to say to members of the military, with varying degrees of sincerity, "Thank you for your service." The phrase was used as the title for an acclaimed book in 2013 and for a well-received, if financially unsuccessful, theatrical film in 2017 that was based on the book. The title was presumably meant to be at least partly ironic because both the book and the film dealt with postwar mental problems experienced by some veterans returning from the wars in Iraq and Afghanistan.

According to the book, some 20 or 30 percent have come home with some degree of post-traumatic stress disorder.[95]

Rather remarkably however, nowhere in either the book or the film do returning veterans voice misgivings about the point or purpose of the dangerous mission for which they volunteered. That is, no one is ever shown reflecting on whether the military venture was worth the service for which soldiers are so routinely, if sometimes robotically, thanked – whether it was worth the cost that they and the nation bore. The closest to a commentary is the observation in the book that, during what was imaginatively labeled "Operation Iraqi Freedom," the mentally shattered soldier at the center of its story used FUCK IRAQ as a screen saver on his computer, blaming his travails on the country to which he was sent without invitation rather than on the people who sent him there.

However, under its closing credits, the film runs a dirge-like song by Bruce Springsteen, especially commissioned for the film, called "Freedom Cadence." It pointedly, if scarcely intelligibly, proclaims,

> Some say freedom is free,
> But I tend to disagree.
> I say freedom is won
> Through the barrel of a gun.

It would seem to be useful to assess what the United States has been getting – whether freedom or anything else – for the half-trillion dollars plus that it has been expending on its military each year. That involves, in particular, an evaluation of the degree to which US military policy since World War II has been successful in dealing with perceived threats. I find that the achievements of the American military since World War II, not to put too fine a point on it, have not been very impressive.

The military and others continue to maintain that it was the existence of the United States military that kept the Soviet Union or China from launching World War III. However, an evaluation in Chapter 1 strongly suggests that the Communist side never saw direct Hitlerian war against the West as being a remotely sensible tactic for advancing its revolutionary agenda. That is, there was nothing to deter.

Moreover, military failure has been frequent. For all the very considerable expense, the American military has won no wars during that period – especially if victory is defined as achieving an objective at an acceptable cost – except against enemy forces that essentially didn't exist. The American military triumphed in a comic opera war over tiny forces in Grenada – equipped with, it seems, only three vehicles, one of which was rented.[96] It also prevailed over scarcely organized thuggish ones in Panama and Kosovo. And, although the Iraqi opponent in the Gulf War of 1991 often looked impressive on paper, it turned out to lack quite a few rather elemental qualities: defenses, strategy, tactics, training, leadership, and morale, as will be discussed in Chapter 3. More recently, there has been a successful war against the especially vicious and amazingly self-destructive insurgent group, Islamic State, or ISIS. However, the principal American contribution has been in air support; others have done the heavy lifting – and the dying.

There are also a few wars in which it could probably be said that the US was ahead at the end of the first, second, or third quarter – Korea, Vietnam, Somalia, Afghanistan, Iraq, and Libya. But the final results of these were certainly less than stellar: exhausted stalemate, effective defeat, hasty withdrawal, and extended misery. Indeed, for the entirety of the present century, American military policy, especially in the Middle East, has been an abject failure. In particular, at the cost of hundreds of thousands of lives, Iraq and Afghanistan have undergone more travail and destruction than they would likely have undergone even under the contemptible regimes of Saddam Hussein and the Taliban.[97] The US military has also shown in Vietnam, Somalia, Iraq, and Afghanistan that it is often incapable not only of defeating insurgents at an acceptable cost, but also of training locals to effectively defend themselves after the Americans have left.

Although perhaps chastened somewhat by the experience in Iraq and Afghanistan (as it was after Vietnam), the United States continues to maintain a huge military force-in-being, held in readiness for the next venture – or adventure. Keeping such a force might make sense, despite the abundant record of failure, if there existed coherent threats that required such a force. In this book I seek to evaluate how much of a military the United States could plausibly be said to require today to protect itself and to advance its interests. As suggested, it concludes that the answer is "not much," arguing that, although there are certainly problem areas and issues in the world, none of these seems to present a security threat to the United States large or urgent enough to justify the maintenance of a large military force-in-being.

And there is a related issue. Having a large military force-in-being tempts leaders to eschew complacency and to apply military force to solve problems for which it is inappropriate, inadequate, and often counterproductive. It was in the wake of the disastrous Vietnam War that defense analyst Bernard Brodie wistfully reflected that "One way of keeping people out of trouble is to deny them the means for getting into it."[98] More than 40 years later, Brodie's admonition continues to be relevant.

PART I

ASSESSING THE THREAT RECORD

1

Korea, Massive Extrapolation, Deterrence, and the Crisis Circus

At the conclusion of World War II, the Western victors faced two major international problems: what to do about the defeated countries, Germany and Japan, and what to do about an emerging conflict – the Cold War – with another victor, the Soviet Union. Since it involved a lot of interesting conflict, the latter problem has inspired a much greater literature. But it seems quite possible that in time the Cold War contest will be remembered as something of a historical curiosity. By contrast, the successful solution of the Japan/ Germany problem – in which those countries became moderate and prosperous allies and peaceful competitors whose view of the world is much like that of the Western victors – may well come to be seen as a much more momentous development historically. Of necessity, the Japanese and the Germans were the principal charters of their own destinies. However, the efforts of the victors to guide, nudge, assist, browbeat, bribe, and encourage them deserve credit as well. One of Napoleon's maxims is "Never interrupt your enemy when he is making a mistake." In the aftermath of World War II, the victors' slogan might have been, "Never interrupt your friends when they are successfully solving a problem." The victors certainly helped, or tried to help, with the process of securing the peace, but they also realized that those now running the former enemy states were central to this process, and they were often wise enough to let them carry the ball when things were going well.

An important facilitating factor was the disgust and contempt of the German and Japanese people with the militaristic regimes that had led them into the horrors of the just-ended catastrophe.[1] Both peoples were fully ready for a return to the comparative liberalism of the 1920s, however flawed, and willing to accept the leadership, at least for a while, of the occupiers. In the case of Germany, the defeated accepted dismemberment, divided occupation, and substantial loss of territory in the east, deprivations rather worse than those inflicted on them by the victors in 1918.

In the process, the defeated countries worked themselves into various congenial cooperative arrangements – seen most impressively in the growth of the Common Market or, later, European Union. Given the destructive war they had just endured, they recovered economically with remarkable speed. As noted in the Prologue, it had taken the German economy over ten years to recover from First World War. It took only about five for the Second.

THE COLD WAR BEGINS: THE KOREAN WAR AND MASSIVE EXTRAPOLATION

In addition to dealing with former enemies, Western policymakers after 1945 needed to size up international Communism and to evaluate its potential as a threat – or monster.

According to the ideology on which the Soviet regime had been founded in 1917, world history is a vast, continuing process of progressive revolution. Steadily, in country after country, the oppressed working classes will violently revolt, destroying the oppressing capitalist classes and aligning their new regimes with other like-minded countries, eventually transforming the world.

As he put it in 1945, Soviet dictator Josef Stalin envisioned a situation that would have socialism in one country where the dictatorship of the proletariat would be consolidated, and that would be used as a base to aid and inspire subversive revolutionary movements throughout the world.[2] Stalin also anticipated that there would be a harvest of congenial revolutions after the war as well as internecine rivalries among capitalist states, developments that Communist doctrine had long held to be inevitable.[3]

It was obviously understandable that the capitalist countries of the West found this threatening. However, aggressive, conquering Hitlerian war by the Soviets themselves does not fit into this scheme at all, and it would foolishly risk everything. The Communists in Russia were surely in a good position to understand and appreciate the risks of world war: it was the Great War of 1914–18, after all, that destabilized the Russian Czarist regime, greatly facilitating their opportunistic takeover in 1917. In the aftermath of World War II, it became common to characterize some governments and societies as "totalitarian" and to place Stalin's Soviet Union and Hitler's Germany in the same category. Thus, George Orwell's famous and influential novel *1984*, published in 1948, was set in a Soviet-style country and strongly suggests that war was actually necessary for the depicted totalitarian state to function and to maintain its control. For all the novel's value, this was a caricature of the Soviet Union, and to take this to be a serious representation of Soviet ideological thinking would be misguided. For Hitler, direct aggressive war was a requirement in order to carry out his theoretical goals, which mainly envisioned forceful territorial expansion and colonization to the east rather like what happened in the United States in the opposite direction in the nineteenth century.[4] The Soviets may have endorsed revolution and class warfare, but they did not have similar ambitions.[5]

In fact, in the aftermath of World War II, many people felt the likelihood of direct military aggression by the Soviets to be exceedingly small. Thus, US diplomat George Kennan concluded in 1948 that "we do not think the Russians, since the termination of the war, have had any serious intentions of resorting to arms."[6] But no one, of course, could be sure, and there were dicey confrontations over the status of the occupied and divided city of Berlin – which in considerable measure inspired the West to form the anti-Soviet North Atlantic Treaty Organization. There was also alarm when China fell to the Communists in a civil war there in 1949.

By 1950, Soviet foreign policy had mostly experienced discouragement or at least a form of stalemate as the West became alarmed and united against it.[7] It had consolidated a sort of empire in areas in Eastern Europe that it occupied at the end of World War II, and the Communist advance in China was encouraging. However, there was little sign either of the harvest of revolutions or of the vicious rivalries among capitalist states that had been anticipated – indeed, with the formation of NATO, they were aligning themselves against the Soviets. At the same time, international Communism was planning a military enterprise that inspired great alarm in the West. In late 1949, Kim Il-sung, the leader of Communist North Korea, broached the idea of attacking South Korea. A degree of warfare, mostly at the revolutionary level, had been going on in the south between the two entities at least since 1948.[8] A full-out military attack across the border, it was argued, would settle the matter. As one Soviet leader, Nikita Khrushchev, put it later, Kim was "absolutely certain" that, if prodded with the "point of a bayonet," an internal explosion "in South Korea would be touched off."[9] Although Stalin had misgivings, Kim insisted that South Korea would quickly fall into the Communist camp before the West even had much of a chance to react. Eventually, both Stalin and the Chinese Communists accepted the scheme.[10]

The ensuing Korean War, which lasted from 1950 to 1953, proved to be crucial in the Cold War. It provoked unwarranted fears of an imminent World War, and these in turn were taken to require the assemblage of a vast arsenal of weapons (accompanied by a lot of exquisite, rationalizing theory) that were designed to deter a war with the Soviet Union that neither side had any intention whatever of starting. What Stalin approved was a distant war of expansion by a faithful ally, a war that was expected to be quick, risk-free, and cheap. And, in allowing Kim to proceed, Stalin made it clear that if things went badly, Kim would have to depend on China, not on the Soviet Union, to help.[11] To be further on the safe side, he also took precautionary steps to limit the war by withdrawing not only Soviet military advisors from North Korea, but most Soviet equipment as well. "One thing remains clear," notes Sovietologist Adam Ulam: "the extreme reluctance of the Soviets to become involved militarily in any phase of the Korean conflict."[12]

The venture may have been envisioned by its perpetrators as a limited probe in an obscure corner of the world, but it proved to be a resoundingly counter-productive fiasco when the United States intervened on the side of the belea-guered South Koreans shortly after the invasion began in June 1950.

President Harry Truman bluntly concluded at the time that this was an instance of what would be called "direct aggression." As he put it at the time, "The attack upon Korea makes it plain beyond all doubt that Communism has passed beyond the use of subversion to conquer independent nations and will now use armed invasion and war."[13] As he recalled later, "I felt certain that if South Korea was allowed to fall Communist leaders would be emboldened to override nations closer to our own shores ... .If this was allowed to go unchallenged it would mean a third world war, just as similar incidents had brought on the second world war."[14] How could he, or anyone, be *certain* about that?

A National Security Council document darkly suspected that Korea was the first phase of a general Soviet plan for global war, and the CIA authoritatively opined that the Soviet rulers might "deliberately provoke" such a general war before 1954.[15] A direct analogy with Hitlerian aggression was readily applied. The public was also alarmed: a poll in August 1950 found 57 percent of the public opining that the United States was now actually in World War III, while only 18 percent held that the fighting would stop short of another world war.[16]

A major figure in advancing the extravagant alarmist perspective was Secretary of State Acheson. In utter contempt for the capacity of the average American citizen to understand foreign policy, he notes in his memoirs the necessity to be "clearer than truth" while abandoning qualification for simpli-city and nuance for bluntness. and he grandly dismissed contrary arguments from people who actually knew about the Soviet Union and its ideology as leading to a debate that was stultifying, sterile, and semantic.[17] A few people at the time challenged this cosmic and erroneous interpretation – State Department Counselor and Soviet specialist Charles Bohlen among them – but they were ignored even though their interpretation was plausible (if perhaps complacent) and could not be rejected by the evidence available at the time – or, as it happens, since.[18]

Within a few months, the North Korean onslaught had been reversed by American and South Korean troops. However, rather than simply expelling the invaders, the US-led coalition decided to pursue them as they retreated back into the North despite warnings from the Chinese that they might intervene under that condition. China did so with devastating effect in the last months of 1950. At that point, recalls defense analyst Bernard Brodie, many, particularly the Joint Chiefs of Staff, were "utterly convinced" that the Soviets "were using Korea as a feint to cause us to deploy our forces there while they prepared to a launch a 'general' (total) war against the United States through a major attack on Europe." Indeed, continues Brodie, "they had convinced themselves that an outbreak of general war in Europe was both probable and imminent" – in fact "only two or three weeks away" – an example, he suggests, of "the dangerous extravagances in intelligence analysis that derive from the *idée fixe*."[19]

The three-year war was likely the most costly since 1945: millions perished. It ended in a military stalemate codified in an armistice signed in the summer of 1953, a few months after Stalin's death, that left the Korean peninsula divided in the middle at about the same place as in 1950.

Despite the horrific costs, it could be argued that the Korean War, at least in longer-term perspective, may be the only combat venture by the US military since World War II that was worth carrying out. It prevented tens of millions of people from being incorporated into a country controlled by what was to become one of the most contemptible regimes in history. In an important sense, the only winners of the Korean War were the South Korean people – or at least those that survived the war. But of course no one knew that in 1950, and the protection of the Korean people was not the primary motive for the intervention.[20] Moreover, for a couple of decades South Korea suffered under control that was essentially authoritarian. It is highly unlikely, however, that the war prevented further aggression of that sort. Historian Alistair Horne has recently asked, had the 1950 attack succeeded, "who knows what apocalyptic, speculative ventures Stalin may have tempted to try with the overwhelming power of the Red Army presence in Europe?"[21] However, from the perspective of the Communists, the event was a unique opportunity and yet an extreme one in its own terms of risk. It seems unlikely, accordingly, that, even if successful, such a venture would have been attempted elsewhere. But the American intervention must surely have much enforced that proclivity.

The war was a huge setback for the Communists.[22] It also proved to be unacceptably painful for the United States, which lost over 35,000 soldiers in the war. Under a dictum that might be called a "Korea syndrome," there was a strong desire not to do that again – on both sides.

The war in Korea may not have been repeated, but it proved to be a major turning point.[23] Policymakers not only rejected milder interpretations of the Communist aggression in Korea out of hand, but they also extrapolated massively and then proceeded to spend extravagantly based on those fanciful extrapolations. The American defense budget quadrupled – something that previously had been thought to be politically and economically infeasible – and to confront the much-feared threat of a frontal Soviet invasion of Western Europe, NATO was rapidly transformed from a paper organization (big on symbolism, small on actual military capability) into a viable, well-equipped, centrally led multinational armed force.[24]

An alarmist and monochromatic perspective continued throughout the Cold War, and the United States developed a costly policy in which it tried not so much to destroy the Communist monster as to deter it by threatening nuclear punishment for any major Soviet aggression.

As it happens, however, the fact that the Soviet Union did not launch a massive aggressive war cannot really be credited to American policy. Indeed, as has been noted, the USSR clearly had no interest whatever in instituting major war whether nuclear or not, or even in planning one, no matter how the United States happened to choose to array its arsenal. Insofar as the Soviets wanted to "take over" other countries, they anticipated that this could come about through revolutionary or civil war processes within those countries, ones that, assisted and encouraged by the Communist states, would bring into control congenial, like-minded people and groups that would willingly join the Communist camp. Military measures designed to deter direct, Hitler-style military aggression simply have no relevance in that case – and that perspective would have prevailed even if the United States was not directly in the path of such advances.

Brodie, one of the few defense analysts of the time seriously to consider the premises of American policy, came to the Bohlenesque conclusion by 1966 that it was "difficult to discover what meaningful incentives the Russians might have for attempting to conquer Western Europe – especially incentives that are even remotely commensurate with the risks."[25] And in 1977 Kennan argued that the Soviet Union "has no desire for any major war, least of all for a nuclear one ... Plotting an attack on Western Europe would be ... the last thing that would come into its head." And late in the Cold War, he said, "I have never believed that they have seen it as in their interests to overrun Western Europe militarily, or that they would have launched an attack on that region generally even if the so-called nuclear deterrent had not existed."[26]

After it was all over, a great amount of documentary evidence became available, and as Robert Jervis notes, "the Soviet archives have yet to reveal any serious plans for unprovoked aggression against Western Europe, not to mention a first strike against the United States." And, after researching those archives, Vojtech Mastny concludes that "All Warsaw Pact scenarios presumed a war started by NATO" and that "The strategy of nuclear deterrence [was] irrelevant to deterring a major war that the enemy did not wish to launch in the first place." As Andrian Danilevich, a top Soviet war planner, put it in a 1992 interview, "We never had a single thought of a first strike against the U.S. The doctrine was always very clear: we will always respond, but never initiate."[27]

It could be argued, of course, that his perspective stemmed from American deterrence policy. However, those who would so contend need to demonstrate that the Soviets ever had the desire to risk anything that might in their wildest imagination come even slightly to resemble the catastrophe they had just endured. In addition, they were under the spell of a theory that said they would eventually come to rule the world in a historically inevitable process to which they would contribute merely by safely inspiring and encouraging like-minded revolutionaries abroad – a mindset that was not, and could not be, deterred.

Actually, things were quite impressively ludicrous in the Soviet Union. Throughout they scampered to keep up with the United States – "we had the psychology of an underdog," recalled one Soviet general in 1994.[28] Indeed, as will be discussed in Chapter 2 it is likely that the desperate, costly, and profoundly unnecessary military scramble that went on for decades helped speed Communism's demise.

Thus, the extravagant alarmism that inspired the Cold War arms race was essentially based on nonsense. In the process, however, the United States spent somewhere up to 10 trillion dollars on nuclear weapons and delivery systems – enough to purchase everything in the country except for the land by one calculation.[29] There were also enormous short- and long-term opportunity costs. If those deterrence monies had instead been invested in the economy, one estimate suggests, they would have generated an additional 20 or 25 percent of production each year *in perpetuity*.[30] And there was also a substantial loss entailed in paying legions of talented nuclear scientists, engineers, and technicians to devote their careers to developing and servicing weapons that have proved, it certainly seems, to have been significantly unnecessary and essentially irrelevant. All this was primarily to confront, to deter, and to make glowering and menacing faces at a perceived threat of direct military aggression that, essentially, didn't exist. In all, it was the stuff of comedy – or, more accurately, farce.[31]

Farce is also evident in the American reaction, often bordering on the hysterical, to the Soviet Union's dramatic launch in 1957 of Sputnik, the first artificial space satellite. When Sputnik was launched, one astrophysicist predicted with certainty that the Soviets would soon be on the moon – perhaps within a week – while physicist Edward Teller declared that the United States has lost "a battle more important and greater than Pearl Harbor." A prominent political aide extravagantly opined that "the Russians have left the earth and the race for the control of the universe has started."[32]

The impact of the space race can hardly be overstated. For the better part of a decade the Soviets scored triumph after triumph as the United States struggled desperately to get into the game. Impelled in no small degree by the accompanying public relations blitz launched by Soviet leader Nikita Khrushchev, many came to believe that the remarkable Soviet achievement in space said something tangible about the basic comparative worth of capitalism and Communism. For example, a hastily-assembled, if august and authoritative committee, The President's Commission on National Goals, was soon extrapolating wildly, declaring the democratic world to be in "grave danger" from Communism's "great capacity for political organization and propaganda" and from the "specious appeal of Communist doctrine." And one government estimate helpfully (and massively) extrapolated CIA statistics in 1960 to conclude that the Soviet Union's Gross National Product, which seemed to be surging at the time, might be triple that of the United States by the year 2000.[33] Such fears and fantasies eventually proved absurd.

Most importantly, Sputnik gave dramatic punch to the almost completely misguided message of the Gaither Report, which was in the works at the time. The Report espied a "missile gap" and asserted confidently that the United States was falling behind in the arms race and in a few years would be much inferior to the Soviet Union in intercontinental missiles: "The evidence clearly indicates an increasing threat which may become critical in 1959 or 1960."[34] The Report recommended substantial spending increases in an attempt to keep up in missilery and also in conventional local war capability since it was fancied that, with the American nuclear capacity neutralized or worse, the Soviet enemy would likely be tempted to spin off other Koreas, particularly in Asia and the Middle East.[35]

This calculation proved to be alarmist fantasy – or farce – of the purest order. It was based less on clear indications in the evidence than on some assumptions about Soviet capacities to build missiles – which may have been correct – and about Soviet intentions to do so – which were decidedly in error. The Gaither Report and other analyses projected that the Soviet missile strength in the early 1960s would stand at 700 (in extrapolations by the Air Force whose budget stood to rise with high Soviet numbers) or merely at 200 (in extrapolations by the Navy whose budget did not). The actual figure turned out to be four, though the Air Force continued doggedly to suggest for a while that barn silos, medieval towers, a Crimean War memorial, and various mysterious-looking buildings in isolated areas were actually cleverly disguised missiles.[36]

Such views remained dominant even after an elaborate war/crisis simulation game set up by Harvard's Thomas Schelling failed to come up with any sort of scenario or provocation that could get a war, particularly a nuclear war, started. Nonetheless, some officials declined to sign up for retirement plans figuring they were not likely to live that long, and others cheerlessly concluded it to be "perfectly conceivable . . . that the U.S. might have to evacuate two or three times every decade."[37] It was in 1979, over 40 years ago, that the prominent political scientist Hans Morgenthau confidently declared: "In my opinion the world is moving ineluctably towards a third world war – a strategic nuclear war. I do not believe that anything can be done to prevent it. The international system is simply too unstable to survive for long."[38] He had plenty of company in his shrill and, as it turned out, wildly misplaced alarmism.

Meanwhile, farce continued to reign. As it turns out, Khrushchev's stratospheric claims about how many ICBMs his factories were producing was at best a bluff, at worst a lie. And he refused any international inspections not because he had much to hide as was widely assumed in the West, but because he didn't want the West to know how weak the Soviet military was.[39] In fact, because the United States had desperately built up its own arsenal, a missile gap did materialize by 1962 – but it was the opposite of what had been predicted: the United States had two to four times more than the Soviets.

Nonetheless, deterring an essentially non-existent threat became a central, even overwhelming, preoccupation, and the result was a truly massive emphasis on exquisite theorizing, something that Robert Johnson has characterized as "nuclear metaphysics."[40] And, as Fred Kaplan has aptly observed, "In the absence of any reality that was congenial to their abstract theorizing, the strategists in power treated the theory as if it *were* reality. For those mired in thinking about it all day, every day, in the corridors of officialdom, nuclear strategy had become the stuff of a living dreamworld."[41]

Central to that living dreamworld was its unexamined assumption that the only way to persuade the other side not to attack was through the careful development of weapons that could credibly threaten to inflict unacceptable punishment on the aggressor. Deterrence has almost always been looked at strictly as a military issue, and definitions routinely characterize it as "the threat to use force in response as a way of preventing the first use of force by someone else" or as "altering the behavior of a target by using, or threatening to use, force."[42] Starting with a perspective like that, there has been a tendency to concentrate on what military capabilities will effectively threaten the attacker with high costs and on what diplomatic and military actions can be taken to make the threat appear credible.

By contrast, a broader and more fully pertinent concept would vigorously incorporate nonmilitary considerations as well as military ones into the mix, making direct and central application of the obvious fact that states do not approach the world solely in military terms.[43] When deterrence is recast this way, it becomes clear that the vast majority of wars that never happen are prevented – deterred – by factors that have little or nothing to do with military concerns. If outcomes are principally determined by military considerations in our chaotic state of international "anarchy," as so many have suggested, why is it that there are so many cases where a militarily superior country lives contentedly alongside a militarily inferior one?[44]

Deterrence would hold when two countries, taking all the various costs, benefits, and risks into account, vastly prefer peace to war. It's the sort of thing that has prevailed for a century between the United States and Canada. Even more strikingly, there is the comfortable neighbor relationship that has developed between Germany and France despite centuries of enmity and despite the fact that France could readily devastate Germany within minutes with its nuclear arsenal. And, insofar as direct warfare is concerned, it held for the relationship between the United States and the Soviet Union during the Cold War.

However, as it was developed, the deterrence logic with its overwhelmingly military focus not only tended to induce and to justify calls for increased defense expenditures, but it encouraged exaggerations of the military threat posed by the other side. Central to the process was the somber and focused examination of worst-case scenarios. Good analysis, of course, should include a consideration of extreme possibilities – even ones that envision monsters. However, particularly where nuclear weapons are concerned, these often become so mind-concentratingly appalling that they push aside other considerations and become essentially accepted, even embraced, as the norm. During the Cold War, as Johnson puts it, the process involved "making the most pessimistic assumptions possible about Soviet intentions and capabilities" and then assuming that the capabilities (which turned out almost always to have been substantially exaggerated) would be used "to the adversary's maximum possible advantage." During the Cold War, notes Strobe Talbott, scenarios about what the Soviet Union might do often had "a touch of paranoid fantasy about them."[45]

Brodie was one of the few who were capable of stepping back from the doom-eager thinking processes. In 1966, he expressed support for "the capability of dreaming up 'far out' events," but he also demanded that it be accompanied by a "disciplined judgment" about their likelihood. To do otherwise, he pointed out, is to assume that "the worst conceivable outcome has as good a chance as any of coming to pass."[46] And in 1978, he railed against the preoccupation with what he called "worst-case fantasies" and pointedly observed that the defense establishment was inhabited by people of

> a wide range of skills and sometimes of considerable imagination. All sorts of notions and propositions are churned out, and often presented for consideration with the prefatory works: "It is conceivable that ..." Such words establish their own truth, for the fact that someone has conceived of whatever proposition follows is enough to establish that it is conceivable. Whether it is worth a second thought, however, is another matter. It should undergo a good deal of thought before one begins to spend much money on it.[47]

Similarly, Kennan found "childishness" in the practice of making "sweeping assumptions about Soviet intentions" that were "the most extreme, most pessimistic, least sophisticated, and most improbable" and concerned problems "we do not really have."[48] Asked later about the nuclear buildup he had done so much to foster, former defense secretary Robert McNamara, once one of the most important proponents of nuclear metaphysics, reflected: "Each individual decision along the way seemed rational at the time. But the result was insane."[49]

Interestingly, President Dwight Eisenhower does seem, almost uniquely, to have grasped the fundamental reality that the Soviets had no interest whatever in a direct military confrontation and therefore that an ever-enlarged military was scarcely required to deter them. As his press secretary recorded in 1954, although Eisenhower was concerned about what he called "a sort of peaceful infiltration," he insisted, "after many long, long years of study on this problem," that "everything points to the fact that Russia is not seeking a general war and will not for a long, long time, if ever."[50] He may have been particularly impressed by the destruction he saw when he flew to Moscow in 1945 to meet with Stalin, recalling in his memoirs, "From the region of the Volga westward almost everything was destroyed. ... I did not see a house standing."[51] He also recalled conversations with his Soviet counterpart, Nikita Khrushchev, concluding it improbable that the Soviets would gamble everything on a surprise attack.[52]

That is, while the Soviets may have had the capacity to launch a major war against the West, Eisenhower maintained that they essentially had no desire to do so and that nuclear war was accordingly quite unlikely, apocalypse distant, and the nation's nuclear deterrent essentially, even excessively, adequate.[53] In the margins of his copy of a 1951 speech by an Admiral asserting that the "national strategy" of the Soviets "does not contemplate any g[l]obal war of her own choosing" because "the risk of losing is too great," Eisenhower scrawled, "I've preached [this] for 5 years!"[54]

But Eisenhower never really summoned the political courage to present his position openly and forcefully. He did make a bit of an effort in a 1954 speech in which he noted that those in the Kremlin "love power" and that, "whenever they start a war, they are taking the great risk of losing that power." And "when dictators over-reach themselves and challenge the whole world, they are very likely to end up in any place except a dictatorial position. And those men in the politburo know that." He concluded, somewhat evasively, that "these things are deterrents upon the men in the Kremlin" and "are factors that make war, let us say, less likely."[55]

McGeorge Bundy notes of Eisenhower, however, that "even in meetings of the National Security Council he seems to have preferred not to press his own point of view." Bundy reports on an incident in 1959 when, after hearing a report presenting "a gloomy assessment of the growing threat from the USSR," Eisenhower "stopped his usual doodling, raised a hand, and said, 'Please enter a minority report of one'." Concludes Bundy: "I find it a large missed opportunity for leadership that the man with the rank, the record, and the personal understanding to make this argument fully and persuasively appears to have made it, as far as the record now shows, only to himself."[56]

Instead, in public Eisenhower chose to rail against what he called the "military-industrial complex," warning that "in the councils of government, we must guard against the acquisition of unwarranted influence, whether sought or unsought, by the military-industrial complex."[57] In this, he attacked the lobbying movement for its successful machinations, but he did not confront the faulty and underexamined premise about dire Soviet intentions that gave that movement its effectiveness, its political potency. And he did that only as he was leaving office.

In an article published in 1961, the first year of the Kennedy administration, Morton Halperin declared the response of the Eisenhower era to defense requirements – massively extrapolated from the Korean War experience and exquisitely amplified by an army of nuclear metaphysicians – to be "complacency." In contrast, he called for "a strong, vigorous President" to overcome "bureaucratic and political opposition to the implementation of new, vitally needed programs."[58]

In this instance, complacency proved to be the far more nearly correct response to threats and challenges that, as it happened, didn't exist. No new military programs were "vitally needed" because there was nothing to deter. Moreover, complacency would have saved considerable money and might even have helped keep the United States from wandering into the debacle of Vietnam, a central consideration of Chapter 2.[59]

THE CRISIS CIRCUS

As it developed, the Cold War came furnished with a set of crises, and it was commonly envisioned that disaster would inevitably emerge from one or another of them. Their principal author was Nikita Khrushchev during his tenure as leader of the Soviet Union. He was seeking to manipulate the various antagonisms or "contradictions" among capitalist states that Leninist theory had long held to be the natural and inevitable condition of the capitalist state of being. Stalin had been familiar with this tactic, and Khrushchev claimed in 1960 that it was related to Soviet victory in World War II: "We smashed the aggressors, and in so doing we made use also of the contradictions between the imperialist states."[60]

Although postwar developments in the capitalist world had not been as vigorously contradictory as an ardent Leninist might desire, all was far from well in the West, and it gave the Soviets great pleasure in 1960 to announce that, what with the "mounting disintegration of the colonial system" and all, "a new stage has begun in the development of the general crisis of capitalism."[61] Moreover, when Khrushchev met various Western leaders, he discovered that they did not present a united front. Instead, they spoke to him in many tongues (some of them forked), and from time to time they even contradicted each other – proof to him that Lenin had been right all along.

Khrushchev's idea, then, was to see what he could do to make these shades of disagreement work to the Soviet benefit. His scheme was to exploit "intra-imperialist contradictions," as he called them, pitting the Western countries against each other and seeking out opportunities for "kindling distrust" of the United States in Europe.[62]

To accomplish this, Khrushchev sometimes built tensions to crisis levels through threats, bluster, and displays of force. He employed the technique first at the time of a crisis in 1956 over the Suez canal, and he seems to have concluded that it worked quite well there: it was his "stern warning" that "stopped the war," he publicly claimed later.[63] He soon honed his blusterous technique over disagreements about the status of the divided city of Berlin. In 1961, he had been confronted by a problem in Soviet-controlled East Germany: many residents were fleeing by going to West Berlin where they were embraced by the West German authorities and then flown out. In August, he stopped the damaging exodus by abruptly constructing a wall around West Berlin. Although this was something of an admission of failure about the appeals of East Germany, the Western countries were caught flat-footed by Khrushchev's *fait accompli* and did little except to disagree about what to do.

Most famously, Khrushchev tried again in issues concerning Cuba, a newly Communist country led by Fidel Castro. The Americans were in various degrees of hysteria about Castro's takeover in the nearby island, and in 1961, John Kennedy's first year as president, the United States put together an invasion by various exiles at Cuba's Bay of Pigs that was intended to topple Castro's government. Although the enterprise went so badly that it can reasonably be called "a perfect failure," Castro believed the Yankees would try again. Khrushchev was also concerned that the "missile gap," impelled in considerable part by his threatening bloviations, had come out the wrong way: after a certain amount of panicky building, the Americans now had a lot more missiles than he did.

He thus sought to solve two problems that didn't exist: 1) a potential US invasion which was not at all likely after the Bay of Pigs fiasco, and 2) a strategic "imbalance" that was irrelevant because neither side had the slightest intention of initiating a nuclear exchange whatever the disparity of the arsenal. He would try the *fait accompli* route again by secretly implanting a bunch of short-range missiles (which he had in abundant supply) in Cuba to deter the unlikely attack and to help right the irrelevant balance.

However, the Americans spotted the missiles in mid-transfer, blockaded Cuba, and got very mad. Hence, the crisis. Although there were some dicey moments particularly in the first day or so, and although there were some hotheads on both sides, the leaders were determined to keep the crisis from escalating.[64]

For his part, Khrushchev saw the horrors of potential war before him, and he had no intention of working closer toward that calamity. "I have participated in two world wars," Khrushchev wrote Kennedy at the height of the crisis, "and know that war ends only when it has carved its way across cities and villages, bringing death and destruction in its wake."[65] Khrushchev's memoirs seem to support the conclusion that from the start the Soviets "were preoccupied almost exclusively with how to extricate themselves from the situation with minimum loss of face and prestige."[66] The Soviets never even went on a demonstration alert.

Kennedy was also intensely concerned about escalation. In particular, he had been greatly impressed by Barbara Tuchman's best-selling book *The Guns of August,* and he concluded from it that in 1914 the Europeans "somehow seemed to tumble into war ... through stupidity, individual idiosyncrasies, misunderstandings, and personal complexes of inferiority and grandeur." He had no intention, he made clear, of becoming a central character in a "comparable book about this time, *The Missiles of October*."[67]

The crisis was resolved when the Soviets openly agreed to remove the offending missiles from Cuba while the United States secretly agreed to remove comparable short-range NATO missiles from Turkey. However, Kennedy was apparently quite willing to consider formally removing the missiles from Turkey if that is what it took to get the Cuban missiles out. Indeed, 25 years after the event, Kennedy's Secretary of State, Dean Rusk, disclosed that Kennedy had actually established mechanisms for arranging the missile trade should it come to that.[68] As two analysts who have worked with the transcripts of the American meetings have observed, even if the Soviets had held out for a deal that was substantially embarrassing to the United States, the odds that the Americans would have gone to war "were next to zero."[69]

There were also concerns at the time that the two contestants might somehow get into a war by accident. However, the historical record suggests that wars simply do not begin that way. In his extensive survey of wars that have occurred since 1400, Luard concludes, "It is impossible to identify a single case in which it can be said that a war started accidentally; in which it was not, at the time the war broke out, the deliberate intention of at least one party that war should take place." Geoffrey Blainey, after similar study, very much agrees: although many have discussed "accidental" or "unintentional" wars, "it is difficult," he concludes, "to find a war which on investigation fits this description." Or, as Henry Kissinger has put it dryly, "Despite popular myths, large military units do not fight by accident." And, after investigating 40 crises with some sort of nuclear connection, analyst Bruno Tertrais concludes, "solid command and control arrangements, sound procedures, constant vigilance, efficient training, and cool-headedness of leadership have ensured – and can continue to ensure – that nuclear weapons will continue to play only a deterrence role." And then adds: "'Luck' has very little to do with it."[70]

Even if an accident takes place during a crisis, it does not follow that escalation or hasty response is inevitable, or even very likely. As Brodie points out, escalation scenarios essentially impute to both sides "a well-nigh limitless concern with saving face" and/or "a great deal of ground-in automaticity of response and counterresponse."[71] None of this was in evidence during the Cuban missile crisis when there were accidents galore. An American U-2 spy plane was shot down over Cuba, probably without authorization, and another accidentally went off course and flew threateningly over the Soviet Union. These events were duly evaluated and then ignored. Actually, the Americans had specifically decided that if a U-2 plane were shot down over Cuba, they would retaliate by destroying the antiaircraft site responsible.[72] When the event came to pass, however, the policy was simply not carried out.[73]

One episode during the Cuban missile crisis has frequently been put forward as particularly ominous and threatening. But, overall, it reads more like a comedy of errors. It began when the Soviets sent four submarines, each with a single nuclear-tipped torpedo, to the Atlantic during the crisis. Amazingly, it appears that many (perhaps all) in the top Soviet leadership did not realize the subs were old diesel ones, not nuclear powered, and therefore ordered them to get to the area at an impossible speed. Consequently, they were going full power, full time, sometimes blowing engines. Moreover, the subs were not designed for the tropics and so temperatures, and tempers, inside them went well over 100 degrees Fahrenheit. Sailors were dropping like flies.[74]

Patrolling the area, the US Navy spotted the subs and was essentially dropping toys (grenades, practice depth charges) on them.[75] Nonetheless, these were noisy enough to convince those toyed with that they were under real attack.[76] Above all, the Russians didn't know what was going on because they could only get communications if they surfaced at least to periscope depth, and the United States didn't know each sub had a nuclear torpedo.

In all this, the commander of one of the submarines, according to the testimony of a radio officer, let out with an "outburst" in which he ordered that the sub's sole nuclear torpedo be launched against a patrolling American surface ship.[77] However, two other officers had to agree to launch and, according to the testimony, one of them demurred. In addition, there was a "special officer" who actually slept with the nuclear torpedo (maybe Dr. Strangelove isn't all that big an exaggeration after all), and he had one set of keys which were necessary to load it. He was also responsible for maintaining the torpedo and assembling it for combat use, but only if such an order had been received from Moscow.[78] No such orders to the torpedo's bedmate were ever made, of course.[79] However, had they been issued, he presumably would go into action only if he was assured that any such order had originated from Moscow which would mean all three commanders would have had to lie to him. And he would have known it was a lie because he would surely know that communication with Moscow was impossible under water. In addition, the radio officer who is the primary source of this story actually concluded in a separate interview that an intentional launch was "very unlikely," although he did worry about an accident or about "malfunctioning equipment."[80] However, this seems impossible because the torpedo was not armed. Disassembled torpedoes assemble and then launch themselves by accident only in Disney animations.

It has been suggested that, if the nuclear torpedo had been launched, the alarmed Americans might have used nuclear depth charges and that this might have started a "chain of inadvertent developments."[81] But even the first step in the unspecified "chain" is not particularly plausible: the Americans could easily have taken out the ancient diesel subs they had already located with conventional weapons. Moreover, even if the torpedo had been launched it might well have missed and/or failed to detonate. And if it did detonate, the only sensible response would be that this could not possibly be part of a first strike (nobody could be that stupid) and that it must be some sort of accident or misadvertence – something a terrified Khrushchev would confirm passionately as he withdrew from the field to prove it. Kennedy was already uneasy about even the use of "practice" depth charges against the Soviet submarines.[82]

Moreover, military action was unlikely even if the missiles had been successfully implanted in Cuba. It is very clear that Kennedy would have formally and openly offered to remove NATO missiles from Turkey in order to get the Cuban ones retracted, and it is equally clear that Khrushchev and the Soviet leadership would have agreed.

But even failing that, the missiles scarcely would have changed the international nuclear situation very much: they would have added only marginally to the Soviet Union's ability to hit the United States with nuclear explosives and, as the discussion in this chapter has repeatedly suggested, the Soviets were overwhelmingly unlikely to do that unless they were attacked first. That is, if Khrushchev's gambit had been successful and if the missiles had been duly installed in Cuba and their removal not negotiated, the only consequence would be that, like other nuclear forces, they would have spent the next decades gathering dust.

Except recently, perhaps. Americans are being allowed to visit Cuba after a pointless and fundamentally absurd travel ban was finally lifted by Barack Obama in 2016. If the missiles had remained in Cuba, the regime would now likely be polishing them up and putting them forward as a tourist attraction. Perhaps there would even be a Trump Tower nearby, affording the tourists, (for a price of course) an aerial view of the aging military instruments that had caused so much concern in 1962.

There were two longer-term consequences from the Cuban missile crisis.

First, Khrushchev (and his successors) thereafter gave up engineering provocative crises in order to exacerbate the supposed "contradictions" among capitalist states – there were essentially none for the rest of the Cold War. The sentiment behind this change is evident in a speech Khrushchev gave to Soviet textile workers a year after the crisis. He recalled the loss of his son in World War II and the millions of other deaths suffered by the Russians, and he then laid into his critics: "Some comrades abroad claim that Khrushchev is making a mess of things, and is afraid of war. Let me say once again that I should like to see the kind of bloody fool who is genuinely not afraid of war." The Soviet press reported that this vivid statement about the stupidity of war was cheered more loudly and wholeheartedly than any other by his audience. Or there was his earthy comment to some naval officers shortly after the crisis: "I'm not a czarist officer who has to kill himself if I fart at a masked ball. It's better to back down than to go to war."[83]

And second, the Soviets somehow preposterously concluded that they had humiliatingly lost their Caribbean gambit because they did not have enough nuclear weapons. "You got away with it this time," one Soviet diplomat bitterly asserted at the United Nations, "but you will never get away with it again." In 1964, Khrushchev was ousted for "hare-brained scheming," and his replacement, Leonid Brezhnev, launched a massive, drunken-sailor-like military, and particularly nuclear, buildup that the country could scarcely afford. It was a policy that, as Max Frankel puts it, "contributed mightily to the economic collapse and political ruin of the Soviet Union."[84] That process will be discussed in more detail in Chapter 2.

2

Containment, Vietnam, and the Curious
End of the Cold War

If the policy of deterrence sought to solve a problem that didn't exist, the associated policy of containment at least sought to deal with one that did.

It is commonly argued that containment worked. Thus diplomat Chas Freeman declares that it was "the grand strategy of containment that brought us a bloodless victory in the Cold War." Daniel Drezner characterizes that strategy as "persistently effective," and Scott Sagan seeks to extend the concept, arguing that a strategy of containment, together with deterrence can "work on North Korea, as it did on the Soviet Union."[1]

However, the policy itself was logically flawed, and it was to impel the United States into a costly "test-case" war in Vietnam against an enemy that proved to be essentially undefeatable. In the end, the problem containment was fabricated to deal with went away only when the policy itself lapsed – a development that helped Communism to self-destruct and that led directly to the end of the Cold War when an exhausted and much over-extended Soviet Union abandoned its expansionist ideology.

CONTAINMENT AND INDIRECT AGGRESSION

Whatever their preoccupation with nuclear deterrence, Western policymakers were aware that any Soviet expansionism was not so likely to be expressed primarily in endeavors like the Korean War. Although they were unduly and excessively alarmed by the potential for such exercises in "direct aggression" as discussed in Chapter 1, they expected "indirect aggression" to be more common. This involved subversion, diplomatic and military pressure, revolution, and armed uprising – all inspired, partly funded, and heavily influenced by Moscow and later by Beijing.

The policy of containment was designed to deal with this threat, and it was formally set in motion as the United States responded to crises on the periphery of Europe in the early postwar years. In Greece, Communists were waging a civil war against the Western-oriented monarchist government, and pressure was being applied by the Soviet Union on the Turkish government to gain various territorial and naval rights. Both threatened countries needed help, and the United States came through with military and economic aid accompanied by the ringing declaration of the Truman Doctrine of March 12, 1947, that "it must be the policy of the United States to support free peoples who are resisting attempted subjugation by armed minorities [Greece] or by outside pressures [Turkey]."

In putting forth this policy, President Harry S. Truman made it clear that no crisis was an island unto itself. If "Greece should fall," the effect on Turkey "would be immediate and serious." Then "confusion and disorder might well spread throughout the entire Middle East." Moreover, this would have a "profound effect" upon important countries in Europe which were already "struggling against great difficulties to maintain their freedoms and independence while they repair the damages of war." This was an early expression of what would later be called the domino theory, and it derives directly from the experience before World War II. In part, such subversion had allowed Hitler to take over Austria in 1938 and Japan to take over Manchuria in 1931.

Containment policy was free of explicit limits. If all else failed, US combat troops could quite possibly be sent over as part of the aid package – although nothing in the Truman Doctrine guaranteed this would occur. (As it happened, however, that decision never had to be made by Truman because troops were never required: the Greek Communists were defeated by 1949, and the Turks were able successfully to stand up to Soviet pressures.) The policy pronouncement also suggests that containment would be applied any place in the world where, in the American judgment, international Communism was, or appeared to be, on the march.[2]

The Truman Doctrine also saw economic stability as important in opposing the spread of Communism, something that in the end would facilitate peace. This lesson too was derived in part from the experience of the 1930s, because it was concluded that economic chaos had spawned Hitler and thus eventually world war. As Truman put it in his 1947 speech,

> The seeds of totalitarian regimes are nurtured by misery and want. They spread and grow in the evil soil of poverty and strife. They reach their full growth when the hope of a people for a better life has died. We must keep that hope alive. .... If we falter in our leadership, we may endanger the peace of the world.

The quintessential intellectual presentation of the containment policy remains George Kennan's article "The Sources of Soviet Conduct," published in *Foreign Affairs* in 1947. It is concerned about Soviet military strength, but it argues that what makes that strength threatening is an ideology that is fundamentally expansionist. In the first paragraphs of the article, Kennan argues that the outstanding features of Communist thought are 1) "the capitalist system of production is a nefarious one which inevitably leads to the exploitation of the working class by the capital-owning class"; 2) "capitalism contains the seeds of its own destruction," which must result inevitably and inescapably in a "revolutionary transfer of power to the working class"; 3) countries where revolutions have been successful "will rise against the remaining capitalist world"; 4) capitalism will not perish "without proletarian revolution"; and 5) a "final push" is "needed from a revolutionary proletariat movement in order to tip over the tottering structure."[3]

The operative expressions in Kennan's article were "The main element of any U.S. policy toward the Soviet Union must be that of a long-term, patient but firm and vigilant containment of Russian expansive tendencies" and "a policy of firm containment, designed to confront the Russians with unalterable counter-force at every point where they show signs of encroaching upon the interests of a peaceful and stable world."[4] In the long run, it was hoped, the Soviets, frustrated in their drive for territory and expanded authority, would become less hostile and more accommodating. Diplomacy would encourage that desirable development and remain open to it. Kennan stressed weaknesses: the Soviet population was exhausted and disillusioned, economic development was spotty, and there were looming uncertainties in the impending transfer of power that would follow the demise of Soviet dictator Josef Stalin, something that might "shake Soviet power to its foundations." Moreover, the Soviets were also likely to find maintaining control over Eastern Europe far from easy.[5]

As early as 1948 some of this seemed to be coming true: an important schism in the Soviet empire developed when Stalin sought to bring Yugoslavia, led by a loyal but independent Communist Party, under tighter control. Although the Yugoslav party had been ideologically even more aggressive and belligerent toward the West than the Soviets, this breach in Communist solidarity was quickly welcomed with offers of aid and friendship by American policymakers, who nevertheless have often since been accused of being insensitive to differences among members of the international Communist movement.

In general, Kennan concluded, there was a "strong" possibility that Soviet power "bears within it the seeds of its own decay, and that the sprouting of these seeds is well advanced."[6] How long it might take for collapse to occur was not predictable of course, but Kennan apparently believed that it wouldn't take too long, estimating 10 to 15 years.[7] This timing strongly suggests that Kennan, remembering the conflicts that erupted after the death of the Soviet founder Vladimir Lenin in 1924, was putting his primary emphasis on the transfer of power issue: Stalin was nearing 70 when Kennan was formulating the policy. Later, in 1950, Kennan argued that even if it took an extremely long time – like 30 years – for the "defeat of the Kremlin" to occur, the "tortuous and exasperatingly slow devices of diplomacy" were surely preferable to a "test of arms" which was unlikely to bring about "any happy or clear settlement" of international differences.[8]

Actually, as it turned out, the "defeat of the Kremlin" still had not occurred even by 1980. The Soviet regime managed to survive Stalin's death (which took place in 1953) quite well, and for decades it managed to maintain control over resentful, sophisticated people in the middle of Europe.

INDIRECT AGGRESSION IN THE DEVELOPED WORLD

An especially insidious form of "indirect aggression," one with chillingly wide-ranging potential, was internal subversion in the West.

Indirect aggression was seen to be in operation when, in complicity with the neighboring Soviet Union, the Communist Party in democratic Czechoslovakia fomented a coup in 1948, taking over the country and bringing it into the Soviet camp. There was great fear that a similar process might take place elsewhere in Europe, especially in Italy and France where there were large and well-organized Communist parties. But Communism's appeal gradually waned on that continent. After the limited, and at-the-time alarming, case of Czechoslovakia, Communism did not expand further on that continent.

In the quest to deal with indirect aggression, many within the United States increasingly envisioned even the small domestic Communist Party to be a potential threat. Ideologically committed to the violent overthrow of sitting governments and allied with a hostile foreign country, domestic Communists had a subversive agenda that included, or seemed to include, agitation, conspiracy, sabotage, and espionage.

Fears rose as evidence from defecting American and Canadian Communists in 1945 and 1946 suggested that the operatives of the Communist Party generally really did believe in the conspiratorial revolutionary ideology that filled their speeches, directives, and publications.[9] In the following years, alarm about the threat presented by such "enemies from within" grew with two spectacular espionage cases. First, a respected former

State Department official, Alger Hiss, was accused of having sent huge quantities of classified documents to the Soviets before World War II. Then, a former Communist, British physicist Klaus Fuchs, admitted that he had sent atomic secrets to the Soviets during the war, and the trail from Fuchs soon led to the arrests of various co-conspirators and ultimately to the celebrated trial of two American Communists, Julius and Ethel Rosenberg, who were convicted of being atomic spies.

In 1949, the Soviet Union tested its first atomic bomb, and it was commonly assumed that the Soviets could not have done so without the secret plans purloined for them by domestic sources and that this possession emboldened Stalin in his plan for world conquest. There was little or no effort at the time to try to refute (or even examine) these understandable, but entirely speculative, assumptions, and later research strongly suggests that neither happens to be true.[10]

This experience was set in high relief with the invasion of South Korea by forces from Communist North Korea in June 1950, bolstered later in the year by hordes of troops from Communist China. As discussed in Chapter 1 almost everyone simply assumed that the Korean War was being directed from Moscow and was part of a broad militarized quest for "world domination." And the Korean War also convinced many that US Communists were devoted to a system dedicated not only to the revolutionary overthrow of the American government but also ultimately to a direct invasion of the country itself. Accordingly, fears about the dangers presented by the enemy within became greatly heightened and then fully internalized. The execution in 1953 of the Rosenbergs might never have taken place had the Korean War not occurred.[11] Fears about "the enemy within" were extensively and successfully exploited by various politicians, of whom Senator Joseph McCarthy is the best remembered.

In that atmosphere politicians scurried to support billions upon billions to surveil, to screen, to protect, and to spy on an ever-expanding array of individuals who had come to seem suspicious. During 1972 alone, 65,000 new intelligence files were opened and added to the half-million already in existence.[12] Extravagant proclamations about the degree to which "masters of deceit" and "enemies from within" presented a threat to the republic found a receptive audience. Thus, J. Edgar Hoover, the highly respected, even revered, director of the FBI, confidently asserted in a 1958 book that the American Communist Party was working "day and night to further the communist plot in America" with "deadly seriousness"; that a "Bolshevik transmission" was in progress that was "virtually invisible to the non-communist eye, unhampered by time, distance, and legality"; that it was "creating communist puppets throughout the country"; and that it had for "its objective the ultimate seizure of power in America."[13] And that's all on just one page.

In fact, despite huge anxieties about it at the time, there seem to have been no instances in which domestic Communists engaged in anything that could be considered espionage after the conclusion of World War II. Moreover, at no time did any domestic Communist ever commit anything that could be considered violence in support of the cause. For example, FBI informant Herbert Philbrick's best-selling confessional book *I Led Three Lives*, published in 1952, at no point documents a single instance of violence or planned violence by domestic Communists.[14]

In his book *Communazis*, Alexander Stephan systematically describes and evaluates the essential absurdity – or farcical nature – of the situation: the high efficiency and gross overkill as hundreds of agents were paid to intercept and catalogue communications, to endlessly record goings and comings, and to sift enterprisingly through trash bins of people who were highly unlikely to pose much of a subversive threat.[15] As the Cold War continued, there apparently was no audience for the proposition that the threat presented by domestic communists was overblown. That is, no one – *no one* – ever seems to have said in public,

> Many domestic communists adhere to a foreign ideology that ultimately has as its goal the destruction of capitalism and democracy and by violence if necessary; however, they do not present much of a danger, are actually quite a pathetic bunch, and couldn't subvert their way out of a wet paper bag. Why are we expending so much time, effort, and treasure on this issue?

It is rather astounding that that plausible, if arguable, point of view seems never to have been publicly expressed by anyone – politician, pundit, professor, editorialist – during the Cold War.

INDIRECT AGGRESSION IN THE DEVELOPING WORLD: VIETNAM AS A TEST CASE

Although never able to gain much of a hold in the developed world (certainly including the United States), international Communism could cast its eye with more pleasure on less developed areas. In 1949, China was taken over by Communist insurgents under the command of Mao Zedong. In addition, dozens of new nations were emerging, most of them carved out of colonial empires that were gradually dismantled in the postwar era. Most of the new states and many of the old ones in what came to be called the "Third World" had leaders and elites who, although not Communists in the classic sense, seemed susceptible because they bubbled over with ideas about economics, politics, and society that could comfortably be labeled progressive by Communist ideologues.[16] Thus, a successful anticolonial war in Indo-China against the French brought in a Communist regime in North Vietnam in 1954, and Cuba alarmingly joined up after Fidel Castro's victory there in 1959. Communists were also able to take control of portions of Laos in 1961. In addition, there were potentially congenial regimes in decolonized Indonesia after 1949 and in Algeria after 1962.

The Communist successes in China, North Vietnam, Cuba, and Laos were all preceded by a cut-off or draw-down of support of the incumbent regimes by the United States: Truman with the opposing nationalists in China, Eisenhower with French forces in Indo-China and with the Batista regime in Cuba, and Kennedy with anti-Communist elements in Laos.[17] That pattern was soon to be replicated in South Vietnam where, by 1965, insurgents, increasingly aided and supported by Communist North Vietnam, appeared to be on the verge of victory. It seemed that the only way to rescue the situation was to send in American troops and that was done. The alternative would have been to succumb to complacency. The effect of the American military inter-vention may well have been simply to delay, at a total cost of well over a million lives, a Communist takeover by 10 years.

Vietnam was seen to be an important testing ground of the efficacy of such wars. As Defense Secretary Robert McNamara put it at the time, the conflict was taken to be "a test case of the capacity of the U.S. to help a nation meet a Communist 'war of liberation'." And North Vietnamese leaders agreed: "South Vietnam is the model of the national liberation movement of our time. If the special warfare that the United States imperialists are testing in South Vietnam is overcome, then it can be defeated anywhere in the world." Final victory in the "sacred struggle," intoned the country's chief leader, Le Duan, would be "an active contribution to strengthen the world revolution." Lin Piao, then defense minister for Communist China, also put the issue in global terms in September 1965. Since World War II, revolution for various reasons had been temporarily held back in North America and West Europe, he noted, but it was growing vigorously elsewhere. Thus, ultimately the whole cause of world revolution hinged on the revolutionary struggles of the Asian, African, and Latin American peoples, and he urged that socialist countries should regard it as their internationalist duty to support such struggles.[18]

Unlike many other military ventures, this one was extensively thought through before US troops were sent in: premises were evaluated, options considered, and potential costs (fairly accurately) calculated.[19] In the end, decision-makers agreed with the 1965 assessment of reporter David Halberstam. Although he was later to become a severe war critic, at that time he said he considered Vietnam to be "a strategic country in a key area" and "perhaps one of only five or six nations in the world that is truly vital to U.S. interests." He opposed withdrawal because of the domino fixation: "the pressure of Communism on the rest of Southeast Asia" would then "intensify and throughout the world" as "the enemies of the West" became "encouraged to try insurgencies like the one in Vietnam."[20]

When the American decisions of 1965 to send troops to Vietnam were taken, then, a grim, if fanciful, consensus existed in the United States about the necessity and wisdom of such ventures. There seemed to be a special urgency at the time because China was crowing belligerently about supporting such wars and because China-linked Communists seemed to be on the verge of taking over in the important and nearby country (or domino) of Indonesia. Complacency, it seemed, was simply unacceptable.

Although the process of consideration was exemplary in many ways, in the end simplicity and spook – or farce – prevailed. It is perhaps demonstrated in Johnson's wild and absurd, even deranged, extrapolation about the situation, one that, in its certainty, rivals Truman's about how the Korean War was necessary to prevent World War III:

> I was as sure as any man could be that once we showed how weak we were, Moscow and Peking would move in a flash to exploit our weakness. . . . As nearly as anyone can be certain of anything, I knew they couldn't resist the opportunity to expand their control over the vacuum of power we would leave behind us. And so would begin World War III.[21]

Such spooky extrapolations about threat were deadly in their consequences. They implied, or sucked, the United States into a costly, spectacularly unnecessary war.

As it happened, however, within a year of the 1965 decision to send American troops in large numbers to fight in Vietnam, the Cold War value of doing so declined substantially. First, there was a violent anti-Communist reaction in previously Communist-leaning Indonesia in which hundreds of thousands of domestic Communists and their families were murdered. And second, the Chinese, although still verbally belligerent, mostly turned their energies inward as they embarked upon a bizarre ritual of romantic self-purification known as the Great Proletarian Cultural Revolution.[22]

The war inspired an extensive and very public anti-war opposition in the United States. Its tactics of public disruption, however, may have actually been counterproductive.[23] This is because opposition to the war came to be associated with violent disruption, stink bombs, desecration of the flag, profanity, and contempt for American values. Indeed, it generated negative feelings among the American public to an all but unprecedented degree. In an election poll conducted by the University of Michigan in 1968, the public was asked to place various groups and personalities on a 100-point scale. Fully one-third of the respondents gave Vietnam War protesters a zero, the lowest possible rating, while only 16 percent put them anywhere in the upper half of the scale. Not only did these associations tend to affect public opinion in a negative way, they also tended to frighten away more "respectable" would-be war opponents from joining the cause.

However, the protest movement may have had some impact in presidential elections: it was quite possibly instrumental in electing Richard Nixon. Twice. In 1968, it trashed the campaign of Hubert Humphrey and, in 1972, it nominated George McGovern, the worst presidential candidate any party has put forward in modern times.[24]

Popular support for the war in Vietnam did decline as casualties accrued. But it is unlikely the anti-war movement had much to do with that: support declined at much the same pace as for the Korean War, which did not have a public anti-war protest movement (nor was it a "television" war like the one in Vietnam).[25] As will be discussed in Chapter 4, the anti-war movement in the Iraq War seems to have learned some lessons from the experience of their counterparts in Vietnam.

The military strategy chosen to confront – or to contain – the Communists in Vietnam was attrition. The basic idea was to send over large numbers of American troops to seize the initiative and to carry the war to the enemy and in the process cause it to reach its breaking point. It would become "convinced that military victory was impossible and then would not be willing to endure further punishment," in the words of the general in charge, William Westmoreland.[26]

There were at least three ways the American strategy might have been successful, all with historical precedents. Weakened, they might fade away – "choose to reduce their efforts in the South and try to salvage their resources for another day," as McNamara put it – something like what had happened previously in Greece, the Philippines, and Malaya.[27] Another possible path to success was through a combination of military effectiveness and diplomatic maneuver: denied military victory, the Communists might have tried to cut a deal. They had previously done this in Korea in 1953, in Indo-China against the French in 1954, and in Laos in 1961. And a third possibility was that the Soviet Union and/or China, important North Vietnamese allies and suppliers, might become discouraged and, wary of the costs and escalatory dangers of the war, pressure their combative little client Southeast Asia into a more accommodating stance as they had in 1954.

American policymakers, then, did have some plans for success in the war. The idea was to push the North Vietnamese Communists until they broke. As Leslie Gelb and Richard Betts characterize the thinking of the time, "How could a tiny, backward Asian country *not* have a breaking point?"[28] Specific predictions included General Westmoreland's timetable, which seemed to suggest a reasonable hope for the defeat and destruction of enemy forces by the end of 1967, and conclusions by top Defense Department officials of a 50-50 chance of success by 1967 or 1968.[29] Despite assertions that intelligence reports of the time were "invariably pessimistic," these projections, given the uncertainties of the time, seem quite reasonable even in retrospect. Potential costs were also soberly assessed, and calculations about probable American casualties proved to be quite accurate.[30]

The war effort in Vietnam failed because the military (and others) misjudged the casualty tolerance of the Communist forces. As Secretary of State Dean Rusk observed in 1971, "I personally underestimated the resistance and determination of the North Vietnamese. ... I thought that when we had established a position in Vietnam which would be clearly impossible for them to overrun militarily that then the chances were very high that they would pull back – maybe only for a time – but pull back or take part in some serious negotiation."[31]

This misestimation proved to be a crucial mistake, but history suggests that, however unfortunate, it was quite reasonable. It turns out that the willingness of the Communists to suffer battle deaths in Vietnam was, proportionate to size, almost unique in modern warfare. If the battle death rate as a percentage of prewar population is calculated for each of the hundreds of countries that have participated in international and colonial wars since 1816, it is apparent that Vietnam was an extreme case. Even discounting heavily for exaggerations in the body count, the Communist side accepted battle death rates that were about twice as high as those accepted by the fanatical, often suicidal, Japanese in World War II. Furthermore, the few combatant countries that did take loss rates as high as the Vietnamese Communists were mainly those like the Germans and Soviets in World War II who were fighting to the death for their national existence, not just for expansion, like North Vietnam.[32]

In Vietnam, it seems, the United States was up against an incredibly well-functioning organization – patient, firmly disciplined, tenaciously led, and largely free from corruption or enervating self-indulgence. Although the Communists often experienced massive military setbacks and periods of stress and exhaustion, they were always able to refit themselves, rearm, and come back for more.[33] As General Creighton Abrams put it, "You give them 36 hours and, goddam it, you've got to start the war all over again."[34] Or as Westmoreland put it tersely, "Any American commander who took the same vast losses . . . would have been sacked overnight."[35] In this respect, it may well be that, as one American general concluded, "they were in fact the best enemy we have faced in our history."[36]

The extraordinary Communist tenacity could not have been confidently anticipated. Evidence from the war they had earlier conducted against the French certainly was of little help: in their major battles in the war against the Americans and South Vietnamese the Communists suffered tens of thousands of battle deaths, while in their major massed battle against the French in 1954 they had lost about 7,900 men – and apparently had been pushed to the limits of collapse as a result.[37]

Over the course of the war, as it happens, the massive losses suffered did repeatedly inspire dissention both in the Communist ranks and among top decision-makers, particularly in connection with hugely costly Communist offensives in 1968 and 1972 that were supposed to ignite uprising in the south, but utterly failed to do so. There was also pressure from the Soviets and the Chinese to modify the tactics and the strategy. However, the regime in the north, including in particular Le Duan, the man – or monster – crucially in charge, was able to outflank and often purge or murder Communist Party dissenters, to stifle protest in the military ranks, and to brush off foreign advice.[38] It was characterized, as Pierre Asselin puts it, by a "callous disregard for the death and suffering of their own compatriots."[39] Although such a supreme exercise in irresponsible fanaticism would have thoroughly dismayed the tactically cautious Lenin, Le Duan and his like-minded collaborators were able continuously to stream hundreds of thousands of soldiers to the south to be ground up by the American war machine.

It did not come out the way American strategists had planned, but the war did represent a triumph for the strategy of attrition: after a long, costly struggle, it was the American will that broke. After a Communist offensive in 1968 that seemed to demonstrate that the end of the war was likely to be a long way off, the American administration under Lyndon Johnson essentially decided to cease the American escalation and to begin to turn the war over to the South Vietnamese, a policy that was essentially continued under his successor, Richard Nixon.[40] The American casualty rate dropped, troops were withdrawn, and by May 1971, the United States no longer had a direct combat role – though it provided extensive air support to help the South Vietnamese turn back a Communist offensive in 1972. Then, in 1973, the United States agreed to withdraw its already substantially reduced direct military participation in the war and to allow Communist troops to remain in the south poised for action. In response, the North Vietnamese agreed to give the Americans their prisoners back – an essential element from the perspective of the United States.[41]

Another component of the American failure in Vietnam was that, despite enormous effort and expense, its military was unable to fashion the South Vietnamese military into an effective fighting force – in particular, to create an effective leadership corps.[42] In 1975, the ill-led, unmotivated, exhausted, and corrupt South Vietnamese forces, substantially abandoned by the United States in, and after, the face-saving agreement of 1973, collapsed to a Communist onslaught in 55 days. In 1972, they had been able to hold the line against the Communist offensive until US bombing could be brought in. Not this time.

It seems unlikely that the Vietnam War could have been won by the United States at any reasonable cost.

In Senate testimony in 1969, General Westmoreland was asked if he thought the war could be won. "Absolutely," he replied, and others have agreed.[43] For example, H. R. McMaster has taken the chiefs to staff to task – indeed accusing them of a dereliction of duty – because "they did not recommend the total force they believed would ultimately be required in Vietnam," accepting instead "a strategy they knew would lead to a large but inadequate commitment of troops, for an extended period of time, with little hope for success."[44] The implication is that there was a force level that would actually have worked.

To be convincing, however, these analysts need evidence that the North Vietnamese "breaking point" had been, or could have been, reached. The Communists in Vietnam have been virtually unique in modern history in their willingness to tolerate casualties, and their remarkable tenacity and resiliency after major setbacks suggest that their breaking point might have been very high, possibly even near to extermination levels. As military analyst Konrad Kellen put it at the time, "Short of ... being physically destroyed, collapse, surrender, or disintegration was – to put it bizarrely – simply not within their capabilities."[45] Even using nuclear weapons on North Vietnam and the infiltration trails might not have worked unless they had been dropped at near-annihilation levels; and exactly how they could have been used effectively in the internal war in the south, which is where the war ultimately had to be won, is difficult to imagine. An invasion of North Vietnam might have led to a major response by the Chinese or the Soviets, and the war against North Vietnam might have been "won" in the same sense that the invasion of North Korea in 1950 "won" the war against that country. But even without such an escalation by North Vietnam's larger allies, the United States might well have found itself bogged down in a lengthy, costly, agonizing guerrilla war conducted throughout Indo-China – a war rather like the one the French fought, and lost, in 1954.

THE CONTAINMENT LAPSE AFTER VIETNAM

In the end, any mellowing of Soviet expansionism was due not to containment's success, but to its failure.

In 1975 three countries – Cambodia, South Vietnam, and Laos – abruptly toppled into the Communist camp. Then, partly out of fear of repeating the Vietnam experience, the United States went into a sort of containment funk: it effectively adopted a policy of complacency (or perhaps of appeasement) as it watched from the sidelines as the Soviet Union, in what seems in retrospect to have been remarkably like a fit of absent mindedness, opportunistically gathered a set of Third World countries into its imperial embrace: Angola in 1976, Mozambique and Ethiopia in 1977, South Yemen and Afghanistan in 1978, Grenada and Nicaragua in 1979.

The Soviets at first were quite gleeful about these acquisitions – the "correlation of forces," as they called it, had decisively and most agreeably shifted in their direction.[46] For example, a Soviet spokesman enthused in 1979, "The feat accomplished in Nicaragua reflected the intensification of revolutionary processes on the Latin American continent and doubtless will be an inspirational stimulus in the struggle . . . against imperialism and its henchmen."[47]

However, almost all the new acquisitions soon became economic and political basket cases, fraught with dissension, financial mismanagement, and civil warfare, and turned expectantly to the Soviet Union for maternal warmth and sustenance. Most disastrous for the Soviet Union was the experience in Afghanistan. In December 1979, they sent a large contingent of troops there, apparently planning to nip an anti-Communist rebellion in the bud and avoiding a long, enervating war like the one the Americans had suffered in Vietnam. Instead, they soon found themselves bogged down in exactly that sort of war. They were up against several groups that regarded it as their holy duty to fight the foreign intervention even if the war took decades. The rebels obtained sanctuary in neighboring Pakistan and were granted various forms of aid, including increasingly sophisticated weapons, from China (now very much at odds with the Soviets), the United States, Saudi Arabia, and elsewhere. Their Afghan adventure also severely undercut the credibility and respect the Soviets had sought for decades to develop in the Third World, particularly in Muslim areas.[48]

President Jimmy Carter was electrified by the Soviet invasion, and he quickly embraced instead what Raymond Garthoff has called "the *least* likely Soviet motivation – pursuit of a relentless expansionist design." Similarly, national security adviser Zbigniew Brzezinski envisioned the invasion as "a strategic challenge" and fancied Afghanistan as a central element in an "arc of crisis" anchored in North Africa on one end and in India on the other – "one of those intellectual constructs that dramatizes a threat but hardly contributes to clear thinking," as Robert Johnson aptly characterizes it.[49]

There were other problems for international Communism in general and for the Soviet Communism in particular. In 1978, the Vietnamese Communists invaded neighboring Cambodia after a number of border clashes and toppled the even more brutal Communist government there. With substantial financial aid from the Soviets, they continued their occupation despite lingering guerrilla opposition – Vietnam's Vietnam some called it – and despite a punitive attack across their northern border by the Chinese Communists in 1979 who were angered at what they took to be Vietnamese imperialism. The Soviets' empire in Eastern Europe had also became a severe economic drain and a psychic problem. The economic bill to the Soviet Union for maintaining its growing collection of dependencies around the world rose dramatically.[50] It soon came to realize that it would have been better off contained.

But this suggests that the policy of containment was logically flawed. The Soviet system really did prove to be as rotten and as destined to self-destruct as Kennan had more or less accurately surmised in 1947. However, if this is so, the best policy would not have been to contain it, but to give it enough rope – to let it expand until it reached the point of terminal overstretch. Indeed, one of Kennan's favorite quotes comes from Gibbon: "there is nothing more contrary to nature than the attempt to hold in obedience distant provinces."[51]

ENDING THE COLD WAR

In March 1985 the reins of the Soviet Union were given over to 54-year-old Mikhail Gorbachev. He found plenty to be concerned about. Not only were the costs rising for maintaining the bloated military and the empire, but there were major domestic problems like slackening economic growth rates, persistent agricultural inadequacies, industrial stagnation, energy shortages, severe technological deficiencies, declining life expectancy, rising infant mortality rates, and rampant alcoholism.[52] Moreover, these distressing phenomena were presided over, and in many important respects caused by, an entrenched elite of bureaucrats and party hacks who compensated for any administrative and intellectual failings with a truly virtuosic flair for bureaucratic infighting that allowed them to hang on to their privileges. In many important aspects, then, the system was, not to put too fine a point on it, rotten to the core.

Adding to all this was the overbearing burden of defense expenditures which had burgeoned after the Cuban Missile Crisis and which now took up at least twice the percentage of gross national product as for the United States. The economic prognosis was also clouded by two unpleasant developments in world trade: declining prices for the Soviet Union's largest export, oil, and increased competition in the Third World for its second largest, arms. The colonies in Eastern Europe were also stagnating and were becoming a considerable burden on the Soviet Union and on its long-suffering and often-resentful citizenry.[53]

Kennan was clearly woefully wrong in the emphasis he put on the Soviet Union's succession dilemma – the great uncertainty arising from the transfer of power from one individual or group of individuals to others. However, while the process took much longer than he seems to have anticipated, Kennan was essentially right about the disillusionment and skepticism of the Russian population, about the fundamental precariousness of Soviet economic development, and about the dangerous congealment of political life in the higher circles of Soviet power.[54] In fact, Nikita Khrushchev got the contest right in his "kitchen debate" with Richard Nixon in 1959: "So let's compete! Let's compete! Who can produce the most goods for the people, that system is better and it will win." It didn't come out the way Khrushchev expected, however – from his perspective, the wrong side won the competition.[55]

In addition, Communist expansionary ventures proved to be impotent, ineffective, and often counterproductive, and the biggest disaster for the advance of international Communism – the violent anti-Communist massacres in Indonesia in 1965 – came as a complete surprise to American policymakers. Various lunatic Communist enterprises, such as Mao's Great Leap Forward in the 1950s and his Great Proletarian Cultural Revolution a decade later and Pol Pot's genocide after victory in Cambodia in 1975, were wildly self-destructive, but they were scarcely generated by anything the United States did.

It took 40 years – far longer than Kennan had anticipated – but, plagued by economic, social, and military disasters, the Soviets finally were able, as he had hoped, to embrace grim reality, and decisively to abandon their threatening ideology.

Gorbachev took the lead and gave up on just about everything Lenin had preached for, Stalin had murdered for, Khrushchev had finagled for, and Brezhnev had spent for. It does not follow, however, that economic and social travail would *necessarily* lead to a mellowing of ideology. Leaders, in this case Gorbachev, had to *choose* that policy route. Faced with the same dilemmas, a conservative leader might have stuck to the faith while suffering gradual decline (like the Ottoman empire) or such a leader might have adopted more modest reforms to maintain the essential quality of the system – and the privileges of its well-entrenched elite.[56]

Gorbachev's Soviet Union began to act like an old-fashioned, self-interested participant in the world community, rather than like a revolutionary, system-shattering one.[57] And, in the process and most importantly, it abandoned its threateningly expansionary ideology and its devotion to impelling ideas about the class struggle. In 1985 Gorbachev announced that his country required not only a reliable peace, but also a quiet, normal international situation.[58] By 1986 he began forcefully to undercut Communist ideology about the class struggle and about the Soviet Union's internationalist duty as the leader of world socialism.[59] And by 1988, the Soviets were admitting the inadequacy of their earlier thesis that peaceful coexistence is a form of class struggle, while the Kremlin's chief ideologist explicitly rejected the notion that a world struggle was going on between capitalism and Communism.[60] As part of the process, Gorbachev promised in 1987 to withdraw from Afghanistan and was to do so by February 1989.

Then, in a major speech at the United Nations in December 1988, Gorbachev specifically called for "de-ideologizing relations among states" and, while referring to the Communist revolution in Russia as a most precious spiritual heritage, proclaimed that "today we face a different world, from which we must seek a different road to the future."[61] There were also passages in Gorbachev's UN speech that could be taken to suggest the Soviet Union would not use force to maintain its control over the countries of East Europe.[62] With that change, the whole premise upon which containment policy rested was shattered, and the Cold War came to an end.[63]

Referring to Gorbachev's UN appearance, Secretary of State George Shultz has said, "If anybody declared the end of the Cold War, he did in that speech."[64] By the spring of 1989, that conclusion had been widely accepted including by the new George H. W. Bush administration, which issued a set of statements about going "beyond containment."[65]

If the Cold War essentially did come to an end at that point, this would suggest that it could not have been about a number of issues and themes.

It was clearly not about the existence of the Soviet Union, and dating the demise of the Cold War to coincide with its collapse at the end of 1991 makes little sense. Actually, the United States made considerable effort to keep the country from collapsing. Most notably, earlier in 1991 President George

H. W. Bush had gone to Ukraine to give a speech in which he essentially urged the various Soviet Republics to work it out and to remain within the country.[66] If there was a Cold War raging at that time, the United States and the Soviet Union were on the same side.

Nor was the Cold War about the fact that the Soviet Union had happened to adopt Communism as its domestic economic and governmental form. Neither in his UN speech nor in his later pronouncements did Gorbachev indicate that he intended to abandon Communism or Communist Party control in the Soviet Union. Moreover, the end of the Cold War came while the Soviet Union still controlled Eastern Europe.

Nor was the Cold War about the military balance or the distribution of capabilities more generally and the "bipolarity" they have been said to induce.[67] In fact, about the only thing that did *not* change at the end of the Cold War was the military, and particularly the nuclear, balance. This suggests that the arms balance was more nearly an indicator of international Cold War tensions than the cause of them.[68]

The Cold War did not end, then, because the United States adopted adept policies to counter or "contain" the Communists by waging "test-case" wars in Vietnam or by avidly questing after Communists within. As Stobe Talbott puts it, the Soviet system went "into meltdown because of inadequacies and defects at its core, not because of anything the outside world had done or threatened to do."[69] The internal contradictions the Soviets came to confront were a direct result of misguided domestic and foreign policies, and these contradictions would have come about no matter what policy the West chose to pursue. Soviet domestic problems derived from decades of mismanagement, mindless brutality, and fundamental misconceptions about basic economic and social realities. Their defense dilemmas came from a conspiratorial ideology that creates external enemies and then exaggerated the degree to which the enemies would use war to destroy them. And their foreign policy failures stemmed from a fundamentally flawed, and often highly romantic, conception of the imperatives of history and of the degree to which foreign peoples will find appeal in the Communist worldview.

The ending of the Cold War also suggests that it was about ideology.[70] It ended when the Communists abandoned their class war doctrine, not when economic or military or territorial issues were settled. As ambassador Jack Matlock puts it, "The cold war could not end, truly and definitively, until the Soviet Union abandoned its system's ideological linchpin, the class struggle concept."[71] And a broader lesson from this seems to be that ideas really matter. As stressed in this book, they are very often forces themselves, not flotsam on the tide of broader social or economic or military patterns.

In formulating his influential and widely discussed theory of international politics usually called "realism," "structural realism," or "neorealism," Kenneth Waltz chose substantially to downplay attributes such as "ideology, form of government, peacefulness, bellicosity or whatever." What chiefly makes the system tick, according to Waltz, is the "distribution of capabilities." States differ in their capabilities and from these differences springs the structure. For Waltz, a country's capability includes its "size of population and territory, resource endowment, economic capability, military strength, political stability and competence." In the Cold War period, two countries were far more "capable" than any others by these more or less objective measures, and from this condition, concludes Waltz, stemmed the essential conflict: "the United States is the obsessing danger for the Soviet Union, and the Soviet Union for the United States, since each can damage the other to an extent no other state can match." The Cold War between them, therefore, "is firmly rooted in the structure of postwar international politics, and will last as long as that structure endures."[72]

In contrast, it certainly appears that any "bipolarity" during the Cold War was a consequence of ideology, not "capabilities." Since the United States and the USSR remained far more "capable" by the Waltz criteria than any other countries in the world, each side should have continued to "focus its fears on the other, to distrust its motives, and to impute offensive intentions to defensive measures."[73] However, the United States found the Soviet Union to be an "obsessing danger" not because the Soviet regime brandished big weapons or because it had such a substantial "resource endowment" or occupied so much space on the earth's surface, but because the Soviets espoused an ideology that was threatening. The Cold War came about because of a clash of ideas, and its demise principally resulted from an important change in those ideas, not from a major change in the distribution of capabilities.[74]

3

Military Intervention and the Continued Quest for Threat after the Cold War

In a *New Yorker* cartoon published sometime in the midst of the Cold War, two locals who happen to be standing at the North Pole are gazing skyward at two missiles, one labeled USSR, the other US, hurtling past each other in opposite directions. One remarks, "Well, I guess that's the end of the world as they know it."

Beginning in 1989, we did come to the end of the world as we knew it then, but, as it happens, no missiles were ever launched.

Virtually all the major problems that had plagued big-country (sometimes known as Great Power) international relations for nearly half a century were resolved with scarcely a shot being fired, a person being executed, or a rock being thrown. Among them: the unpopular and often brutal Soviet occupation of East Europe; the artificial and deeply troubling division of Germany; the expensive, virulent, crisis-prone, and apparently dangerous military contest between East and West; and the ideological struggle between authoritarian, expansionist, violence-encouraging Communism and reactive, sometimes-panicky capitalist democracy. In the process, the key problem, securing the peace, was very substantially solved. After the remarkably bloodless dissolution of the Soviet Union in 1991, Russia retained a nuclear arsenal vastly larger than the one the Soviet Union controlled during most of the Cold War, but there was little concern that those weapons would be used. And post-Cold War prophesies of international instability in East Asia proved to be essentially empty.[1]

For many, however, the immediate post-Cold War period did not really feel too much like a wonderful golden age. This chapter is concerned with the quest to find threats to worry about and monsters to pursue during the first decade of the new era. It also discusses a new opportunity brought forward by the ending of the Cold War: former enemies could work together to police the world, or selected portions thereof.

SECURING THE PEACE

The developed countries may have been in substantial agreement about most major issues, and there may have been little or no fear of armed conflict among them. But notable problems remained. High among these, certainly, was managing the entry of Russia and China, the main losers of the Cold War, into the world community – a process that generally went rather well in the first post-Cold War decade. Indeed, by the dawn of the new century the post-Communist era seemed substantially to be over, and a considerable stability had enveloped most of the area after a rather turbulent decade. Problems remained, of course – especially concerning China's deep desire to bring Taiwan back into its fold – but, for the most part, the losers of the Cold War came to see the world in much the same way as the winners.

If the Cold War essentially ended by the spring of 1989 as argued in Chapter 2, the settlement of outstanding issues concerning arrangements in central and eastern Europe became the first major task of the post-Cold War era. This was accomplished with astonishing speed. Even as it was happening, George Kennan predicted that "we will be lucky if the task is substantially accomplished before the end of the century," and Henry Kissinger anticipated that it would take three or four years to see a de facto unification of Germany, a process that was accomplished, de jure, in one.[2] And Soviet Communism received its *coup de grâce* almost overnight after a failed *coup d'état* in Russia in 1991.

Equally impressive is the alacrity with which the post-Communist countries in what had previously been called "East Europe," with Western support and urging, took up capitalism and democracy. The transition was hardly problem-free, but, compared to the gloomy predictions common at the time about minds that had been permanently warped by decades of Communist indoctrination, the shift has been a quite remarkable success. And historically unprecedented: as economist Lawrence Summers has noted, at the time there was not a single book or article on the problem of transforming an economy from the communist to a market system.[3] Many analysts at the time argued that the potential for economic development in the post-Communist countries in Europe was severely limited because over its reign of 40 years or more Communism had systematically stifled the entrepreneurial spirit – people expected everything to be furnished them and had lost the capacity to work. The experience of the 1990s, however, suggests that there has been plenty of entrepreneurial spirit within the societies – particularly among the young.[4]

The transitional experience in many post-Communist countries and else-where suggests that democracy as a form of government and capitalism as an economic form are really quite simple, even natural, and, unless obstructed by thugs with guns, they can form quite easily and quickly without any special development, prerequisites, or preparation.[5] Democracy had spread through-out Latin America between 1975 and 1990, and it took hold fairly easily in much of east central Europe, as did capitalism. Important in this process was that the newly liberated countries in Eastern Europe increasing looked west-ward at the prosperous countries in Western Europe for their role models, and they were attracted to the European Union and NATO – two clubs they could join if they came up to standards. For the most part, they were quite willing to try.

The eastward expansion of the North Atlantic Treaty Organization created deep concern in Russia, however, a concern heightened with NATO's 1999 bombing to facilitate the secession of the province of Kosovo from Serbia as discussed toward the end of this chapter.[6] The full effect of these ventures emerged only in the next century and will be considered in Chapter 6.

THE QUEST TO IDENTIFY THREATS

Farce did not go into decline with the end of the Cold War. With the demise of the Soviet Union, there was a quest to identify new threats.

Actually, however, the effort had already begun a few years earlier when a somewhat improbable devil du jour was spotted: insidiously peaceful Japan. As Gorbachev's Soviet Union was bringing the Cold War to an end, Americans were becoming concerned about a new "threat" to national secur-ity perceived at the time to be presented by economically impressive, if substantially demilitarized, Japan. In a major best seller of 1987, historian Paul Kennedy confidently listed a set of reasons why Japan was likely to expand faster than other major powers, stressed the country's "immensely strong" industrial bedrock and its docile and diligent work force, and predicted that, unless there were a large-scale war, an ecological disaster, or a world-wide slump like the 1930s, Japan would become "*much* more powerful" economically.[7] Many people found this prospective development threatening, especially after the diabolical Japanese shelled out a lot of money to buy Radio City Music Hall and a major Hollywood film studio. By the spring of 1989, the Japanese "threat" was seen rather preposterously by the American people to be nearly comparable to the one posed by the still heavily armed Soviet Union.[8]

Those of the then-fashionable America-in-decline, or FLASH! JAPAN BUYS PEARL HARBOR! school quickly moved into action. For example,

Harvard's Samuel Huntington assured us that a need had suddenly arisen to fear not "missile vulnerability" but "semiconductor vulnerability." And "economics," he apparently seriously warned, "is the continuation of war by other means."[9] Danger signals were espied when Japan became the largest provider of foreign aid and when it shockingly endowed professorships at Harvard and MIT. One book of the time was even entitled *The Coming War with Japan*. Some analysts confidently insisted that Japan by natural impulse would soon come to yearn for nuclear weapons, even though the Japanese themselves seemed to remain viscerally uninterested in them.[10]

Such concerns, however, soon faded and then evaporated when Japan's "threatening" economy began to stagnate in the 1990s – particularly by 1993.

It was in that year that Bill Clinton's new Central Intelligence Agency chief, James Woolsey, testified darkly (and not, perhaps, without a degree of institutional self-interest) that "we have slain a large dragon, but we live now in a jungle filled with a bewildering variety of poisonous snakes."[11] Thus, applying his metaphor, the post-Cold War jungle had snakes whereas the Cold War jungle was inhabited not only by the snakes but by a dragon as well. Some people might have considered that to be, as jungles go, a notable improvement. When big problems (dragons in Woolsey's characterization) go away, small problems (snakes) can be elevated in perceived importance, and, in the wake of the Cold War, several of the snakes were dutifully so elevated.[12]

One surefire snake, or monster, was readily and quickly identified: uncertainty. Thus, Bill Clinton proclaimed in his 1993 Presidential inaugural address that "the new world is more free but less stable," and later in the year former Central Intelligence Agency chief Robert Gates contended that we now lived in a world that was "far more unstable, turbulent, unpredictable and violent." Meanwhile former national security adviser Zbigniew Brzezinski published a book in which he argued that global change was now "out of control," implying apparently that there was a time when it was notably *in* control.[13] He found turmoil everywhere and blamed much of it on material wealth, on self-indulgence, and on that perennial recipient of potshots, television (soon to be replaced by the internet). This theme was echoed by some international relations scholars as they tried to come to grips with a field undergoing tremendous change, in which old categories no longer worked very well. Thus as Stanley Hoffmann put it, "the problem of order has become even more complex than before."[14]

Conclusions about the comparative complexity of the world in the wake of the Cold War stemmed in part from a remarkably simplified recollection of what went on during the Cold War. The phenomenon is related to the tendency to look backward with misty eyes, to see the past as much more benign, simple, and innocent than it really was. For example, there is Woolsey's curious recollection that the Cold War threat could be character-ized "precisely and succinctly" because our adversary was "a single power whose interests fundamentally threatened ours."[15] But the Communist threat was shifting, multifaceted, and extremely complicated. And most of the time there were two central sources of threat, China and the USSR, not one. Moreover, China and the Soviet Union, while jointly threatening the West, were often intensely at odds with each other – nearly at war a few times – over both strategy and tactics, complicating things further. The Cold War also added an especially difficult layer of complexity to US relations with a whole host of countries. At one time the United States had to treat Mobutu of Zaire as a dictator who had brought his country to ruin but who was on the right side in the Cold War. After the Cold War it could treat him merely as a dictator who had brought his country to ruin. In that very important respect, international policy became far *less* complex than it was during the Cold War.

Woolsey helpfully enumerated other snakes: "the proliferation of weapons of mass destruction and the ballistic missiles to carry them; ethnic and national hatreds that can metastasize across large portions of the globe; the international narcotics trade; terrorism; the dangers inherent in the West's dependence on Mideast oil; new economic and environmental challenges." Except perhaps for concerns about supposedly metastasizing ethnic and national hatreds, all of the bewildering poisonous snakes Woolsey specified were already out there in full measure during the Cold War: proliferation, terrorism, drugs, oil dependence, and economic and environmental "chal-lenges" were scarcely new concerns. However, without the Soviet dragon to worry about, such problems were elevated in importance.

In the process, the phrase "weapons of mass destruction" was greatly expanded. The concept had once been taken to be simply a dramatic synonym for nuclear weapons, or was meant to include nuclear weapons and weapons yet to be developed that might have similar destructive capacity. After the Cold War it was taken to embrace chemical, biological, and radiological weapons even though those weapons for the most part are simply incapable of committing destruction that could reasonably be considered "massive," particularly in comparison with nuclear ones. Then, in 1992 the phrase was explicitly rendered into American law to include those weapons, and, in the process, the definition was extended far further to include any bomb, grenade, or mine and any projectile-spewing weapon that has a barrel with a bore of more than one-half inch in diameter. That would include potato guns and missile-propelled firecrackers if their designers intended them to be a weapon.[16] It turns out, then, that Francis Scott Key was exultantly, if innocently, witnessing a WMD attack in 1814 and that the "shot heard round the world" by revolutionary war muskets was the firing of a WMD.

Rather new on the scene was anxiety about the threat apparently presented by ethnic and national hatreds, and there were special new concerns about this in Europe with civil wars that erupted in the former Yugoslavia and in a few places in the former Soviet Union in the early 1990s.

A central issue in the aftermath of the Cold War was the establishment of mechanisms for dealing with such residual disorder in what George H. W. Bush, who became president in 1989, was given to calling "the new world order." Since 1918, developed countries had engaged in three kinds of warfare. For differing reasons, all of these were now firmly in the past. One was the cluster of wars known as World War II, another was colonial war, and the third was warfare emerging from the Cold War contest as considered in the previous two chapters. A fourth application, or potential application, of warfare, although not without precedent, was developed in the wake of the Cold War to deal with two very notable sources of artificial death and destruction. One of these is civil war, the chief remaining form of war as can be seen in Figure 0.1. And the other is government: in fact, over the course of the bloody twentieth century, far more people were killed by their own governments than were killed by all wars put together.[17] In the process, militarily pathetic countries were sometimes seen to pose a major security threat, and a new emphasis on what came to be called "rogue states" became the rage.

In principle, the international community is ill-prepared to deal with civil conflict and with vicious or criminal or cosmically incompetent domestic governments because it is chiefly set up to confront problems that transcend international borders, not ones that lurk within them. However, having substantially abandoned armed conflict among themselves, the developed countries can, if they so desire, expand their efforts and collaborate on international police work to deal with civil war and with destructive domestic regimes. Moreover, as international law has developed, it has become accepted that the Security Council of the United Nations can intervene in civil wars or declare a state government too incompetent or too contemptible to be allowed to continue to exist, and it can accordingly authorize military intervention.[18]

The opportunities are considerable. Much civil warfare, though certainly not all, can be policed because it is chiefly perpetrated by poorly coordinated, if often savage, thugs. Moreover, many of the most vicious governments are substantially of the criminal variety and could be readily toppled by disciplined policing forces sent from outside because a criminal or near-criminal force tends to be cowardly and incompetent when confronted by an effective one. In the decade after the Cold War, there were a number of instances in which disciplined policing forces principally, but not always, from developed countries applied military force in other countries in an effort to correct conditions they considered to be sufficiently unsuitable.

In the next century, after the terrorist attacks of September 11, 2001, the process was extended by the United States to deal with threats thought to be presented by Afghanistan and Iraq as will be discussed in Chapter 4. The disastrous results of those endeavors have led to a dismissal of all such efforts to stop civil wars or to displace destructive regimes as vapid, arrogant, and extremely ill-advised efforts to establish "liberal hegemony" or "liberal world order."[19] However, this characterization seems far too grand. As Christopher Preble puts it, the post-Cold War policing efforts "had an ad hoc quality about them" and "seemed purely reactive," not "part of a broader U.S. campaign to shape the world order to suit its interests."[20] That is, the efforts were characterized by vast proclamation and half-vast execution.[21] Moreover, as Robert DiPrizio and Rajan Menon have stressed, interventions that were seemingly humanitarian have tended to be carried out more for national interest reasons than for humanitarian ones.[22]

In the decade after the Cold War, developed countries were able to engage in these ventures at remarkably little cost to themselves, particularly in casualties, though they often seem to have had little concern about the casualties they might themselves have been inflicting in the process. The experience suggests that a sufficiently large, impressively armed, and well-disciplined policing force can often be effective in pacifying thug-dominated conflicts and in removing thuggish regimes. But it also suggests that, because their interests were only modestly engaged, the policing forces could readily be withdrawn if they met costly resistance.

The first case in point came at the end of 1989 when the United States invaded Panama to depose Manuel Noriega, a thug who had abrogated an election there in order to continue running the place himself. He also played around in the drug trade and was a CIA informant. During his election campaign of 1988 and particularly during his first year as president, George H. W. Bush had made drugs a high-priority issue, and he seems to have seen the Panamanian dictator as "an unpleasant symbol of American impotence in the face of illegal drugs."[23] Outraged at the Panamanian dictator's insolent statements and behavior, Bush ordered 24,000 American troops into action at the end of 1989. They were up against 16,000 troops in the substantially criminalized Panamanian Defense Forces of whom 3,500 were reckoned to be capable of combat; few fought with much vigor.[24] Noriega gave himself up and was sent to Florida where he was tried by an American court, convicted by an American jury, and locked up in an American prison where he died in 2017. In Panama, a new government, not ideal, but a distinct improvement by most standards, was set up. Although the venture seems to have had no significant impact one way or the other on the drug trade, it was a rare victory for the American military, and in some important respects it had been presaged by their effort in the Cold War-related invasion of the tiny island of Grenada in 1983 by Bush's predecessor, Ronald Reagan.[25]

Bush also became alarmed by the antics of Saddam Hussein, a former street thug and certifiable monster who was now the president and resident dictator of Iraq.[26] Saddam had become particularly aggrieved by the behavior of his neighbor country, Kuwait. Iraq was in desperate economic straits, and he argued that Kuwait should forgive a debt Iraq had incurred by fighting the mutual enemy, Iran, in a costly and exhausting war Saddam initiated in 1980 and that had ended in 1988, and that Kuwait was violating agreements by over-producing oil. In various meetings over the issue, Kuwait, urged on by British Prime Minister Margaret Thatcher, refused to budge, and Kuwait's Crown Prince and Prime Minister reportedly shouted in a meeting on August 1, 1990, that if the Iraqis needed funds they should send their wives out onto the street to earn money for them. Iraq's invasion of oil-rich Kuwait the next day seems to have been motivated by outrage over this affront as much as anything else.[27] It caught almost everyone by surprise, including Arab rulers in Kuwait and other countries in the Middle East who had brushed off Iraq's troop buildup as a bluff.[28]

This act of war in an area of importance alarmed most world leaders, particularly Bush and Thatcher. Bush saw it as a form of naked aggression comparable in its way to that of Adolf Hitler in the 1930s – in fact, Bush was given to declaring that Saddam was "worse than Hitler."[29] But he did not find similarities, of course, with his pique-motivated venture into Panama a few months earlier. Encouraged by Thatcher, Bush led a determined international effort to impose a punishing economic blockade on Iraq and on the conquered Kuwait whose oil revenues Saddam had apparently been planning to capture. Cooperating were not only the Western countries, but most Arab ones includ-ing Saudi Arabia, which agreed to increase its oil output to compensate for the shortfall in international supplies caused by the boycott of Iraq and occupied Kuwait. Moreover, in the wake of the Cold War, Iraq's former friend and ally the Soviet Union joined the boycott – something that took Saddam by surprise.[30] In short order, Iraq's economy was fractured, making these sanctions far more punishing than any others ever previously imposed.

By October, Bush had decided that the economic sanctions were not working fast enough, and shortly after the 1990 Congressional election he announced that troop levels in the Middle East would be substantially increased in order to attain an offensive military option. The hope was that this threat, combined with the sanctions, would cause Iraq to withdraw as demanded. At the end of the month, Bush was able to sharpen the threat by getting the United Nations Security Council to authorize the use of force unless Iraq left Kuwait by January 15, 1991. Bush's earlier policy in the Gulf had been strongly supported by the political leadership of both parties, but his unilateral November escalation, with its apparent rush to war before sanctions would be given a full chance to take effect, alarmed many. Eventually, Bush formally asked Congress to authorize him to use force after the UN deadline, and, after extensive debate, a majority – a rather slim one in the Senate – did so in a vote that substantially followed party lines. During the runup to the war, Bush was unable to increase support for his war among the public.[31]

Throughout, Bush became emotionally absorbed, even obsessed, by the crisis, developed a hatred for Saddam (as he had previously for Noriega), and felt he was being tested by real fire. And, to some, he seemed to yearn to have a war.[32] To a considerable degree, he was the war's singular author.

In this mood, he insisted that there could be no deals: in his view, Saddam must withdraw unconditionally and ignominiously, suffering maximum humiliation for his aggression. There were also growing concerns that Iraq might be able to produce a crude atomic bomb, complicating the eventual use of force. Military planners, meanwhile, were concluding that a war against Iraq's forces could easily be won. Saddam Hussein apparently became convinced that war was inevitable and that a humiliating backdown would be suicidal for him.[33] Accordingly, he called Bush's bluff and refused to move his occupying troops. There was a growing sense, too, of helpless fatalism in Washington – a feeling that the United States simply could not back down from the expensive and heightened troop commitment that had been unilaterally instituted by the president two months earlier.[34] At any rate, the public was greatly concerned. A few days before the war began, 22 percent of the public said they thought about the crisis every few minutes and another 27 percent said they did so at least once an hour; only 10 percent were so blasé as to claim they thought about it at most once a day.[35]

Unleashed by Congress, Bush proclaimed that there would be a great promise of a new world order in victory and began the war with a bombing campaign that started on the moonless night of January 16, 1991, a few days before huge antiwar demonstrations were scheduled to take place in Washington. Six weeks later, ground troops went in, and they routed the occupying Iraqi forces in 100 hours. The number of US fatalities in the war turned out to be 146, and of these a maximum of 54 were killed directly by the Iraqi defenders.[36] It appears that far more Americans were conceived during the Gulf affair than were killed in it – one report puts the number of pregnancies among American military personnel in the area at over 1,200.[37]

It is rather common for American military analysts substantially to ignore the enemy when they assess a war, and this pattern seems to hold for the Gulf War of 1991. But wars, of course, have at least two sides, and to assess them fully it is vital to systematically and directly deal with the policies, strategies, and tactics of both combatants. The lopsided outcome of the war was quite surprising: as commanding General H. Norman Schwarzkopf put it at the end of the war, "We certainly did not expect it to go this way."[38] In other words, there was a very considerable failure in intelligence. Iraqi troop strength had been greatly overestimated and so had its ability to wage effective war. There is an important similarity here with the Vietnam War. As discussed in Chapter 2, the outcome of that conflict was chiefly determined not by American strategy, tactics, or firepower, but by the unexpected, even astounding, ability of the Communists to maintain morale and fighting cohesion despite losses that, as a percentage of the population, were almost unprecedented historically. And the unexpected outcome of the Gulf War was chiefly determined not by the quality of the American machines or by the craftiness of their military planning and maneuvers, but by the fact that it is easy to run over an enemy that is vastly outnumbered and has little in the way of effective defenses, strategy, tactics, planning, morale, or leadership. As a senior US commander has suggested, it proved to be the perfect war in part because the United States and its allies were confronted with the perfect enemy.[39] Indeed, when the ground war finally began at the end of February 1991, the campaign quickly became more a matter of crowd control than anything else – desert roundup, one writer has called it.[40] The Iraqi forces seem mainly to have been going through the motions and had little or no real intention of fighting a war, and their will to fight, if any, had been substantially broken before a shot was fired or a bomb dropped. As one American Marine suggested, "On a combat scale of 1 to 10, it was a 1."[41] Saddam Hussein had promised the mother of all battles, but his troops and commanders delivered instead the mother of all bug-outs. To a substantial degree, the Americans gave a war and no one showed up.

The chief military lesson of the prosecution of the Gulf War is, in John Heidenrich's words, that "military effectiveness need not be synonymous with human slaughter."[42] Although the US military often seems to want to believe that military effectiveness is synonymous with kicking butt, the real achievement for US combat forces in the Gulf War may well be in the way they routed their confused, ill-led, terrified, but rather well-armed enemies without killing many of them.

However, although Iraqi military deaths in the Gulf War itself – probably a few thousand – were probably not remotely as high as it first seemed, the war did lead to a great deal of death. Egged on by President George H. W. Bush and by US propaganda, groups opposing Saddam Hussein within Iraq – Kurds in the north, Shiite Muslims in the south – seized the opportunity and rebelled, expecting help from the victorious American troops. Then, even while triumphantly proclaiming the Vietnam syndrome to be a thing of the past, Bush proceeded to apply it: after blasting the pathetic Iraqi defenders out of their bunkers, he refused to intervene to get Saddam or to help the rebels because he did not want American troops to become involved in a Vietnam-style quagmire.[43] As the United States watched from the sidelines, the remnants of Saddam's army brutally put the rebellions down: the army, so inadequate against a military foe, showed itself quite capable at slaughtering unarmed civilians. Tens of thousands apparently died – two sources arrive independently at an estimate of 35,000.[44] This caused a massive and well-publicized exodus of pathetic, fleeing Kurds toward, and into, Turkey, an important NATO ally. Eventually the administration was goaded into movement and, particularly to help the refugee-besieged Turks, it helped to establish a safe zone in the north of Iraq for the Kurds and, much later, a no-fly zone in the south to help the Shiites.

In the runup to his war, Bush adamantly insisted that the war must inflict maximum humiliation on Saddam Hussein, and that, accordingly, there could be "no deals."[45] Indeed, as one reporter tallied at the time, in the first 15 minutes of one television interview, Bush ruled out compromise 19 separate times.[46] As a result of this mindset, war was inevitable if the United States insisted, as it did, on "unambiguous humiliation," in the words of Robert Tucker and David Hendrickson.[47] On the other hand, a deal would not necessarily have led him into other ventures elsewhere. And it is worth noting that, when his back was to the wall, he had agreed to punishing (but not suicidal) deals with Iran in 1975 and again in 1990 and that, after his invasion of Iran in 1986 went seriously awry, he tried to broker a deal to withdraw.[48]

Thus, there were viable alternatives to war – with its deadly aftermath – to resolve the crisis created by Iraq's invasion of Kuwait. In particular, Tucker and Hendrickson argue that the United States should have applied a patient strategy of "punitive containment" which would extend security guarantees to Saudi Arabia and other Gulf states while lacing Iraq in economic sanctions until "it withdrew from Kuwait and gave satisfactory guarantees of good behavior in the future."[49] The sanctions would be continued "indefinitely," and they would not require, even by implication, the removal of Saddam Hussein. To obtain these concessions, Iraq would withdraw from Kuwait, of course – perhaps in stages. Furthermore, it would agree to reduce its armed forces to levels consistent with defense, but not with effective offense, thereby reducing its ability to repeat its aggression. As part of this, it would continue to accept repeated inspections to assure that it was not producing nuclear weapons.

It would have been something of an exercise in appeasement perhaps, but there would have been little in Saddam's adventure to encourage other aggressors. Although, he would have emerged with his "dignity" intact and although he would doubtless have done a lot of crowing about that, his expansion would have been stalemated, he and Iraq would have suffered very substantially for his aggression. And Kuwait would have been liberated without a war that eventually – mostly in the aftermath – brought about the deaths of tens of thousands. Bush and others would not have had the pleasure of kicking butt, but the public would in all probability have accepted a deal along these lines if Bush had led them to it.

When American troops are sent abroad into dangerous situations, there is usually a "rally round the flag" effect: the commander in chief's approval ratings rise abruptly.[50] But it is important to note that this phenomenon tends to be fleeting. The public does not seem to be very interested in rewarding – or even remembering – foreign policy success. This seems to have been in effect even for the Gulf War. The war that had once so obsessed the press soon became such a distant memory that commentators were unable to remember it well enough to remark upon how little people remembered it.[51] And, despite easy triumph, the war's chief – even singular – author went down to electoral defeat a year later against an opponent who, on paper at least, did not seem to have the background and qualifications to present a major challenge. More generally, the fact that Bush found little lasting electoral advantage in a large, dramatic, and substantially single-authored victory like the Gulf War suggests that presidents can expect there to be little or no long-term political gain from successful international ventures.[52]

In the dozen years following the Gulf War, the United States and, occasionally, its allies kept up a military campaign of focused bombing to harass and intimidate the Iraqi regime and to enforce no-fly zones.

Economic sanctions were also applied. Before the 1991 war, the goal of the sanctions had been to pressure Iraq to leave Kuwait. During and after the war, however, the United States and the UN substantially escalated the requirements for sanctions to be lifted, demanding reparations and insisting that Iraq must allow various inspection teams to probe its military arsenal, particularly to make sure it had no nuclear, biological, or chemical weapons.

Iraq was peculiarly vulnerable to sanctions because so much of its economy was dependent on the export of oil, because it had not recovered from its lengthy war against Iran that took place between 1981 and 1988, and because the effects of sanctions were enhanced by the destruction of much of its rather advanced infrastructure during the Gulf War and by the truculent, even defiant, policies of the regime. Multiple studies concluded that the sanctions were the necessary cause of hundreds of thousands of deaths in the country, most of them children under the age of five – the most innocent of civilians. This came about because of inadequate food and medical supplies as well as breakdowns in sewage and sanitation systems and in the electrical power systems needed to run them – systems destroyed by bombing in the Gulf War that had often gone unrepaired due to sanctions-enhanced shortages of money, equipment, and spare parts.[53] Studies based on later intelligence conclude in particular that high estimates of a half-million or more child deaths are likely exaggerated due to regime manipulation of the numbers.[54] However, while the numbers may be in dispute, there is little doubt that the sanctions brought about extensive suffering.

Early on, Bush announced that the economic sanctions would be continued until Saddam Hussein was out of there. In 1997, President Bill Clinton's Secretary of State, Madeleine Albright, stated that sanctions would not be lifted even if Iraq had complied with its obligations concerning weapons of mass destruction. The British made similar statements.[55] Unlike many dictators, Saddam Hussein had no other place to go – he was reasonably safe only in office and in control in Iraq. Therefore, the rather mild-sounding notion that he should be removed from office – that he should "step aside" in Bush's words – was effectively a death sentence to him. Not surprisingly, he remained uncooperative about allowing the sanctions to have this effect, regardless of the cost to the Iraqi people – whose suffering could be used to portray Iraq as the aggrieved party. He also apparently also sought to rebuild his military capabilities.

Policymakers were clearly aware of the suffering the sanctions were causing. As Robert Gates, who was then President George H. W. Bush's deputy national security adviser, put it in 1991, while Saddam remains in power, "Iraqis will pay the price."[56] One might have imagined that the people carrying out this policy with its horrific and well-known consequences would from time to time have been queried about whether the results were worth the costs. But this seems to have happened only once, on television's *60 Minutes* on May 12, 1996. Madeleine Albright, then the American ambassador to the United Nations, was asked, "We have heard that a half a million children have died. I mean, that's more children than died in Hiroshima. . . . Is the price worth it?" Albright did not dispute the number and acknowledged it to be "a very hard choice." But, she concluded, "we think the price is worth it," pointing out that because of sanctions Saddam had come "cleaner on some of these weapons programs" and had recognized Kuwait. A Lexis-Nexis search suggests that Albright's remarkable dismissal on a prominent television show of the devastation sanctions had inflicted on innocent Iraqi civilians went completely unremarked upon by the country's media. In the Middle East, by contrast, it was widely and repeatedly covered and noted. Among the outraged was Osama bin Laden, who repeatedly used the punishment that sanctions were inflicting on Iraqi civilians as a centerpiece in his many diatribes against what he considered to be heartless and diabolical American policy in the area.[57]

In the meantime, support for the sanctions was waning with only the United States and Britain remaining as dedicated advocates. The sanctioners hoped that their policy would encourage or help facilitate a coup, an assassination, an army revolt, a popular uprising, or a rebellion or invasion by armed dissidents. However, while such an undertaking was certainly possible, the prospects never seemed very bright. The memory of Saddam's brutal suppression of the 1991 rising against him provided a strong disincentive to a repetition, and the opposition, both within the country and outside it, was splintered and infiltrated by agents.[58] The sanctions did not loosen his control, and he seemed exceedingly unlikely to become enticed to relinquish leadership, and life, over concern about the sufferings inflicted upon the Iraqi people by economic sanctions and by his policies.

In 1992, American troops were sent to Somalia as part of a UN effort to deal with a famine there caused by criminal and clan-based warfare and predation carried out by armed gangs, usually high on qat, a local amphetamine.[59] The troops almost immediately brought order to the chaotic situation, and food distribution proceeded with little problem and few casualties, and most of the American troops were withdrawn. However, efforts to disarm the clans and their semi-associated hoodlums – an essentially hopeless enterprise given the number of weapons in the country and neighborhood – ran into resistance. A raid on October 3, 1993, in the capital, Mogadishu, did manage to capture several associates of one of the contending warlords, but in the process a couple of US helicopters were shot down. The body of a fallen US

Ranger was trapped in one of the crashed helicopters, and his comrades, already pinned down by Somali fire, were unwilling, according to their code, to leave it behind. Accordingly, they staged a firefight until equipment could be brought in to free the remains and to rescue them. In the process, 18 Americans were killed, one was captured, the body of another was dragged through the streets and photographed, and hundreds of Somalis were killed.[60] In strict military terms, the October venture could have been considered a success. Although plans went awry and emergency measures had to be hastily improvised to compensate – something that is, of course, hardly uncommon in warfare – the rescue mission was accomplished with low casualties to the United States and high ones to the enemy. There had been considerable support for the effort when the troops went it, but public support for the venture was dampening even before the Americans were killed in the October firefight. After that, support for the venture dropped even further, criticism became rampant, and President Bill Clinton judiciously retreated. With that, other contingents from the UN force were withdrawn as well. Once they left, Somalia descended again into chaos, though perhaps at a somewhat attenuated level. Despite the enormous number of lives that the international mission appears to have saved, American policy there has been labeled a failure in large part because a few Americans were killed in the process. In essence, when Americans asked themselves how many American lives a humanitarian venture was worth, the answer came out rather close to zero: a poll conducted a few days after the firefight found 60 percent agreeing that "Nothing the US could accomplish in Somalia is worth the death of even one more US soldier."[61]

In the wake of the Gulf War, the war's chief instigator, President George H. W. Bush, triumphally exclaimed, "By God, we've licked the Vietnam Syndrome once and for all."[62] After the firefight in Mogadishu in 1993, however, Americans succumbed to the Somalia Syndrome. For the rest of the century, troops were sent into policing situations only when the environment was "permissive" or when they would be conducting high-altitude bombing alone. Thus, when genocide erupted in Rwanda in 1994, the United States, under the spell of that syndrome, worked to keep itself, and the international community, out of it. Indeed, it refused to use the word "genocide," concerned that to do so would trigger legal obligations to intervene.[63]

Much of the writing about that genocide, in which some 500,000 to 800,000 perished in a matter of weeks – mostly by being hacked to death with machetes – gives the impression that the conflict was one of all against all, friends against friends, neighbors against neighbors, even Cain against

Abel. Friends and neighbors (and even brothers perhaps) did kill each other, but it seems that by far the greatest damage stemmed from the rampages of murderous Hutu thugs guided by a government and essentially acting as mercenaries in attacks on Tutsis. In all, it appears that more than 90 percent of the over-13 male Hutu population did not participate in killings.[64] This hardly seems to justify the notion that the situation was one of all against all or neighbor against neighbor. The genocide was mostly carried out by drunken or drugged militia bands, criminals released from jail, and youth gangs. The prospect for enrichment by looting was vastly escalated during the genocide and was used as a specific incentive by the leaders – many of whom were happy to take booty as well. Rape and sadism were also common.

The deadly mayhem was finally, quickly, and decisively put down by military intervention – albeit one that came out of Africa. The Tutsis did have a comparatively capable and disciplined army, and when they eventually were able to get it into Rwanda in 1994, they had to battle for the capital city, Kigali, but took over the rest of the country with a minimum of fighting. For the most part, Hutu authorities ordered their forces and other genocidal marauders to flee when confronted with a capable military force. These forces, so adept at preying on civilians, simply collapsed when confronted with the reasonably coherent military force put together by the Tutsis.

Elsewhere in the early 1990s, the federation of south Slav states known as Yugoslavia began to fall apart.[65] There were substantial Serb minorities in areas in two of the seceding republics, Croatia and Bosnia, and these declared their loyalty to the republic of Serbia and sought forcibly to secede from those seceding republics.[66] Such secondary secession was not accepted by the republics' leaders, and civil warfare broke out – rather shockingly because Europe had been free from civil war for over 40 years.

The need for an explanation for the situation, preferably a simple one, was handily supplied by pundits like the fashionable travel writer and congenital pessimist Robert Kaplan. In a book and, probably much more importantly, in a front page article in the Sunday *New York Times Book Review* in 1993, he portentously proclaimed the Balkans to be "a region of pure memory" where "each individual sensation and memory affects the grand movement of clashing peoples." These processes of history and memory had been "kept on hold" by Communism for 45 years "thereby creating a kind of multiplier effect for violence." With the demise of that suppressing force, he argued, ancient, seething national and ethnic hatreds were allowed to spontaneously explode into nationalist violence.[67] This perspective informed some of the reluctance of the Bush administration to become involved in Bosnia, and it was also embraced by the Clinton administration. It was elaborated into a cosmic world view by Samuel Huntington as the Japan "threat" he had once been so concerned about receded in 1993. Although Huntington acknowledged that there had been little or no ethnic violence in Yugoslavia before World War II, he extrapolated very broadly, even heroically, from these civil wars, proclaiming them to be harbingers of an entirely new orientation for world politics in which whole civilizations clash, particularly in "fault line" areas where various civilizations happen to abut each other.[68] Western "civilization" primarily supported the creation of a state in Bosnia that would be dominated by people from the Islamic "civilization," but this troubled Huntington so little that he ignored the issue entirely.[69]

In contrast to this perspective, the violence that erupted in Yugoslavia principally came from the actions of recently empowered and unpoliced thugs, and, as in Rwanda, it was put down by local armed forces that had achieved a degree of disciplined coherence.[70] After years of supposedly influential media propaganda and centuries of supposedly pent-up ethnic and civilizational antagonism, ordinary Serb soldiers were finally given an opportunity to express these supposed proclivities in government-sanctioned violence. Overwhelmingly, however, they responded to the opportunity by pointedly declining to embrace it: professing they did not know why they were fighting, they often mutinied or deserted en masse. Meanwhile, back in Serbia itself, young men mainly reacted by determined draft-dodging. This phenomenon is almost too vividly illustrated by the experience of General Slavko Lisica who tried to shame Serb conscripts in Croatia into fighting by declaring that all those who were not prepared to "defend the glory of the Serbian nation" should lay down their arms and take off their uniforms. To his astonishment, he says, "they all did, including their commanding officer." Furious, he shouted at them "to remove everything including their underpants, and with the exception of one man they all removed their military issue underpants and marched off completely naked. I was still hoping they would change their mind, but they didn't." Later, he says, the recruits managed to commandeer a cannon and used it to shell his headquarters.[71]

Because Serbs from Serbia proper were unwilling to fight outside their own republic, Belgrade had to reshape its approach to the wars in Croatia and Bosnia in major ways and this, as Steven Burg and Paul Shoup observe, "led all sides came to rely on irregulars and special units."[72] In all, there were at least 83 of these groups operating in Croatia and Bosnia, comprising 36,000 to 66,000 members. As part of this process, it appears that thousands of prison inmates, promised shortened sentences and enticed by the prospect that they could "take whatever booty you can," were released in Serbia for the war effort.[73] The key dynamic of the conflicts, then, was not in the risings of neighbor against neighbor, still less in the clashings of civilizations. Rather it was in the focused predations of comparatively small groups of violent thugs and criminals recruited and semi-coordinated by politicians. Identity, ethnicity, nationalism, civilization, culture, religion proved more nearly to be an excuse or pretext for their predations than an independent cause of them.[74]

Dealing with the wars that broke out in Croatia in 1991 and in Bosnia in 1992 proved difficult for the leading developed states. They did much huffing and puffing, passed self-important resolutions, held peace conferences, and authorized the United Nations variously to provide humanitarian aid and to establish a set of ambiguous safe areas – lightly defended enclaves where refugees from ethnic cleansing could be housed and fed.

Serb forces in Croatia and Bosnia remained criminal-dominated and became increasingly so. However, their local opponents began to develop real armies. Only a year after Serbs had effectively partitioned their country, the new Croatian army launched an attack on several important targets in Serb-held territory and encountered little resistance. In 1995, using plans partly devised by retired American generals, the army pushed from most of the rest of Croatia the remaining Serb opposition, which for the most part simply ran. Similar results were soon achieved in neighboring Bosnia by organized Croat and Bosnian forces.

There had been much talk from time to time among the leading states, particularly those in NATO, about bombing Serb positions. This was tried a few times, but in each case it came to an embarrassed end when Serbs calmly took West European peacekeepers, particularly those in "safe areas," into custody and essentially held them for ransom. By the time of the Croat and Muslim offensives, however, there were no longer peacekeepers to kidnap. This was because the Serbs had brutally extinguished the safe areas, sending their foreign overseers packing, and because peacekeepers had been quietly removed from other vulnerable areas.[75]

Consequently, when an excuse presented itself, extensive bombing of Serb positions began and continued for several weeks. Although the bombing campaign probably helped to concentrate the Serb mind, it does not seem to have been necessary to obtain the resulting agreement, signed at Dayton, Ohio, in 1995, that ended the war. Before the bombing even began, the Serb military position was falling apart to Croatian ground attacks – the importance of which, as United States negotiator Richard Holbrooke notes, was not appreciated by policy planners at the time.[76] Moreover, the Bosnian Serbs had already agreed to let Serbian President Slobodan Milošević negotiate for them, giving him virtually total control over their fate. Since he had been repeatedly urging them for more than two years to accept various peace plans offered by the West, this appointment was close to an admission of defeat. Also relevant is the fact that the final agreement involved substantial concessions on the part of the *Bosnian* government.[77]

At the end of 1995, well after the Dayton agreement had been signed, Clinton sent policing troops into what he hoped would be a "permissive" environment in Bosnia. It was not a popular mission, and it was opposed by Republicans who would have raised the roof if things had gone awry (as would the Democrats if Bush's Gulf War of 1991 had failed). But the environment remained "permissive," and the policing troops had little to do.

Thugs were also put down by disciplined forces – in this case ones from Australia – in East Timor in 1999. Before and after a government-approved referendum in which East Timorese voted overwhelmingly for independence from Indonesia, thuggish militia groups under the control, or at least influence, of the Indonesian army went on a rampage, looting, pillaging, raping, and torching. Australia led and mostly manned a force of several thousand policing troops sent by a several countries – a coalition of the willing – under UN auspices. When these troops arrived, the militia groups simply disappeared.

Something similar happened in Sierra Leone in 2000 when several hundred disciplined British troops arrived to police a chaotic civil war that had broken out in the former British colony. By 2002, the country had come back from the dead. The war was declared over with the surrender of tens of thousands of rebels and renegades, Britain trained a new local army, and elections were held.[78] The country has remained peaceful and reasonably democratic. However, it is at or near the bottom of all countries in terms of development and health, and corruption remains endemic.[79]

What happened in the Serbian province of Kosovo at the end of the 1990s often resembles the process seen earlier in Croatia and Bosnia, except that it may have taken place at a more focused degree of brutality.[80]

The ruling Serbs under the leadership of Milošević substantially created the problem, especially after 1989, by officially discriminating against ethnic Albanians who constituted the vast majority of Kosovo's population. Then, when some Albanians resorted to anti-Serb terrorism in 1998, the Serbs foolishly moved against them with excessive violence that included massacres and the creation of masses of refugees, especially in rural areas. Although the terrorists of the Kosovo Liberation Army did not enjoy great support among the Albanians, particularly in the cities, the Serb depredations, carried out mainly by special paramilitary units under the direction of the Ministry of the Interior in Belgrade, greatly increased the support for the terrorists by essentially forcing Albanians to make a Bosnia-like decision: they had to choose between rule by brutish racist thugs from their own ethnic group or rule by brutish racist thugs from the other ethnic group. The KLA, which numbered no more than 150 before the massacres, quickly increased to an estimated 12,000.

Kosovo is much closer to Serbia's core interests, or, at any rate, sentiments, than Bosnia or Croatia, and Serbs had been dutifully weaving fanciful myths and legends about the region for a good 600 years. Nonetheless, following the earlier pattern found in the wars in Croatia and Bosnia, an amazingly large percentage of Serbian youth was entirely able to contain its enthusiasm for actually *fighting* for dear old Kosovo. As one Serb journalist put it, "you won't find anyone prepared to send their children into the battlefield." Belgrade's newspapers cited despairing letters from army conscripts on this issue, and some policemen were dismissed for refusing assignment to Kosovo. Many of the Serb policeman who did go were sent as a demotion or as punishment for misbehavior.

In a doomeager willingness to repeat the mistake of 1998, Milošević allowed himself in 1999 to believe assurances that a really substantial offensive could wipe out the KLA in five to seven days. Since he needed dedicated fighters for this, he found many of them in the same place as before: criminals were released from prison to join and to form paramilitary forces.

In the meantime, NATO was threatening to bomb if the offensive took place. Concerned about this, those running the Serb offensive appear to have tried to keep it under some degree of control: efforts were made to keep it localized and focused mainly on KLA stronghold areas. Serbian "special police," presumably in an effort to deter, pointedly announced to Western journalists that they "would kill every Albanian in sight" if NATO bombed. Ethnic Albanians and others in Kosovo expressed the fear that this was not an idle threat.

Dismissing such threats as "foolish Serbian bravado," NATO launched airstrikes in March 1999 under the assumption, as US President Bill Clinton admitted later, that after "a couple of days" of bombing the Serbs would halt their offensive. Instead, the bombing had a sort of Pearl Harbor effect on the Serbs: like the Americans in 1941, they were sent into a state of outraged fury. The Serbs couldn't take their fury out directly on Brussels, London, or Washington, but they did have an enemy conveniently close at hand: the Albanians of Kosovo. Serb forces in Kosovo went into an orgy of vengeful violence and destruction that lasted for several weeks and was apparently intended to carry out the goal, previously considered unrealistic probably, of driving the majority of Albanians from Kosovo.

However, the violence seems to have been almost entirely committed by marauding, if sometimes uniformed, thugs rather than by conscripts in the army, and it often involved pure sadism, mindless violence, debauched boozing, and focused, if opportunistic, looting of the homes of wealthy Albanians. The experience generated what a soldier called "one of the best jokes of the war": a "Rambo," asked why he had quit the war, responds, "I couldn't carry a gun and a television set at the same time."[81]

NATO had become substantially self-entrapped on the Kosovo issue. Its bluff had been embarrassingly called, and its leaders had come to believe that its credibility and relevance were crucially at stake, even to the point of maintaining that the organization (at the time celebrating its fiftieth anniversary) would disintegrate if it did not stand up to the challenge. For all that, however, NATO was careful to make sure that it suffered few, if any casualties itself, whatever might be happening to the Albanians it was seeking to protect. In order to preclude the possibility that they could be taken hostage, international monitors who had been placed in Kosovo under an earlier agreement were withdrawn in anticipation of the bombing campaign. Moreover, to keep the bombers outside the range of potential anti-aircraft defenses, the bombing was conducted from very high levels, considerably reducing its accuracy and effectiveness. And no ground action was anticipated or planned for.

After nearly three months of bombing, Milošević finally did give in. The bombing was halted, and a deal was worked out that gave Kosovo effective, if not internationally recognized, independence, together with a great deal of international guidance and largesse. No one knows precisely why Milošević finally decided to capitulate. He probably came to conclude that, despite early indications of dissension within the ranks, NATO would not split over the bombing policy and thus could keep it up forever and that Russia, though critical of the bombing, would not come to his aid. He may also have feared an eventual invasion that would directly topple him, possibly from neighboring Hungary, which had only very recently been admitted to NATO. In addition, the deal he got had rather better terms than the one he had previously been offered by NATO.

Many countries in the West, including the United States, recognized Kosovo as an independent country in 2008. Neither Serbia nor Russia followed suit.

THE FIRST POST-COLD WAR DECADE

The record in the 1990s suggests that the recovery from the Cold War was handled rather well. There were great concerns that what happened in Yugoslavia after its disintegration might also occur in countries to its north or even, most disastrously, among or within countries that had previous made up the Soviet Union. Substantial concentrations of Hungarians, for example, are found in several countries neighboring Hungary itself. And, indeed, there were troubles in a few areas, including the brutal suppression of an independence movement in Chechnya within Russia. In general, however, this concern receded by the end of the 1990s as the countries in what has sometimes been called "the former East Europe" mostly attained a fair amount of stability and joined Western economic institutions. Rather than metastasizing across large portions of the globe as Woolsey had feared in 1993, civil wars mostly remained contained in other portions of the globe and then declined in number by the end of the century: see Figure o.1. And most of these, on examination, seemed to have been the clash more nearly of predatory thugs than of civilizations.

The experience also suggests that policing is not likely to be terribly difficult or costly when disciplined forces are mainly up against criminal ones or against ones representing criminal or substantially criminalized regimes. In Panama, Somalia, Rwanda, Croatia, Bosnia, Kosovo, East Timor, and Sierra Leone disciplined forces triumphed easily and at remarkably low cost to themselves in casualties – though in the case of Somalia the peacekeepers found that cost to be insufficiently low given the value of the stakes to them.

The intimidating, opportunistic thugs in these conflicts have been successful mainly because they are the biggest bullies on the block. However, like most bullies (and sadists and torturers), they tend not to be particularly interested in engaging a formidable opponent. Moreover, they substantially lack organization, discipline, coherent tactics or strategy, deep motivation, broad popular support, ideological commitment, and, essentially, courage. Therefore, a sufficiently large, impressively armed, and well-disciplined policing force can be effective in pacifying thug-dominated conflicts and removing thuggish regimes. The thugs would still exist of course, and many might remain in the area, but, insofar as they remained unpacified, they would be reduced to sporadic and improvised crime and violence, not elevated to town or area mastery.

The Gulf War of 1991 was a policing war of a rather different order. It turned back the invasion of a neighboring country by a country that could likely be considered to be run by a criminal, or thuggish, regime. Iraq had elements of a reasonably coherent conventional army but, because it was ill-led and displayed little sign of motivation, it proved to be a pushover when confronted with a military without those key defects, and it obligingly collapsed from, or even before, the first military contact.

Once policing forces restore peace to a country, it can often endure. Somalia was a marked failure, but, after a decade of especially brutal civil war, Sierra Leone remains quite peaceful some 20 years after the British policing invasion. Something similar can be said for Rwanda: it has remained peaceful for decades after enduring a horrific episode of genocide. And peace, if not perfection, has been fabricated in Panama, Kosovo, and East Timor, not to mention Kuwait.

Most impressive, perhaps, is the case of Bosnia. Huntington deemed it a quintessential instance of a fault-line war of clashing civilizations that "rarely ends permanently" because "when one side sees the opportunity for gain, the war is renewed," and he prophesied that, should the United States withdraw, the war there would very likely erupt again because the former combatants "have every incentive to renew the fighting once they have refreshed themselves."[82] But, as noted, the international peacekeepers sent in at the end of 1995 found they had little to do, and they were duly pulled out when their year-long mandate expired. And for a quarter century now there has not been any ethnic violence, much less ethnic warfare, in the country, whatever the "incentives" and no matter how deeply those "ancient" ethnic hatreds had supposedly been engrained. Bosnia suffers from many ills, such as government mismanagement and high unemployment. And the voters, much to the dismay of their foreign well-wishers, have routinely elected the "wrong" people to office. There is considerable corruption and something of a population exodus by people seeking a better life elsewhere.[83] But the goal of peacemaking is to stop people from killing each other; to get them to love one another is a bit beyond the mandate.[84]

As suggested earlier, it is much too grand to consider these ventures to constitute exercises in "liberal hegemony" or a "liberal world order." Nonetheless, the record does suggest that, although policing wars are not likely satisfyingly to order the world, they can be used at least to eliminate some of the criminal regimes and to pacify some of the criminalized civil wars that are a major source of unnatural death and deprivation in the world.

This conclusion does not hold, however, when regime or insurgent forces are willing to fight and die for their cause, particularly if they envision the policing forces not as a liberating force, but as a foreign invader and occupier.

Thus, reacting to the Soviet invasion seeking to prop up a local Communist regime in 1979, Afghan warriors, Mujaheddin, fought a guerrilla war with tenacity and substantially with discipline against the well-armed, but often ill-led and incompetent invaders, leading them to withdraw in 1989.

An invasion by Israel of Lebanon in 1982 seems, overall, to have followed a similar pattern. Outraged by a series of terrorist attacks and shellings perpetrated by Palestinian forces based in bordering Lebanon, the Israelis moved in with massive force. Many Arabs in southern Lebanon resented the Palestinian presence in their midst, and they welcomed the Israelis with flowers and smiles. But the Israelis overran numerous Arab villages, killing some 1,900 civilians in the first stages, and this quickly turned, as Sandra Mackey puts it, "a confederate against the Palestinians into a formidable adversary of the State of Israel."[85] The use of roadside bombs and persistent attacks, many of them suicidal, by dedicated opponents against Israeli occupiers in southern Lebanon eventually proved successful: they sufficiently increased the cost of the occupation (controversial in Israel from the start), and in 2000 the Israelis withdrew their forces. By the time Israel withdrew, vastly more Israelis among the occupying forces had been killed by harassing Arab attacks than had been killed by terrorists before 1982.

This issue will be considered more fully in Chapter 4 in connection with the American invasions of Afghanistan and Iraq in the new century. The Soviet and Israeli experiences suggest there are precedents.

4

Al-Qaeda and the 9/11 Wars in Afghanistan, Iraq, Pakistan

In Chicago in 1968, shortly after what was essentially a police riot in an attempt to subdue anti-war demonstrators at the Democratic National Convention, the city's mayor, Richard J. Daley, memorably defended his troops, insisting at a press conference, "Gentlemen, get the thing straight once and for all – the policeman isn't there to create disorder, the policeman is there to preserve disorder."

In the new century, American military policy has done both: the United States first created disorder and then it preserved it. Throughout, foreign and domestic policy has been a quixotic quest to extinguish threats to US security that, as with the Cold War, substantially do not exist.

On September 11, 2001, al-Qaeda, a small group headquartered in Afghanistan and led by an exiled Saudi, Osama bin Laden, managed to carry out a terrorist attack in which 19 men hijacked and commandeered four airliners in the United States and crashed three of them into buildings. As noted earlier (and it can't be said too often) scarcely any terrorist attack, before or since, in a war zone or outside, has managed to inflict even one-tenth as much total destruction. But that the attack would prove to be an extreme outlier was not appreciated at the time – nor, in many respects, has it since.

As with the assassination of President John Kennedy in 1963, there has been a great reluctance to accept that such a monumental event could have been carried out by a fundamentally trivial entity, and there has been a consequent tendency to inflate al-Qaeda's importance and effectiveness. In the process, massive extrapolations have been made – similar to those made over North Korea's attack on the South – to present terrorism as a threat to the survival, to the very existence, of the United States or even of the world system.[1]

In the process, fears about rogue states and about the proliferation of weapons of mass destruction were much enhanced by fancies that such states might one day decide suicidally to hand over some of their precious and potentially traceable arsenal to terrorists – irresponsible groups they could not control. And wild extrapolations have precipitated costly anti-terrorism and anti-proliferation wars and huge increases in security spending.

The much-exaggerated alarm made politically possible an armed invasion of Afghanistan in 2001 to depose an unpleasant regime that, despite some appearances, had essentially nothing to do with 9/11. And in 2003, the process was extended to another such regime as the American military was sent to Iraq in another war of aggression to remove the fully containable and fully deterrable regime of the pathetic Saddam Hussein. There has also been a third war – the spillover one in Pakistan, which the United States has avidly promoted. As suggested earlier, there has been a tendency to see these exercises as misguided elements of a coherent plan to establish a "liberal world order" or to apply "liberal hegemony."[2] However, the overwhelming impetus was far more banal: to get the bastards responsible for 9/11.

In its most dynamic – or, as the military like to put it, kinetic – aspects, American military policy during the current century has been an abject, and highly destructive, failure. Misguided and unnecessary (that is, stupid) wars of aggression and occupation have been launched in which trillions of dollars have been squandered and well over 200,000 people have perished, including more than twice as many Americans as were killed on 9/11.

These wars and the process that led to them are the central concern of this chapter. It begins with a survey of terrorism since 9/11 focusing particularly on the chief demon group, al-Qaeda, and it then discusses America's reaction to that group's most spectacular, and pretty much only, achievement.

The following chapter deals with other post-9/11 quests including foul-ups in Libya and Syria as well as those directed against international terrorism around the world in what was grandly dubbed the Global War on Terror. Particularly important in this was a military venture that actually proved to be comparatively successful: the one against Islamic State, or ISIS, an especially vicious and self-destructive insurgent group with a genius for creating enemies that emerged in Syria and Iraq in 2014.

AL-QAEDA

For almost all of the period since September 11, 2001, the chief terrorist group of concern has been al-Qaeda, a fringe element of a fringe movement with grandiose visions of its own importance.[3]

It seems reasonable to suggest, but unpleasant to point out, that, if the United States had followed a policy of security isolationism, the 9/11 attacks, and therefore the consequent wars in Afghanistan and Iraq, would never have taken place. The accepted narrative, as put forward by President George W. Bush, holds that the attacks were from people "who hate us for what we are rather than for what we do." But it is clear the attackers' central motivation was to affect America's foreign and military policy in the Middle East – to cease stationing troops in Saudi Arabia, to stop destroying Iraq with economic sanctions under the spell of the anti-proliferation obsession, and to reduce its support for Israel and for corrupt Muslim governments. As it happens, journalist James Fallows could not find supporters of the dominant public narrative in the American foreign and defense establishment at the time of the attacks: "There may be people who have studied, fought against, or tried to infiltrate al-Qaeda and who agree with Bush's statement. But I have never met any. The soldiers, spies, academics, and diplomats I have interviewed are unanimous in saying that 'They hate us for what we are' is dangerous claptrap."[4]

However, al-Qaeda has done remarkably little since it got horribly lucky in 2001. Moreover, Islamist terrorism from any source has remained a rare phenomenon except in war zones where, by a deft definitional shift that conflates terrorism and insurgency, what would previously have been called war is now being labeled terrorism – a phenomenon that is discussed more fully in the Chapter 5.

Although the 9/11 attacks were in many respects clever and well planned, their success was more the result of luck than of cleverness. In fact, it is not at all clear that the planners really appreciated why they might be successful.

As pilot Patrick Smith points out, "it was not because they exploited a weakness in airport security by smuggling aboard box cutters. Rather, what they actually exploited was a weakness in our mindset – a set of presumptions based on the decades-long track record of hijackings. In years past, a takeover meant hostage negotiations and standoffs; crews were trained in the concept of 'passive resistance.'"[5] It was this policy that made the 9/11 hijackings possible. However, the policy was obviously shattered by that experience as demonstrated on the fourth plane in which passengers and crew, having learned of what had happened on the earlier flights, fought to overcome the hijackers.

Nonetheless, apparently completely oblivious to this highly likely development, the 9/11 planners had also been working on a second-wave hijacking in which the targets would be skyscrapers in Los Angeles, Seattle, Chicago, and New York.[6] This means they did not appreciate the fact that the first attack would make a replication vastly more difficult. Moreover, the planners' mindset continued even *after* the 9/11 experience. Impressed by new airline security measures instituted by the Americans (but not, it appears, by the crucial change in mindset), they judged that the prospects for success in a second hijacking were low at least for the short term, but they continued to keep the prospect in mind.[7]

In addition, there were many miscues in the execution of the 9/11 plot. Most impressively, Mohamed Atta, one of the ringleaders of the plot and the pilot of the plane that crashed into the North Tower of the World Trade Center, almost missed his flight. As Michael Kenney notes, 9/11 was characterized less by flawless execution than by steadfast, malleable militants practicing slipshod tradecraft. Two were completely unprepared for their assigned roles of piloting the suicide aircraft and couldn't get training in the United States because they couldn't speak adequate English. Another al-Qaeda trainee was so incompetent that two days into his aviation training his flight instructor reported him to the FBI as a potential hijacker. He called attention to himself by, among other things, insisting on receiving advanced training for flying large commercial aircraft, asking how much fuel a jumbo jet could carry and how much damage it would cause if it crashed into anything, and getting extremely agitated when asked about his religious background.[8]

It appears that bin Laden's strategic vision for the attacks was, like that of the Japanese at Pearl Harbor, profoundly misguided. He was impressed in particular by the American reaction to losses in peacekeeping exercises in Lebanon in 1983 and in Somalia in 1993, concluding that this demonstrated impotence, weakness, and false courage. Accordingly, he appears to have believed that the country would respond to a large direct attack at home by withdrawing from the Middle East.[9] But it had, to say the least, the opposite effect. Indeed, the key result among jihadis and religious nationalists was a vehement rejection of al-Qaeda's strategy and methods.[10] With 9/11 and subsequent activity, bin Laden and gang mainly succeeded in uniting the world, including its huge Muslim portion, against their violent global jihad.[11]

What bin Laden clearly failed to understand was that the United States withdrew from Lebanon and Somalia, not simply because of the losses, but because it did not value the stakes very much in those humanitarian ventures. By contrast, the American public concluded from 9/11 that the country's very survival was at stake in the conflict with bin Laden's form of terrorism. Accordingly, its willingness to confront the danger (and to exact revenge) was, as after Pearl Harbor, monumental. As Fawaz Gerges puts it, bin Laden had picked the "wrong yardsticks by which to measure the American response."[12]

Initially there was panic in al-Qaeda at the unexpected ferocity of the American response.[13] Then bin Laden reformulated his theory. His policy, he now proclaimed, actually was one of bleeding America to the point of bankruptcy.[14] But that was more nearly a convenient rationalization than a fair representation of his goals when he had planned the attack. Initially, he apparently expected that the United States would essentially *under*react to the 9/11 attacks.

Of course, the result of America's massive and self-destructive overreaction to 9/11 may well lead it to substantially withdraw from the Middle East. Thus, by luck, bin Laden's original goal may be eventually achieved, but not at all in the way he planned it.

Impressively, bin Laden appears to have remained in a state of self-delusion even to his brutal and abrupt end in 2011 at the hands of raiding US commandoes. He continued to cling to the belief that another attack like 9/11, or even bigger, might force the United States out of the Middle East. Wallowing in delusion, he now decided that the American losses suffered in these ventures (some 5,000 soldiers he estimates) had not been nearly sufficient to enrage the American people to force the politicians to withdraw from the Middle East. Consequently, he argued, al-Qaeda must concentrate on large operations within the United States – presumably killing many tens of thousands of people since he noted that even 57,000 deaths in Vietnam did not work.[15] His death, however glamorized in America portrayals, was scarcely much of a set-back to al-Qaeda.

Al-Qaeda central, holed up in Pakistan after its abrupt enforced exit from Afghanistan, has consisted of perhaps one or two hundred people who, judging from information obtained in Osama bin Laden's lair, have been primarily occupied with dodging drone missile attacks, complaining about the lack of funds, and watching a lot of pornography.[16]

Since 9/11, the record of accomplishment of this monster group has been rather meager.[17] It has served as something of an inspiration to some Muslim extremists, has done some training, seems to have contributed a bit to the Taliban's far larger insurgency in Afghanistan, and may have participated in a few terrorist acts in Pakistan.

Al-Qaeda has also issued a considerable number of videos filled with empty, self-infatuated, and essentially delusional threats.[18]

Even isolated and under siege, it is difficult to see why al-Qaeda could not have perpetrated attacks at least as costly and shocking as the shooting rampages (organized by others) that took place in Mumbai in 2008, at a shopping center in Kenya in 2013, in Paris and San Bernardino, California, in 2015, or in Orlando and Berlin in 2016. None of these required huge resources, presented major logistical challenges, required the organization of a large number of perpetrators, or needed extensive planning. And, although *billions* of foreigners have been admitted legally into the United States since 2001, not one of these, it appears, has been an agent smuggled in by al-Qaeda.[19]

President George W. Bush recalls that, in the immediate wake of 9/11, "it seemed almost certain that there would be another attack" and that "we believed more attacks were coming, but we didn't know when, where, or from whom." Or, in the words of deputy CIA director John McLaughlin, "There was a pervasive feeling that 9/11 was not the end of the story." And another important official, John Poindexter, saw the attacks as "an opening salvo, not a final shot."[20]

In subsequent years, that gloomy perspective, despite the absence of much in the way of confirming evidence, was internalized and institutionalized in a great many ways, and even though Islamist extremist terrorists have been able to kill an average of but six people a year in the United States since 2001. The result has been two decades worth of wild overreaction and preposterous extrapolation substantially resistant to counterinformation or counterargument. And trillions of dollars have been expended to deal with a problem that, insofar as it affects the United States, is limited, even trivial – or in Marc Sageman's crisp characterization, "rather negligible."[21]

As part of this, there has been a massive tendency to inflate the group's importance and effectiveness.[22] At the preposterous extreme, the remnants of the tiny group have even been held to present a threat that is existential. Thus, in 2002, national security adviser Condoleezza Rice insisted that, after 9/11, "there is no longer any doubt that today America faces an existential threat to our security – a threat as great as any we faced during the Civil War, the so-called 'Good War', or the Cold War."[23] Michael Scheuer, formerly of the CIA, was soon repeatedly assuring us that our "survival" is at stake, that we are engaged in "war to the death," and that time is short.[24] Following this line of thinking, it has become fashionable in some circles extravagantly to denote the contest against Osama bin Laden and his scruffy little band as "The Great War of Our Time" or even (depending on how the Cold War is classified) as World War III or World War IV.[25]

Included has been a consequent tendency to assume terrorists to be clever, crafty, diabolical, resourceful, ingenious, brilliant, and flexible – opponents fully worthy of the exceedingly expensive efforts being made to counter them. In stark contrast, when seeking to describe their subjects, the authors of a set of case studies of terrorists who have focused on the United States since 9/11 chiefly apply different descriptors: incompetent, ineffective, unintelligent, idiotic, ignorant, inadequate, unorganized, misguided, muddled, amateurish, dopey, unrealistic, moronic, irrational, foolish, and gullible.[26] Or there is Brian Jenkins' assessment of domestic terrorists: "their numbers remain small, their determination limp, and their competence poor."[27] There has also been a tendency to exaggerate the importance and potential destructiveness of their plots. Thus, although the efforts of the Times Square bomber of 2010 are sometimes held to have "almost succeeded," the bomb was reported from the start to be "really amateurish" with a hopeless array of design flaws.[28]

The exaggeration of terrorist capacities has been greatest in the many much overstated assessments of their ability to develop nuclear weapons or devices. It has been widely predicted for two decades now that, because al-Qaeda operatives used box cutters so effectively on 9/11, they would, although under siege, soon apply equal talents in science and engineering to fabricate nuclear weapons and then detonate them on American cities. A popular estimate was that such a disaster might well happen by 2014.[29] Given the decidedly limited capabilities of terrorists, this concern seems to have been substantially overwrought: thus far, terrorist groups seem to have exhibited only limited desire and even less progress in going atomic. That lack of action may be because, after a brief exploration of the possible routes, they – unlike generations of alarmists – have discovered that the tremendous effort required is scarcely likely to be successful.[30]

Chasing such essentially non-existent entities is an expensive, exhausting, bewildering, chaotic, and paranoia-inducing process. Impelled by extravagant perceptions of threat, there had been that almost mind-boggling expansion of the apparatus designed to counter the terrorist enemy within. Thus, the United States has created or reorganized *about two entire counterterrorism organizations* for every terrorist arrest or apprehension it has made of people plotting to do damage within the country.[31] And the FBI has dutifully followed up some 10 to 20 million terrorism tips and leads since 2001.[32] At times, in fact, it seems to be an exercise in dueling delusions: a Muslim hothead has delusions about changing the world by blowing something up, and the authorities have delusions that he might actually be able to overcome his patent inadequacies to do so.

As with the quest to uncover domestic Communists during the Cold War as discussed in Chapter 2, US intelligence was operating under an apparently unanimous alarmist mentality after 9/11, and it came extravagantly to imagine by 2002 that the number of trained al-Qaeda operatives in the United States was between 2,000 and 5,000.[33] None, or virtually none, of these ever made an appearance. But the chase will continue, of course, because no one wants to be the one whose neglect somehow leads to another catastrophe – or in the hyperbole of an official at the FBI's National Threat Center, "it's the one you don't take seriously that becomes the 9/11."[34]

Tallying the expenditures on domestic homeland security and adding opportunity costs – but leaving out related overseas costs such as those entailed by the terrorism-induced wars in Iraq and Afghanistan – the increase in expenditures on domestic homeland security since 9/11 easily exceeds $1 trillion.[35] This has not been enough to move the country into bankruptcy – arch-terrorist Osama bin Laden's stated goal after 9/11 – but it clearly adds up to real money, even by Washington standards.

It is possible to argue, of course, that the damage committed by jihadists in the United States since 9/11 is so low because "American defensive measures are working," as Peter Bergen puts it.[36] At the extreme are the repeated assertions of former Vice President Dick Cheney that security measures put into place after 9/11 have saved thousands of lives, a figure he escalated by 2009 to "perhaps hundreds of thousands of lives."[37]

There have been few efforts to refute or even examine such extravagant and evidence-free claims – for the most part, they are simply allowed to lie there. However, although security measures should be given some credit, it is not at all clear that they have made a great deal of difference: the measures do not seem to have reduced the amount of terrorism significantly.[38] The capacities of the people involved in terrorist plots are singularly unimpressive. and their schemes, especially when unaided by facilitating FBI infiltrators, have been incoherent and inept, their capacity to accumulate weaponry rudimentary, and their organizational skills close to non-existent.[39] And it is unlikely that much terrorism has been deterred by security measures. Extensive and costly security measures have undoubtedly taken some targets (like airplanes) off the list for just about all terrorists.[40] However, no dedicated would-be terrorist should have much difficulty finding other ones if the goal is to kill people or destroy property in order to make a statement – the world is filled with such targets. The fact that terrorism is such a rare phenomenon, particularly in the developed world, likely derives from what might be called the grand or ultimate deterrent, not from security measures. In the end, terrorism simply doesn't recommend itself as a course of practical political action because of the futility and fundamental absurdity of the enterprise. In general, in fact, it tends to be counterproductive. Thus, in her analysis of civil wars, Virginia Page Fortna concludes that insurgencies that employ a systematic campaign of indiscriminate violence against public civilian targets pretty much *never* win.[41] Similarly, Max Abrahms finds that, whether they are in a war situation or not, terrorists who target civilians tend to fail in their policy goal: such targeting "is highly correlated with political failure."[42]

That there is so little terrorism, then, is not because of the efficacy of security measures or because it is so difficult to pull off – lucrative targets are ubiquitous and headline-grabbing mayhem is easy to commit. To a considerable degree, terrorism is rare because as Bruce Schneier puts it bluntly, "there isn't much of a threat of terrorism to defend against."[43]

Al-Qaeda's remarkably limited record suggests that Glenn Carle, formerly the CIA's deputy national intelligence officer for transnational threats, was right when he warned in 2008,

> We must not take fright at the specter our leaders have exaggerated. In fact, we must see jihadists for the small, lethal, disjointed and miserable opponents that they are. Al-Qaeda has only a handful of individuals capable of planning, organizing and leading a terrorist organization, and although they have threatened attacks, its capabilities are far inferior to its desires.[44]

THE FAILED WARS IN AFGHANISTAN AND PAKISTAN

Although the direct perpetrators of the 9/11 attacks were, of course, killed in the crashes, there was a focused effort to go after the group responsible for the attacks, and all eyes turned to Afghanistan.

Since 1996, the country had been under the control of the Taliban. While affording peace and a degree of coherent government to the country after a horrific civil war, the group did not generate much support abroad due to its extreme Islamist fundamentalism. Among its few friends were Saudi Arabia and Pakistan.

In 1996, Osama bin Laden, an exile from Saudi Arabia and more recently Sudan, showed up with his entourage. However, the relationship between the two groups was often very uncomfortable.[45] Although quite willing to extend its hospitality to its well-heeled visitor, the Taliban insisted on guarantees that he refrain from issuing incendiary messages and from engaging in terrorist activities while he and his followers were in the country. Bin Laden repeatedly agreed and equally frequently broke his pledge. At times, the Taliban had their troublesome "guest" under house arrest, and veteran correspondent Arnaud de Borchgrave says he was "stunned by the hostility" expressed for bin Laden when he interviewed the top Taliban leader.[46] As Vadim Brown puts it, relations were "deeply contentious, and threatened by mutual distrust and divergent ambitions."[47] Meanwhile, the Saudis tried for years to get the Saudi renegade extradited, and they appear to have been close to success in 1998.

However, the deal fell through after the Americans bombed Afghanistan in response to some al-Qaeda attacks on two of its embassies in Africa.[48]

After it was established that the terrorists who flew airliners into New York's World Trade Center and Washington's Pentagon in September 2001 were linked to and apparently trained by al-Qaeda, the United States demanded of the Taliban government that those Afghan residents the United States considered responsible for the attack be turned over to it. When the Taliban rejected this request, the administration of George W. Bush, bolstered by favorable resolutions passed in NATO and Congress, supported by an outraged domestic public, and crucially aided by cooperation from Pakistan, very actively threw its considerable military support to the efforts of anti-Taliban forces occupying some 10 percent of the country in the north.[49]

Armed forces in Afghanistan at the time were mostly a shifting collection of warlord bands, and just about anybody with about 10,000 dollars could set one up. It was a game the United States proved fully capable of playing. Operating warily (the cautionary wisdom was, "You can't buy an Afghan but you can rent one"), Special Forces teams and agents from the Central Intelligence Agency entered the country armed with large metal suitcases each packed with $3 million in US currency in nonsequential $100 bills. With such sums, platoons of combatants were hired, each liberally paid between $100 and $1,000 a month and each furnished with a shiny new weapon embossed with a serial number (in sensible concern that the combatants might sell the weapons while claiming they had lost them, they were only paid if they could produce their numbered weapon on pay day). In addition, the Americans supplied two other crucial commodities. One was leadership and tactical direction. The Afghans had a tendency to fight only until their ammunition ran out and to retire before finally securing their objective even when they had gained the upper hand. The Americans made sure their hired charges never ran out of ammunition, and they forcefully urged them on to complete each military task. The other was the deft coordination of precision, and sometimes massive, bombardment from the air.[50]

After eight years of chaotic and often brutal rule, the Taliban had become deeply unpopular in the war-exhausted country, and its poorly trained forces, which a few years earlier had united the country by conquering or bribing the warlord bands that had been tearing the country apart, now mostly disintegrated under the air and ground onslaught. Many al-Qaeda members did stand and fight, but few Afghans joined them except under duress. That virtually no one seems to have been willing to fight for the Taliban in Afghanistan in 2001 was perhaps also due to the successful effort to eradicate the lucrative drug trade in the year previous.[51] (The effort, as it happens, had no effect on street prices in Europe or the United States.)

The invasion proved to be a remarkable success. Anticipations were that it might take years to finally dislodge the Taliban and al-Qaeda, and plans were being made to send 50,000 or 55,000 American troops into the fray if necessary. But the ground and air onslaught rather quickly engendered the perception that victory was inevitable and this attitude, combined with suitable remuneration, converted an increasing cascade of Taliban fighters (behaving like chickens, according to their religious leader) and enticed warlords to switch sides without a fight. The country was secured in two months at a cost to the CIA of some $70 million. Along with the people providing the massive airpower and with some Marines which helped with the final occupation, the total American personnel involved in the conflict consisted of about 110 CIA officers and 316 from Special Forces. Two Americans were killed by the enemy in the operation, three died from friendly fire, and ten from accidents. The Navy and Air Force delivered some 6,500 strike missions from the air, and 57 percent of the ordnance was precision guided.

Later, an operation was undertaken to dislodge residual al-Qaeda elements from bases in remote mountainous terrain using a combination of US and allied forces and Afghan proxies. The venture was only a qualified success since many of the most important al-Qaeda and Taliban leaders were able to escape – a result sometimes attributed to an over-reliance on the somewhat undermotivated and unreliable Afghans. Eleven Americans were killed in the operation, as well as three friendly Afghans.

A plausible position after 9/11 – one arising, perhaps, from a sense of complacency – would have been to argue that, rather than launching a war that proved to be disastrous, an alternative reaction to 9/11 might have been to expand police and intelligence work and to work with sympathetic allies to pressure the Taliban to turn over al-Qaeda members in the country.[52] Almost all countries in the world were very eager to cooperate after the 9/11 shock, and this included two of the very few that had supported the Taliban previously: Pakistan and Saudi Arabia. Indeed, as noted earlier, the Saudis had been trying for years to get Saudi renegade Osama bin Laden extradited. Moreover, the Taliban would need Saudi support in order to have even a prayer of establishing a coherent government in Afghanistan.

Thus, the insecure regime in Afghanistan might have been susceptible to international pressure, perhaps even to the point of turning Osama bin Laden and his top associates over to international justice, which is more than the invasion accomplished. Indeed, as the bombing began, the Taliban reportedly offered to give him up to any country other than the United States without seeing evidence of guilt. But that was not good enough for President George W. Bush, who eschewed any "negotiations" whatever.[53] To the degree that this didn't work, the United States could have applied policing, intelligence, selective bombing, and commando raids to go after al-Qaeda and its leadership rather than outright invasion. That this policy might have been politically possible is suggested by the derisive assertion of a member of the Bush administration in 2004 that a Clinton-like administration, even under the impetus of 9/11, might have refrained from "any form of decisive operations involving ground troops in areas of high risk" including Afghanistan.[54] That such a restrained policy option was not even considered in 2001 (or scarcely in the years thereafter) is testimony to how much the attacks changed things. As with Pearl Harbor, there was a clear lapse in rational decision-making – that is, a failure to consider plausible alternative policies.[55]

In the wake of the 2001 war, a new, rather broadly based government was set up, many Afghans returned to their tortured country, and foreign aid and assistance contributions were sent in by a large number of countries. A fair amount of security was set up, particularly in the capital, Kabul, but much of the country continued to be run by, or plagued by, entrepreneurial warlords following traditional modes of conduct. The central government set about the daunting task of trying to defeat the warlords – or else to coopt them: "Now we call them 'regional leaders'," noted one of Afghanistan's new government officials.[56]

Even in the early years, things scarcely went smoothly.[57] However, they were soon to get much worse.

Forced by the invasion into exile in Pakistan, the Taliban gradually regrouped there, and by 2006 it had re-ignited a civil war in Afghanistan. The group soon controlled substantial areas in the south mostly inhabited by ethnic Pashtuns. Its operators were essentially free to come and go from base areas in the Pashtun section of neighboring Pakistan. The remote international border can't be closed except perhaps by contingents of troops in the hundreds of thousands.[58] Inevitably, then, Pakistan was drawn into the fight. Even though Pakistan receives $2–3 billion in American aid each year, large majorities of Pakistanis – 74 percent by 2012 – came to view the United States as an enemy.[59] As negative achievements go, that foreign policy development is a strong gold medal contender.

Graeme Smith, a Canadian journalist stationed in Afghanistan, suggests that the counterinsurgency theory applied there has been, to put it mildly, "flawed." The essential notion was that American soldiers, not knowing either the culture or the language and on a one-year tour of duty, "could walk into the world's most conservative villages, make friends, hunt their enemies, and build a better society." But "none of that," he concludes, "proved successful."[60] Instead, the Taliban was finding that the notion of attacking foreign invaders regularly rallied tribesmen to their cause.[61]

By 2008, a classified National Intelligence Estimate assessed the situation to be "bleak," noting that "the Afghan government has failed to consistently deliver services in rural areas," that the Taliban and other insurgent groups were beginning to fill the void, and that "the Taliban have effectively manipulated the grievances of disgruntled, disenfranchised tribes." It further maintained that even if the Afghan army and police could be trained into an effective force of several hundred thousand, that improbable development would still be "insufficient if Pakistan remains a safe haven for insurgents."[62] By 2010, briefers were pointing out to top generals that no counterinsurgency on record had succeeded when the insurgents had access to a deep cross-border sanctuary. They did add, however, that one could "hope" the situation in Afghanistan would prove to be an exception.[63]

There were major training failures as well. After seven years, some 200,000 Afghans were under arms, but only one battalion of 1,000 was deemed to be capable of carrying out operations independently.[64] And by 2016, top American commanders were noting that, after a decade and a half of training by the US at enormous cost, the Afghan army was still not ready, in part because it still lacked effective leaders. To set things right, they said, would require the United States to keep working at it for, variously, several more years, decades, or generations.[65]

In the process, there has been an almost mind-boggling increase of corruption. One stomach-turning example: "Afghan soldiers died of starvation at the National Military Hospital because pervasive bribery left the facility stripped of supplies."[66] Overall, estimated a governmental study in 2012, of the almost $100 billion in reconstruction aid that had been doled out by then, 85 percent had been siphoned off (including by American contractors) before it could reach its intended recipients.[67] In one listing of corruption, Afghanistan ranked 166 – third from the bottom.[68] Also disconcerting is the tolerance for Afghan soldiers and commanders to abduct boys as sex slaves.[69]

As they gained and held land, particularly in the south of the country, the Taliban have set about trying to prove, with considerable success, that they can govern with more effectiveness and less corruption than the entity in Kabul supported so lavishly by the United States.[70]

It is common to see the cause or initial impetus of the Afghanistan fiasco in the early decision of the Bush administration to divert the focus of policy from Afghanistan to Iraq in preparation for the invasion of that country – which proved, of course, to be another fiasco. But, as analysts Michael Mandelbaum and Steve Coll suggest, the notion of successfully social-engineering Afghanistan was flawed from the start.[71] In particular, it seems likely that the Taliban revival would have happened, and would have proceeded apace, whether the Americans were there in greater numbers or not: the development was essentially unstoppable.

The search for the breaking point in Vietnam was discussed in Chapter 2. Something similar, but even less tractable, seems to hold for Afghanistan. In Vietnam, the United States was not able to break the will of the Communists, but it was able to deliver horrific punishment that, by any reasonable historical standard, should have been successful in breaking the enemy's will – and it actually did so in some cases, although not enough to cause the Communist forces to pull back. In Afghanistan, the Taliban only needs to maintain a comparatively low level of violence. They can hit and run, retire to Pakistan for refreshment, and then come back to inflict more damage. If they can't be cut off, they can likely continue the effort forever, or until the hated foreign invader gets sufficiently tired of the contest and goes away – whichever comes first. In both cases, the key issue is one of patience. The Taliban have nowhere else to go; the Americans do.

The dilemma is suggested by a 2010 comment by President Barack Obama,

> It is very easy to imagine a situation in which, in the absence of a clear strategy, we ended up staying in Afghanistan for another five years, another eight years, another 10 years. And we would do it not with clear intentions but rather just out of an inertia. Or an unwillingness to ask tough questions.[72]

In the subsequent decade, Afghan policy has been notable principally for the inertial guidance Obama was concerned about. NATO allies have gradually faded away as the long war has become ever longer, and, to a considerable degree, the United States has been left to hold the bag. It, too, could leave or pull back. It did so in Somalia in 1993 as well as in Lebanon in 1983 – where Israel also withdrew from occupation in 2000. However, the United States seems to think in owns the war in Afghanistan. In the process, the "tough questions" that are either essentially ignored or answered with knee-jerk, unexamined responses are: "why are we still there?" and "should we still be there?" Simplicity and spook continue to flourish and persist.[73] In the words of Lord Salisbury, "nothing is more fatal to a wise strategy than clinging to the carcasses of dead policies."[74]

By far the most common justification for remaining in Afghanistan is that it is important to keep al-Qaeda from establishing itself there once again where it would be free to again plot attacks on the United States. That is, it is effectively contended that, although 9/11 was substantially plotted in Hamburg, Germany, just about the only reason further attacks haven't taken place is that al-Qaeda needs a bigger base of operations and that base must be in Afghanistan.[75]

Ambassador Richard Holbrooke, who worked on Afghanistan policy under Obama as America's special envoy to South Asia, contended in 2009 that "the fundamental difference between Afghanistan and Vietnam is 9/11. The Vietcong and the North Vietnamese never posed a threat to the United States homeland. The people of 9/11 who were in that area still do and are still planning. That is why we're in the region with troops." If the Taliban returned to control in Afghanistan, Holbrooke maintained with consummate certainty, "without any shadow of a doubt, al-Qaeda would move back into Afghanistan, set up a larger presence, recruit more people and pursue its objectives against the United States even more aggressively." That, he insisted, is "the only justification for what we're doing."[76]

This notion is stressed by virtually all promoters of the war. Barack Obama applied it in 2009.[77] And, in 2017, General David Petraeus, who had commanded American forces in Afghanistan for a while, ardently contended in an article written with the Brookings Institution's Michael O'Hanlon that "America's leaders should not lose sight of why the U.S. went to, and has stayed in, Afghanistan: It is in our national interest to ensure that country is not once again a sanctuary for transnational extremists, as it was when the 9/11 attacks were planned there."[78] President Donald Trump reflected that thinking when he authorized an increase of troops to Afghanistan in 2017. His "original instinct," he noted, was "to pull out," but he had been persuaded by the military (whose record on predicting events in Afghanistan has been rather miserable) to believe that "the consequences of a rapid exit are both predictable and unacceptable." Noting that "the worst terrorist attack in our history, was planned and directed from Afghanistan because that country was ruled by a government that gave comfort and shelter to terrorists," he was sure that "a hasty withdrawal would create a vacuum that terrorists . . . would instantly fill, just as happened before September 11th."[79] And the next year, when he was asked, "Can you explain why 17 years later we're still there?" he replied: "We're there because virtually every expert that I have and speak to say if we don't go there, they're going to be fighting over here. And I've heard it over and over again." He seems to have been speaking to a rather select group of "experts."[80]

This key justification for staying in Afghanistan – indeed, the *only* one, according to Holbrooke – has gone almost entirely unexamined. It fails in several ways.

1. It is unlikely that a triumphal Taliban would invite al-Qaeda back. As pointed out earlier in this chapter, relations between the two groups were anything but comfortable during the 1990s. The Taliban insisted, in agreeing to advance hospitality to bin Laden's foreign band, that al-Qaeda stay out of the terrorism business, and Osama bin Laden repeatedly promised to do so and equally repeatedly went back on his word. Then, bin Laden's 9/11 ploy not only shattered the agreement, but brought armed destruction upon his hosts.[81] The last thing the Taliban would need should it take over Afghanistan is an active terrorist group continually drawing fire from the outside.

Moreover, unlike al-Qaeda, the Taliban has a very localized perspective. The main Taliban fighters in Afghanistan are quick to point out that they are running their own war, and it seems clear that al-Qaeda plays only a limited role in their efforts. "No foreign fighter can serve as a Taliban commander," insists one Taliban leader. And, according to the American commander of US detention centers in Afghanistan, less than 6 percent of his prisoners come from outside the country, and most of these are from Pakistan: "This is a very local fight," he observes. CIA Director Leon Panetta estimated in 2010 that there were "maybe 60 to 100, maybe less" al-Qaeda operatives in Afghanistan. An extensive study of the Taliban operation in Afghanistan includes al-Qaeda as part of the coalition but mentions it only very occasionally when discussing the details of the insurgency.[82]

2. It is not at all clear that the remnants of al-Qaeda central would even *want* to establish a base camp in a war-ravaged, impoverished, insecure, and factionalized Afghanistan even if it were invited to return. It would have to uproot itself from Pakistan where it has been operating for more than a decade, and reestablish itself in new, unfamiliar territory. It is difficult to see how an Afghan "haven" would be safer than the one al-Qaeda occupies now. In fact, Douglas Saunders of Canada's *Globe and Mail* reports that most allied commanders in Afghanistan he had talked with think it "very unlikely" that al-Qaeda would establish a base there even if the Taliban were to take over.[83]

3. If al-Qaeda were to return, the United States would still be able to bomb and raid – indeed it might well be in a better position to do so than in Pakistan. American efforts to go after al-Qaeda in Pakistan are hampered by concerns about the sensitivities of the Pakistanis and about the fact that Pakistan can retaliate by cutting off or cramping logistics lines. But there would be no such constraints in a Talibanized Afghanistan: the United States could bomb and/ or send in drones or commandoes without concern about the sensitivities of the "host" country. Moreover, there are likely to be plenty of people on the ground (including Taliban) resentful of yet another "visit" by Arabs and other

foreigners, and they might be quite happy to help the Americans with intelligence and targeting. Also the United States would know the turf better as it has been occupying the country for nearly two decades. Thus, al-Qaeda would scarcely be able to obtain "sanctuary" in Afghanistan.

4. Although the 9/11 plotters received both guidance and funding from al-Qaeda in Afghanistan, much of the actual plotting was carried out in an apartment in Hamburg, Germany. The notion that terrorists need a lot of space and privacy to hatch plots of substantial magnitude in the West has been repeatedly undermined by tragic terrorist episodes in Madrid in 2004, London in 2005, Paris in 2015, and Brussels and Istanbul in 2016. As noted earlier in this chapter, al-Qaeda has not really done all that much since 9/11, and the patent inadequacies and incompetence of the essentially trivial group would scarcely be erased by uprooting itself and moving to new foreign turf. The group's problems do not stem from failing to have enough space in which to operate or plan.

A second, less common, justification for continuing the war in Afghanistan is that a Taliban takeover there would somehow "destabilize" its huge neighbor, Pakistan, perhaps leading to the seizure of its atomic arsenal by terrorists or other assorted bad guys. It's the sort of "worst case fantasy" that Bernard Brodie once warned about, and requires an exquisite sequence of things to go wrong. Actually, given that Pakistan has essentially been harboring the Taliban and generally enjoys good relations with it (and did before 9/11), a Taliban takeover that brought stability – in the sense of freedom from civil war – to Afghanistan might just as well serve to help stabilize Pakistan.

The best justification for continuing the forever war in Afghanistan is essentially humanitarian. As after the fall of the Communist regime in 1992, the country could descend into another catastrophic civil war.[84] Working against this, however, is the intense desire of the Afghan people to live at peace after decades of disaster as seen in the overwhelming popularity of a short ceasefire between Taliban and government forces in June 2018 in which people in all areas and walks of life implored combatants on all sides to stop the fighting.[85]

Over the years, there have been sporadic efforts to find a negotiated solution to the war in Afghanistan.[86] Lessons for such a deal might be applied from the January 1973 agreement between the United States and the Communist Vietnamese that settled the war there for a while.[87] It contained several elements that might be applied to the present, essentially stalemated, situation in Afghanistan in which Afghan forces are incapable of being able to seize, hold, and then coherently govern areas controlled by the Taliban and in which substantial elements in the Taliban recognize that a takeover of government strongholds, in particular the heavily-populated capital area of Kabul, is likely impossible.[88]

These elements include 1) a ceasefire in place, 2) withdrawal of US military forces, 3) continued resupply of the central regime by the United States, and 4) an exchange of prisoners – the Taliban has been interested for years in getting the release, in particular, of some of people still held in Guantanamo.[89] Also a pledge might be required that the Taliban will not allow its territory to be used by international terror groups. The United States might still retain a considerable presence in the country, but any transfers of funds or munitions would be handled by civilians and any training or other military contributions would be handled by private contractors.

An agreement with the Taliban would not bring the end of all fighting because there are spinoff and independent insurgent elements throughout the country – though it is at least conceivable that some of these could be brought into the agreement.

However, the settlement might well prove to be only temporary. That is what happened in Vietnam when, after a decent interval of two years, the Communists launched an offensive and the US-supplied South Vietnam military and government folded in 55 days as the United States wrung its hands from afar and then promptly, and with remarkably little obvious regret, moved on to other concerns as discussed in Chapter 2.[90] Later on, as it happened, the United States and the Communist regime in now-unified Vietnam became bosom buddies commiserating with each other over their mutual concern about China, the glowering giant to Vietnam's north.

It is possible that Afghan forces, trained and funded by the United States, would similarly collapse when pushed, but that is far from a certainty. For one thing, the Taliban, as a military force, is far weaker than the Communists in Vietnam were in 1975.

On the brighter side, over time the main Afghan forces might develop a degree of cooperation and coordination if a ceasefire were arranged even though the country would likely remain effectively partitioned. A great deal has changed since the American invasion, and a wired-in generation has been developed particularly in cities. And at least some in the Taliban realize that a full return to the Islamic Emirate that existed there before the invasion is no longer possible.[91]

But partition has been the effective condition for some time – indeed, it is how the country has traditionally been organized. The difference would be that the war, a decades-long disaster for all involved, would be ended or at least substantially tempered.

THE FAILED WAR IN IRAQ

Once a seeming success in Afghanistan had been achieved in 2002, the American administration turned its attention to Iraq, the country with the rather unimpressive military it had engaged and summarily defeated in and around Kuwait in 1991.

There was wide consensus, particularly among developed countries, that Saddam Hussein's criminal regime in Iraq was a contemptible one. Moreover, it was reasonable to expect that a conventional military invasion by a disciplined foreign army could eliminate the regime – it seemed entirely possible that Iraq's ill-led and demoralized army, which fought almost not at all when challenged in the Gulf War of 1991 as discussed in the previous chapter, would put up little armed resistance to such an attack.

Nonetheless, there was not much stomach for such a war in the 1990s. For example, defense department adviser Richard Perle, one of most ardent proponents of war in 2003, had published an article in 2000 that, while strongly advocating a policy hostile toward Saddam, recommended only protecting and assisting resistance movements within Iraq, not outright invasion by American troops.[92]

In the wake of the September 11, 2001 terrorist attacks in the United States, however, things changed. Indeed, as CIA director George Tenet contends, the Iraq War would likely not have happened without 9/11.[93] President George W. Bush, who came into office proposing a humble foreign policy, proclaimed shortly after 9/11 that the country's "responsibility to history" now was to "rid the world of evil." Then, a few months later, Bush specified in a major speech that, while evil could presumably be found everywhere, a special "axis of evil" existed, and it lurked in North Korea, Iran, and Iraq.[94]

Bush began to think much more seriously about launching a war to remove Iraq's leader – rather in the way his father had deposed the hapless Manuel Noriega in Panama in 1989 but had failed to topple Saddam in 1991. And in 2002, encouraged further by the Afghan venture that seemed at the time to have been so successful, and by sweet memories of his father's apparent success in the Gulf War of 1991, the Bush administration began to set its sights on one. It had no wish to be, or appear to be, complacent of course.

Efforts to tie Iraq to international terrorism mostly proved futile, but fears that the dictatorial and unstable Saddam could develop weapons of mass destruction remained high, now embellished by the argument that he might palm them off for dedicated terrorists to explode in the United States. This argument enjoyed quite a bit of support with the American public and Congress, still reeling from the September 11 attacks. As John Mearsheimer puts it, "What drove the United States to invade Iraq was the perceived need to deal with the proliferation and terrorism."[95]

Operative in the run-up to the Iraq War was what Jacques Hymans calls a "Washington threat consensus," and it seems to have been based on three propositions.[96] First, Iraq would eventually rearm and would likely fabricate WMD, including a small supply of atomic arms. Second, once so armed, Saddam Hussein would be incapable of preventing himself from engaging in extremely provocative acts such as ordering a military invasion against a neighbor or lobbing weaponry against nuclear-armed Israel, despite the fact that such acts were extremely likely to trigger a concerted multilateral military attack upon him and his regime. And third, with his army outfitted with such weaponry, Saddam could somehow come to dominate the Middle East.

The first proposition remained a matter of some dispute. At worst there was a window of several years before the regime would have been able to acquire significant arms, particularly nuclear ones. Some experts, however, seemed to think it could be much longer, while others questioned whether Saddam's regime would ever be able to gather or make the required fissile material.[97] Obviously, if effective weapons inspections had been instituted in Iraq, they would have reduced this concern greatly.

The second proposition rested on an enormous respect for what could be called Saddam's "daffiness" in decision-making. Saddam did sometimes act on caprice, and he often appeared to be out of touch – messengers bringing him bad news rarely, it seems, got the opportunity to do so twice.[98] He does seem to have been an egomaniac, although egomania is rather standard equipment for your average Third World tyrant. At the same time, as noted in Chapter 3, Saddam had shown himself capable of pragmatism. When his 1980 invasion of Iran went awry, he called for retreat to the prewar status quo; it was the Iranian regime that kept the war going. After he invaded Kuwait in 1990, he quickly moved to settle residual issues left over from the Iran-Iraq War so that he had only one enemy to deal with.

Above all, he seems to have been entirely nonsuicidal and was primarily devoted to preserving his regime and his own personal existence. Much of his obstruction of arms inspectors in the 1990s seems to have arisen from his fear that intelligence agents among them could fatally triangulate his where-abouts – a suspicion that press reports suggest was not exaggerated.[99] Even if Saddam did acquire nuclear arms, it seems most likely that he would have used them as all others have since 1945: to deter an invasion rather than to trigger one (and, also, of course, to stoke his ego). He was likely to realize that any aggressive military act in the region was almost certain to provoke a concerted, truly multilateral counterstrike that would topple his regime and remove him from existence.

The third proposition was rarely considered in discussions of the war, but it is important. One can't simultaneously maintain that Iraq's military forces can easily be walked over – something of a premise for the war makers of 2003, and one that proved to be accurate – and also that this same demoralized and incompetent military presented a coherent international threat. In many ways the "dominance" myth, repeatedly promulgated by promoters of the war in Iraq, is like the "safe haven" myth in Afghanistan. It maintains that if Saddam Hussein could just lay his hands on a chemical bomb or two, or maybe on fancier "weapons of mass destruction," he would be able to "dominate" the Middle East. Rarely considered were the inconvenient facts that the impoverished and hated dictator controlled only a shard of his country – the Kurds had established a semi-independent entity in the north, and the antipathy toward Saddam's rule was so great in the Shiite south that government and party officials often considered it hostile territory. Moreover, Saddam so feared a military coup and so distrusted his army (which he would presumably need to "dominate") that he issued it little ammunition and would not allow it to enter Baghdad with heavy equipment.[100]

Even if Saddam did order some sort of patently suicidal adventure such as lobbing an atomic weapon at some target or other, his military might very well disobey – or simply neglect to carry out – the command. After all, his initial orders in the 1991 Gulf War were to stand and fight the Americans to the last man. When push came to shove, his forces treated that absurd order with the contempt it so richly deserved.[101]

Exactly how this domination business was to be carried out was never made very clear. The United States possesses a tidy array of thousands of nuclear weapons and for years had difficulty dominating downtown Baghdad – or even keeping the lights on there. But the notion apparently is that should an atomic Iraq rattle the occasional rocket, all other countries in the area, suitably intimidated, would supinely bow to its demands. Far more likely is that any threatened states would make common cause with each other against the threatening neighbor, perhaps enlisting the convenient aid eagerly proffered by other countries, probably including the United States, and conceivably even Israel.[102]

Nevertheless, the "domination" argument was repeatedly used with dramatic urgency by many for the dangers supposedly posed by Saddam Hussein in Iraq. Thus, in the run-up to his 2003 war against Saddam Hussein's Iraq, President George W. Bush insisted that a nuclear Iraq "would be in a position to dominate the Middle East," even as Senator John McCain contended that a nuclear Saddam "would hold his neighbors and us hostage." Later, Bush maintained that a nuclear Iran would become "the predominant state in the Middle East," lording it over its neighbors.[103]

The nuclear theme was repeatedly applied in the run-up to the war. In 2002, Bush pointedly and prominently warned that "The United States of America will not permit the world's most dangerous regimes to threaten us with the world's most destructive weapons." Most famous, perhaps, is National Security Adviser Condoleezza Rice's dire warning in September 2002. Two years earlier she had contended that there should be "no sense of panic" about an Iraqi bomb and that weapons like that in the hands of Iraq would be "unusable because any attempt to use them will bring national obliteration." But now, she ominously warned, we may not be able to wait for firm evidence before launching a war: "We don't want the smoking gun to be a mushroom cloud" – a snappy construction Bush applied in a major speech the next month.[104] As the Defense Department's Paul Wolfowitz pointed out, nuclear weapons, or at any rate weapons of mass destruction (WMDs), were the "core reason" used for selling the war.[105] At a press briefing on April 10, 2003, shortly after the fall of Baghdad, White House press secretary Ari Fleischer insisted, "We have high confidence that they have weapons of mass destruction. That is what this war was about and it is about."[106]

The costly venture in Iraq, then, was almost entirely billed it as a venture required to keep Saddam Hussein's pathetic rogue state from developing nuclear and other presumably threatening weapons and to prevent him from palming off some of these too eager and congenial terrorists. Karl Rove, one of Bush's top political advisers, reflected in 2008 that, absent the belief that Saddam Hussein possessed WMD, "I suspect that the administration's course of action would have been to work to find more creative ways to constrain him like in the 90s."[107]

More lives have been extinguished – or in military euphemism, wasted – in the unnecessary war against him than at Hiroshima and Nagasaki combined. But the war's authors, it must be admitted, did manage successfully to eschew complacency.

However, when no connections to international terrorists and no weapons of mass destruction or programs to create them were found in Iraq, the war's instigators quickly moved – "shifted rapidly," in the words of neoconservative Richard Perle – to promote the advancement of democracy as the reason for the war. That is, as Bruce Russett notes, the democracy argument, a rather incidental one before the war, rose in significance only after the security arguments for going to war proved to be empty.[108] Or as, Francis Fukuyama has crisply put it, a prewar request to spend "several hundred billion dollars and several thousand American lives in order to bring democracy to . . . Iraq" would "have been laughed out of court."[109] Indeed, the American public, when given a list of foreign policy goals, has rather consistently ranked the promotion of democracy lower – often *much* lower – than such goals as combating international terrorism, protecting American jobs, preventing the spread of nuclear weapons, strengthening the United Nations, and protecting American businesses abroad.[110] As it happens, the word "democracy" nowhere appears in Bush's address to the nation of March 19, 2003 announcing the war.

War supporters applied a common argument maintaining that, rather than simply being a process of interest aggregation, democracy actually creates, inspires, or requires certain desirable modes of thought or congenial policy preferences. However, although democracy is a (comparatively) desirable gimmick for aggregating policy preferences, it does not create the policy preferences themselves. This should be clear from experience. Over the course of time, democracies variously have banned liquor and allowed it to flow freely; raised taxes to confiscatory levels and lowered them to next to nothing; refused women the right to vote and granted it to them; despoiled the environment and sought to protect it; subsidized certain economic groups and withdrawn subsidies; stifled labor unions and facilitated their creation; banned abortion and subsidized the operation; tolerated drug use and launched massive "wars" upon the practice; embraced slavery and determinedly sought to eradicate it; persecuted homosexuals and repealed or systematically failed to enforce the laws that did so; seized private property and turned over state assets to the private sector; and tolerated the organization of peaceful political opposition and voted themselves out of existence by withdrawing the right to do so. Moreover, democracies have welcomed or committed naked aggression and fought to reverse it; devolved into vicious civil war and avoided it by artful compromise; embraced colonialism and rejected the practice entirely; tolerated and sometimes caused humanitarian disaster in other parts of the world and sought to alleviate it; adopted protectionist economic policies and been free traders; and gone to war with enthusiasm and self-righteousness and sought to outlaw the institution.[111]

Associated is the idea that there is a causal correlation between democracy and peace. This notion has been brewing for some time. Woodrow Wilson's famous desire to "make the world safe for democracy" was in large part an anti-war motivation. He and many others in Britain, France, and the United States had become convinced that, as Britain's Lloyd George put it, "Freedom is the only warranty of Peace."[112] With the growth in the systematic examination of the supposed peace–democracy connection by the end of the century, such certain pronouncements became commonplace.

It was left to George W. Bush to put this mystique into practice. If democracy inevitably creates favorable policy preferences and encourages a peaceful quest for the better life, it follows that forcefully jamming it down the throats of the decreasing number of non-democratic countries in the world must be all to the good. Bush had already done something like that in Afghanistan with what looked at the time to be a fair amount of success. Moreover, as discussed in the Chapter 3, Bill Clinton had bombed Bosnia and Serbia with the same lofty goal at least partly in mind; George H. W. Bush had crisply slapped Panama into shape in 1989; Ronald Reagan had straightened out Grenada in 1983, and the Australians had recently done it in East Timor and the British in Sierra Leone. Critics have argued that democracy can't be spread at the point of a gun, but cases like these, as well as the experience with the defeated enemies after World War II, suggest that it sometimes can be, something that supporters of the administration were quick to point out.[113] Even Bruce Russett, a prominent democratic peace analyst, eventually, if rather reluctantly, concedes the possibility.[114]

However, George W. Bush and some of his supporters – particularly those in the neoconservative camp – extrapolated to develop an even more extravagant mystique. Not only would the invasion crisply bring viable democracy to Iraq, but success there would have a domino effect: democracy would eventually spread from its Baghdad bastion to envelop the Middle East. Vice President Dick Cheney attested to Bush's "abiding faith that if people were given freedom and democracy, that would begin a transformation process in Iraq that in years ahead would change the Middle East."[115]

In the process, it was argued that new democracies would also adopt all sorts of other policies including, in particular, love of, or at least much diminished hostility toward, the United States and Israel. Such extravagant, even romantic visions filled neoconservative calls to arms. In their book *The War Over Iraq*, Lawrence Kaplan and William Kristol applied due reverence to the sanctified correlation – "democracies rarely, if ever, wage war against on another" – and then extrapolated fancifully to conclude that "The more democratic the world becomes, the more likely it is to be congenial to America."[116] In an article proposing what he called "democratic realism," Charles Krauthammer urged taking "the risky but imperative course of trying to reorder the Arab world," with a "targeted, focused" effort that would (however) be "limited" to "that Islamic crescent stretching from North Africa to Afghanistan."[117] And Kaplan and Kristol stressed that "The mission begins in Baghdad, but does not end there. . . . War in Iraq represents but the first installment. . . . Duly armed, the United States can act to secure its safety and to advance the cause of liberty – in

Baghdad and beyond."[118] With that, laments Russett, democracy and democratic peace theory became "Bushwhacked."[119]

However, although Bush's simple faith in democracy may perhaps have its endearing side, how deeply that passion is (or was) really shared by his neoconservative allies could be questioned. Although they hyped democracy, David Frum and Richard Perle carefully cautioned that "in the Middle East, democratization does not mean calling immediate elections and then living with whatever happens next," but rather "opening political spaces," "creating representative institutions," "deregulating the economy," "shrinking and reforming the Middle Eastern public sector," and "perhaps above all" changing the educational system.[120] Most interesting is a call issued by neoconservatism's champion Norman Podhoretz in the run-up to the war. He strongly advocated expanding Bush's "axis of evil" beyond Iraq, Iran, and North Korea "at a minimum" to embrace "Syria and Lebanon and Libya, as well as 'friends' of America like the Saudi royal family and Egypt's Hosni Mubarak, along with the Palestinian Authority." However, Podhoretz proved to be less mystical (or simply less devious) than other neocons about democracy by pointedly adding: "the alternative to these regimes could easily turn out to be worse, even (or especially) if it comes into power through democratic elections." Accordingly, he emphasized calmly, "it will be necessary for the United States to *impose* a new political culture on the defeated parties."[121]

Although Podhoretz may be more realistic than others about democracy, his extravagant notion that the United States would somehow have the capacity to impose a new political culture throughout the non-Israeli Middle East is, like Krauthammer's comparable vision to "reorder the Arab world," so fantastic as to border on the deranged. Indeed, after looking beneath the boilerplate about democracy and the democratic peace, what seems to have principally motivated at least some of these people was a strong desire for the United States to use military methods to make the Middle East finally and once and for all safe for Israel. John Mearsheimer and Stephen Walt point out that such policy advocacy is entirely appropriate: democracy is centrally characterized by the contestings of isolated, self-serving, and often tiny special interest groups and their political and bureaucratic allies. It does not follow, of course, that policies so generated are necessarily wise, and Mearsheimer and Walt consider that the results in this case were detrimental to American (and even Israeli) national interest.[122] Yet, their contentions that the "Israel Lobby" in the US was "critical" or "a key factor" in the decision to go to war or that that decision would "have been far less likely" without the lobby's efforts need more careful analysis. In particular, it is not clear that things would have turned out differently even if Israel had not existed. The neocons may have been stridently pro-Israel and their stridency might have been enforced by urgent fears for that country's fate due to a civil-war-like intifada that was going on in Israel at the time.[123] However, most of them were ardent hawks as well, and likely to advocate for war regardless. And if the Middle East became safer for Israel, it might become so for Muslim states in the region as well – a plausible, if arguable, proposition.

Whatever the resonances of 9/11, there was no political imperative to launch a costly ground war against Iraq although the Bush administration was working from a position of some strength with the public. Hostility toward Saddam Hussein had been generated at the time of the 1991 Gulf War that reversed Iraq's seizure of neighboring Kuwait, and throughout the subsequent decade, polls document a fair degree of support for the use of military force to depose Saddam – a bit more than 50 percent.[124]

That percentage jumped to nearly 75 percent in the wake of the 9/11 terrorist attacks. However, despite the fact that polls found around half of the population professing to believe Saddam had been personally involved in the attacks, support for war against Iraq dwindled during the next several months to about where it had stood before 9/11. The administration launched a concentrated campaign to boost support for going to war in August and September 2002 but, despite strenuous efforts, it was unable notably to increase support for doing so: from September 2002 to the launching of war in March 2003, attitudes did not change notably.[125]

Bush did manage to get his war, of course. But this was because, as president, he was able to order troops into action, not because of his ability to move the public to his point of view. This suggests, then, that a great deal sometimes lies in the president's ability to deploy troops and thus to commit the country's honor and destiny. With such moves he could make an issue important and convey a compelling sense of obligation as well as of entrapment and inevitability. But in this case it was presidential policy – aided by the fact that Congress was intimidated by the experience with the Gulf War of 1991 – that redirected foreign policy, not the public's inchoate fears and anxieties about terrorism. There was no political requirement for a war against Iraq.

The heedless and essentially arrogant drive for war generated little backing abroad, however, and the Americans were never able to get a resolution of support from any international body – they tried hard both in NATO and in the UN. The leaders of most countries, including those bordering Iraq, never seemed to see that country as nearly as much of a threat as did the distant United States. They found the evidence that Iraq possessed or was developing weapons of mass destruction – banned for the country by various United

Nations resolutions – unconvincing or incomplete, and, along with many American analysts, felt the militarily pathetic Saddam could readily be deterred and contained.

France was notably opposed. Or, in retrospect, it was trying to keep the United States from embarking on a huge foreign policy debacle, one that was to lead to more American deaths than 9/11 and hundreds of thousands of additional deaths of people living in the war zone the United States was about to create. Its efforts generated an especially childish response in the United States in which "French fries" were often redubbed "freedom fries." However, "Pardon my freedom" did not become a catch phrase nor did Americans come to use freedom dressing on their salads, eat freedom bread or toast, go through freedom doors, or engage in freedom kissing.

Most impressively, Turkey refused to allow its territory to be used as a staging area for the Americans' misbegotten and ill-fated war, resisting both verbal bludgeoning and flagrant bribery.[126] In general, as Fawaz Gerges notes, the Muslim world, which had scarcely objected to the war on Afghanistan, was very hostile to the one in Iraq.[127]

Determined to see it out, Bush shrugged off international disapproval and, after fabricating a rather small and personalized coalition of the willing that included, mainly, the British and some Australians, sent the American military into action. Simplicity and spook reigned: as Paul Pillar has observed, "The most extraordinary aspect of . . . the launching of a war in Iraq in 2003 was the absence of any apparent procedure for determining whether the war was a good idea."[128]

As expected, the Iraqi military performed in about the same manner as in 1991: basically, it disintegrated under the onslaught and seems to have lacked any semblance of a coherent strategy of resistance. A reporter's observation from the later war could hold as well for the earlier one:

> The battlefields I walked over revealed signs of panicky flight: Iraqi gas masks and uniforms abandoned; armored vehicles left in revetments where they could not see advancing U.S. armor, much less shoot at it; blanket rolls left out in the open. I searched for bodies and bloodstains but saw neither on battlefields where Iraqi vehicles hit by Marines were still smoking. Defenders must have run before Marine fire reached them. Iraqi officers deserted their men . . . and this abandonment almost certainly triggered full flight by all ranks.[129]

In all, Iraq's army in 2003 was in even worse shape than in 1991, and it collapsed with even greater alacrity.

Total battle deaths for the invading forces during the war were well under 150 – even lower than had been borne in the Gulf War of 1991. In a matter of weeks, then, Iraq was relieved of two vicious regimes: the 25-year-old one of Saddam Hussein and the 13-year-old one of international sanctions.

The fat lady sang in George W. Bush's father's war: once Iraq was expelled, the Kuwaiti regime could come back from exile and take over, and American troops could go home to parade victoriously in American cities. No such pleasant fate greeted their descendants in 2003 who had to remain to build a viable national government out of the rubble that remained after Saddam; the sanctions, and the war had taken their toll.

It had been hoped that the Iraqis would greet the conquerors by dancing happily in the streets and somehow coordinate themselves into a coherent, and appreciative, government. But, although many were glad to see Saddam's tyranny ended, the invaders often found the population resentful and humiliated, rather than gleeful or grateful. Moreover, bringing order to the situation was vastly complicated by the fact that the government-toppling invasion had effectively created a failed state which permitted criminality and looting. The United States had insufficient forces to police the country, having first ignored and then disparaged the prewar contention of General Eric Shinseki that hundreds of thousands of policing troops would be required.[130]

Shunned by the Bush administration, the international community was not eager to join in the monumental reconstruction effort – particularly after the UN headquarters in Baghdad was bombed by a terrorist on August 23, 2003. The inability of the conquerors to find any evidence of those banned and greatly feared weapons of mass destruction, much less links to international terrorism, only enhanced this reluctance.

Meanwhile, Iran and, to a somewhat lesser degree, Syria fully realized that they were on the explicit hit list provided almost daily by Bush and his coterie of cheer-leading neocons: if they needed reminding, Richard Perle exultantly suggested shortly after the invasion of Iraq that a short, "two-worded," message should now be delivered to other hostile regimes in the area: "You're next."[131] Accordingly, those two countries worked closely and successfully with, and provided sanctuary for, friendly Iraqis in order to make the American tenure in Iraq as miserable as possible. An extensive US Army study of the war, in fact, strikingly concludes that "Iran appears to be the only victor."[132] Although it strongly argues that "the overwhelming majority of decisions in the Iraq War were made by highly intelligent, highly experienced, leaders," it concludes that the "failure to achieve our strategic objectives" stemmed from reasoning that contained "systemic failures," and high among these was that "U.S. leaders seemed to believe that other regional nations would not react," a "belief" that was almost breath-taking in its naiveté.[133]

In addition to Iran and Syria, others were dedicated to sabotaging the victors' peace and to killing the policing forces. After the American invasion of Afghanistan in 2001, Abu Musab al-Zarqawi, an especially bitter and violent jihadist who sympathized with al-Qaeda's ideology and agenda, moved with 30 supporters from Afghanistan to Iraq. Pursued by Saddam Hussein's security services, this tiny band had difficulty linking up with antiregime elements. However, that problem was conveniently removed, of course, in 2003 by the Americans, whose war and subsequent disorder and chaos played perfectly into Zarqawi's hands. Soon he was the leader of a small army of dedicated and brutal terrorists numbering perhaps in the thousands, recruited or self-recruited from within and abroad. It was only in late 2004 that Zarqawi linked himself up with al-Qaeda (although bin Laden harbored considerable misgivings about Zarqawi's violent hostility to Shia Muslims who constitute a majority in Iraq), and this connection may have helped in attracting recruits and in generating financial and logistical support for Zarqawi's insurgents. They were further benefited by the tendency of the Americans to credit them with a far larger portion of the violence in Iraq than they probably committed, a process that also helped to burnish Zarqawi's image in much of the Muslim world as a resistance hero.[134]

Ayman al-Zawahari, then al-Qaeda's second in command, once described the war in Iraq as "the greatest battle of Islam in this era."[135] However, whatever their connection to al-Qaeda, the mindless brutalities of his protégés in Iraq – staging beheadings at mosques, bombing playgrounds, taking over hospitals, executing ordinary citizens, performing forced marriages – eventually proved to be self-destructive, turning the Iraqis against them, including many of those who had previously been fighting the American occupation either on their own or in connection with Zarqawi. In fact, his fighters of al-Qaeda in Iraq, as they were called, seem eventually to have managed to alienate the entire population: data from polls in Iraq in 2007 indicate that 97 percent of those surveyed opposed efforts to recruit foreigners to fight in Iraq, 98 percent opposed the militants' efforts to gain control of territory, and 100 percent considered attacks against Iraqi civilians "unacceptable." In Iraq as in other places, "al-Qaeda is its own worst enemy," notes Robert Grenier, a former top CIA counterterrorism official. "Where they have succeeded initially, they very quickly discredit themselves."[136]

Helped enormously by the alienation between jihadist marauders and Iraqi tribes, the US military was able for a while to bring civil warfare under some degree of control in Iraq by 2009. However, the campaign to do so – the surge, it was called – cost over 1,000 American lives, a number seven times greater than had been lost in the 2003 invasion.[137]

In the meantime, as casualties mounted, Americans were souring on the war as they had for the wars in Korea and Vietnam. All three military ventures were quite substantially supported by the public as the troops were sent in and, in all cases, support decreased as casualties – whether of draftees, volunteers, or reservists – suffered. The decline was steeper in the early stages of the war as reluctant approvers were rather quickly alienated, and the erosion slowed as support progressively became reduced to the harder core – the pattern is essentially logarithmic.[138] There is one important difference between the wars, however. After two years of war, support for each war on a key measure had slumped to around 50 percent. At that point around 20,000 Americans had been killed in Vietnam and Korea, but only about 1,500 in Iraq.[139] That is, casualty for casualty, support dropped off far more quickly in the Iraq War than in either of the earlier two wars. This suggests that the public placed a far lower value on the stakes in Iraq than it had in the earlier wars. Korea and Vietnam were seen, initially at least, to be important and necessary components in dealing with international Communism. Also contributing to the difference in casualty tolerance may be the fact that the main threats Iraq was deemed to present to the United States when troops were sent in – fears of its "weapons of mass destruction" and of its connections to international terrorism – quickly became, to say the least, severely undermined. With those justifications gone, Iraq became something of a humanitarian venture with little relevance to US security.

As popular support for the war waned in the United States, a highly effective movement in opposition to the Iraq War emerged. Refusing to commit the mistakes of their counterparts during the Vietnam War, opponents of the Iraq War never became associated with anti-American values and, rather than expressing themselves in noisy and often unruly public demonstrations, they worked assiduously within the Democratic Party. And, seeking to avoid another mistake made by its Vietnam predecessors, the movement was careful not to attack members of the military or the military itself and joined in on the "thank you for your service" litany discussed in the Prologue to this book. This may have contributed to the high regard the military retained among the public even though it was unable to pacify Iraq and Afghanistan at an acceptable cost.

Working within the Democratic Party, the movement was instrumental in engineering the party's 2004 nomination for the presidency of the most credible anti-war candidate, John Kerry.

Bush barely won the 2004 election, which would likely have been a walkover for him without the Iraq War – he was still basking in a historically-unprecedented surge in approval generated by 9/11. Moreover, the economy was doing well, and the venture in Afghanistan looked, at the time at least, to be a remarkable success.[140] Then, in the 2006 and 2008 elections the protest movement worked to field congenial candidates for House and Senate, many of them Iraq War veterans. This substantially increased in each case the number of Democratic seats. And, in 2008, Iraq War opponents were the cornerstone of the success of Barack Obama, the only major presidential candidate to have opposed the Iraq War before it began.

Obama, however, proved to be something of a disappointment to them after he took office. There was little policy change on the wars – Obama accepted the Bush deadline on Iraq and was substantially supportive of the war in Afghanistan. And he appointed no one to foreign policy office who (like him) had clearly and publicly opposed the Iraq War before it started.[141]

After peaking at over 170,000, US troop levels declined and pretty much all were out at the end of 2011. But some came back again after the rise in 2014 of the Islamic State group – though the contribution was configured so that the Americans suffered few casualties. This episode will be discussed more fully in Chapter 5.

BUILDING DEMOCRACY?

Efforts to force democracy on Iraq are not necessarily doomed. Using minimal – but realistic – definitions of democracy, Iraq (and to a degree, Afghanistan) is acting quite a bit like a standard democracy, albeit one with exceptionally high rates of violence. Politicians are squabbling continuously. Interest groups are seeking to loot the public treasury as best they can. People are rather freely expressing themselves even where this may entail the airing of ethnic and racial hatreds (those who use violence to do so are not democratic, however), and politicians are seeking to manipulate the system to advantage their supporters. There is, however, some suppression of protest and of the media, and this is scarcely democratic. If the violence and suppression eventually come under control and if demands for security do not lead to a takeover by a strongman, it is possible that the country might become recognizably democratic.

However, even if democracy does survive in Iraq, it is to be expected that those in charge will remain loyal to the wishes of their constituencies. As noted in Chapter 3, peace builders in Bosnia repeatedly discovered that elections lead to the rise of people who can best engage and manipulate the political process to attract voters, and these are not necessarily the ones preferred by intervening foreign well-wishers. In late 2005, nearly two-thirds of those elected to the Iraqi parliament explicitly advocated a stronger role for Islam in politics.[142] Thus if the people detest Israel and the United States and let that passion influence their vote, they will (freely) elect politicians who voice – indeed, stoke – hatred for Israel and the United States. That may well mean, as Podhoretz had suggested in 2002, intensified hostility to Israel, friendliness with Shia Iran, and ungrateful animosity toward Iraq's naive, clumsy, and destructive democratic liberators.

There is a considerable danger that the disastrous chaos visited upon the area by the American invasion will come to be associated with democracy, substantially discrediting the institution more broadly. Indeed, polls in 2012 found that strong majorities of those with opinions in Turkey, Egypt, Jordan, Tunisia, and Pakistan felt that the United States actually opposes democracy in the Middle East.[143]

Insofar as the invasions of Afghanistan and Iraq were motivated by a romantic notion that the forceful intervention would instill blissful democracy on a grateful people there and that this would in turn impel other countries in the area not only to follow suit, but in time to love the United States and Israel, it has been a fiasco of monumental proportions.[144] On the brighter side, however, there is at least some hope that the experience will terminally undercut aspects of the democracy mystique as promulgated so assiduously by George W. Bush and his ménage of artful neocons.

5

Chasing Terrorists Around the Globe and Other Post-9/11 Ventures

The wars the United States instituted in Afghanistan, Iraq, and Pakistan were not the only military expeditions the country engaged in after 9/11. There were interventions in Libya and in the Syrian civil war, and these were characterized by vast proclamation and half-vast execution – that is, they were more like some of the ventures in the 1990s (Chapter 3) than like the 9/11 wars (Chapter 4). In addition, the Global War on Terror, designed to harass and defeat various al-Qaeda affiliates and other unpleasant groups deemed to be of the terrorist persuasion, was continued and far-flung. This included, in particular, the successful campaign against Islamic State, or ISIS, or ISIL, an especially vicious, if ultimately self-destructive, insurgent group that emerged in 2014. Although the campaign against that entity was essentially humanitarian, Americans managed to envision that the fanatical group somehow presented a dire threat to the United States itself – even an existential one.

I begin, however, with an examination of a definitional modification which had the effect of greatly magnifying the perceived importance and frequency of terrorism.

DEFINITIONAL SHIFT: CONFLATING TERRORISM AND WAR

Although 9/11 may not have "changed everything," its impact on language, on how terrorism has come to be understood and explained, has been substantial.[1] Some of this may come about because "terrorism," just about always a pejorative term, became much more so with that dramatic event.

Outside of war zones, the number of fatalities committed by terrorists of all stripes has been, with very few exceptions (such as 9/11 of course), remarkably low. There were 3,372 fatalities from terrorist incidents within the United States during the 38-year period from 1970 and 2013: the attacks in 2001 represented almost all of these and most of the rest come from the attack by a domestic (and non-Islamist) terrorist on a federal building in Oklahoma City in 1995. In all, even with 9/11 included in the count, this generates an annual fatality risk for the period of 1 in 4 million for the United States. And for the period since 9/11, the number of people killed by Islamist terrorists in the United States averages about six per year. The yearly rates for the period in other developed countries are also low: 1 in 1,200,000 for the UK (including Northern Ireland), 1 in 4,300,000 for Canada, 1 in 8,000,000 for Australia (including the Bali attack of 2002). During the same period the yearly chance of dying in an automobile accident in the United States was 1 in 8,200 – about 40,000 deaths per year.[2]

The vast majority, then, of what is now commonly being tallied as terrorism has occurred in war zones. This is especially true for fatalities. In 2014, for example, 78 per cent of all deaths from terrorism occurred in only five countries, all of them undergoing civil war: Iraq, Nigeria, Afghanistan, Pakistan, and Syria.[3]

There are scores of definitions of terrorism, but the following seem to capture much of the variety. In a book dealing with the Global Terrorism Database they have developed at the University of Maryland, Gary LaFree, Laura Dugan, and Erin Miller note that "most commentators and experts agree on several key elements, captured in the definition we use here: 'the threatened or actual use of illegal force and violence by non-state actors to attain a political, economic, religious, or social goal through fear, coercion, or intimidation.'"[4] And Michael Stohl, after extended consideration, defines terrorism as "the purposeful act or the threat of the act of violence to create fear and/or compliant behavior in a victim and/or the audience of the act or threat."[5]

There is some disagreement among definitions, but they generally agree on three components. They suggest that terrorism involves the 1) pursuit of a policy goal by 2) applying violence 3) in order to create fear and compliant behavior on the part of the enemy.

The problem is that these three elements do not differentiate terrorism from war. As Carl von Clausewitz stressed, the whole effort in war – at least in non-criminal ones – is to obtain political goals. In his most famous formulation, "war is merely the continuation of policy with other means" – that is, war "is a true political instrument." And the means to attaining the goal, stresses Clausewitz, involve using violence to coerce and to inflict fear and intimidation in order to break the enemy's will. In battle, says Clausewitz "the loss of morale" is the "major decisive factor."[6] Wars, then, do not involve the annihilation of the enemy, but the breaking of the enemy's will, generating surrender or policy change, something that sometimes comes quite quickly as with

France after the German invasion in 1940, and sometimes only after a long period of attrition as with the United States in Vietnam as discussed in Chapter 2.

Terrorism differs from war not in its essential method or goal, not in its efforts to intimidate and create fear, and certainly not in the fact that it applies violence. Analyst John Horgan is certainly correct to suggest that "terrorism is fundamentally a form of psychological warfare."[7] But, as Clausewitz stresses, so is war.

Terrorism differs from war in the frequency and probably the intensity with which violence is inflicted. When political violence is sporadic, it is called "terrorism." If the violence becomes frequent and sustained, it will look like, and traditionally has been called, "war."[8] Thus, in the past, when terroristic violence by substate actors (or elements) became really extensive within a country, the activity was no longer called terrorism but rather civil war or insurgency. The Irish Republican Army, for example, was generally taken to be a terrorist enterprise, while fighters in Sri Lanka in the 1990s were considered to be combatants or insurgents in a civil war situation. And the violence Vietnamese Communists inflicted on the civilian population in the early and middle 1960s – assassination, ambush, harassment, sabotage, assault – was generally considered to be an element in an insurgent or guerrilla war, not terrorism, because the violence was so sustained.[9] Among terrorism definitions, Marc Sageman seems to capture this important distinction best when he defines terrorism as "a public's characterization of political violence by non-state actors during domestic peacetime."[10]

Before 9/11, terrorism was generally seen to be a limited phenomenon, and terrorism was often called the weapon of the weak. If terrorists began to engage in violence that was no longer fitful or sporadic, the enterprise was relabeled war or insurgency, and the goal for those engaged in countering such warfare was to reverse the process – to reduce insurgent activities to more bearable terrorist levels and then to end it entirely if possible. The US military applied the distinction to the war in Iraq. In the early days when violence was sporadic, those opposing the American presence were called "terrorists." When the violence became more continuous, they became "insurgents."[11]

That definitional condition could change if terrorists were to become capable of visiting very substantial destruction with episodic attacks. In that case, the activity would still be considered terrorism because it would remain sporadic, but the damage inflicted could hardly be said to be limited. That could have happened if 9/11 had proved to be a harbinger. But it didn't, and, as noted earlier, the tragic event seems increasingly to stand out as an aberration.

Since 9/11, however, standard definitions of terrorism have been expanded to the point where virtually any violence perpetrated by rebels in civil wars is now being called terrorism. As a result, there has been a marked exaggeration in the perceived frequency and importance of terrorism.

In the wake of 9/11, "terrorism" has increasingly been slung around in an effort to discredit enemies. Thus, in the civil war in Syria, the United States branded those fighting the government of Bashar al-Assad to its own convenience. Islamic extremist fighters were "terrorists" while those insurgents approved by the United States were labeled the "moderate opposition." Assad himself is more consistent, if equally self-serving: any violent opposition to a sitting government, he says, is "terrorism."[12] The rather confusing process could also be seen when Islamic State, or ISIS, was commonly labeled a band of terrorists even though it occupied territory, ran social services, and regularly confronted armed soldiers in direct combat. In any armed conflict before the current century, that would be called an insurgency.[13]

Assad's perspective, one that has become increasingly popular since 9/11, would allow us to retire the concept of "civil war" just about entirely. That is, if one wishes to embrace the broader application of the definition of terrorism that substantially took hold after 9/11, a huge number of violent endeavors that had previously been called civil wars would have to be recategorized, and the amount of terrorism in the world in years past would accordingly mushroom.[14]

This can be taken a step further. Stohl's definition is, in his words, "actor-neutral," and he points out that terrorism, as he sees it, is very frequently committed by states, as well as by non-state actors.[15] In this spirit, much of the bombing by the United States in World War II, including that of Hiroshima, would be designated as state terrorism. A definition used by Jason Burke also does not require that terrorism must be carried out by substate actors, and he points out that "lots of different actors" apply terrorism, "state and substate, local and international."[16]

If that element of the definition is adjusted, the entire category of "war," including those of the international variety, could substantially vanish. Military historian Matthew Waxman points out that, in war, "punishment of civilians is a commonly used strategy of coercion."[17] Almost all violence at whatever level that has a policy or political goal would become "terrorism."

Whatever the definition, the post-9/11 conflation of insurgency (or even of all warfare) with terrorism makes it seem that the world is awash in terrorism, something that stokes unjustified alarm even in those countries outside war zones in which terrorism remains a quite limited hazard. For example, applying data from the Global Terrorism Database, it is possible to argue that there has been a "staggering" increase in terrorism deaths over this century.[18] However, that is because much of the violence from what would previously have been considered to be civil wars – as in Iraq, Afghanistan, Syria, and Nigeria – has been designated to be terrorism, and because a similar approach has not been fully applied to such wars in earlier decades.[19]

The expansion of the definition of terrorism so that it threatens to embrace all violent behavior that is directed at an ideological or policy goal leads, then, to a misoverestimation of terrorism's importance and impact. When properly differentiated from insurgency, terrorism has had a quite limited effect on human affairs – indeed, any significant historical impact seems to have derived much more from the reaction or overreaction it inspired or facilitated than from anything the terrorists accomplished on their own. That could be seen not only in the reaction to 9/11, but in the response to the terrorist assassination of an archduke in 1914 that was used to propel Europe into World War I.[20]

Nonetheless the process will likely continue to flourish. The incentives are to play to the galleries and to inflate the threat: there is likely to be considerably more purchase in servicing anxiety over terrorism than in seeking to counter it. Thus, officials seem incapable of pointing out that an American's chance of being killed by a terrorist is one in 4 million per year, and to suggest that terrorism might pose an acceptable risk (or even to discuss the issue) appears to be utterly impossible.[21] Accordingly, the misoverestimation of terrorism will likely long be with us.

LIBYA, SYRIA, AND VAST PROCLAMATION

The Iraq War, like the one in Afghanistan, was a response to 9/11. In the decades before those wars, US policy toward conflicts around the world had been substantially humanitarian. The United States got involved from time to time, but rarely showed a willingness to sacrifice American lives in the process. As discussed in Chapter 3, for example, intervention on the ground in Bosnia was held off until hostilities had ceased; bombs but no boots were sent to Kosovo; and in Somalia, the United States withdrew its troops after 19 of them died in a firefight.

There have been two comparable exercises in the twenty-first century, one in Libya, the other in Syria. Both replaced coherent if unpleasant regimes with chaos and murderous disorder.

When a rebellion broke out in Libya against the long-term rule of its often-flaky dictator, Muammar Gaddafi, in 2011, the United States watched from afar in sympathy with the rebels. As violence grew, however, the United States rather reluctantly responded to importunings from Britain and France to join them in entering the conflict by using airpower to help the opposition.[22] However, after some initial gains, the venture proved to be a debacle for Libya's putative liberators: Gaddafi was brutally murdered by members of the opposition, and the country descended into chaos. Then, as Christopher Dandeker puts it laconically, "initially modest objectives . . . were expanded, even though resources to achieve them were not increased proportionately."[23] As the situation devolved into chaotic civil war, the interveners gracelessly left, letting the Libyans, liberated from the order supplied by the toppled regime, to preserve disorder on their own.[24] It was much like American policy in Somalia a decade earlier.[25] Another problem emerged out of the fact that Gaddafi was a reformed rogue who had become quite cooperative with the West in the preceding decade.[26] The 2011 venture involved essentially turning on him, a move that will likely make it more difficult to remove tyrants in the future.[27]

A rebellion also broke out in Syria in 2011 with the objective of ousting that country's dictator, President Bashar al-Assad. With the help of outside forces linked variously to Iran, Assad was able to survive, and the country devolved into a protracted civil war in which, by some counts, there were 1,200 more-or-less independent rebel groups, variously supported by Western countries, including the United States, and by Muslim states in the area.[28] One of the most bizarre consequences of the post-9/11 terrorism obsession occurred early in this war when Assad reportedly released jihadists from his jails so that they could join the insurgency against him in order to "convince the world that we are facing Islamic terrorism."[29] Then, in 2015, fearing that the fast-emerging ISIS might take over the country, Russia began to provide air support for the Assad regime.

It seems clear that foreign assistance simply had the result of systematically stoking the disaster. That is, the outside states have mainly managed to preserve disorder in an especially chaotic civil war that might have ended early but for the diverse supporting cast of interveners. The war resulted in massive death and destruction as well as in a huge exodus of refugees. For years, much of the "fighting" in Syria consisted of the mindless lobbing by all sides of ordnance on civilian areas.[30]

Although US President Barack Obama rather grandly insisted on March 20, 2013 that "Assad must go" – adding "I believe he will go" – he was reluctant to do much to bring that about. Earlier, however, in an effort to deter chemical weapons use, he had effectively (and irresponsibly) promised to send in American troops with guns blazing if a rebel group could ever managed to get itself gassed by regime forces. In August 2012, he was asked what could lead him to use military force and he responded that he drew a "red line" at chemical weapons. If the regime used them, warned Obama, "That would change my calculus."[31] Then on August 21, 2013, there was a sarin gas attack in a rebel-held area, and the regime was held to be responsible by most analysts. The Obama administration dramatically proposed military action – an air strike – in response to chemical weapons use in Syria. It sought Congressional approval of such a venture, and leaders of both parties in Congress rather quickly fell into line on the issue as did lobby groups for both Israel and Saudi Arabia as well as "foreign policy luminaries" as Ben Rhodes, an Obama aide, calls them.[32] Moreover, these bipartisan leadership cues were accompanied by disturbing photographs of the corpses of Syrian children apparently killed in the attack. Nonetheless, as members of Congress discovered when they went home, the American public was decidedly unwilling to support the punitive bombing of Syria – a venture likely to risk few if any American lives – out of concern that it would lead to further involvement in the conflict there.[33] And it remained suspicious of, and therefore immune to, repeated assurances from Obama that he had categorically ruled out putting boots on the ground in Syria. "One after another," continues Rhodes, "members of Congress of both parties – including people who had demanded that we take action in Syria – announced they would vote against authorizing it." Obama's bombing never took place, though with the aid of the Russians, a face-saving arrangement was made in which the Syrian government abandoned its chemical weapons stocks.[34]

In time, two unpleasant propositions about the lengthy and costly civil war had become true although they were still substantially absent from policy discussions. The first of these is the fact that the Assad forces were pretty much winning the war. In February 2018, for example, a US intelligence community report concluded that, "The Syrian opposition's seven-year insurgency is probably no longer capable of overthrowing President Bashar al-Assad or overcoming a growing military disadvantage." It chose to render that assertion in italics.[35] The second proposition is a stark observation put forward in a think tank report in 2015 by Ambassador James Dobbins and his colleagues: "any peace in Syria is better than the current war."[36]

Those whose chief concern was the welfare of the Syrian people might well have concluded from this that the United States and other intervening states should work primarily to bring the suffering to a substantial close, and that this would likely mean cutting off support to most rebel combatants in Syria and working with, even directly supporting, Assad and his foreign allies. This would, of course, constitute a massive reversal in policy – as well as a grim admission that the Russians had been essentially right in the civil war.[37]

There would be a risk, of course, that, once something of a peace had been secured, Assad's forces would embark on murderous rampages against former enemies. But it is more likely that this danger could be effectively dealt with if the United States and other interveners were inside the tent rather than outside it.

As early as 2014, Graham Fuller, a Middle East specialist and former vice chairman of the CIA's National Intelligence Council, pointed out that, although Assad "is hardly an ideal ruler," he "is rational, has run a longtime functioning state," and scarcely represents a threat to the United States. Moreover, he is supported by many in Syria who "rightly fear" the "domestic anarchy" that might come after his fall. The lessons of Libya are clearly relevant here. Fuller concluded that "The time has now come to bite the bullet, admit failure, and to permit – if not assist – Assad in quickly winding down the civil war in Syria."[38] This suggestion was highly unfashionable at the time – it was never even brought up as a hypothetical policy possibility in the administration.[39] And then, like the Dobbins assessment, it was overwhelmed by hysteria over the rise in 2014 of the vicious and headline-grabbing ISIS group.

THE SUCCESSFUL WAR AGAINST ISIS IN IRAQ AND SYRIA

The rather unimpressive post-9/11 achievements of al-Qaeda central, holed up in Pakistan, were discussed in Chapter 4. But there were a number of affiliated or franchised al-Qaeda elements in other countries as well. Indeed, in seeking to argue in 2012 that al-Qaeda was "resurgent," analyst Seth Jones pointed almost entirely to the activities of the organization's affiliates, not of the core group.[40] Various of these variously affiliated groups in places like Iraq, Syria, Yemen, Afghanistan, Somalia, Libya, and Nigeria inflicted damage in ongoing civil wars, but little to the "far enemy," which is al-Qaeda's stated central goal. For the most part, they haven't even tried. Moreover, the groups seem to be overwhelmingly focused on local issues, not on international projection.[41] The chief exception to this was the al-Qaeda branch in Yemen which made a few attempts to attack the United States. The most notable is was the underwear bomber of 2009, who was outfitted by a Yemeni who was constantly called a master bomb-maker. However, the device he came up with was almost impossible to detonate and far too small to bring down the airliner if it had gone off.[42] The group also made two attempts to smuggle bombs on to cargo planes, but both plots were disrupted.[43] Overall, extremist Islamist terrorism in total claimed some 200–400 lives yearly worldwide outside of war zones, about the same as bathtub drownings in the United States.[44]

This changed, however, with the rise of ISIS, or Islamic State, which burst into official and public attention in 2014 with some military victories in Iraq and Syria – particularly when it handily took over Iraq's second largest city, Mosul, in June of that year.

ISIS was a spin-off, or a defecting enterprise, from the al-Qaeda in Iraq group once led by Abu Musab al-Zarqawi that was discussed in Chapter 4. And, like it, ISIS was devotedly, murderously, and self-destructively anti-Shia. Indeed, Islamic State had actually been summarily kicked out by al-Qaeda central itself because, instead of focusing on doing damage against the far enemy, the United States in particular, the new group was mainly devoted to killing and terrorizing fellow Muslims and neighboring Christians that it didn't like.[45]

In some important respects, the terrain was promising for ISIS. The United States military had essentially withdrawn from Iraq by the end of 2011 after its success in the surge that, at a cost of 1,000 American lives, had substantially defeated al-Qaeda in Iraq and provided a moment of respite in the country. However, this achievement soon fell apart in considerable measure because of foolish, even vicious, decisions directed against the Sunni minority by the government in Iraq led by Prime Minister Nouri al-Maliki that the United States had created and left behind.[46] ISIS might have been successful if it had been able to keep its mindless savagery under control and if it could have made common cause with aggrieved Sunni groups in Iraq. For a while in fact, ISIS seemed like an attractive alternative for many Sunnis. But not for long.

ISIS was eventually overcome by a set of defects, many of them similar to those of the group from which it emerged, Zarqawi's al-Qaeda branch in Iraq. As Middle East specialist Ramzy Mardini presciently put it in 2014, "the Islamic State's fundamentals are weak"; "it does not have a sustainable end-game"; its "extreme ideology, spirit of subjugation, and acts of barbarism prevent it from becoming a political venue for the masses"; its foolhardy efforts to instill fear in everyone limits "its opportunities for alliances" and makes it "vulnerable to popular backlash"; "its potential support across the region ranges from limited to nonexistent"; and it "is completely isolated, encircled by enemies."[47] As Daniel Byman notes, it had a "genius for making enemies" and could not make common cause even with other Sunni rebel groups.[48]

Any suggestion that the group had much military prowess was questionable from the start. This was evident even in its greatest achievement: the conquest of Mosul. As it happens, the venture was essentially a fluke, and, like many other ISIS victories, owed its success primarily to the often-monumental incompetence of the Iraqi army. ISIS was apparently planning to hold part of the city for a while in an effort to free some prisoners.[49] However, the defending Iraqi army and the Federal Police numbering perhaps 60,000 (even taking into account the fact that many soldiers had purchased the right to avoid showing up for duty by paying half their salary to their commanders) obligingly simply fell apart in confusion and disarray, abandoning weaponry and the city itself to the tiny group of seeming invaders even though it outnumbered them by perhaps 30 to one.[50]

The defending Iraqi army had been trained, indeed created, by the American military at a cost to US taxpayers of more than $20 billion.[51] Thus, not only did the US military prove unable to contain the (unexpected) violence that followed its invasion of Iraq, but, as in Vietnam, it could not train an Iraq army to replace it after it withdrew.

In the same time, ISIS was committing mindless and self-defeating atrocities guaranteed to generate a dedicated opposition. For example, it massacred some 1,700 unarmed captured Shia military cadets by shooting, beheading, and choking them and pushing the bodies into shallow mass graves. It then triumphantly web-cast videos of the event. In another venture, it captured a prison outside Mosul and summarily executed 600 of the prisoners who happened to be Shia.[52]

Nonetheless, the American public at first saw the situation in Iraq as a minor problem. At any rate, having withdrawn from Iraq, it was not prepared to send American troops to help when civil war seemed to erupt yet again in the beleaguered country. Thus, one poll found only 17 percent willing to send American ground troops to fight ISIS immediately after it surprisingly routed the Iraqi forces in Mosul.[53] Moreover, initially at least, the Islamic State had a local focus, seeking to establish what it called a caliphate in the Middle East, not on adventures abroad.

However, outraged at Islamic State's brutalities, the United States and other Western nations began bombing its positions after the fall of Mosul. In response to this, ISIS members, unable to attack the combatant countries directly, retaliated by performing and webcasting several beheadings of defenseless Western hostages in the late summer and fall of 2014.

This caused alarm greatly to escalate and proved to be spectacularly counterproductive. Following the web-cast beheadings of Americans – tragic and disgusting, but hardly of the order of the magnitude of destruction wreaked on 9/11 – some 60 to 80 percent of the American public came to view ISIS as a major security threat to the United States. And the beheadings boosted support for intervention to over 40 percent. For a while in February 2015, after the death (apparently in a Jordanian airstrike) of an American captive, Kayla Mueller, support spiked even higher – to upwards of 60 percent.[54] A similar phenomenon took place in Europe.

The ISIS phenomenon transfixed the American public: elites who stoked alarm found a receptive audience. Democratic Senator Dianne Feinstein insisted that "The threat ISIS poses cannot be overstated" – effectively proclaiming, as columnist Dan Froomkin suggests, hyperbole on the subject to be

impossible.[55] Equally inspired, Senator Jim Inhofe, born before World War II, extravagantly claimed that "we're in the most dangerous position we've ever been in" and that ISIS is "rapidly developing a method of blowing up a major U.S. city."[56] And Defense Secretary Chuck Hagel soared ever skyward, saying, "we've never seen a threat" like this before, a "comprehensive threat" with sophistication, armaments, strategic knowledge, funding, capacity, ideology. "It's new. The threat is significantly worse than we've seen before, not just in Iraq, but in the Middle East."[57] A poll conducted in the spring of 2016 asked the 83 percent of its respondents who said they closely followed news stories about ISIS whether the group presented "a serious threat to the existence or survival of the US." Fully 77 percent agreed, more than two-thirds of them strongly.[58] Additionally indicative, perhaps, is an episode in 2015 in which a woman in Salem, Illinois, misunderstood a telephone message stating that retired minister Michael Ice and his wife were coming to her church, and called the Sheriff to report with alarm that "the ISIS" were coming.[59]

With the surge of public alarm, the media responded in kind.[60] For example, the childish verbiage spewed out on ISIS websites was often taken seriously and seen to be ominous by commentators. In one, ISIS threatened the Russians: "We will make your wives concubines and make your children our slaves ... Soon, very soon, the blood will spill like an ocean ... .The Kremlin will be ours." Another bloviated, "Know, oh Obama, that we will reach America. Know also that we will cut off your head in the White House and transform America into a Muslim province."[61] And the preposterous, grandiloquent ravings of Islamic State forefather Abu Musab al-Zarqawi (who was killed in 2006) that "We fight here, while our goal is Rome" were gravely and ominously relayed as if they had some serious meaning.[62]

The media also quickly became canny about weaving audience-grabbing references to the arrestingly diabolical ISIS into any story about terrorism. Especially impressive was the ingenious ploy of the editors at the *Daily Beast* when it published a thoughtful article entitled, "How ISIS's 'Attack America' Plan Is Working."[63] The teaser for the article left out the word, "How," cleverly transforming the message of the piece in an effort, presumably, to attract frightened readers and to service their alarm. In contrast, Brian Jenkins' characterization tends to fit: "It's not a threat. It's a tweet."[64]

Outrage at the tactics of ISIS was entirely understandable and justified, and the group certainly presented a threat to the people under its control and in its neighborhood and could contribute damagingly to the instability in the Middle East that followed serial intervention there by the American military. However, as with al-Qaeda after 9/11, it scarcely presented a challenge to global security.

ISIS was led by millenarian crackpots. Its numbers were small, and it differentiated itself from al-Qaeda, initially at least, in that it did not primarily seek to target the far enemy, preferring instead to carve out a state in the Middle East for itself, mostly killing fellow Muslims who stood in its way. Unlike al-Qaeda Central, it welcomed foreign fighters into its ranks in sizable numbers, and sought to administer the territory it occupied. That is, it was far more like an insurgent group than like a terrorist one. Its counterproductive brutalities, such as staged beheadings of hostages, summary executions of prisoners, and the rape and enslavement of female captives, left it without allies and outside support – indeed, it became surrounded by enemies.

After its startlingly easy gains of 2014, the vicious group's momentum substantially halted, and its empire came under siege and went into retreat: its advances were stopped and then reversed.[65] And, by holding territory, it presented an obvious and clear target to military opponents.

After an additional expenditure of more than $1.6 billion by the United States, the Iraqi army, or significant portions thereof, revived considerably from its disastrous collapse in 2014. In part, minds became concentrated and spines steeled by the fact that ISIS had foolishly developed a reputation for massacring people who surrender to it. Along with allied groups, particularly Kurdish forces and Shia paramilitary groups, it did most of the on-ground fighting while the United States supplied air support.

By late 2014, ISIS was being pushed back from Kobani, a strategically-located area in northern Syria, and it was finding that its supply lines were overstretched and that its ranks of experienced fighters were being thinned. The group's magazine claimed that ISIS was ready to burn 10,000 fighters in the fight and would never accept losing. However, they left after losses of a few hundred.

ISIS also found that actually controlling and effectively governing wide territories to be a major strain. And it had to work hard to keep people from fleeing its brutal lumpen caliphate. On close examination in fact, its once highly vaunted economic capacity – selling a lot of oil and antiquities, for example – proved to be illusory. By 2015, Jamie Hansen-Lewis and Jacob Shapiro were arguing that Islamic State was

> extremely unlikely to be sustainable from a financial perspective. Its economy is small compared to its enemies, its institutions are not conducive to economic growth, and it is reliant on extractive industries that in all other non-democratic countries foster the creation of kleptocratic elites. ... Even if it endures as a fragile state, it will be vulnerable to internal strife.[66]

Even in late 2014, there were reports indicating that there were major problems with providing services and medical care, keeping prices from soaring, getting schools to function, keeping the water drinkable. As the territory it controlled diminished – thereby reducing the number of people it could tax (or extort) – ISIS was forced by the end of 2015 to reduce the salaries of its fighters by half. And, most grimly, by 2016, it ceased supplying free energy drinks and Snicker bars to them. Along the line, ISIS created a quixotic currency, the "Gold Dinar," after grandly proclaiming that the death of America's oppressive banknote would bring that country to its knees. However, by 2016, ISIS scrapped its fanciful new currency and came to rely on US dollars, however oppressive. There were also clashes among senior commanders over allegations of corruption, mismanagement, and theft. Not only had the tax, or extortion, base been much reduced and oil sales disrupted, but the huge cash windfall from the seizure of banks during the group's season of expansion in 2014 was now mostly gone.

Moreover, to the degree that ISIS, unlike the more wary al-Qaeda central, welcomed fighters from abroad, the group was more likely to be penetrated by foreign intelligence operatives. Indeed, the fear of informants in the ranks fueled paranoia, and executions of suspected spies and traitors to the cause became common. There was another problem. By most accounts, their most effective fighters were those imported from Chechnya and nearby areas. Many of these arrived in early 2014 because, fearing terrorism at the time of the Sochi Winter Olympics, Russian authorities were opening borders and urging them to leave. In the latter half of that year, however, the Russians reversed the policy. In late 2015, ISIS tried to push back by launching three badly coordinated offensives in Northern Iraq using, among other things, armored bulldozers. The offensives were readily beaten back.[67] By 2016, ISIS had lost some 40 percent of its territory overall, 65 percent in Iraq. Overall, the flow of foreign fighters going to ISIS may have dropped by 90 percent by 2016 even as opposition to the group among Arab teens and young adults had risen from 60 percent to 80 percent. A poll conducted in January 2016 found that 99 percent of Shiite and 95 percent of Sunni Iraqis said that they opposed the group.[68] Throughout, there was near-total rejection of ISIS's interpretation of Islam by scholars and theorists, including those very sympathetic to jihad.[69]

Indeed, less than two years after proclaiming its caliphate and the start of a glorious new epoch in world history, the group was beginning to prepare its supporters for the possibility, even the likelihood, of total territorial collapse while urging its supporters on with such cheerless proclamations as "a drowning person does not fear getting wet."[70]

In defense and in decline, ISIS relied primarily not on counteroffensives, but on planting booby traps, using snipers, and cowering among civilians. Such tactics were very much on view as the Iraqi army and its allies took back the city of Mosul in 2016 and 2017. To maintain its human shield, ISIS murdered hundreds of people who tried to escape, sometimes hanging the corpses from electrical pylons as a warning.[71] The battle for the Old City in East Mosul was the most brutal. The streets were too narrow for armored vehicles, and the fighting was house to house. Any escape routes were cut off, and the Iraqi army executed any surrendering forces on the spot – leaving them with no option but to fight to the end. Bombing reduced the area, much of which had been inhabited continuously since the seventh century, to rubble, and there were tens of thousands of deaths, both military and civilian. One American bomb blew up a building housing two ISIS snipers, and killed 105 civilians in the process.[72]

Because of Islamic State tactics, it seems possible that the overall costs for defeating it might have been lower if the tactics to do so had been more measured, allowing the patent defects of the organization to help defeat it – to let it self-destruct.[73] But that policy was not adopted.

Driven from the cities and towns it occupied in 2014 and 2015, ISIS sought to exact revenge and to remind the world of its continued existence by launching sporadic and vicious terrorist attacks in the Middle East and in the West and by inspiring them abroad in any country at all, not just ones participating in the fight against ISIS. As early as September 2014, a top ISIS spokesman was urging foreign supporters who happened to reside in countries that were waging war against the group in the Middle East to kill disbelievers, whether civilian or military, in any manner. The "spiteful and filthy French" were singled out for special attention.[74] Fears in the West soon focused on the dangers presented by potential homegrown terrorists who might be inspired by ISIS's propaganda or example.

In a reactive ploy that became routine for the group, ISIS claimed responsibility for – or, more accurately, boorishly celebrated – terrorist attacks abroad in Paris, Brussels, Nice, Munich, Berlin, London, Manchester, and Barcelona. But there is little indication that ISIS central planned or significantly participated in them. Indeed, in the case of the Brussels attack, notes Benjamin Friedman, ISIS claimed that the attackers opened fire with automatic rifles, repeating errors that were in initial reporting from the scene. Moreover, like the web-cast beheadings of 2014 or the burning alive of a captured Jordanian pilot in early 2015, such terrorism was spectacularly counterproductive and tended, as Friedman continues, to provoke nationalistic anger, unifying nations against attackers rather acquiescence in their demands.[75] Moreover, the damage residual inspirees managed to commit remained limited, if tragic.

In this connection, there was a trendy concern about the way ISIS could use social media to attract and to instruct followers. However, as Daniel Byman and Jeremy Shapiro and others have pointed out, the foolish willingness of would-be terrorists to spill out their aspirations and their often-childish fantasies on social media has been, on balance, much to the advantage of the police seeking to track them.[76] ISIS also engaged in long-distance "coaching": a few ISIS operatives tried through internet communication to stir up violence by sympathetic would-be jihadists around the world – a development that some saw as a new "threat."[77] But the record of cyber coaching is spotty at best – in one case, for example, the cyber coach connected his eager American charge to a prospective collaborator in the United States who happened to be an FBI operative.[78]

Continuous failure on the battlefield had a dampening effect on enthusiasm, much of which had been impelled by the sudden – and, for some, exhilarating – expansion of ISIS in 2014. By one count there were only two Islamist terrorist plots by locals in the United States in 2014, neither of them ISIS-related. In 2015, this rose to 19, 14 of them ISIS-related – that is, both plots related to *and* unrelated to ISIS increased significantly. In 2016, however, the number of plots declined somewhat to 14 of which 11 were ISIS-related, most of them bone-headed failures. The numbers for 2017 were 13 and 11, while for 2018 they dropped to 2 and 1.[79] In addition, by 2016, the FBI was reporting that the trend for Americans seeking to join ISIS was decidedly downward.[80]

Throughout, there was great fear in the West that foreign militants who had gone to fight with ISIS would be trained and then sent back to do damage in their own countries. And, although ISIS continued to focus primarily on defending its shrinking lumpen caliphate in Syria and Iraq, by 2015 it appeared to have decided to lash out abroad to strike, in particular, foreign countries fighting it perhaps in part to divert attention from its territorial losses.

Alarm about this danger was raised in many quarters, but taking pride of place may well be a lengthy article in the *New York Times* in August 2016, about "a global network of killers" that ISIS had created and empowered. It featured a huge picture on its front page of a German petty criminal who had joined Islamic State in Syria and then defected because, he said, he was put off by all the violence. In a jailhouse interview, the thug eagerly and with seeming authority asserted that many ISIS fighters had returned to Europe and were poised to commit terrorist mayhem: "They have loads of people . . . hundreds definitely . . . living in European countries and waiting for commands to attack the European people." The article also included confirmation of this claim by intelligence and defense officials who spoke on condition of anonymity.[81]

There had been attacks by such returnees in the year previous to the article. At least some of those in the small group that perpetrated an attack on Paris in November 2015 and another in Brussels a few months later may have received training and/or support from ISIS. In the years since then, however, none of those hundreds of returned European "foot soldiers" (as the article called them) has sprung into action – rather suggesting, it appears, that those identified by the thug and police either didn't exist or went on to other pursuits.[82] As Daniel Byman and Jeremy Shapiro detailed in 2014, foreign fighters tend to be killed early (they are common picks for suicide missions); often become disillusioned, especially by in-fighting in the ranks; and do not receive much in the way of useful training for terrorist exercises back home. They are also at risk of arrest by authorities who find them fairly easy to track in part because of their foolhardy use of social media.[83]

It should also be observed that, even if all the terrible outrages committed in Europe in 2015 and 2016 are taken to be ISIS-related, far more people on that continent perished yearly at the hands of terrorists in most years in the 1970s and 1980s.[84] The existence and survival of the continent were scarcely imperiled.

DOES THE MILITARY APPROACH USED AGAINST ISIS HAVE WIDER POTENTIAL?

Foreign policy analyst David Ignatius has suggested that in its war against the Islamic State, the United States military may well have found a winning combination.[85] In this, American advisers and special operations forces in substantial numbers work closely in the field with the troops they advise. In addition, the Americans supply a great deal of coordinated fire support, particularly from the air. In the process, US battle deaths have been kept extremely low – as Ignatius points out, in three years of fighting, just five Americans had been killed in action in Syria and Iraq. What makes this campaign so unusual, notes Linda Robinson, an analyst at the Rand Corporation, is that US forces are not providing the muscle of the frontline combat troops. Rather, she suggests, quoting General Joseph Votel, the campaign was conducted "by, with, and through" others.[86]

It is not at all clear that this approach has much wider potential, however. The strategy against ISIS worked because of a couple of complementary features not likely to be found in many other conflicts.

First, as Ignatius stresses, the "by, with, and through" strategy can succeed militarily in such ventures if – and probably only if – it works with local forces who are prepared to do the fighting and dying. ISIS was vicious, uncompromising, and stupid enough to generate an almost wall-to-wall hostility from the locals. As it grew and governed territory, its character became clearer, and that helped inspire the dedicated and disciplined opposition that Ignatius talks about. "Either we will win or they will kill us all," as one of them puts it bluntly in the film *City of Ghosts*.[87] And second, there was a sense among Americans that the ISIS enemy presented a direct threat to the United States, a sense that stemmed from the vicious group's ultimate idiocy: staging and webcasting beheadings of defenseless American hostages.[88]

Thus, it seems unlikely that the war-fighting approach applied against ISIS in Iraq and Syria will prove to have wide applicability. It is unlikely to work in Afghanistan, for example. First, as discussed in Chapter 4 the Taliban is nothing like ISIS. It has some real appeal and is not corrupt – or, at any rate, it is far less corrupt than the central government supported by the United States. And, second, it scarcely inspires existential angst in the US public.

PART II

EVALUATING PRESENT THREATS

6

The Rise of China, the Assertiveness of Russia, and the Antics of Iran

In the first five chapters of this book, I have argued that American foreign and military policymaking at least since 1945 has been dominated by a worst-case approach and by an entrenched alarmism and a quest for monsters to destroy that repeatedly exaggerates threat. In retrospect, none of the espied threats has really required a large military force-in-being, and efforts to deal with them by military means have mostly failed to achieve policy ends at an acceptable cost.

The grand mistake in dealing with perceived threat during the Cold War was to infer desperate intent from apparent capacity. During the war on terror, which has dominated the post-Cold War era, it has been to infer desperate capacity from apparent intent.[1] Of the threats perceived in both periods, many essentially did not exist at all or were destined to self-destruct, and very few proved susceptible to being solved, or even coherently dealt with, by military means. Complacency would often have been a wiser policy.

The process of threat inflation, or monster identification, continues. Indeed, it has generated a coterie of professional alarmists: as a former planner at the Pentagon puts it, his job was "to look for all the bad stuff. Scanning for threats is what we get paid to do."[2] After examining an important US Defense Department policy document, Benjamin Friedman observed in 2008 that, rather than estimating the varying likelihood of potential national security threats and then coming up with recommendations on that basis, it "contends simply that 'managing risk' compels the United States to prepare for all of them while concluding that we should retain the weapons and forces we have, with a few tweaks."[3] Military historian Gregory Daddis has looked over the 2015 National Security Strategy and notes that the document stresses the "risks of an insecure world" and the "persistent risk of attacks" suggesting that "we live in a dangerous world ... one in which only vigilant nations – led, naturally, by the United States – preemptively rooting out evil can survive."[4]

And in 2018, the Defense Department, then under the command of retired General James ("Mad Dog") Mattis, issued its National Defense Strategy, which espied an "increasingly complex security environment" and an "ever more lethal and disruptive battlefield" to the point where the very character of war had changed. To deal with this, it advocated "a consistent, multiyear investment to restore warfighting readiness and field a lethal force."[5] That is, in its view, the American military had allowed itself to become insufficiently lethal.

Later in the year, the Mattis document was evaluated by the Commission on the National Defense Strategy for the United States, a carefully picked bipartisan group of alarmists. In a report published by the US National Institute of Peace, it concluded that the NDS, while admirable and "a constructive first step," had not gone near far enough, and at one point it helpfully supplied a litany of alarmism over the previous years:

> In 2010, the Quadrennial Defense Review Independent Panel warned of a coming "train wreck" if America did not retain adequate military capabilities in an increasingly competitive world. In 2014, the National Defense Panel warned that the U.S. military had become "inadequate given the future strategic and operational environment."

Then, rising to the occasion, the Commission concluded that, by 2018, America, far from merely having to worry about train wrecks and inadequacies, had actually managed to reach "the point of a full-blown national security crisis" because "the strategic landscape is growing steadily more threatening." Thus, the "security and wellbeing of the United States are at greater risk than at any time in decades" and "if the nation does not act promptly to remedy these circumstances, the consequences will be grave and lasting." The remedy it supplies recommends taking a "holistic approach." In this, one first scrutinizes the entire federal budget – "especially mandatory spending" such as social security – to look for places to cut. Then, one looks hard at tax levels, which are presumably far too low to fund the military requirements meeting the challenges espied on the "strategic landscape." This is necessary, it grandly concluded, because "It will be a tragedy – of unforeseeable but perhaps tremendous magnitude – if the United States allows its national interests and national security to be compromised through an unwillingness or inability to make hard choices and necessary investments."

Analyses like these have often chosen to ignore not only the abject failure of American foreign and military policy in this century as discussed in previous chapters, but also a highly significant development assessed in the Prologue: in substantial part because there has been a remarkable rise in aversion to international war, a major war among developed countries, one like World War II, is extremely unlikely to recur. Although there is no physical reason why such a war cannot come about, barring the rise of another Hitler, it is entirely possible to regard such wars as obsolescent, if not completely obsolete.[6] There have been wars throughout history, of course, but the remarkable absence of the species' worst expression for three-quarters of a century (and counting) strongly suggests that realities may have profoundly and perhaps permanently changed.

Some suggest, however, that this agreeable condition may some day be punctured either by the rise of China as a challenger country or by excessive assertiveness by Russia backed by its large nuclear arsenal. Indeed, the 2018 Commission deemed this to be the "most important" element in a "most challenging security environment."

This chapter deals with that danger. There is also a consideration of the threat, if any, presented in the Middle East by Iran. The chapter also discusses the issue of complacency and appeasement and it assesses whether the current contest justifies the label "a new Cold War."

The following chapter considers potential problems with rogue states and with the proliferation of weapons of mass destruction, particularly nuclear ones. It also assesses other potential dangers and threats such as those presented by international terrorism, international criminals, and cyber geeks, and it considers the military requirements for policing wars – humanitarian interventions designed to deal with civil wars and with incompetent and/or venal regimes.

As noted earlier, Newt Gingrich contends that defense budgets should be directly related to the amount of threat we have. The examination in these two chapters suggests that, although there are certainly problem areas and issues in the world, none of these presents a security threat to the United States large or urgent enough to justify the maintenance of a large military force-in-being.

Chapter 8 then explores what an armed force might look like in a world in which there is a pronounced aversion to international war, and it evaluates the key issue of risk (or comparative risk). It also deliberates on the arrogance that seems to accompany military predominance, and it assesses public opinion on these issues.

Greg Jaffe, Pentagon correspondent for the *Washington Post*, mused in 2012 that the alarmist narrative prevails: "no one is rushing to discuss the implications of a world that has grown safer."[7] While the exercise in the next three chapters may not start the rush that Jaffe calls for, it may help to provide a useful first step.

THE RISE OF CHINA AND THE ISSUE OF "HEGEMONY"

After a remarkable period of economic growth, China has entered the developed world – it has come to rank second in the world in gross domestic product (though around seventieth in per capita GDP). In a globalized economy, it is of course better for the United States and for just about everyone if China (or Japan or Brazil or India or Russia or any other country) becomes more prosperous – for one thing, they can now buy more of our stuff (including debt).[8] However, eschewing such economic logic, there has been a notable tendency to envision threat in China's rapidly increasing wealth.

John Mearsheimer criticizes what he calls the US commitment to global dominance in the post-Cold War era, which, he concludes, has had huge costs and brought few benefits. He also worries that the country could be transforming itself into a national-security state. Nonetheless, he deems it important that the United States keep China in check. This he considers to be one of a very few core strategic interests for which the country should use force.[9] As he puts it bluntly, the United States "must prevent China from becoming a hegemon in Asia."[10]

There is a considerable literature arguing that, by a string of measures and for whatever it is worth, the United States will remain by far the strongest country in the world for decades to come.[11] Nonetheless, writing with Stephen Walt, Mearsheimer argues that

> the chief concern is the rise of a regional hegemon that would dominate its region, much as the United States dominates the Western Hemisphere. Such a state would have abundant economic clout, the ability to develop sophisticated weaponry, the potential to project power around the globe, and perhaps even the wherewithal to outspend the United States in an arms race. Such a state might even ally with countries in the Western Hemisphere and interfere close to U.S. soil. Thus, the United States' principal aim . . . should be to maintain the regional balance of power so that the most powerful state in each region . . . remains too worried about its neighbors to roam into the Western Hemisphere.[12]

Actually, it is not clear that the United States "dominates" anything (nor is it clear what the word "hegemon" even means). As historian David Bell puts it bluntly, despite all its strength, "the United States seems frustratingly unable to impose its will on the rest of the world."[13] This can be seen, in particular, in the Western hemisphere. The United States can't stop the invasion of drugs and immigrants from its south, and the country's neighbors do not seem to quake in fear of America's nuclear weapons or of the prowess of its Marines – whose record in Latin America during the last century was less than stunning.

But their attention can be arrested if the United States credibly threatens to stop buying their sugar, coffee, oil, bananas, or beer. It is in that sense that an economically expanding China may someday come to "dominate" Asia. As Fareed Zakaria puts it, China's "greatest advantage in the global trading system" comes "from its sheer size."[14]

Nonetheless, the fear is that China, as it becomes ever wealthier, will invest a considerable amount in military hardware and will consequently come to feel impelled to target the United States or to carry out undesirable military adventures somewhere and particularly in America's "hegemonic" hemispheric neighborhood.[15] The clear implication of this perspective is that American military force should be applied to keep that from coming to be. "If China continues its impressive rise," Mearsheimer and Walt argue, "it is likely to seek hegemony in Asia," and the United States "should undertake a major effort to keep it from succeeding." This would include "deploying enough firepower to the region to shift the balance in its favor" while "recognizing that it is sometimes necessary to come onshore."[16] Or, as Walt puts it, if some country seems "likely to dominate" an area deemed to be of vital significance to the United States, it should intervene "with military force" to keep that from happening.[17]

Aaron Friedberg is also quite concerned about the necessity of "balancing" against China, an enterprise he grandly labels a "Struggle for Mastery in Asia." He warns rather extravagantly (and inspecifically) that if an illiberal China were to displace the United States as the preponderant player in this region, there would be grave dangers to American interests and values throughout the world and that if Beijing comes to believe that it can destroy US forces and bases in the Western Pacific in a first strike using only conventional weapons, there is a chance that it might someday try to do so. However, even he concludes that China is unlikely to engage in outright military conquest, and he notes that it is important to remember that both China's political elites and its military establishment would approach the prospect of war with the United States with even more than the usual burden of doubt and uncertainty, that the present generation of party leaders has no experience of war, revolution, or military service, and that the Chinese army has no recent history of actual combat. Moreover, even if it could somehow reduce its reliance on imported resources, the vitality of the Chinese economy will continue to depend on its ability to import and export manufactured products by sea – something, obviously, that an armed conflict (or even the nearness of one) would greatly disrupt.[18]

This line of thought has something of a recent precedent. As discussed in Chapter 3, Japan's impressive economic rise in the late 1980s led to a somewhat similar alarmism. And later, Friedberg was among those who worried that northeast Asia would become "a cockpit of great power conflict."[19] But such ardent prophesies of international instability in East Asia have proven to be essentially empty.[20]

Now, applying something like the same thought processes to China, the alarmed effectively seem to suggest that it is better for developed countries if China, and presumably the rest of the world, were to continue to wallow in comparative poverty and that the United States should use military force if it is necessary to make sure that happens.

From time to time, China may be emboldened to throw its weight around in its presumed area of influence. Such weight-throwing (much of it rather childish in character) is unpleasant to watch, as well as counter-productive to China's economic goals to the degree that it inspires hostility in the region, making the neighbors wary and pushing them closer to the United States.[21] But, as noted, China does not seem to harbor Hitler-style ambitions about extensive conquest as even Friedberg and Walt acknowledge.[22]

Above all, China has become almost the quintessential trading state. Its integration into the world economy and its increasing dependence on it for economic development and for the consequent acquiescence of the Chinese people are crucial. Armed conflict would be extremely – even overwhelmingly – costly to the country, and, in particular, to the regime in charge. And Chinese leaders, already rattled by internal difficulties, seem to realize this. As Bell puts it, "there is little reason to think that the country has any interest in seriously damaging the United States, its largest trading partner and debtor."[23] The best bet, surely, is that this condition will essentially hold. Moreover, as Ambassador Chas Freeman points out, "There is no military answer to a grand strategy built on a non-violent expansion of commerce and navigation."[24] A minimally armed United States wouldn't be tempted to try.

Indeed, there is a danger of making China into a threat by treating it as such, by refusing to consider the unlikelihood as well as the consequences of worst-case scenario fantasizing, and by engaging in endless metaphysical talk about "balancing." In this respect, special consideration should be given to the observation that, as Susan Shirk puts it, although China looks like a powerhouse from the outside, to its leaders it looks fragile, poor, and overwhelmed by internal problems. Provocative balancing talk, especially if military showmanship accompanies it, has the potential to be wildly counter-productive. In this respect, special heed should be paid to her warning that "historically, rising powers cause war not necessarily because they are innately belligerent, but because the reigning powers mishandle those who challenge the status quo."[25] That is, a warning by Richard Betts bears consideration: "No evidence suggests that Chinese leaders will have an interest in naked conquest ... The most likely danger lies in the situation in which action China sees as defensive and legitimate appears aggressive to Washington."[26] "Unfortunately," observes Thomas Christianson, "exaggerated rhetoric" from the United States has "seemingly confirmed national Chinese narratives about U.S. efforts to encircle and contain China."[27] And Lyle Goldstein, after going over hundreds of relevant Chinese-language articles, finds "a plainly evident common theme." Chinese specialists "are convinced that Washington seeks to contain and even derail China's rise."[28] This seems a prime example of conditions in which complacency triumphs over doing stuff. Instead, however, the farcical "security dilemma" is updated and perpetuated.

China seemed to have decided to become more assertive about controlling tiny piles of rocks, sometimes known as islands, in the South China Sea and to establish a greater presence in the area. As Freeman points out, "China has not expanded its maritime territorial claims, which date back to at least the early 20th century," but it disputes the occupation of some of those claims by Malaysia, the Philippines, and Vietnam that started in the 1970s. In the meantime, it has "transformed its tenuous holdings in the South China Sea into an impressive array of artificial islands and installations from which no other claimants can hope to dislodge it."[29]

The concerns here seem to be two-fold.

First, the sea lanes are crucial to China – fully two-thirds of the commerce that flows through that waterway originates in or is destined for China. Thus, it is likely to be worried from time to time about whether it can count on the continuous benevolence of the US Navy, which has unilaterally presented itself to be the policing agency for what it likes to call "the global commons" – a fancy term for what other people call the oceans – a phenomenon to be discussed a bit more fully in Chapter 7. After all, policing agencies in cities not only keep the streets open and the traffic flowing, but sometimes deem it necessary to close off some avenues from time to time. The concern has led to an elaborate Chinese scheme, called the Belt and Road Initiative, to establish sea and land lanes to maintain and enhance China's ability to maintain trade with the rest of the world – no matter what the American police may take it into their head to do on the "global commons." Unsurprisingly, many in the United States extravagantly envision this as a key part of a diabolical plot by the Chinese to "rule the world."[30]

Second, as China has become more prosperous, the demand at home for fish has dramatically increased, a phenomenon unlikely to taper off as the country becomes even more rich. Consequently, disputes with its neighbors over fishing areas have increased.[31]

To deem these developments to be some sort of global threat is excessive. Even if China were to come to imagine that it controls that body of water, it will still have an intense interest in the free flow of ships through it. And fishing disputes have been around ever since the invention of fish and of people (whichever came second) and are more nearly the inspiration for farce than for cosmic Sturm und Drang.

There is also the issue of China's oft-stated desire to incorporate (or re-incorporate) Taiwan into its territory and its apparent design on other offshore areas. These do create problems – though the intensity of the Taiwan issue waxed and waned over the years.[32] World leaders elsewhere should sensibly keep their eyes on this because it could conceivably lead to armed conflict for which American military forces might appear relevant. But it is also conceivable, and far more likely, that the whole problem will be worked out over the course of time without armed conflict. The Chinese strongly stress that their perspective on this issue is very long term, that they have a historic sense of patience, and that they have reached agreement with Russia and other neighbors, giving up some territory on which they had historical claims. In time, if China becomes a true democracy, Taiwan might even join up voluntarily and, failing that, some sort of legalistic face-saving agreement might eventually be worked out. In the meantime, Taiwan does not show signs of alarm, and it is underspending on defense.[33] That is, it is simply finding other, better, and far more interesting uses for its money. In addition, China's challenges with unrest in Hong Kong may well deflate any expansionary efforts for the time being.

Analysts also point to a large number of domestic problems that are likely to arrest the attention of the Chinese leaders in future years: as Freeman points out, "China has its hands full." Among the problems:

> environmental devastation, slowing growth, a rapidly aging population and shrinking labor force, enormous levels of industrial overproduction, accumulating local debt, a still-inadequate social safety network, and an increasingly oppressive political system. . . . It has an unfinished civil war with Taiwan and uneasy relations with fifty-five ethnic minority groups – 8 ½ percent of its population – at least two of which are in a near state of rebellion.[34]

China's massive effort to deal with Muslim identity and possible secession in its vast western provinces has been particularly graceless and is potentially highly counterproductive.[35] In particular, alarmed by terrorist acts that killed dozens over several years, officials overreacted and have somehow come to believe that they can concentrate perhaps a million potential separatist Muslims in "re-education" camps, letting them plot together in between mandatory sessions in which they are told how wonderful the Chinese are. It also has problems with a restive and vocal population in Hong Kong and has cracked down, a process that is scarcely likely to woo Taiwan into its embace.

There is also a monumental, endemic problem with corruption characterized by collusive economic looting and privilege-seeking by officials, businessmen, and gangsters. In his study of China's crony capitalism, economist Minxin Pei argues that the process not only wastes "precious resources that could have been invested more productively," but also diverts energies and talents into sectors "that are unlikely to be the growth engines needed to upgrade the Chinese economy." The result is likely to be "long-term economic stagnation," and Pei finds it "inconceivable" that the antiquated Chinese Communist Party can reform the economic and political institutions because "these are the very foundations of the regime's monopoly of power."[36]

To this dismal litany, one might add a brain drain to the West, a lack of secure property rights, and an inadequate legal system. Meanwhile, pollution kills a million and a half Chinese per year.[37]

China's per capita income is only one-fifth that of the United States or Singapore, and its own plans stress the need to accelerate a transition to consumption-led demand, to restructure or close inefficient state-owned companies (which comprise fully a third of the economy), to promote innovation and entrepreneurship, and to avoid unsustainable levels of debt.[38] It has launched a full-scale attack against its monumental corruption problem, but at a time when it should be liberalizing its economy, it increasingly demands ideological conformity, expands surveillance, and restricts speech.[39] As part of this, it maintains a massive program, employing some 2 million people, to censor the internet.[40] As Jon Lindsay puts it, "economic openness promotes growth, but China sees political openness as a threat to its legitimacy."[41]

On top of this, China's (or President Xi Jinping's) elaborate Belt and Road Initiative is increasingly showing signs of being not only a case of overreach, but one of "strategic disfunction" in the words of Tanner Green. An expenditure of hundreds of billions on the grandiose project has failed to deliver either returns for investors (including state-run banks) or political returns for China. It "persists only because it is the favored brainchild of an authoritarian leader living in an echo chamber" – for other Chinese to attack it is "to attack the legitimacy of the party itself."[42]

As Freeman points out, "China's rise is a real, not imaginary, challenge to the status quo and to U.S. leadership," but he stresses that "it is mainly economic, not military and it can be peaceful or not, as our interaction with it determines." It certainly feels it deserves to play a greater role on the world stage, but it does not seem to have territorial ambitions (beyond integrating Taiwan at some point), and it does not have the wherewithal or, it seems, the

ambition to "run the world." As Freeman continues, "History has given
Chinese a healthy apprehension about the damage war can do to their
homeland. China is not in search of monsters to destroy beyond its still
partially unsettled borders."[43] Or as Fu Ying, Chairperson of the Foreign
Affairs Committee of China's National People's Congress, puts it more
bluntly, "China views the U.S.-dominated world order as a mess and this is
why it does not want to take over. Why should China repeat the mistakes
which the U.S. did?"[44]

Complaints that China has not always played within the rules of international trading and has often engaged in unfair practices including the theft
of intellectual property are justified – as they were against the United States
when it was expanding in the nineteenth century. But as it has grown up,
China has had a reasonably good record of complying with complaints against
it brought up in the World Trade Organization, a trajectory that can be
encouraged by wise policy.[45] At the same time, fulminations that seem to
suggest a desire for "regime change" in China are unlikely to be either wise or
effective, not the least because, as Lyle Goldstein points out, they can be used
against genuine indigenous efforts to promote human rights and they founder
on the fact that "the United States manages to quietly and yet very actively
cooperate with states that have even worse human right records, such as Saudi
Arabia."[46]

Analyst Colin Grabow finds that China could well become "the responsible
stakeholder that many have long urged it to be." At any rate, "rather than
reflexively viewing China's economic initiatives as an affront to U.S. interests,"
efforts should be made to "harness China's emerging taste for economic
leadership." And through cooperation, the two countries "could become
successful partners in the promotion of trade and prosperity."[47] This seems
a sensible course to pursue as a matter of general policy even if it might
entail scaling back somewhat American claims to "leadership" in China's
neighborhood and ceding elements of that role (such as it is) to Beijing.[48]

China's many problems suggest that Paul Kennedy's estimation of 2010
seems still to hold: "As to a rising China becoming a new global hegemon,
I have the most serious doubts; its internal weaknesses are immense, and,
externally, it is likely to trip over its own shoelaces."[49]

RUSSIAN ASSERTIVENESS

The notion that a major war among developed countries is wildly unlikely has
frequently been taken to have been challenged by the experience of the armed
dispute between Russia and neighboring Ukraine that began in 2014. It

resulted in the peaceful, if extortionary, transfer of Crimea, a large peninsular chunk of Ukraine, to Russia, and then in a sporadic, and ultimately stalemated, civil war in Ukraine in which ethnic Russian secessionist groups in a portion of Ukraine's east were supported by Russia.

The fear, in particular, is that Russia's successful expansion – justified, it says, in part by the desire to protect persecuted ethnic Russians in a neighboring land – will cause, or tempt, it to expand elsewhere reflecting the manner in which Hitler expanded in order, he said, to protect ethnic Germans from persecution particularly in areas to his east. Indeed, NATO planners busily check roads in Western Europe to see if they are suitable for military transport in the event that Russia launches a full-scale invasion of the continent.[50] And in 2018, at the badgering of President Donald Trump, NATO countries all agreed to increase their defense spending to 2 percent of gross domestic product by 2024, something he implied was a triumph although it merely reaffirmed a commitment they had made at the time of the Crimean takeover in 2014.[51]

In the settlement that led to the unification of Germany in 1990, the United States verbally promised that, although East Germany would now become part of a NATO country, there would be no further expansion of the alliance to the east.[52] A few years later, however, NATO began just such an expansion very much against many agitated concerns by specialists. Among these was George Kennan who warned that "the Russians will react quite adversely" and called the policy "a tragic mistake," pointing out that "there was no reason for this whatsoever. No one was threatening anyone else."[53]

The expansion was carried out with good intentions. and there were many statements seeking to mollify Russian concerns including offering it a sort of adjunct position in the alliance with the possible further prospect of actual membership.[54] Nevertheless, although the Russians were powerless to stop the expansion, they greeted it with considerable dismay and opposition, voiced not just by Communists and by ultra-nationalists, but by very many in the Western-oriented elite. This should have been a warning. But it wasn't. As Christopher Fettweis observes, "In the 1990s, Russian protests regarding NATO expansion – although nearly universal – were not taken seriously, since U.S. planners believed the alliance's benevolent intentions were apparent to all."[55]

The situation was strained further in 1999 when NATO bombed Serbia, a country with considerable historical links to Russia, securing the secession of the Kosovo province as Russia stood by helplessly, a development discussed in Chapter 3. Russia sometimes sees this as precedent for its Crimean seizure.

As he was taking office as president of Russia in 2000, Vladimir Putin did tell a British interviewer, "Russia is part of European culture and I can't imagine my country cut off from what we often refer to as the 'civilized world'."[56] However, the strains from NATO expansion and from the Kosovo experience were already in place, and they gradually escalated in the new century as Putin's regime became increasingly autocratic and as the United States, and particularly Secretary of State Hillary Clinton, together with its West European allies issued strong support for anti-Putin protests that took place in Russia in 2011–12.[57]

Russia's concern about NATO enlargement focused especially on the possible Westernization of Ukraine, the large new country to its west that had previously been part of the Soviet Union. One American observer who had served in the Obama administration supplies an arresting parallel: "The United States would hardly sit by idly if Russia formed an alliance with Mexico and Canada and started building military installations along the US border."[58]

Unlike the neighboring countries to its west in what had previously been known as "East Europe," Ukraine, although fairly open and democratic, had become a basket case economically despite an enormous potential. A few statistics may serve. After the breakup of the Soviet Union in 1991, Ukraine's per capita GDP was higher than Poland's; 25 years later, it was less than one-third that of Poland.[59] In a study comparing 25 post-Communist countries, Ukraine comes out dead last in economic growth.[60] Ukraine is now the poorest country in Europe.[61]

In this, it was like other, smaller counties that essentially lie between Russia and Western Europe: Moldova, Georgia, Armenia, Azerbaijan, and Belarus. These countries have been characterized not by the substantial political liberalization and economic development that has variously taken place in Poland, Hungary, the Czech Republic, Slovakia, Latvia, Lithuania, Estonia, Bulgaria, and Romania, and in countries that emerged out of Yugoslavia after its breakup in 1991. Rather, the "in-between" countries, led by the most important, Ukraine, suffer from a set of what Samuel Charap and Timothy Colton call "post-Soviet pathologies": dysfunctional governmental institutions, economies lacking functioning markets, a rule of law that is weak or absent, patronal politics, close links between political power and control of major economic assets, and "pervasive corruption."[62]

In the case of Ukraine, this phenomenon has been exacerbated by outside efforts from Russia and from Europe to influence the country. These have made it easier for Ukraine to avoid desperately-needed reforms.[63] Among these are huge economic distortions concerning energy. The world average for energy consumption per dollar of GDP is 10 British thermal units. For the US it is 7.5, for the UK 3.8, for Ukraine 56.3.[64]

Things came to a head when mass protests by Western-oriented Ukrainians broke out in the capital city, Kiev. Their duly elected president, who was perhaps even more corrupt than his equally duly elected predecessors, had been juggling various opposing aid offers from the West and from Russia. When he more or less accepted the (higher) Russian bid, protests broke out, and these endured through the cold and snowy winter of 2013–14 heightened by sporadic violence by security forces and by elements within the protest movement, particularly those from the highly anti-Russian far right.[65]

In February 2014, Ukraine's president fled to Russia abruptly leaving the extravagant private zoo he had created behind.[66] In the subsequent chaos, parliament removed provisions that had previously allowed the use of Russian as an official language under some conditions.[67]

Largely ignored in these development were the interests of Russian speakers in the country, some 30 percent of the population, who are concentrated in the east and south and were decidedly unsympathetic to the Kiev protests.[68] This was particularly the case in the large Crimea peninsula to the south where Russia, by an agreement brokered when the Soviet Union split up in 1991, maintains a substantial naval base for its Black Sea Fleet. Putin was alarmed at the developments in Kiev where anti-Russian ideologues now occupied one-third of the cabinet seats. He was also deeply concerned that the new government might abrogate or fail to renew the lease on the naval base, seen to be vital national asset.[69] And he was doubtless miffed that Western leaders had boycotted the winter Olympics he had hosted a few months earlier.[70]

He bolstered troop strength at the naval base, and soon men in green uniforms without insignia (known as "little green men") were fanning out in Crimea occupying military and government facilities.[71] Crimean Russians often felt neglected over the years by government in Kiev, and they feared after the fall of the president that they would be violently persecuted.[72] The local Crimean authorities organized a referendum on secession and on March 16, 2014, a vote, boycotted by many, was held in which 97 percent of those who voted supposedly supported leaving Ukraine and joining Russia. Backed enthusiastically by his parliament and by the citizenry of Russia, Putin graciously accepted the request.

Meanwhile, in Donbas – areas abutting Russia in eastern Ukraine – local Russians, emboldened by the events in Crimea, organized a secession movement, setting up their own ad hoc governments. Ukrainian armed forces, led initially mainly by volunteer paramilitaries, were sent to put them down.[73]

Aided by infiltrators from Russia, the secessionists were able to hold them to a stalemate. Over 10,000 were killed in the violence.[74]

Ukraine cut off financial subsidies, electricity, and water supplies to Crimea, and tourism, an important Crimean industry, dropped precipitously. But Russia, at considerable cost, worked to alleviate these problems, and in 2018 a 12-mile $3 billion bridge – the contract went to one of Putin's buddies, a former judo partner – had been constructed to link Crimea with Russia, a country that, otherwise, ranks ninety-fourth in the world in infrastructure. Putin drove the first truck across the span himself.[75] Efforts to integrate Crimea into Russia have been extensive, and Russian retirees (especially military ones) are encouraged to move there even as those opposed to the Russian takeover often emigrate to Ukraine.

If the goal of Russia was to keep Ukraine from seeking to embrace the West while, in Robert Person's words, "establishing a pliant pro-Russian regime in Kiev," its efforts failed miserably.[76] As one observer predicted at the time, "Far from dissuading Ukrainians from seeking a future in Europe, Moscow's moves will only foster a greater sense of nationalism in all parts of the country and turn Ukrainian elites against Russia, probably for a generation."[77] Or as Daniel Treisman observed in the aftermath, "If Putin's goal was to prevent Russia's military encirclement, his aggression in Ukraine has been a tremendous failure, since it has produced the exact opposite."[78]

In addition, Russia's experience in the 2014 conflict and crisis in Ukraine suggests that countries cannot engage in such enterprises without automatically paying a substantial economic price – it is something like an economic doomsday machine. Because of its antics, Russia suffered a decline in the value of its currency, capital flight, a drop in its stock market, and a decline in foreign investment. And, perhaps most importantly, there was a very substantial drop in confidence by investors, buyers, and sellers throughout the world, a condition that is likely to last for years, even decades.[79] As Charap and Colton stress, "Moscow is at serious risk of permanently alienating the entire EU, which as a bloc has long been Russia's largest trading partner and direct investor."[80] One prominent British observer puts it even more starkly, suggesting that the events "mark the end of an era, the end of the hope that Russia could be incorporated into a united and peaceful Europe."[81] As part of this, Russia's behavior has set off a determined effort by Europeans to reduce their dependence on Russian energy supplies – a change that could be permanent. And the costs of the conflict and of supporting its new distant dependencies have been visited by Russia on itself. Crimea was less well off economically than most of Ukraine and required subsidies from Kiev.[82] And the Donbas region was heavily subsidized by Ukraine as well.[83] These burdens have now shifted to Russia.

There have been other economic costs as well. Economic sanctions have been visited on Russia by other states. Although especially costly to Europe, they were embraced after rebels in eastern Ukraine (perhaps accidentally) shot down a civilian airliner with a missile presumably supplied by Russia.[84] Unrelated to the crisis, there was a severe drop in prices for oil on the international market, a development that is especially harmful to Russia: for every decline of $25 in the price of oil, Russia experiences a nearly 2 percent decline in GNP, and oil and gas sales fund about 36 percent of the Russian annual budget. The economic pain inflicted by the oil price drop has been much greater – perhaps four times greater – than that of the sanctions.[85]

There is likely as well to be a special political cost for Putin. Since he came to power in 2000, there has been a steady improvement in Russia each year in GDP per capita. That process was reversed in 2014. From 2014–17, real disposable income fell by 15 percent.[86] Aspirational purchases as for homes and cars have shifted to ones devoted to daily needs.[87] And Russia's Stabilization Fund, built up when oil prices were high and meant to fund pension payments and to support the ruble, was significantly depleted and may run out of money entirely. Over time, some may see this as a break with his promise to provide the stability and order necessary to allow economic progress to take place.[88]

The developments in Ukraine in 2014 were unsettling, of course. However, it is impressive that the United States and Western Europe never even came close to seriously considering the use of direct force to deal with the issue. Although the crisis created, as Steven Pinker notes, "just the kinds of tensions that in the past had led to great-power wars," nothing like that took place.[89] In fact, the West behaved in much the same way it would have behaved if it had not possessed a great and expensive military capacity. Indeed, President Barack Obama, who presided over the episode, was given to taunting his hawkish critics: "Now, if there is somebody in this town that would claim that we would consider going to war with Russia over Crimea and eastern Ukraine, they should speak up and be very clear about it."[90]

The events inspired concerns that Putin had or has wider intentions.[91] The natural next step, suggest some, would be some sort of invasion of the Baltic states of Latvia, Lithuania, and/or Estonia. Each, like Ukraine, has a Russian minority which, in many cases, has not blended in well with the majority culture and might even consider itself to be persecuted.

West Point's Robert Person has looked at the parallels and finds them wanting.[92] To begin with, Ukraine has what Person calls "a deep symbolic meaning for Russia." It had been part of the Russian empire since the sixteenth century and is often considered to be "the cradle of eastern Slavic civilization." Moreover, Crimea did not become part of Ukraine until it was "gifted" to that Soviet republic in 1954 by Nikita Khrushchev in a process that was quixotic and arbitrary and never actually made official even by the regulations of Soviet or Communist law.[93] And, of course, Crimea's Russian naval base added special significance. By contrast, continues Person, Latvia, Lithuania, Estonia, unlike Ukraine, have frequently enjoyed an independent status, and Russians "have long recognized that the Baltics are culturally and historically different from Russia." Moreover, Russians in the Baltics do not seem to have separatist interests not least in part because they have much higher standards of living than do their counterparts on the other side of the border. And because the Baltic states are members of the European Union and its associated Schengen zone, their citizens would no longer enjoy the associated ease of travel to the continent if they became part of Russia.[94]

In all, then, the notion that Putin's Russia is on an expansionary mission, so commonly voiced at the time of the 2014 events, seems to have little substance.[95] It has not even sought to officially annex separatist areas in eastern Ukraine. A special issue of the journal *Daedalus*, published in 2017, ran a series of essays dealing with Russia's future. None envisioned territorial expansion.[96]

Definitions of superpower status common during the Cold War generally stressed the possession of stocks of nuclear weapons. If that criterion continued to be embraced, Russia should still probably be considered a superpower. However, as Dmitri Trenin points out, Russia "has few formal allies, no satellite states, and … no ideology to compare with the comprehensive dogma of Marxism-Leninism." Moreover, "although it is still a nuclear superpower, it lags far behind the United States in non-nuclear military capabilities. Economically, Russia – with its estimated 1.5 percent of the global gross domestic product – is a dwarf."[97] Its GDP ranks twelfth in the world, but is only one-fifteenth that of the United States and about half that of California. Moreover, GDP growth in Russia has been weak with recent figures at about 1.8 percent per year, and it relies heavily on selling energy abroad: nearly 50 percent of its exports are in oil and gas. Its population is shrinking and may, according to medium-term projections, be reduced to 125 million by 2094 from the current level of about 148 million. For an economy that is more people-intensive than other advanced economies, this spells trouble. As Barack Obama pointed out derisively, if undiplomatically, in his final news conference as president, "Their economy doesn't produce anything that anybody wants to buy, except oil and gas and arms. They don't innovate."[98]

Russia suffers from the same problems as the "in-between" counties as discussed above while being burdened in addition by a much larger military budget – although weak GDP growth has also been reflected in a shrinking military budget, down about 5 percent in 2018 from 2017. Like China, it has devolved into a form of crony capitalism where property rights are insecure, capital flight is common, corruption is rampant, and economic stagnation is likely. As Anders Åslund concludes, the state has been captured by a small group of top officials with the topmost being Vladimir Putin, who has 20 palaces, four yachts, 58 aircraft, and a collection of watches worth $600,000.[99]

The (rather bizarre) Ukraine episode of 2014 seems, like the Korean invasion of 1950, to be a one-off – a unique, opportunistic, and probably under-considered escapade that proved to be unexpectedly costly to the perpetrators. As with the Korean case, massive extrapolation is unjustified and ill-advised. That is, the Ukrainian venture, contrary to much initial speculation, does not seem to be a game-changer.[100]

As Trenin points out, Moscow's most important objective is to reassert its role as a great power with a global reach. However, it does not seek to impose its own model on the world. In all this, neither side envisions a real shooting war against its adversary and neither wants to allow the situation to become uncontrollable.[101]

Under that perspective, a policy toward Russia and Ukraine – one that might appear complacent to some – could include such elements as the following.[102]

- Give up on the Crimea issue: accept annexation in same way that Russia accepts the dismemberment of Serbia, or perhaps work to give Crimea a status like Guantanamo in Cuba in a permanent lease arrangement; the cost of the annexation experience for Russia is unlikely to inspire other countries to imitate.
- Do away with sanctions, or allow them to decay, since they exact pain but are exceedingly unlikely to alter Russian policy on Crimea: Crimea will go back to Ukraine about the same time Texas goes back to Mexico.
- Seek to settle Donbas, perhaps by freezing the conflict there while deploying a UN interposition force as suggested by Putin in September 2017 and then gradually working toward a restoration of Ukrainian sovereignty.[103]
- Obtain a non-aggression guarantee in the area from Russia, something that should be easy to achieve because the country seems to have no additional territorial claims or fantasies.
- Relax military measures especially in Europe where, after the shock of 2014, Europeans – as their low military expenditures suggest – have decreasingly envisioned military threat to exist.

- Perhaps hedge a bit by training Baltic forces in defense as a deterrent, seeking to evoke memories, especially vivid for the Russians, of Afghanistan or Chechnya.[104]
- Guarantee, or effectively guarantee, that Ukraine will not join NATO – something that is extremely unlikely to happen anyway;[105] or perhaps in the process imply that Ukraine will only join NATO if Russia approves.
- Disconnect EU from NATO.
- Encourage, by tough love, the ill-governed Ukraine to get its act together: if it gets better on the issues of stability and corruption, it will become attractive and admirable; the EU might dangle the possibility of membership if Ukraine is eventually able to successfully pass the tests other countries in East Europe were required to pass before they were allowed into the club.
- Stoke the Russian ego by involving it in international talks with, as suggested in Chapter 5, special emphasis on resolving the residual of the Syrian civil war.[106] Alarm about Russian assertiveness has focused on its intervention in the Syrian civil war, which was impelled by a felt need to stop an ISIS takeover and probably had something to do as well with protecting a tiny military "base" Russia has there.[107] However, this scarcely was an exercise in threatening expansion. For the most part, Russia can work with the United States and others to stabilize the situation – although many policy differences remain about how to get there.[108]

Great concern has also been raised in the United States over the fact that Russian cybergeeks appear to have sought in its 2016 presidential election to undermine the election of Hillary Clinton perhaps out of outrage at what Putin took to be her efforts, as Secretary of State at the time, to undermine his re-election in 2011.[109] Although Clinton still managed handily to win the popular vote, it is argued that, with such ventures, the Russian digital inter-lopers are committing cyberwar or "hybrid war" and seeking to change American values and to cause Americans to doubt the integrity of the election process and of democracy itself.

However, the outrage cloaks hypocrisy of staggering proportions.[110] The United States (always, of course, with the very best of intentions) has been assiduously intervening in foreign elections for decades – perhaps even for centuries. Exhibit number one is surely the Italian election of 1948 in which the CIA furnished a million dollars to congenial parties and may have published forged letters designed to discredit leaders of the Communist Party.[111] Meanwhile, there was a concerted effort to get Italian-Americans to write home urging relatives and friends to vote the right way.[112] In the late 1950s, fearing the growing popularity of the Japanese Socialist Party, the United States provided millions of dollars in secret campaign funds to opposition politicians.[113] Then there is a comment by a member of the political opposition in Serbia in 2001 who expressed his appreciation for funds that had been supplied the year before by agencies of the US government. "We never would have been able to launch such an extensive campaign without it," he said.[114]

As a public service, Michael Brenner of the University of Pittsburgh has, with a little help from his friends, provided a list of countries where the United States has intervened in elections (he points out that the US has also participated in a number of coups, but these are not included). Going back a few decades, his list includes a large number of countries such as Greece, Turkey, Italy, France, and Portugal. More recently there have been Macedonia, Serbia, Albania, Bosnia, Ukraine, Russia (especially Yeltsin's 1995–96 campaign), Algeria, Lebanon, Palestine, Cyprus, Iraq, Pakistan, Afghanistan, Kyrgyzstan, Tajikistan, Yemen, Vietnam, Indonesia, Japan, South Korea, Philippines, Congo and several other countries in Africa, and, in Latin America, every country multiple times including within the last 15 years Haiti, the Dominican Republic, Honduras, Panama, Nicaragua, Venezuela, Colombia, Paraguay, Peru, Ecuador, Bolivia, Brazil, and Argentina. Brenner's list is an ongoing project. It does not include Canada, and just possibly there are some Canadians who might find that omission to be unjustified.

Indeed, a more extensive study demonstrates that, over the centuries, intervention by major countries in foreign elections has been common, even routine, though the evidence strongly suggests that overt interventions are much more likely to be effective than covert efforts like those of the Russian geeks.[115]

In general, political campaigns, as anyone who has suffered through one knows, are wall-to-wall fake news as incumbents strategically distort their record in office and their challengers do the same in reverse. With more participants or more effort, the fake news heap simply becomes higher and deeper.

Kathleen Hall Jamieson had done a study of the Russian effort to manipulate the 2016 election. It is subtitled "How Russian Hackers and Trolls Helped Elect a President," and it finds that the Russians probably did "help" albeit, it seems, only by increasing the size of the heap: their efforts scarcely seem to have been decisive. The opportunity was certainly there, however. In three key states, only some 78,000 votes in all separated the two candidates: some six-tenths of 1 percent of the total vote.[116] Campaign information rarely changes many votes: as Diana Mutz points out, "the scholarly consensus" on the degree to which campaign advertising shifts votes is that the impact "is marginal at most."[117] The challenge in the 2016 election was surely within that margin.

The problem, as Jamieson acknowledges, is that "we have no good way to isolate the effects of troll-generated and hacked content from multiple other sources and forms of electoral communication" including, for example, the barrage of campaign advertising and news coverage, the effect of the various missteps of the Clinton campaign, peculiarities in turnout rates (and the weather), and the attractions of third-party candidates (who garnered 5 percent of the total vote).[118] In total, the Russian contribution, though sometimes beguilingly (or even diabolically) clever, was tiny: on Facebook, where the Russian manipulation supposedly principally took place, it totaled perhaps four thousandths of 1 percent of the content in Facebook's news feed over the same period.[119] And a lot of this would be "wasted" because it would be embraced by people who were already committed or were in states that went solidly for one or the other candidate. Moreover, Facebook users are scarcely the most politically attuned: over any period of three months, only 4 percent of them click on an opinion piece.[120]

The Russians seem to have had less than 100 people working as trolls focusing on the United States – most of them college students or recent graduates. They were required to watch *House of Cards* on Netflix to enhance (or establish) an understanding of American politics, and they were devoted to seeking to shake things up by posting on controversial subjects more than trying directly to support one candidate or the other. According to one report, only "two dozen of the trolls' posts scored audiences of a million or more worldwide; the vast majority had less than a thousand page views." Said one troll: "we were just having fun."[121]

Hackers, apparently from Russia, also had fun getting into electronic mail connected with the Democratic National Committee. One dump of this information embarrassingly showed that Committee leaders, who were supposed to be neutral on who the party candidate for president would be, were decidedly in favor of Clinton – a revelation of almost stupefying banality to anyone who knows anything about American politics.[122] Another dump showed that Clinton, like every other politician in the history of the planet, was capable to saying one thing to one group and another to another. In addition, one campaign adviser, the leaks revealed, felt that her political instincts "can be terrible."[123]

In the end, Russia's cyber invasion was wildly counterproductive for the perpetrators. Presumably they hoped to see if they could get the economic sanctions imposed upon them reduced – and they might well have seen the election of Donald Trump as conducive to that outcome. However, since the election meddling was caught, the result was to generate bipartisan support for the sanctions against Russia at a time when the two American parties could agree on little else.

In all, the interference scarcely seems to present a cosmic threat. And American democracy is entirely likely to survive.

IRAN AS "HEGEMON" IN THE MIDDLE EAST?

The antics of Iran in the Middle East (and of the United States in response) suggest an opportunity for a policy of complacency that could be pretty much a poster child for the approach. Any real threat to the United States from Iran is almost nonexistent, and the opponent is substantially bound, even more than was Communism in the Cold War, to self-destruct if only the United States will let it do so.[124]

It all began in 1979 when a Islamist theocratic regime overthrew the Western-oriented Shah who was at the time out of the country for cancer treatment. In the chaos, a few dozen Americans working at the embassy in Iran were effectively put under house arrest – a rather flagrant violation of international conventions that had been around for millennia. Rather than simply appointing a special committee from, say, the State Department to deal with the issue (a policy the Secretary of State later acknowledged in his memoirs would have been wiser), President Jimmy Carter took over negotiations himself and became totally preoccupied with the issue. He was not unmindful, presumably, of the fact that his rather miserable approval ratings from the outraged American public had soared in a rally-round-the-flag effect when the diplomats were taken hostage first by a mob, and then by the regime. After an agonizing 444 days during which the American media, servicing the demand from its customers, managed to remain mesmerized by the venture, the hostages were released unharmed.[125]

In the meantime, Saddam Hussein's Iraq, seeing a military opportunity for success in a rival country which had descended into chaos, launched an invasion – a blatant act of naked aggression much applauded by the United States. The invasion degenerated, like most of Saddam's ventures, into fiasco as the Iranians rallied. The costly international war that ensued lasted eight years.

In its aftermath, the theologians in charge in Iran have established a regime that, like the equally theological Taliban in Afghanistan for which few fought in 2001, is notable for its incompetence, economically illiterate policies, and unpopular social practices, all increasingly laced with corruption. Since the 1990s it has allowed a degree of democracy in which citizens are allowed to vote for competing presidential candidates. Although these candidates have been carefully selected by the regime for their religious purity, the voters have almost always elected the one who is most nearly reformist. In effect, they have repeatedly voted the regime out of office. Overall, it certainly seems, the Iranian people want to get out from under the stifling autocratic theologians and to join the world.[126]

In part because of pain from the humiliating hostage "crisis" which has lingered to an amazing degree in the American consciousness, the policy of the United States toward Iran has mostly been one of hostility. In the aftermath of 9/11, the Iranians actually offered to be helpful to the United States, but this offer was unceremoniously rejected. Instead, President George W. Bush prominently placed Iran in his "axis of evil" trio and then proceeded to launch a war of naked aggression against another member, Iraq. The Iranian response was not only to make America's adventure in Iraq as miserable as possible as discussed in Chapter 4 – the effort was a considerable success – but also to seek to develop nuclear weapons as a deterrent against an American attack.[127] In 2015, however, Iran agreed to a treaty negotiated with the United States and other countries to cease its nuclear weapons program at least for a decade in exchange for the release of Iranian funds that had been impounded in the West. But then President Donald Trump withdrew from the treaty in part, it certainly seems, because it was negotiated by the Obama administration and therefore could not possibly be good.

Iran has also sought to expand its "influence" in the Middle East, perhaps, some fear, even to becoming a "hegemon" there. Like other countries in the area, it has been strongly opposed to the Jewish regime in Israel, and it has helped and supplied arms to relevant like-minded substate entities in the area. It has also aided fellow Shia elements in neighboring Iraq and in more distant civil wars in Syria and Yemen, in the process generating opposition from its chief Sunni opponent, Saudi Arabia. And, needless to say, it has contributed to the forces, including the United States, that have successfully combated the Shia-hating ISIS group as discussed in Chapter 5.

However, Iran scarcely possesses the resources necessary to become a "hegemon," even assuming the word actually means something. In the meantime, sanctions against the regime, much intensified by Trump, supply a convenient excuse for domestic economic travails, distract the public from its oft-expressed opposition to the regime and to its grandiloquent meddling in other countries, and alienate other, otherwise friendly, countries in Europe and elsewhere that are punished as a secondary consequence of the sanctions. Let's try vanilla.

COMPLACENCY, APPEASEMENT, SELF-DESTRUCTION, AND THE NEW COLD WAR

It could be argued that the policies proposed here to deal with the international problems, whether real or imagined, presented by China, Russia, and Iran constitute exercises not only in complacency, but also in appeasement. That argument would be correct. As discussed in the Prologue to this book, appeasement can work to avoid military conflict as can be seen in the case of the Cuban missile crisis of 1962. As also discussed there, appeasement has been given a bad name by the experience with Hitler in 1938.

Hitlers are very rare, but there are some resonances today in Russia's Vladimir Putin and China's Xi Jinping. Both are shrewd, determined, authoritarian, and seem to be quite intelligent, and both are fully in charge, are surrounded by sychophants, and appear to have essentially unlimited tenure in office. Moreover, both, like Hitler in the 1930s, are appreciated domestically for maintaining a stable political and economic environment. However, unlike Hitler, both run trading states and need a stable and essentially congenial international environment to flourish.[128] Most importantly, except for China's claim to Taiwan, neither seems to harbor Hitler-like dreams of extensive expansion by military means. Both are leading their countries in an illiberal direction which will hamper economic growth while maintaining a kleptocratic system. But this may be acceptable to populations enjoying historically high living standards and fearful of less stable alternatives. Both do seem to want to overcome what they view as past humiliations – ones going back to the opium war of 1839 in the case of China and to the collapse of the Soviet empire and then of the Soviet Union in 1989–91 in the case of Russia. Primarily, both seem to want to be treated with respect and deference. Unlike Hitler's Germany, however, both seem to be entirely appeasable. That scarcely seems to present or represent a threat. The United States, after all, continually declares itself to be the indispensable nation. If the United States is allowed to wallow in such self-important, childish, essentially meaningless, and decidedly fatuous proclamations, why should other nations be denied the opportunity to emit similar inconsequential rattlings? If that constitutes appeasement, so be it. If the two countries want to be able to say they now preside over a "sphere of influence," it scarcely seems worth risking world war to somehow keep them from doing so – and if the United States were substantially disarmed, it would not have the capacity to even try.

If China and Russia get off on self-absorbed pretensions about being big players, that should be of little concern – and their success rate is unlikely to be any better than that of the United States. Charap and Colton observe that "The Kremlin's *idée fixe* that Russia needs to be the leader of a pack of post-Soviet states in order to be taken seriously as a global power broker is more of a feel-good mantra than a fact-based strategy, and it irks even the closest of allies." And they further suggest that

> The towel should also be thrown in on the geo-ideational shadow-boxing over the Russian assertion of a sphere of influence in post-Soviet Eurasia and the Western opposition to it. Would either side be able to specify what precisely they mean by a regional sphere of influence? How would it differ from, say, US relations with the western-hemisphere states or from Germany's with its EU neighbors?[129]

Applying the Gingrich gospel, then, it certainly seems that, although China, Russia, and Iran may present some "challenges" to US policy, there is little or nothing to suggest a need to maintain a large US military force-in-being to keep these countries in line. Indeed, all three monsters seem to be in some stage of self-destruction or descent into stagnation – not, perhaps, unlike the Communist "threat" during the Cold War. Complacency thus seems to be a viable policy.

However, it may be useful to look specifically at a couple of worst-case scenarios: an invasion of Taiwan by China (after it builds up its navy more) and an invasion of the Baltic states of Estonia, Lithuania, and Latvia by Russia. It is wildly unlikely that China or Russia would carry out such economically self-destructive acts: the economic lessons from Putin's comparatively minor Ukraine gambit are clear, and these are unlikely to be lost on the Chinese. Moreover, the analyses of Michael Beckley certainly suggest that Taiwan has the conventional military capacity to concentrate the mind of, if not necessarily fully to deter, any Chinese attackers. It has "spent decades preparing for this exact contingency," has an advanced early warning system, can call into action massed forces to defend "fortified positions on home soil with precision-guided munitions," and has supply dumps, booby traps, an wide array of mobile missile launchers, artillery, and minelayers. In addition, there are only 14 locations that can support amphibious landing and these are, not surprisingly, well fortified by the defenders.[130]

The United States may not necessarily be able to deter or stop military attacks on Taiwan or on the Baltics under its current force levels.[131] And if it cannot credibly do so with military forces currently in being, it would not be able to do so, obviously, if its forces were much reduced. However, the most likely response in either eventuality would be for the United States to wage a campaign of economic and military (including naval) harassment and to support local – or partisan – resistance as it did in Afghanistan after the Soviet invasion there in 1979.[132] Such a response does not require the United States to have, and perpetually to maintain, huge forces in place and at the ready to deal with such improbable eventualities.

The current wariness about, and hostility toward, Russia and China is sometimes said to constitute "a new Cold War."[133] There are, of course, considerable differences. In particular, during the Cold War, the Soviet Union – indeed the whole international Communist movement – was under the sway of a Marxist theory that explicitly and determinedly advocated the destruction of capitalism and probably of democracy, and by violence to the degree required. Neither Russia nor China today sports such cosmic goals or is enamored of such destructive methods. However, as discussed in Chapters 1 and 2, the United States was strongly inclined during the Cold War massively to inflate the threat that it imagined the Communist adversary to present. The current "new Cold War" is thus in an important respect quite a bit like the old one: it is an expensive, substantially militarized, and often hysterical campaign to deal with threats that do not exist or are likely to self-destruct.[134]

It may also be useful to evaluate terms that are often bandied about in considerations within foreign policy circles about the rise of China, the assertiveness of Russia, and the antics of Iran. High among these is "hegemony." Sorting through various definitions, Simon Reich and Richard Ned Lebow array several that seem to capture the essence of the concept: domination, controlling leadership, or the ability to shape international rules according to the hegemon's own interests. Hegemony, then, is an extreme word suggesting supremacy, mastery, preponderant influence, and full control. Hegemons force others to bend to their will whether they like it or not. Reich and Lebow also include a mellower designation applied by John Ikenberry and Charles Kupchan in which a hegemon is defined as an entity that has the ability to establish a set of norms that others willingly embrace.[135] But this really seems to constitute an extreme watering-down of the word and suggests opinion leadership or entrepreneurship and success at persuasion, not hegemony.

Moreover, insofar as they carry meaning, the militarized application of American primacy and hegemony to order the world has often been a fiasco.[136] Indeed, it is impressive that the hegemon, endowed by definition by what Reich and Lebow aptly call a grossly disproportionate military capacity, has had such a miserable record of military achievement since 1945 – an issue discussed frequently in this book.[137] Reich and Lebow argue that it is incumbent on IR scholars to cut themselves loose from the concept of hegemony.[138] It seems even more important for the foreign policy establishment to do so.

There is also absurdity in getting up tight over something as vacuous as the venerable "sphere of influence" concept (or conceit). The notion that world affairs are a process in which countries scamper around the world seeking to establish spheres of influence is at best decidedly unhelpful and at worst utterly misguided. But the concept continues to be embraced in some quarters as if it had some palpable meaning. For example, in early 2017, the august National Intelligence Council opined that "Geopolitical competition is on the rise as China and Russia seek to exert more sway over their neighboring regions and promote an order in which US influence does not dominate."[139] Setting aside the issue of the degree to which American "influence" could be said to "dominate" anywhere (we still wait, for example, for dominated Mexico supinely to pay for a wall to seal off its self-infatuated neighbor's southern border), it doesn't bloody well matter whether China or Russia has, or seems to have, a "sphere of influence" someplace or other.

More importantly, the whole notion is vapid and essentially meaningless. Except perhaps in Gilbert and Sullivan's *Iolanthe*. When members of the House of Lords fail to pay sufficient respect to a group of women they take to be members of a ladies' seminary who are actually fairies, their queen, outraged at the Lords' collected effrontery, steps forward, proclaims that she happens to be an "influential fairy," and then, with a few passes of her wand, brushes past the Lords' pleas ("no!" "mercy!" "spare us!" and "horror!"), and summarily issues several edicts: a young man of her acquaintance shall be inducted into their House, every bill that gratifies his pleasure shall be passed, members shall be required to sit through the grouse and salmon season, and high office shall be obtainable by competitive examination. Now, *that's* influence. In contrast, on December 21, 2017, when the United States sought to alter the status of Jerusalem, the United Nations General Assembly voted to repudiate the US stand in a nearly unanimous vote that included many US allies. Now, that's *not* influence.

In fact, to push this point perhaps to an extreme, if we are entering an era in which economic motivations became paramount and in which military force is not deemed a sensible method for pursuing wealth, the idea of "influence" would become obsolete because, in principle, pure economic actors do not care much about influence. They care about getting rich. (As Japan and Germany have found, however, influence, status, and prestige tend to accompany the accumulation of wealth, but this is just an ancillary effect.) Suppose the president of a company could choose between two stories to tell the stockholders. One message would be, "We enjoy great influence in the industry. When we talk everybody listens. Our profits are nil." The other would be, "No one in the industry pays the slightest attention to us or ever asks our advice. We are, in fact, the butt of jokes in the trade. We are making money hand over fist." There is no doubt about which story would most thoroughly warm the stockholders' hearts.

In all of this, the admonitions of A. A. Milne might be kept in mind. He was understandably appalled by the Fashoda affair of 1898, which he regarded as an incident in which the British and the French almost got into a war over "a mosquito-ridden swamp" in Africa. When someone soberly countered that "at stake was whether France should be allowed to draw a barrier of French influence across the English area of influence," Milne was catapulted into peak form:

A war about it, costing a million lives, would have seemed quite in order to the two Governments; a defensive war, of course, a struggle for existence, with God fighting on both sides in that encouraging way He has. A pity it didn't come off, when it had been celebrated already in immortal verse.

Tweedledum and Tweedledee
Agreed to have a battle,
For Tweedledum said Tweedledee
Had spoilt his nice new rattle.

"Only it isn't really a rattle," said Tweedledum importantly, "it's an Area of Influence! There's glory for you!" "I don't think I know what an Area of Influence is," said Alice doubtfully. "Silly," said Tweedledee, "it's a thing you have a battle about, of course." "Like a rattle," explained Tweedledum.[140]

7

Proliferation, Terrorism, Humanitarian Intervention, and Other Problems

Beyond the non-threats presented by China and Russia as well as by Iran, it is always possible that real threats lurk out there somewhere, perhaps even one or two for which the maintenance of a large military force might be required, This chapter explores an array of candidates including in particular the proliferation of weapons of mass destruction (with a focus on the case of North Korea) and terrorism. It also more briefly assesses the threat potential of such problems as rogue state behavior, international crime, the need to police the oceans, the potential invasion of cyber geeks, the securing of energy sources, climate change, economic challenges, and the protection of allies. It concludes by evaluating the potential need to have armed forces around to deal with humanitarian interventions.

Singly, or in groups, these problems and issues, to the degree that they are valid concerns at all, scarcely justify massive expenditures to maintain a large military force-in-being, and complacency is, in general, a more fitting response than agitated, and particularly militarized, alarm.

PROLIFERATION

For decades there has been almost wall-to-wall alarm about the dangers supposedly inherent in the proliferation of nuclear weapons – or in some cases, of such lesser "weapons of mass destruction" as chemical and biological ones.[1]

Over the decades, analysts of nuclear proliferation have separated themselves, or have been separated by others, into two camps.[2]

Proliferation alarmists constitute the vast majority, and they occupy a prominent position in what Bernard Brodie once called "the cult of the ominous."[3] They argue that proliferation is a dire development that must be halted – a monster that must be destroyed – as a supreme policy priority. Thus, Graham Allison argues that "no new nuclear weapons states" should be a prime foreign policy principle, and Joseph Cirincione insists that nonproliferation should be "our number one national-security priority."[4] In recent years, such alarmism has been sent into high relief by the apparent efforts of Iran to move toward a nuclear bomb capacity, and it is now focused on North Korea, which tested its first nuclear weapon in 2006.

The other camp, which is quite tiny, consists of proliferation sanguinists who maintain that, on balance, a certain amount of proliferation might actually enhance international stability by deterring war or warlike adventures.[5]

However, there is another possible approach to the proliferation issue that might be called irrelevantist. People in this near-empty camp stress two considerations:

First, it really doesn't bloody well *matter* whether the bomb proliferates or not: proliferation has been of little consequence (except on agonies, obsessions, rhetoric, posturing, and spending), and no country that has possessed the weapons has found them useful or beneficial, nor for the most part have those who abandoned them suffered loss because of this. Thus, the consequences of such proliferation that has taken place have been substantially benign.

Second, alarmed efforts to prevent the proliferation of nuclear weapons, seen particularly in Iraq, have proved to be very costly, leading to the deaths of more people than perished at Hiroshima and Nagasaki combined.

These two irrelevantist propositions are assessed below.

Although we have now suffered through three-quarters of a century characterized by alarmism about the disasters inherent in nuclear proliferation, the substantive consequences of proliferation have been quite limited. The weapons have certainly generated obsession, and they have greatly affected military spending, diplomatic posturing, and ingenious theorizing. However, the few countries to which the weapons have proliferated have for the most part found them a notable waste of time, money, effort, and scientific talent. They have quietly kept them in storage and have not even found much benefit in rattling them from time to time. Insofar as the weapons have been "used," it has been to stoke the national ego and to deter real or imagined threats.

It is sometimes said, or implied, that proliferation has had little consequence because the only countries to possess nuclear weapons have had rational leaders. But nuclear weapons have proliferated to large, important countries run by unchallenged monsters who, at the time they acquired the bombs, were certifiably deranged: Josef Stalin, who in 1949 was planning to change the climate of the Soviet Union by planting a lot of trees, and Mao

Zedong, who in 1964 had just carried out a bizarre social experiment that resulted in an artificial famine in which tens of millions of Chinese perished.[6] Yet neither country used its nuclear weapons for anything other than deterrence and ego-boosting.[7]

There has never been a militarily compelling – or even minimally sensible – reason to use nuclear weapons, particularly due to an inability to identify suitable targets or ones that could not be attacked about as effectively by conventional munitions. And it is difficult to see how nuclear weapons benefited their possessors in specific military ventures. Israel's presumed nuclear weapons did not restrain the Arabs from attacking in 1973, nor did Britain's prevent Argentina's seizure of the Falklands in 1982. Similarly, the tens of thousands of nuclear weapons in the arsenals of the enveloping allied forces did not cause Saddam Hussein to order his occupying forces out of Kuwait in 1990. Nor did possession of the bomb benefit America in Korea, Vietnam, Iraq, or Afghanistan; France in Algeria; or the Soviet Union in Afghanistan.[8]

Proliferation alarmists may occasionally grant that countries principally obtain a nuclear arsenal to counter real or perceived threats, but many go on to argue that the newly nuclear country will then use its nuclear weapons to "dominate" the area. That argument was repeatedly used with dramatic urgency before 2003 for the dangers supposedly posed by Saddam Hussein as discussed in Chapter 4, and it is now being applied to Iran.

Exactly how that domination business is to be carried out is never made clear.[9] But the notion, apparently, is that should an atomic Iraq (in earlier fantasies) or North Korea or Iran (in present ones) rattle the occasional rocket, other countries in the area, suitably intimidated, would supinely bow to its demands. It seems far more likely that if a nuclear country brandishes its weapons to intimidate others or to get its way, it will find that those threatened, rather than capitulating to its blandishments or rushing off to build a compensating arsenal of their own, will ally with others to stand up to the intimidation – rather in the way they coalesced into an alliance of convenience to oppose Iraq's invasion of Kuwait in 1990.

It is also argued that nuclear weapons embolden a country to do mischief with less fear of punishing consequences. However, countries like Iran already seem about as free as they need to be to do mischief (from the US standpoint) in the Middle East and rogue states like the USSR, China, and North Korea do not seem to have stepped up their mischief after gaining nuclear weapons.

There are conceivable situations under which nuclear weapons could serve a deterrent function: perhaps if Iran had had them in 1980 or Kuwait had had them in 1990, Iraq would not have invaded. However, under the conditions in which we have actually lived, it is questionable whether they have yet ever done so. In particular, as discussed in Chapter 1, it is far from clear that a deterrence policy centered around nuclear weapons is what kept the Cold War from becoming a hot one. To expect countries that experienced World War III somehow to allow themselves to tumble into anything resembling a repetition – whether embellished with nuclear weapons or not – seems almost bizarre.

Moreover, the weapons have not proved to be crucial status – or virility – symbols. French President Charles de Gaulle did opine in 1965 that "no country without an atom bomb could properly consider itself independent," and Robert Gilpin concluded that "the possession of nuclear weapons largely determines a nation's rank in the hierarchy of international prestige."[10] In that tradition, some analysts who describe themselves as "realists" have insisted for years that Germany and Japan must soon come to their senses and quest after nuclear weapons.[11]

But, as Robert Jervis has observed, "India, China, and Israel may have decreased the chance of direct attack by developing nuclear weapons, but it is hard to argue that they have increased their general prestige or influence."[12] And, as Jenifer Mackby and Walter Slocombe note:

> Undoubtedly some countries have pursued nuclear weapons more for status than for security. However, Germany, like its erstwhile Axis ally, Japan, has become powerful because of its economic might rather than its military might, and its renunciation of nuclear weapons may even have reinforced its prestige. It has even managed to achieve its principal international objective – reunification – without becoming a nuclear state.[13]

Pakistan and Russia may garner more attention today than they would without nukes, but would Japan's prestige be increased if it became nuclear? Would anybody have more or less interest in Britain or France if their arsenals held 5,000 nuclear weapons, or would anybody pay much less if they had none? Did China need nuclear weapons to impress the world with its economic growth? Or with its Olympics?

In addition, the proliferation of nuclear weapons has been far slower than has been commonly predicted primarily because the weapons do not generally convey much advantage to their possessor. Dozens of technologically capable countries have considered obtaining nuclear arsenals, but very few have done so. Indeed, as Jacques Hymans has pointed out, even supposedly optimistic forecasts about nuclear dispersion have proved to be too pessimistic.[14] In fact, over the decades, a huge number of countries capable of developing nuclear weapons have neglected even to consider the opportunity – for example, Canada, Italy, and Norway – even as Argentina, Brazil, Libya, South Korea, and Taiwan have backed away from or reversed nuclear weapons programs, and Belarus, Kazakhstan, South Africa, and Ukraine have actually surrendered or dismantled an existing nuclear arsenal.[15] Some of that reduction is no doubt due to the hostility (and in some cases the bribery) of the nuclear nations, but experience certainly suggests, as Stephen Meyer has shown, there is no "technological imperative" for countries to obtain nuclear weapons once they have achieved the technical capacity to do so.[16]

In consequence, alarmist predictions about proliferation chains, cascades, dominoes, waves, avalanches, epidemics, and points of no return have proved to be faulty. Insofar as most leaders of most countries (even rogue ones) have considered acquiring the weapons, they have come to appreciate several defects: nuclear weapons are dangerous, distasteful, costly, and likely to rile the neighbors. Moreover, as Hymans has demonstrated, the weapons have also been exceedingly difficult to obtain for administratively dysfunctional countries like Iran.[17]

Although the consequences of nuclear proliferation have proved to be substantially benign, the same cannot be said for the consequences of the nuclear antiproliferation quest. The perpetual agony over nuclear proliferation has resulted in an obsessive effort to prevent or channel it, and it is this effort, not proliferation itself, that has inflicted severe costs. In the presidential campaign of 2008, candidate Barack Obama repeatedly announced that he would "do everything in [his] power to prevent Iran from obtaining a nuclear weapon – everything," while candidate John McCain insisted that Iran must be kept from obtaining a nuclear weapon "at all costs."[18] Neither bothered to tally what "everything" might entail and what the costs might be.

The war in Iraq, with deaths that have run well over 200,000 – greater than those inflicted at Hiroshima and Nagasaki combined – is a key case in point. As discussed in Chapter 4, it is far from clear what Saddam Hussein, presiding over a deeply resentful population and an unreliable army could have done with a tiny number of bombs against his neighbors and their massively armed well-wishers other than seek to stoke his ego and to deter real or imagined threats. He was, then, fully containable and deterrable. Nonetheless, the war against him was a militarized antiproliferation effort substantially sold as a venture required to keep his pathetic regime from developing nuclear and other presumably threatening weapons and to prevent him from palming off some of these too eager and congenial terrorists.

However, the devastation of Iraq in the service of limiting proliferation did not begin with the war in 2003. For the previous 13 years, as discussed in Chapter 3, that country had suffered under economic sanctions visited upon it by both Democratic and Republican administrations that were designed to force Saddam from office (and, effectively, from life since he had no viable sanctuary elsewhere) and to keep the country from developing weapons, particularly nuclear ones. Multiple, although disputed, studies have concluded that the sanctions were the necessary cause of hundreds of thousands of deaths in the country.

There have been other costs and detrimental results.[19] Owing to its antiproliferation fixation, the United States has often allowed itself to become a victim of extortion. Antiproliferation policy also hampers economic development. As countries grow, they require ever increasing amounts of power, and any measure that limits their ability to acquire this vital commodity – or increases its price – effectively slows economic growth at least to some degree and it thereby reduces the gains in life expectancy inevitably afforded by economic development.[20] The antiproliferation obsession has also resulted in the summary dismissal of potentially promising ideas for producing energy. It should also be noted that, because nuclear power does not emit greenhouse gases, it is an obvious potential candidate for helping with the problem of global warming.[21] Thus, because many of the policies arising from the nonproliferation fixation increase the costs of nuclear power, they, to that degree, exacerbate the problem.

Concern about proliferation may be justified, but the experience of three-quarters of a century suggests that any danger is far from overwhelming. It would certainly be preferable that a number of regimes never obtain nuclear weapons. Indeed, if the efforts to dissuade a country from launching a nuclear weapons program succeed, they would be doing it a favor – though, quite possibly, they won't notice.

The invasion of Iraq may have prevented that country from going nuclear – assuming it ever would have been able to put together the effort.[22] However, it scarcely seems likely that there will be much sympathy for repeating that disastrous experience. That is, there will likely be little enthusiasm for applying military force to prevent, or to deal with, further putative proliferation. Thus, despite nearly continuous concern – even at times hysteria – about nuclear developments in North Korea and Iran, proposals to use military force (particularly boots on the ground) to deal with these developments have been persistently undercut.

Accordingly, maintaining huge forces-in-being to deal with the proliferation problem scarcely seems sensible. And, insofar as nuclear proliferation is a response to perceived threat, it follows that one way to reduce the likelihood such countries would go nuclear is a simple one: stop threatening them. More generally, any antiproliferation priority should be topped with a somewhat higher one: avoiding militarily aggressive actions under the obsessive sway of worst-case-scenario fantasies, actions that might lead to the deaths of tens – or hundreds – of thousands of people. If that sounds complacent, so be it.

The costly alarmist perspective on atomic proliferation is evident in policies advocated toward North Korea at various times.[23]

Already the most closed and secretive society in the world, North Korea became even more isolated after the Cold War when its former patrons, Russia and China, notably decreased their support. Its economy descended into shambles, and in incessant fear of attack from the outside, it continued to spend 25 percent of its wealth to maintain a huge military force of over a million troops.[24]

In 1994, some American analysts concluded that there was "a better than even" chance that North Korea had the makings of a small nuclear bomb – though this was hotly disputed by others.[25] Indeed, the Clinton administration was apparently prepared to go to a war with the miserable North Korean regime to prevent or to halt its nuclear development – a war that might kill over a million people.[26] In the meantime, it moved to impose deep economic sanctions to make the isolated country even poorer (insofar as that was possible), a measure which garnered no support even from neighboring Russia, China, and Japan.[27]

In the next years, floods and bad weather exacerbated the economic disaster that had been inflicted upon the country by its rulers. Famines ensued, and the number of people who perished reached hundreds of thousands or more, with some careful estimates putting the number at over 2 million.[28] Although food aid was eventually sent from the West, there seem to have been systematic efforts, particularly in the early days of the the famine, to deny its existence for fear that a politics-free response to a humanitarian disaster would undercut efforts to use food aid to wring diplomatic concessions on the nuclear issue from North Korea.[29] In the end, the United States essentially let itself be extorted: in exchange for a nonnuclear pledge from North Korea, it promised considerable aid to the country – though much of that, as it happened, was never delivered.

Then, shortly after 9/11, President George W. Bush announced that America's "responsibility to history" was now to "rid the world of evil," and a few months later he specified in a major speech that, while evil could presumably be found everywhere, a special "axis of evil" existed, and it lurked, in this order, in North Korea, Iran, and Iraq.[30] As Bush geared up to attack number three in early 2003, North Korea announced that it would be with-drawing from the Nuclear NonProliferation Treaty. As Mitchell Reiss observes, "one of the unintended 'demonstration' effects" of the American antiproliferation war against Iraq "was that chemical and biological weapons proved insufficient to deter America: only nuclear weapons, it appeared, could do this job."[31] It is likely a lesson North Korea drew, and in time it had a nuclear capacity and, apparently, the ability to deliver at least a few of the weapons to hit American soil.

North Korea's experience reflects that of China several decades earlier. Impelled, like North Korea, primarily by incessant threats from the United States, China began building a bomb, and President John Kennedy was heard to declare that "A Chinese nuclear test is likely to be historically the most significant and worst event of the 1960s."[32] There seems to have been rather serious consideration in Washington about bombing nuclear facilities in China. However, an uncharacteristically calm assessment of the situation was delivered in several State Department internal reports authored primarily by a staffer, Robert H. Johnson.[33] Not only did his point of view come to prevail at the time, but Johnson's predictions, ones that prescribed complacency in the face of imaginable (or fancied) threat, came to pass. China continued to act rather roguish for another decade or so and then began to mellow.[34] Moreover, it ended up building far fewer of the bombs than it could have, and the existence of its arsenal has proved to be of little historical consequence. And it turned out that "historically the most significant and worst event of the 1960s" stemmed not from China's nukes, but from Kennedy's tragically misguided decision to begin to send American troops in substantial numbers to Vietnam largely to confront the Chinese threat that he came to believe lurked there.

The China experience is likely relevant to the later one with North Korea, and in that case the obsession about proliferation potentially stands in the way of an extremely important development. It seems entirely possible that the peninsula is at one of the most important turning points in its history: there is the prospect of forging a potentially permanent normalization of relations between North and South that would markedly reduce the prospect of armed conflict between the two countries and that would be one of the most significant developments in Korea's long history.

North Korea sports perhaps the most pathetic, insecure, and contemptible regime in the world, and survival is about the only thing it has proved to be good at. It surely knows that launching a nuclear bomb somewhere against a set of enemies that possess tens of thousands is a pretty terrible idea. This would be the case even if the missile actually manages to complete the trip and even if the warhead actually detonates, neither of which is very likely given the country's technological prowess: 88 percent of the flight tests of some of its missiles have failed (5 to 10 percent is normal).[35]

The hysteria its nuclear program has inspired is simply not justified. And North Korea does continually insist that its nuclear program is entirely for "defensive" purposes. Moreover, if its goal were to commit self-destructive mayhem, it has long possessed the capacity to do so. With the artillery it has amassed in its south, it could pulverize much of South Korea, including its capital city, Seoul.[36]

North Korea's ego-stoking has, of course, already started.[37] And the threat it needs to deter has not been difficult for it to identify. Since the 1950s, the United States has persistently and unambiguously wanted to take out the regime, and it has, at times, actively schemed to do so. North Korea's wariness about negotiating away its nuclear capacity can only have been enhanced by the experience of Libya's dictator, Muammar Gaddafi, who cut a deal with the Americans to do that in 2003.[38] When Gaddafi was confronted with an insurrection in 2011, the Obama administration militarily intervened, speeding his downfall and brutal execution.

In all this, it should be kept in mind that it is the people of North Korea who suffer. Particularly since the end of the Cold War, the consequences have been dire. Famines and food shortages have led to stunted growth and potentially to brain damage in the people affected.[39] And that continues to the present day.[40] If the goal is to enjoy "life, liberty, and the pursuit of happiness," economic development would at least begin to deliver on the first, and most fundamental, of these qualities. The others might come in time.

Until recently, North Korea's official policy was focused on *Juche*, or self-reliance – particularly a self-reliant economy. However, in 2013, its leader, Kim Jong-un, announced a two-track policy, *byungjin noseon* ("parallel lines"), stressing two important themes: becoming a nuclear power and furthering economic development.[41] The policy sought to guarantee North Korea's security with a nuclear weapons and missile program designed particularly to deter the distant but threatening United States. And the policy sought to generate economic development, perhaps with the experience of China, Vietnam, or even Singapore in mind – countries where economic development has occurred without toppling the regime.

Kim seems increasingly to be comfortable with progress on the first goal – even at times to declaring it to have been "perfected."[42] Indeed, in 2018, he declared that North Korea would now focus on economic development because the goal of becoming a nuclear power had been achieved.[43]

There has been some progress on the economic development goal – mostly, it appears, in the growing presence of private markets that at one time would have been closed down by the regime.[44] For the most part, as Stephan Haggard and Marcus Noland point out, progress has been de facto rather than de jure, but it is nonetheless real.[45] Analyst Chung Min Lee believes Kim "genuinely wants to transform North Korea into an economic powerhouse," and he points out that Kim has authorized farmers to keep more of their harvests, factories to have more leeway to make their own decisions on quality control, prices, and wages, and small enterprises to conduct a greater number of direct business-to-business interactions.[46]

Kim seems to be serious about economic development, but there could, of course, be setbacks whether caused by his capricious ruling methods, opposition within the party, or fears of setting in motion developments that could go out of control. However, the direction so far is distinctly positive, and judicious efforts by, in particular, South Korea, to nudge it along could lead to a much more relaxed atmosphere and a highly desirable normalization of relations on the peninsula.

This does not mean that unification is in the offing. The economic and cultural divergence of the two Koreas over the last seven decades has been extensive, and the notion that they could or should be unified at any time soon is at best romantic and at worst dangerous. The unification of the two Germanys was a remarkably difficult and costly process even though those two entities were far less different from each other than the two Koreas have grown to be today. A much better model might be found in the peaceful and mutually advantageous coexistence of Germany and Austria – two separate countries that share a common language, history, and cultural heritage. It is very sensible for the South to expand economic and social contacts with the North, and to seek family reunifications. But a conscious drive for unification would be unwise for the South and threatening to the regime in the North.

It seems reasonable to suggest that, even taking the difficulties into account, there is at least a 60 percent chance that a permanent normalization would eventually result. And, of course, if the venture fails, no one is much worse off than they are now. Accordingly, it seems well worth a concentrated effort – even if the venture seems to smack of complacency and even of appeasement.

Thus, it is sensible to actively explore possibilities for normalization while downplaying the nuclear issue for the time being. That is, for progress to happen, it is vital that the nuclear weapons issue be detached from the consideration. In the long run, the nuclear issue could be raised again and there might be progress on the issue, but only if the North feels secure.

The chief tension-causing entity in the Korean area is the United States. Utterly obsessed by the North Korean nuclear arsenal that was apparently created in response to existential threats emanating from Washington while embracing extreme, even hysterical, worst-case-fantasies about what the North Koreans might do with such weapons, the United States has adopted an intensely hostile and threatening posture that only increases the North's frightened desire to have nuclear weapons and the systems to deliver them.

The hostility fuels North Korea's nuclear development in another, rather perverse, way: it often seems that the only way the country can garner attention is when it advances its nuclear program. With friends like that, South Korea scarcely needs enemies. Indeed, it may well be time for South Korea – now very much a grown-up country – fully to take charge of its own destiny.

The sanctions on North Korea are designed in considerable part to force the regime to cut back, or even cut off, its nuclear program. Given the current state of tensions and distrust – and the long history – this is essentially a nonstarter for the North, and the sanctions seem to be having little or no effect except to make the North Korean people even more miserable.[47] In addition, the sanctions include a set of secondary sanctions on other countries that hamper efforts in the South to reach out to the North at this crucial time. The sanctions, then, are doubly foolish.

Historically, Korea has been a relatively poor country. When one adds to this fact its twentieth-century experience with Japanese occupation, the destruction and turmoil of World War II and the Korean War, and the misguided policies and corruption of some of its early leaders after 1945, the economic progress South Korea has made in the last few decades approaches the miraculous. And it is overwhelmingly apparent that history is on the side of democratic, capitalistic South Korea while the North is a bizarre, sometimes almost comical, relic (or caricature) of a bygone era. Korea has a very long history, and its sheer duration could be taken to suggest that there is no need to take risks or act impetuously to speed up historical processes, especially when they are almost inevitably going to work to South Korea's long-term benefit. What is most required is judicious, watchful patience – a specialty of the complacent.

TERRORISM

The issue of terrorism, mainly of the international variety, has certainly dominated American foreign and especially military policy in this century. The concern was impelled, of course, by the trauma induced by the terrorist attacks on the United States that took place on September 11, 2001. As discussed in Chapter 4, any "threat" from terrorism has been massively exaggerated in the re-telling.[48] Moreover, as noted in Chapter 5, its apparent incidence, particularly in war zones, has been inflated since 9/11 by conflating terrorism with what had previously been called "insurgency."

The problem of terrorism in the United States and most of the West, then, has proved to be limited – or "rather negligible" as Marc Sageman puts it.[49] Nonetheless, even though other issues – particularly economic ones – have crowded out terrorism as a topic of daily concern, 9/11 clearly has achieved perpetual resonance in the American mind. Indeed, there has been a long-term, routinized, mass anxiety – or at least a sense of concern – that has shown little sign of waning over the years since 2001.[50] For example, in late 2001 some 40 percent of the public professed to be worried that the respondent or a family member might become a victim of terrorism, a level that has held ever since. And the percentage finding another terrorist attack "causing large numbers of American lives to be lost" in the near future to be likely has held at over 70 percent ever since 9/11.[51]

The most plausible explanation for the remarkable absence of erosion in concern is that special fear and anxiety has been stirred by the fact that Islamist terrorism is taken to be part of a large and hostile conspiracy and network that is international in scope and rather spooky. In the words of Clem Brooks and Jeff Manza, it is seen to be a "subversive enemy" that is "foreign in origin but with possible domestic supporters organized in covert cells, hidden yet seemingly everywhere, and providing a direct and open challenge."[52] There were hundreds of terrorist attacks in the 1970s, but these were mainly domestic in apparent origin and scope: for the most part, they did not have a significant foreign or external referent. That quality holds as well for the highly destructive 1995 Oklahoma City attack. In the aftermath of that bombing, over 40 percent of the public said it worried about becoming a victim of terrorism. However, unlike the situation after 2001, this percentage declined considerably in the next few years.

A potentially instructive comparison in this regard is with concerns about domestic Communists during the Cold War as discussed in Chapter 2. Like Islamist terrorists within our midst, many Americans believed domestic Communists were connected to, and agents of, a vast, foreign-based conspiracy to topple America. Extravagant alarmist proclamations about the degree to which such "masters of deceit" and "enemies from within" presented a threat to the republic found a receptive audience.[53]

In 2010, anthropologist Scott Atran mused, "Perhaps never in the history of human conflict have so few people with so few actual means and capabilities frightened so many."[54] That continues to be true today, and, because of the special formlessness, even spookiness, of terrorism's hostile foreign referent in this case, it is likely to be exceptionally difficult to get people to believe that the threat has really been extinguished – or at least that it is no longer particularly significant. If people want to be afraid, nothing will stop them.

And it is probably best to see public opinion as the primary driver in the excessive and somewhat bizarre counterterrorism process that took place after 9/11. To the degree that the public remains terrorized, it seems likely to continue to demand that its leaders pay due deference to its insecurities. Indeed, it took until 2015, nearly a decade and a half after 9/11, before public officials, including in this case Barack Obama, the president of the United States, were willing to suggest that terrorism, even that presented by ISIS, did not, as it happens, present a threat to the country that was existential in nature, an observation that is "blindingly obvious" as security specialist Bruce Schneier puts it.[55] Obama seems to have been ready to go further, but never summoned the political courage to do so during his presidency. Out of concern that Obama would seem insensitive to the fears of the American people, his advisers fought a constant rearguard action to keep Obama from placing terrorism in what he considered its "proper" perspective.[56] As analyst Stephen Sestanovich puts it, "It's not good politics to display your irritation with the American people."[57] As discussed on page 40 above, something similar happened to President Dwight Eisenhower on the notion of whether the Soviet Union really threatened to launch a major war.

Two former counterterrorism officials from the Obama administration, Jennie Easterly and Joshua Geltzer, suggest that significant policy consequences arise from this phenomenon. They argue that

> So long as human nature yields a reaction to terrorism that shakes domestic politics, redirects foreign policy, and upends regional stability, terrorism demands our attention. Of course, so does the quite explicit expectation of the American public that its government protect it from this form of deliberately targeted, violent death in particular – whereas the American public has expressed no such concern about the accidental perils of the bathtub.[58]

The writers are certainly correct when they note that there is far more demand from the public to deal with terrorism than to deal with bathtub drownings and that in a democracy, in particular, officials must yield (or appear to yield) to the demand: attention must be paid. The suggestion is that there are distinct political consequences of the public fears, and that this must be serviced by overreaction and by instituting excessively costly countermeasures. That is, the argument runs, the only way to reduce the fear and consequently the political pressure is to reduce the incidence and/or the virulence of terrorism.

However, it is not clear that the public demand requires specific foreign and domestic policies that are excessive to the danger presented by the threat.

As discussed in Chapter 3, the fearful response to 9/11 may have made the wars in Afghanistan and Iraq politically possible, but it did not mandate them.

Although 9/11 is an extreme case, history clearly demonstrates that overreaction to major international terrorist acts against Americans is not necessarily politically required. Indeed, policies that might strike some as complacent have been applied. Consider, for example, the two instances of terrorism that killed the most Americans before September 2001. Ronald Reagan's response to the first of these, the 1983 suicide bombing in Lebanon that resulted in the deaths of 241 American marines, was to make a few speeches and eventually to pull the troops out. The venture seems to have had no negative impact on his reelection a few months later. The other was the December 1988 bombing of a Pan Am airliner over Lockerbie, Scotland, in which 187 Americans perished. The official response, beyond seeking compensation for the victims, was simply to apply meticulous police work in an effort to tag the culprits, a process that bore fruit only three years later and then only because of an unlikely bit of luck.[59] But that cautious response proved to be entirely acceptable politically. This is suggested as well by the experience with terrorism within the United States. George W. Bush's response to the anthrax attacks of 2001 was essentially the same as Clinton's had been to the terrorist attacks against the World Trade Center in 1993 and in Oklahoma City in 1995, and the same as the one applied in Spain when terrorists bombed trains there in 2004, or in Britain after attacks in 2005, or in France after the Paris killings of 2015: the dedicated application of police work to try to apprehend the perpetrators.

Moreover, political pressures do not precisely dictate the level or direction of expenditure. Although there may be public demands to "do something" about terrorism, nothing in those demands specifically requires American officials to mandate removing shoes in airport security lines, to require passports to enter Canada, to spread bollards like dandelions, to gather vast quantities of private data, or to make a huge number of buildings into forbidding fortresses.

Therefore, policymakers are, in an important sense, free, if not to be completely complacent on this issue, but at least to be rational: to adopt measures that most efficiently enhance public safety using standard risk-analytic and cost-benefit procedures. For the most part, however, they have not done so. For example, after nearly two years of investigation, a committee of the National Research Council of the National Academies of Sciences, Engineering, and Medicine reported in 2010 that it was unable to find any "risk analysis capabilities and methods" that were adequate to support decision-making by the Department of Homeland Security, observing that "little effective attention was paid to the features of the risk problem that are fundamental."[60]

The two former members of the Obama administration also contend that "any administration on whose watch an attack were to occur would immediately face relentless political recrimination." However, it seems likely that politicians and bureaucrats are overly fearful about the consequences of reacting moderately to terrorism. That is, their worries about job security, budget preservation, and political consequence are exaggerated. For example, President Barack Obama was so daring as to say that the United States can "absorb" terrorist attacks and, as noted, that such episodes do not present an "existential risk" to the country.[61] Such seemingly impolitic remarks have drawn considerable attention among the press and politicians.[62] Yet, they hardly seem to have hurt Obama's effectiveness or approval ratings – though they did not alter opinion either, of course. More generally, it should be asked which officials have been damaged by terrorist attacks, and when? Certainly not George W. Bush – when 9/11 occurred on his watch, his job approval ratings went sky high and then declined only quite slowly thereafter.[63] Officials in the United States seem to have survived large attacks like the ones on Fort Hood in 2009, San Bernardino in 2015, and Orlando in 2016, as have those abroad after attacks in London, Paris, Brussels, Barcelona, and Berlin. Who has been sacked?

For all the gloomy difficulties, there ought at least to be an effort to try to communicate the risk terrorism presents in a responsible manner. That is, risk assessment and communication should be part of the policy discussion over terrorism, something that is a far smaller danger than is popularly portrayed, or imagined. At a minimum, efforts should be made to reduce the glory from terrorism by treating terrorists more like common criminals – although this would mean, as Sageman points out, putting a stop to press conferences in which officials "hold self-congratulatory celebrations of their newest victories in the 'war on terror'." He stresses that to allow officials to "exploit the issue of terrorism for political gain is counterproductive."[64] In addition, the persistent exaggeration of the mental and physical capacities of terrorists, discussed in Chapter 4, has the perverse effect of glorifying the terrorist enterprise in the minds of many of its practitioners. But perhaps there is a considerable amount of (self-interested) method in the madness. As Kenneth Anderson puts it provocatively, "what government security measures, or ecosystem of security measures, could survive scrutiny if it were accepted, and taken as the central comparative fact, that the [yearly] chances of an individual U.S. person dying from terrorism in the years 1970–2013 was a mere 1 in 4 million?"[65]

The main military efforts to deal with international terrorism have been the costly ventures in Iraq and Afghanistan. Both of these were much disproportionate to the supposed danger presented, and they have been, in their own terms, and in the long run, very considerable failures. In result, that kind of military approach to terrorism, as suggested earlier, has been substantially discredited, an issue that is discussed more fully in Chapter 8.

To the degree that terrorism requires a response, it is one that calls not for large military operations, but for policing and intelligence work and perhaps for occasional focused strikes conducted from the air and by small ground units while relying on local forces to furnish the bulk of the combat personnel. This is substantially the approach the Obama administration developed to deal with ISIS as seen in Chapter 5. It seems likely to prevail. In addition, efforts to deal with the (questionable) dangers of atomic terrorism as discussed in Chapter 4, mainly require policing and intelligence, international cooperation on locking up and cataloging fissile material, and sting operations to disrupt illicit nuclear markets. They do not require large military forces-in-being.

OTHER PROBLEMS

Over the course of the last several decades, alarmists have often focused on potential dangers presented by rogue states, as they came to be called in the 1990s. These were led by such devils du jour as Nasser, Sukarno, Castro, Gaddafi, Khomeini, Kim Il-sung, Saddam Hussein, Milošević, and Ahmadinijad, all of whom have since faded into history's dustbin.[66] Today the alarm has been directed at Iran as discussed in Chapter 6 and also at North Korea as discussed in this one. However, neither country really threatens to commit major direct military aggression. Iran, in fact, has eschewed the practice for several centuries.

Nonetheless, it might make some sense to maintain a capacity to institute containment and deterrence efforts carried out in formal or informal coalition with concerned neighboring countries – and there are quite a few of these in each case. However, the military requirements for effective containment by their neighbors, by the United States, and by the broader world community are far from monumental and do not necessarily require the United States to maintain large forces-in-being for the remote eventuality.

This is suggested by the experience with the Gulf War of 1991 when military force was successfully applied to deal with a rogue venture – the conquest by Saddam Hussein's Iraq of neighboring Kuwait. As noted earlier, Iraq's invasion was rare to the point of being unique: it was the only case since World War II in which one United Nations country has invaded another with the intention of incorporating it into its own territory. It scarcely appears, as laid out in Chapter 3, that Iraq's pathetic forces required a large force to be thrown at them to decide to withdraw: over a period of half a year, they did not erect anything resembling an effective defensive system and, when the chips were down, they proved to lack not only defenses, but strategy, tactics, leadership, and morale as well.

Countries opposed to provocative rogue behavior do not need to have a large force-in-being because there would be plenty of time to build one up (should it come to that) if other measures such as economic sanctions and diplomatic forays (including appeasement) fail to persuade.

In 2011, a White House report proclaimed that transnational organized crime poses a significant and growing threat to national and international security, with dire implications for public safety, public health, democratic institutions, and economic stability. However, as Peter Andreas points out in a study of the issue, it is not at all clear that international crime is increasing as an overall percentage of global commerce. In fact, trade liberalization has sharply reduced incentives to engage in smuggling practices designed to evade taxes and tariffs, which were historically a driving force of illicit commerce. More importantly, he continues, the image of an octopus-like network of crime syndicates that runs the underworld through its expansive tentacles is a fiction invented by sensationalistic journalists, opportunistic politicians, and Hollywood scriptwriters. In contrast, international crime tends to be defined more by fragmentation and loose informal networks than by concentration and hierarchical organization.[67] Thus, like a parasite, international crime works best when it keeps a low profile and best of all when no one even notices it is there. Thus, *by its very nature* it does not want to take over the international system or threaten national security. It has no incentive to kill or dominate its host.

In an age of globalization and expanding world trade, many, particularly in the Navy, argue that a strong military force is needed to police what is portentously labeled the global commons. However, there seems to be no credible consequential threat in that arena. As Christopher Fettweis points out, "Today, the free flow of goods is critical to all economies, and no state would benefit from its interruption. . . . Free trade at sea may no longer need protection . . . because it has no enemies. The sheriff may be patrolling an essentially crime-free neighborhood."[68] Somali pirates hardly present an occasional inconvenience, and, although there exist choke points in international shipping, there are also exist routes around them in the unlikely event that they should become clogged. And any armed cloggers are likely to be as punished and inconvenienced as the clogged. Huge forces-in-being are scarcely required because, in the unlikely event that the problem really becomes sustained, newly formulated forces designed for the purpose could be developed.[69]

Moreover, as discussed in Chapter 6, the "policing" navy seems to be *causing* problems. Indeed, it is the "global commons" romanticism that seems to have fueled some of China's outward ploys, especially in the South

China Sea. China has to be worried that American police can not only keep trade lanes open, but close them on the whim of, for example, any effervescent and erratic resident of the White House who should happen to become commander in chief. It is also worth considering that the maintenance of a huge and costly military force by the distant United States might well fail to be a credible deterrent to localized assertive behavior by China because it is likely to be aware that there is little enthusiasm in the United States for sending large numbers of combatant troops abroad to directly confront such limited and distant effronteries.

There is also great concern about an impending, if presumably viral, invasion by cybergeeks to commit sabotage, to steal intelligence, or to spread propaganda. Any military disruptions are likely to be more nearly instrumental or tactical than existential, and they call far more for a small army of counter-cybergeeks than for a large standing military force. In 2003, Defense Secretary Leon Panetta proclaimed cyber to be "without question, the battlefield for the future," but, as Micah Zenko pointedly observed, the Pentagon was spending less than 1 percent of its budget on cybersecurity.[70] If that proves adequate to deal with the problem, it would seem, intuitively, to be something of a bargain.

Cyber, even more than terrorism, is the weapon of the weak. In fact, suggests Jon Lindsay, it seems entirely possible that "chronic cyber friction is a sign that more dangerous threats have been constrained."[71]

Cyber, unlike terrorism, has yet to kill anybody.[72] Nonetheless, we and our possessions are increasingly becoming interconnected, and the internet, key to this process, is vulnerable. For example, the brake pedal on cars is no longer actually connected to the brakes as in days of old, but rather to a potentially hackable computer that tells the brakes what to do. In a recent book, rather cheerlessly entitled *Click Here to Kill Everybody*, Bruce Schneier warns that "everything is becoming vulnerable ... because everything is becoming a computer," and, "more specifically, a computer on the Internet," and warns of "hackers remotely crashing airplanes, disabling cars, and tinkering with medical devices to murder people."[73]

Although it may be possible to commit sabotage using such methods, the record thus far is not very impressive. The United States, apparently in league with Israel, does seem to have explored the offensive use of cyber. Most famously, it managed to hamper Iran's progress toward developing a nuclear weapon. However, the hampering proved to be only temporary, and the effort was ultimately counterproductive in that it encouraged Iran to accelerate its nuclear program at the time.[74] There have also been cyber efforts by the United States to interfere with missile launches in North Korea, but there seems to be no proof that such interference was successful. There were multiple explanations for the failures, and eventually the North Koreans did solve whatever the problem was. As one official warns, "You have to be cautious whenever the enthusiasts of cyberattacks come in and claim victory."[75] There is some concern about disruptive cyberattacks on infrastructure, and, indeed, Russian hackers have caused a couple of power outages in Ukraine. However, they are much outclassed by squirrels who are credited with causing well over a thousand outages – and even jellyfish, who managed to take down a nuclear reactor in Sweden in 2013.[76]

It was in 2002 that the *Washington Post* was relaying on its front page the views of "government experts" that "terrorists are at the threshold of using the Internet as a direct instrument of bloodshed."[77] And a few years later an article in *Forbes* was solemnly assuring us that, while "four years ago al Qaeda operatives were taking flying lessons," they were now "honing a new skill: hacking."[78] Nonetheless, despite such warnings, no terrorist has ever launched a successful cyber-attack – that is, while cyber has vastly expanded during this century, terrorists do not seem yet to have gotten the hang of it. As Michael Kenney has observed, although the United States has experienced "hundreds of thousands of cyber-attacks" in the ensuing years, none rose to the level of cyber-terrorism," which he defines as "politically motivated computer attacks against other computer systems that cause enough physical harm or violence to generate fear and intimidation beyond the immediate victims of the attacks."[79] And even under the worst-case scenarios, cyberattacks are likely to be of limited physical effect.[80] Moreover, if terrorists want to express their concerns through violence, there are much easier methods for committing it than by hacking. Even if it becomes possible for a hacker to kill somebody, shootings and bombings are likely to accomplish the same goal far more reliably.[81]

There are also concerns about intelligence in which classified material, of varying degrees of official secrecy, will be hacked, savored, and perhaps published. However, this is not particularly new. As Lindsay points out, with the telegraph and with later innovations in telephony, radio, and computation, "the sophistication of techniques for electronic interception and deception has increased." Nonetheless, this has not created "lasting decisive advantages" because "the target reacts with operational security and counterintelligence measures."[82]

Moreover, to the degree that invading geeks engage in such espionage, they are likely to find that far too much has been classified: that is, most of what they come across is already pretty well known, while much of the rest is not worth knowing at all. The degree to which classification has been overdone is suggested more generally by the case of Chelsea (then known as Bradley) Manning, who downloaded hundreds of thousands of classified documents that were subsequently made public by Wikileaks in 2010. As it turned out, these documents, while embarrassing to some officials, contained no really significant new disclosures. According to Bill Keller, the *New York Times* editor in charge when the newspaper reported the material, just about all the information was already essentially public, though in many cases it was less textured, detailed, and nuanced.[83] Although prosecutors forcefully argued in Manning's military trial that she was guilty of "aiding the enemy" – surely the key issue in determining whether something should be classified – the judge failed to find her guilty on that charge.[84]

Extravagant concerns that a terrorist group might be able to glean enough information from the web to fabricate an atomic bomb seem to have faded. And concerns that it could be effective in providing useful operational information, particularly about making bombs, seem to be severely flawed. Kenney notes that the internet is filled with misinformation and error, and that it is no substitute for direct, on-the-ground training and experience.[85] Moreover, as David Benson points out, even if the information is valid, "it does not necessarily follow that one can actually carry out the task." Interaction with an instructor is often necessary. Thus, many are unable to prepare food correctly from internet instructions, "let alone master gourmet cooking." And unlike failure at fudge-making, failure at explosive-making carries considerable danger.[86]

If cyber has not been used to actually commit terrorism, it has proved to be a convenient method for terrorist groups to recruit and communicate. But in this, it has simply replaced or embellished other methods. In many cases, the internet has helped terrorists communicate with each other as they try to organize a plot, mainly through email. However, in the American cases, the bulk of the communication – and the most important – was face-to-face.

Many terrorists and would-be terrorists have gone to the internet for information, and they frequently sought out the most radical sites of which there are a large number. However, as Sageman notes, such web searches "merely reinforce already made-up minds."[87] Indeed, for the most part the process simply supplied information that in earlier days might have been furnished by incendiary paper pamphlets – a relatively minor change. It is the message that is vital, not the medium for delivering it. There certainly are abundant opportunities to use cyber to spread propaganda, but the spreading of propaganda and misinformation is scarcely a new phenomenon, and the notion that views so propagated will necessarily be accepted or influential is highly faulty. In particular, cyber scarcely seems necessary for the process of stoking outrage at American foreign and military policy. For the most part, any stoking stems from information readily available in the evening news: the invasion of Iraq, abuse of Iraqi prisoners at Abu Ghraib, torture by the CIA, "collateral" damage from American air and drone strikes, the mounting body count in Iraq and Afghanistan, instances of American troop abuse of Muslim civilians, and Israeli bombings of Lebanon and Gaza.[88]

For the most part, then, any virtual terrorist army in the United States has, as Brian Jenkins puts it, remained exactly that: virtual. "Talking about jihad, boasting of what one will do, and offering diabolical schemes egging each other on is usually as far as it goes." This "may provide psychological satisfaction" and "win accolades from other pretend warriors, but it is primarily an outlet for verbal expression, not an anteroom to violence."[89] To the degree that this has been done on the internet, it seems mainly to have attracted the attention of the FBI. Indeed, on balance, it appears that the internet has mainly benefited the authorities.

Another concern is with cybercrime.[90] A key issue, however, concerns its profitability. Schneier reports that 978 million people were "affected" by cybercrime in 2017 at a cost of $172 billion.[91] That works out to an average of $173 per effect or successful crime – or two days' wages at McDonalds. And since the average is likely distorted by a small number of hyper-successes, the median take is probably much lower. Nor does the consideration include all the time- and effort-consuming forays by criminals who were denied entry or were otherwise stifled. In addition, if crime has multiple authors, the take will have to be divvied up among the perpetrators. It doesn't sound like a very promising business. At that rate, a criminal would have to succeed hundreds of times to reach a poverty wage with the attendant danger that some of the "attacks," whether successful or not, might lead to discovery and pursuit.[92] Cybercrime that involves extortion or blackmail carries with it the usual problems of the genre: communication with the victim has to be completely secure and untraceable as does any ensuing transfer of funds, and these must be sufficiently large to justify the effort. The police are not unacquainted with methods to handle the crime, and they are likely to know quite a bit more about its nuances than the average criminal. And, as discussed in Chapter 6, the idea that voters can easily be manipulated by cyberintruders is highly questionable.

The developed world's dependence on oil imports from the Middle East has been an issue for a half-century now. However, unless the United States plans to invade other countries to seize their oil, the need for a military force-in-being to deal with this problem is far from obvious.[93] Any oil disruptions are likely to be handled by the market: if supply diminishes, prices will increase, and people will buy less. Not much fun, but much more likely than imperial invasion, especially after the experience in Iraq. And even if evil people manage to take over some oil wells somewhere, they will still be constricted in their choices: they can drink it, swim in it, or sell it. Christopher Preble considers the whole preoccupation to be based on a set of fallacies, and he even goes so far as to apply a degree of cost-benefit analysis – unfortunately a great rarity – to the issue. He notes that the United States has spent about $40 billion per year policing the Persian Gulf area when the total value of the oil exported might be something like a quarter of that.[94] Moreover, the problem, such as it is, seems to be in remission as, aided in part by such major technological breakthroughs as fracking, domestic supplies grow and oil prices decline worldwide. This phenomenon is likely to last for a considerable amount of time even as one prime oil supplier, Venezuela, takes itself substantially out of the market through mismanagement of cosmic proportions.

The potential for, and the consequences of, global warming are of great concern to many, and some have envisioned security issues. Thus, in 2013, Admiral Samuel J. Locklear, the chief of American forces in the Pacific, declared that global warming, and specifically rising sea levels, had the greatest potential to – as he put it rather opaquely – cripple the security environment.[95] Interestingly, the Admiral clearly was not speaking out of institutional self-interest because the larger the oceans become, the more important the Navy – though the service would presumably have to bear the costs of adding links to its anchor chains.[96] The need to maintain a military force to deal with climate change is scarcely evident, however. And, of course, the shutting down or mothballing of military vehicles on land, in the air, and on the sea might reduce warming vapors somewhat. Overall, as Mark Stewart points out, any damage to national security that might be expected to come from climate change is likely to require defense spending adjustments that are far from significant.[97]

Some argue that a substantial force-in-being is required to protect allies and friends. However, the most important allies, those in Europe, not only seem to face little threat of a military nature as suggested in Chapter 6, but are likely to be capable of dealing with any that should emerge.[98] In general, they spend less proportionately on defense than the United States, and there have long been complaints from the Americans about that. However, it seems highly plausible that, as Christopher Fettweis puts it, the Europeans "are not shirking their international responsibilities as much as interpreting the threats of the post-Cold War world in a profoundly different way than are policy makers in Washington."[99] If the United States wants to massively overspend on defense, why should they? At the same time, they proved to be excellent friends: most of them tried to warn their distant, elephantine ally about invading Iraq. They did go along for a while on America's invasion of Afghanistan, but then gradually faded away.

The threat environment for some other friends and allies, in particular Taiwan and Israel, is more problematic. However, whatever the conditions of military spending, it would be foolish for either to assume that the United States will come riding to its rescue should the country come under severe military pressure, though it can probably count on moral and financial support at a pinch. Actually, the Taiwan/China issue remains only a fairly remote (and perhaps declining) concern as suggested in Chapter 6. Some concern has been voiced that, if Taiwan were to go nuclear in response to a Chinese invasion threat, South Korea and Japan might follow suit. However, not only is this unlikely, but, as argued earlier in this chapter, the consequences of such a development are hardly dire. Moreover, the intense problems China is facing on controlling Hong Kong suggest it will not be eager at any time soon to attempt to expand to Taiwan. The Palestine/Israel dispute may or may not be resolved by the end the millennium, but the value of maintaining large American military forces seems to be irrelevant to that resolution. Israel's primary problems with violent opposition derive from the actions of sub-state groups, not from the potential for international warfare, and it seems quite capable of handling these on its own. Americans might eventually be part of a force to help police a peace settlement, but, if so, that can be recruited at the time if the need ever becomes evident.

There have been considerable increases in the number of refugees fleeing such war-wracked countries as Syria, Iraq, Libya, and Afghanistan. As detailed in Chapter 5, much of this is because aid by the US and others has served to sustain wars that might have dimmed earlier. And, of course, some of these wars were actually started by the United States – many of the refugees have come from Afghanistan. At any rate, the flow of refugees scarcely justifies the maintenance of a huge military. It is substantially irrelevant to the problem.

The country (and the world) certainly faces major problems of an economic nature, but the military is of little importance here either. Actually, large cuts in military budgets might temper the budget problem.[100] Although some military leaders have pointed to the burgeoning American debt as a security problem, they never seem to suggest an obvious partial remedy that is readily at hand. Nor is there much of a military remedy for AIDS in Africa – sometimes billed as a threat to US security. And the same can be said for other health and humanitarian concerns, including the control of pandemics.

INTERNATIONAL POLICING

One possible use of American military forces in the future would be to deploy them under international authority to police destructive civil wars or to depose regimes that, either out of incompetence of viciousness, are harming their own people in a major way. For a number of reasons, however, humanitarian intervention with military force by developed countries is unlikely to become anything like routine. There are at least three key problems.

First, there is little or no political gain from success in such ventures. If George H. W. Bush failed to receive a lasting boost from the American public for the way he applied the US military at remarkably low cost to drive Saddam Hussein's Iraq out of Kuwait in 1991, it is exceedingly difficult to imagine an operation that could do so.[101]

Second, there is a low tolerance for casualties in such applications of military force: a loss of a couple of dozen soldiers in chaotic fire-fights in Somalia in 1993 led the mighty United States to withdraw.

And finally, the experience with policing wars has been accompanied by an increasing aversion to the costs and difficulties of any nation-building that can often ensue. This aversion was already high in 2000 after messy experiences in the 1990s, particularly the one in Somalia, and it has been immeasurably enhanced by the exceedingly messy and costly wars in Iraq and Afghanistan. The US military has proven to be good at killing people and at breaking things, but not at anthropology.

Even if there is some stomach for putting American troops into humanitarian policing ventures, however, this would not require a large number of troops: most of the successful ventures were accomplished by inserting a few hundred to a few thousand disciplined troops. And, for the most part, the interventions that were successful were conducted by disciplined military forces against ones that usually were substantially criminal or criminalized.[102] A viable policy might be to continue to conduct such ventures but, should they devolve into chaos and civil warfare, to withdraw. Indeed, history suggests that, should the situation deteriorate, the calls would be for removing the troops as in Somalia (and in Libya), not for sending in more.

Actually, some of the problems that policing wars were designed to deal with may be resolving themselves. In the last couple of decades there may have been something of a decline in the number of venal tyrannies and, as Figure 0.1 suggests, in civil wars. There has, however, been something of an increase in the number and particularly in the destructiveness (mainly due to Syria) of civil war in the last few years.[103] Whether this represents a reverse of the trend or a temporary blip remains to be seen, but the latter prospect seems more likely.

Insofar as policing military forces might be useful, the most promising possibility seems to be in the construction of a viable international force through the United Nations, as has been suggested for decades.[104] There seems to have been considerable success in peacekeeping (as opposed to peacemaking) and this may have contributed to the remarkable decline in civil warfare in the 1990s.[105] Thus people in Africa and elsewhere seem to have become fed up with the civil warfare they have suffered in recent decades in which small numbers of thugs, often drunken or drugged, were able to pulverize effective society through their predatory criminal antics, sometimes sustaining them for decades. In consequence of this disgust, there has been a strong willingness to accept and make effective use of outside aid and to establish effective (if hardly perfect) governments to deal with this problem. Among the advantages of working through the UN is that participants would be international civil servants, not constituents of a specific country, whose deaths in action would stir only indirect concern in their home countries. Among the key questions, however, are whether developed countries will be willing to pay for such an enterprise, whether the international organization can put together a truly capable military force, and whether the Security Council can be counted on to manage and deploy it effectively.

The survey of potential threats and monsters conducted in this chapter and in the previous one scarcely suggests that severe dangers lurk out there, on the threshold, or over the horizon, particularly ones that require the maintenance of a huge military force-in-being. As Charles Kenny concludes, "US spending is at an all-time high at a moment when traditional military treats are at an all-time low" and "defense spending is a grossly inefficient tool to confront the more pressing global threats that we do face."[106]

To be sure, always lingering is the ever-reliable problem of complexity and its constant companions, instability and uncertainty, and these concepts, if that is what they are, get routinely trotted out as if they had some tangible meaning, as if they had only recently been discovered, and as if they somehow necessitate more military spending.[107] Of course, whatever their meaning, they can be used to justify decreases in military expenditures in favor of expenditures on intelligence, diplomacy, or soft power.

However, there may nonetheless be a justification for some military forces as a hedge against uncertainty – something that will never, can never, go away. This consideration is a focus of Chapter 8.

8

Hedging, Risk, Arrogance, and the Iraq Syndrome

The perspective in this book is not isolationist. There is no suggestion that the United States should withdraw from being a constructive world citizen. The generally desirable processes of increasing economic inter-connectivity and of globalization make that essentially impossible anyway. Rather, the policy proposition that emerges reflects one Eric Nordlinger once suggested: minimally effortful national strategy in the security realm; moderately activist policies to advance our liberal ideas among and within states; and a fully activist economic diplomacy on behalf of free trade.[1]

Nor does the perspective in this book arise from pacifism – the notion that military force is always necessarily evil or unproductive and that there are no conditions under which it should be instituted or deployed. Indeed, as noted in Chapter 3, some armed interventions have been quite successful at halting civil wars or deposing vicious regimes at an acceptable cost. However, it certainly seems that most wars have been foolish and unnecessary – the "most tragic and stupid folly," as General Dwight Eisenhower put it in the aftermath of World War II. Over the course of the last hundred years, that proposition has come to be widely accepted, particularly as it pertains to international war. In addition, experience certainly suggests that sometimes the most sensible approach may not be to seek to win wars, but to end them: war is often the worst thing there is. Fighting makes little sense if the worst plausible outcome of the war is likely better than the war itself.

A prominent finding in the book is that, even as international war has gone into decline, threat has persistently been inflated and militarized efforts to deal with some of them have been applied, often with tragic results as in Vietnam, Afghanistan, and Iraq. Given the essential absence of any substantial security threats to the United States (and to most of the developed world) that derives at least in part from the rising aversion to international war, and given the generally miserable record of American military intervention over the last three-quarters of a century, it certainly seems that spending huge sums on the military to cover unlikely threats (or fantasies) borders, indeed, considerably oversteps, the profligacy line.

It is often pointed out that defense spending, even in the United States, constitutes only a fairly small percentage of government spending and a quite small percentage of the country's gross national product.[2] Nevertheless, the saving of several hundreds of billions of dollars each year soon adds up even in that comparison. In total, expenditures on defense in the United States since the end of the Cold War have been something like $17 trillion – about the size of the entire national debt. Moreover, there is much bloat and inefficiency.[3]

While the argument proposes that the United States should embrace threatlessness, there are a few final considerations and caveats.

First, even if the United States should substantially disarm, it is probably wise to keep some military forces-in-being in order to carry out limited military missions and to hedge against the potential rise, however unlikely, of a hostile, dedicated, and effective adversary.

And second, it should be acknowledged that the proposed policy carries with it some risk. This, however, is something that must be balanced off against the risks attendant on maintaining a huge military force-in-being.

This chapter evaluates these issues, and it also includes some comments about the arrogance attendant on being number one.

It concludes with an examination of American public opinion, finding that it is generally in line with the perspective in this book. The American public cannot be said to have become newly isolationist or militaristic: it has long been willing to engage internationally, but not to expend American lives in costly and questionable foreign adventures. That is, the 9/11 wars are not harbingers. Indeed, as after Vietnam, there is a wariness about such interventions as an Iraq Syndrome takes hold: let's not do that again. Military intervention, particularly with ground troops, whether of the neoconservative or the liberal persuasion, does not seem to have much of a future.

HEDGING, RISK, AND ARROGANCE

It probably makes sense to hedge a bit by judiciously maintaining small contingents of troops for rapid response and for policing functions, a capacity to provide air support for friendly ground troops in localized combat, a small number of nuclear weapons for the (wildly) unlikely event of the rise of another Hitler, something of an effort to deal with cyber geeks, an adept intelligence capacity, and the development of a capacity to rebuild quickly should a sizable threat eventually materialize. Military alliances may also continue to prove to be useful – though not necessarily simply for military purposes.

The maintenance of some small rapid-response or commando forces of the kind that captured and killed Osama bin Laden seems sensible. Actually, however, although there may have been something of a psychological charge when the chief instigator of 9/11 was abruptly and brutally removed from the scene and from life, it is not at all clear, as discussed in Chapter 4, that there was all that much benefit from the venture in the never-ending war on terror: material gathered in the raid show bin Laden to have been wallowing in delusion and to have become something of an irrelevance by the time he was dispatched.[4] But, of course, while maintaining a capacity to carry out such raids might still be worthwhile, to do so would not require a large military force.

In addition, there may be instances in which it would be useful to be able to send troops, often, perhaps, in coordination with policing forces from the United Nations or from other countries, to establish and maintain peace where a civil war has subsided or to help maintain order in places where a despot has been removed. As discussed at the end of Chapter 7, policing wars are likely to be few due to a low tolerance for casualties in such efforts, an increasing aversion to the costs of nation-building, and the lack of political gain from successful ventures. Moreover, such missions do not require large numbers of troops – a few thousand would surely do – and they are likely to be deployed only when the atmosphere on the ground is permissive or substantially so. If either of those conditions changes and substantial violence once again erupts, the troops are likely to be removed as happened in Lebanon after 1983 and Somalia after 1993 and as essentially happened in the misguided Libyan intervention of 2011.

It would remain potentially wise to maintain a capacity to provide air support, including the use of drone munitions, for friendly ground troops who are dedicately engaged in localized combat as in that against ISIS in Iraq and Syria. Despite near-cosmic failures by US forces to train locals in Vietnam, Iraq, and Afghanistan, some capacity to train friendly forces overseas might be maintained as well. And logisitic and financial support may also be required from time to time. But none of this requires the maintenance of large numbers of combat troops.

It would likely be prudent in addition to retain a small number of nuclear weapons. These should be secure, hardened, and deliverable, but they need not be numerous. It certainly seems, as argued earlier, that nuclear weapons have been essentially irrelevant to world history since 1945. However, there are still imaginable, if highly unlikely, contingencies – such as the rise of another Hitler – in which they might become useful.

Relatedly, it might make some sense to maintain containment and deterrence capacities against aggressive efforts of rogue states should any such appear. However, the military requirements for this by their neighbors, by the United States, and by the broader world community are far from monumental and do not necessarily require the United States to keep large forces-in-being. As seen in the Gulf War of 1991 and in its multi-month buildup, it is scarcely necessary to have large forces on hand to reverse direct aggression from such states in the almost vanishingly rare occasions when that may seem to be necessary.

Although, as argued in Chapter 7, cyber "attacks" might conceivably sometimes be considered to be sabotage, they scarcely constitute war. Obviously, guarding secure information is desirable – though, as many have noted, there is a huge amount of over-classification of material. Nevertheless, maintaining a capacity to deal with this troublesome, if limited, issue even if it scarcely ever rises much above – or indeed even reaches – the level of vandalism, would be useful.

While it certainly appears that standing military forces can safely be substantially reduced, maintaining an adept intelligence capacity probably remains a priority. However, studies should be made to determine whether, on balance, the benefit of a massive intelligence apparatus justifies its very considerable cost.[5]

It also seems sensible to establish something of a capacity to rebuild quickly should a sizable threat eventually materialize. In Richard Betts' formulation, this would be a mobilization strategy in which one would hedge against unknowable future threats by developing plans and organizing resources so that military capabilities can be expanded quickly later if necessary.[6] The United States was very good at that in the early 1940s when global threats emerged.[7] And something similar, on a substantial, but less massive, scale happened when the Korean War broke out suddenly in 1950. In most (but not all) cases, there is likely to be time to rebuild in the unlikely event that substantial threats actually materialize, though there is inevitably waste in crash programs.

Maintaining NATO and some other alliances is likely to be a good idea, although mostly for non-military reasons. As Paul Schroeder has pointed out, military alliances have generally been designed at least in part to control the allies.[8] This valuable characteristic is likely to be pertinent to the current situation: together with the European Union, NATO played a role in stabilizing Europe after the Cold War not so much by its specific military prowess, but by providing an attractive club for newly independent states in the area to join. It is not clear, however, that the defense of allies is a key military necessity. As noted in the previous chapter, Europe seems to face no notable threats of a military nature, the Taiwan/China issue remains a fairly remote concern, and Israel's primary problems derive from the actions of sub-state groups.

It certainly seems, then, that the United States does not now face (nor since 1945 has ever faced) threats that require it to maintain a large military force-in-being. On balance, given an unimpressive threat horizon accompanied by a well-established, even venerable, aversion to international war, very substantial arms reduction seems fully worth the gamble.

However, it should be acknowledged that it *is* a gamble: there would be risk if US military forces were very substantially reduced. But, as the experiences in Vietnam and Iraq suggest, there is risk as well in maintaining large forces-in-being that can be deployed with little notice and in an under-reflective manner. Thus, in the wake of the disastrous Vietnam War, defense strategist Bernard Brodie recalled that the substantial defense buildup that had begun under the presidency of John Kennedy had, to a considerable degree, made the Vietnam disaster possible. He wistfully reflected, as noted in this book's Prologue, that "One way of keeping people out of trouble is to deny them the means for getting into it."[9] That is, having a large military force-in-being tempts leaders to use it in an effort to solve problems for which the application of military force may be singularly unwise.

Decades later, Brodie's admonition continues to be resonate. For the entirety of the current century, American military policy, especially in the Middle East, has been an abject failure. In particular, impelled by a massive overreaction to 9/11 and at the cost of hundreds of thousands of lives and trillions of dollars, the two international wars of the twenty-first century have been waged. And it certainly seems that Iraq and Afghanistan have been made worse off than they were even under the contemptible regimes of Saddam Hussein and the Taliban. Something similar holds for the military venture in Libya. In 2011, political scientist Stephen Walt reflected on what he called the "reasons we keep getting into foolish fights." The first reason he came up with was "Because We Can."[10]

In this connection, one might compare the tumultuous and self-destructive overreaction to 9/11 with that to the worst terrorist event in the developed world before then, the downing of an Air India airliner departing Canada in 1985. The crash killed 329 people, 280 of them Canadian citizens, and journalist Gwynne Dyer points out that, proportionate to population, the fatality rates were almost exactly the same in the two cases. But, continues Dyer, "here's what Canada didn't do: it didn't send troops into India to 'stamp out the roots of the terrorism' and it didn't declare a 'global war on terror'." Dyer points out this was because Canada "lacked the resources for that sort of adventure." And also, he adds, "because it would have been stupid."[11]

Canada essentially adopted a policy of complacency after its 1985 tragedy, and this is extremely likely to have been the right reaction. That is, it fortunately lacked the arrogance – or political narcissism – of the strong, a condition memorialized in an oft-quoted declaration of the mighty Athenians (who later went down to ignominious defeat) as reported by Thucydides: "the strong do what they can and the weak suffer what they must."[12]

As the arrogant (and fundamentally stupid) 9/11 wars fade away (Iraq) or dribble on (Afghanistan), the somewhat prosaic wisdom of the pre-9/11 George W. Bush is looking very attractive. As he put it in one of the debates during the 2000 campaign:

> If we're an arrogant nation, they'll resent us. If we're a humble nation, but strong, they'll welcome us.... I just don't think it's the role of the United States to walk into a country and say, we do it this way, so should you. I think we can help.... I think the United States must be humble and must be proud and confident of our values, but humble in how we treat nations that are figuring out how to chart their own course.[13]

In a thoughtful article in *Foreign Affairs* in the summer of 2002, some nine months before the American invasion of Iraq, political scientists Stephen Brooks and William Wohlforth explore the argument holding that what had once been called the "unipolar moment," in which the United States was unchallenged, was coming to an end. Applying various measures of military, economic, geographic, and technological strength, they concluded that "no state in the modern history of international politics has come close to the military predominance these numbers suggest" and that such dominance was likely to last "for decades to come."[14]

Then, in a concluding section titled "resisting temptation," they urge that, although "now and for the foreseeable future, the United States will have the immense power resources it can bring to bear to force or entice others to do its bidding," it should not "act heedlessly" or become "the global bully," but rather seek to "reap the greater gains that will eventually come from magnanimity." Because of its special status, it was free to act in its own, and the world's, long-term best interests by integrating Russia and China into the global system, teaming with others to deal with environmental problems, disease, migration, and economic problems, and lowering international and domestic trade barriers. The focus, then, should not be on "small returns today" but "larger ones tomorrow."[15]

Even by that time, however, Bush had failed to resist the "temptation" to use the country's military "to force or entice others to do its bidding." As discussed in Chapter 4, under the impetus of 9/11, he had exhibited exactly the kind of arrogance that he had denounced in the election campaign, going so far as to grandly proclaim that "Our responsibility to history is already clear – to answer these attacks and rid the world of evil."[16] This rather remarkable goal – proposing to outdo God who had tried and failed to rid the world of evil with that flood of His some time ago – was blandly accepted by press and public alike at the time, although the *New Orleans Times-Picayune* did modestly suggest that "perhaps the President over-promised."[17]

The problem, then, is that the "primacy" (or whatever it was) that the United States enjoyed not only allowed the chief primate the freedom to be magnanimous, but also to "do stupid shit," as Barack Obama was soon to label it. And in the spring of 2003, Bush led the country into its great foreign policy debacle in Iraq.

Although, as suggested by the pre-9/11 Bush, influence often springs from humility, the ability of military strength to generate desirable outcomes seems to have been greatly exaggerated.[18] Nevertheless, although made at least somewhat more wary by a couple of decades of cascading debacle in and around the Middle East, the United States (led by its foreign policy establishment) too often continues to view itself, in Doug Bandow's quip, as "the globe's dominatrix into whose hands every dispute is properly remitted."[19]

Moreover, the maintenance of a large military force-in-being facilitates and sometimes stimulates not only misguided and foolish exercises in military assertiveness, but fatuous political rhetoric. Thus, American Secretary of State Madeleine Albright notably came up with a modern equivalent of the Athenian pose in 1998 when she declared, "If we have to use force, it is because we are America; we are the indispensable nation. We stand tall and we see further than other countries into the future."[20] That self-obsessed phraseology was routinely echoed, even expanded, by Barack Obama during his presidency. As he said in a speech at West Point in 2014, "The United States is and will remain the one indispensable nation."[21] The suggestion that the United States considers all other nations to be, well, dispensable, has not been lost on them. Asked in 2012 about the degree to which the United States, in making international policy decisions, takes into account the interests of countries like theirs, major-ities, usually overwhelming ones, in almost all countries polled replied "not too much" or "not at all."[22]

It is difficult to keep people who think they are the chief primate from exaggerating threats, from wallowing in arrogance, or from failing to explore the virtues of complacency. But if they are denied the means, they are far less likely, following Brodie's dictum, to do dumb things in consequence.

PUBLIC OPINION AND THE IRAQ SYNDROME

One popular explanation for the American public's palpable unwillingness to countenance military involvement in the Syrian civil war in 2013 was that the country was slumping into a deep isolationist mood, and there was concern about a new isolationism or a growing isolationism or a new non-interventionist fad.[23] In contrast to those envisioning a new isolationism, some commentators, including such unlikely soulmates as Andrew Bacevich, Robert Kagan, John Mearsheimer, Rachel Maddow, Gregory Daddis, and Vladimir Putin, have variously maintained that we have seen the rise of a new American militarism in the last decades or that Americans congenitally hail from Mars.[24]

But both perspectives are flawed.

The American people have not become isolationist: they have not come seriously to yearn for full withdrawal from the world. However, they have long had a deep and abiding wariness about costly and frustrating military engagements.

And the militarism perspective, it seems to me, extrapolates far too much from the wars in Afghanistan and Iraq. These ventures – the 9/11 wars – have proved to be aberrations from usual patterns, not portents of the future. Although they demonstrate that Americans remain willing to strike back hard if attacked, they do not indicate a change in the public's reticence about becoming militarily involved in other kinds of missions – or errands.

Instructive is an examination of the long-term trends in a set of poll questions designed to tap "isolationism." Three versions are mapped in Figure 8.1.[25] They document something of a rise in wariness about military intervention after the Vietnam War and then, thereafter, a fair amount of steadiness punctured by spike-like ups and downs in response to events including 9/11 and its ensuing wars. In the wake of the disastrous military interventions in Iraq and Afghanistan, "isolationism" as measured by these poll questions has gone back to about where it was in the aftermath of Vietnam.

The poll question with the longest pedigree has been asked at least since 1945: "Do you think it will be best for the future of this country if we take an active part in world affairs, or if we stayed out of world affairs?" The question seems to have been fabricated to generate an "internationalist" response. In 1945, after all, the United States possessed something like half the wealth in the world and scarcely had much of an option about "taking an active part in world affairs," as it was so blandly and unthreateningly presented. The authors of the poll question got the number they probably wanted: so queried, only 19

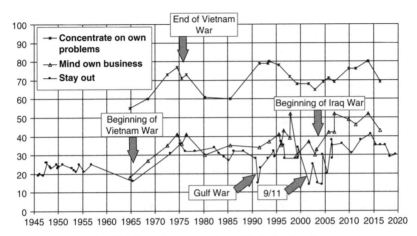

FIGURE 8.1 Public opinion trends on "isolationism," 1945–2019

percent of poll respondents in 1945 picked the "stay out" or "isolationist" option. As can be seen in the figure, however, high levels of "isolationism" can be generated if the question is reformulated by asking respondents whether they agree or disagree that "We shouldn't think so much in international terms but concentrate more on our own national problems and building up our strength and prosperity here at home." In that rendering, the option of staying out of world affairs is only implied, and measured "isolationism" consistently registers 30 or 40 percentage points higher.

In the years following 1945, the "stay out" percentage rose a bit to around 25 percent, but it had descended to 16 percent in 1965 in the aftermath of the 1962 Cuban missile crisis and as the war in Vietnam began. The experience of that war pushed it much higher – to 31 to 36 percent as part of what has been called the "Vietnam Syndrome."

The percentage has stayed at around that level ever since except for some spike-like jolts upward or downward. There was a downward dip during the Gulf War of 1991, at the end of which, as noted in Chapter 3, the war's chief author, President George H. W. Bush, grandly concluded a speech by trumpeting, "By God, we've kicked the Vietnam Syndrome once and for all." Within weeks, however, the "stay out" option had regained its previous attractiveness. There were also interesting spikes suggesting a wariness about military interventions abroad when troops were sent to Bosnia in late 1995 and at the time of the Kosovo conflict in 1999. In these instances, the spikes were upward, even though no American troops were lost in either venture and even though both were deemed successful, at least in their own terms, at the time.

In the current century, the "stay out" percentage dropped to 14, its lowest recorded level ever, in the aftermath of 9/11. It rose the next year, and then plunged downward again in 2003 and 2004 – the first two years of the Iraq War. By 2006, however, it had risen to post-Vietnam levels, where it has roughly remained although a related question, asking whether the United States "should mind its own business internationally" while letting "other countries get along as best they can on their own," did reach new – or almost new – highs in 2013.[26]

Given the bland attractiveness of the "take an active part in world affairs" option, it is impressive that around a third or more of the public since Vietnam has generally rejected it to embrace the "stay out" option. However, this should probably be taken to be more nearly an expression of wariness about costly military entanglements than as a serious yearning for full withdrawal from the world, or "isolationism." There is, for example, no real indication that Americans want to erect steely trade barriers.[27] And polls continually show that the public is far more likely to approve foreign ventures if they are approved and supported by allies and international organizations.[28] Real isolationism should be made of sterner stuff.[29] As Christopher Preble puts it succinctly, "for the most part, Americans want to remain actively engaged in the world without having to be in charge of it."[30]

John Mearsheimer argues that the public has become less enthusiastic about acting as the world's policeman.[31] However, it does not seem that it has ever been very enthusiastic: there has always been a deep reluctance to lose American lives or to put them at risk overseas for humanitarian purposes. That perspective is seen most starkly, perhaps, when Americans were asked in 1993 whether they agreed that "Nothing the US could accomplish in Somalia is worth the death of even one more US soldier." Fully 60 percent expressed agreement.[32] This is not such an unusual position for humanitarian ventures. If Red Cross or other workers are killed while carrying out humanitarian missions, their organizations frequently threaten to withdraw no matter how much good they may be doing. Essentially what they are saying is that the saving of lives is not worth the deaths of even a few of their service personnel.[33]

Thus, civil warfare and vicious regimes have not actually inspired a great deal of alarm except when they seemed to present a direct threat to the United States. As a result, few have inspired military intervention. Rather, the most common official pattern about such situations has been, as suggested earlier in this book several times, vast proclamation followed by half-vast execution.

For example, the United States did a great deal of bloviating about the civil war in Bosnia in the early 1990s, but it held off intervention on the ground until hostilities had ceased. Even then, the public was anything but enthusiastic when American peace keeping soldiers were sent in, and enthusiasm did not rise even when it turned out the atmosphere remained "permissive" and the troops were met with little or no hostility.[34] Indeed, about the only time the public chose to pay much attention to the war in Bosnia, a venture much publicized and much agonized over by elites and by the media in the 1990s, was when an American airman was shot down behind enemy lines and when American troops were dispatched to the area to police the situation.[35]

Intervention in Kosovo in 1999 was by bombing alone, and in Somalia, the United States abruptly withdrew when 19 of its troops were killed. The United States, like other developed nations, mostly remained studiously distant from genocide in Cambodia in 1975–79 and Rwanda in 1994 and from catastrophic civil war in Congo after 1997 or in South Sudan after 2013.[36]

In many respects the Libyan effort of 2011 was quite a bit like the campaign in Somalia in 1992–93: after some initial success, troops and direct military involvement were pulled back when things began to go awry. The reluctance is most evident in the supportive, but distant, response to rebels in the calamitous Syrian civil war.

In general, then, those who suggest there has been a surge of militarism put far too much weight on the temporary successes of the stridently hawkish neoconservative movement in the early part of the George W. Bush administration. In fact, there has never been much support for sending American troops into hostile situations in the last decades – or maybe even century – unless there was a decided provocation. In the 9/11 cases, opinion was impelled not by a propensity toward militarism, but, as with entry into World War II, by an outraged reaction to a direct attack on the United States. Even at that, as seen in Chapter 4, Bush was unable to boost support for going to war with Iraq in his campaign to do so in 2002–3 despite the fact that there was little opposition from the Democratic leadership. Even support for the once-popular, 9/11-induced war in Afghanistan waned. Using the same poll question, initial support for that war was some 15 percentage points higher than it had been at the start of the wars in Korea, Vietnam, and Iraq, but, like those wars, support gradually declined as American casualties were suffered.[37]

People, contrary to a large literature, do not seem to be readily manipulable by opinion elites or by the media on such issues. As noted in Chapter 5, the Obama administration dramatically proposed military action in response to chemical weapons use in Syria, and leaders of both parties in Congress rather quickly fell into line. Nonetheless, the public was decidedly unwilling even to support the punitive bombing of Syria – a venture likely to risk few if any American lives – out of concern that it would lead to further involvement in the conflict there.[38]

Leaders may propose, but that does not mean public opinion will move in concert – that people will necessarily buy the message. And on the occasions when they do, it is probably best to conclude that the message has struck a responsive chord, rather than that the public has been manipulated.[39] If George W. Bush was unable to boost support for invasion during the runup to his war in Iraq, neither was his father able to do so, despite strenuous efforts, for going to war against Iraq in Kuwait in the runup to the 1991 Gulf War as discussed in Chapter 3. On the other hand, public concern about international terrorism, as discussed in Chapter 7, has not altered much in the two decades since 9/11 even though there have been multiple reasons to have expected an erosion of concern to take place.

After Vietnam, there was strong desire – usually called the Vietnam Syndrome – not to do that again. And, in fact, there never were other Vietnams for the United States during the Cold War. The administration was kept by Congress even from rather modest anti-Communist militarized ventures in Africa and, to a lesser extent, in Latin America – though there was bipartisan support for aiding the anti-Soviet insurgency in Afghanistan, a venture, however, that did not involve sending American troops.

A rather comparable Iraq, or Iraq/Afghan, Syndrome now seems likely.[40] Christopher Dandeker parses the situation succinctly: "the interventions in Afghanistan and Iraq represent the high-water mark of the Western belief that states can successfully use military force to intervene in the affairs of failed, rogue, or other states to achieve ambitious foreign policy goals." Further, "the difficulties of achieving success in these interventions, even when 'success' is modestly defined, have shaken confidence and belief in the value of intervention among Western political and military elites and publics." Dandeker also argues that "military interventions will continue," but they will be different from those in Iraq and Afghanistan and "more like the Libyan example of 2011."[41] As noted above and in Chapter 5, however, the behavior in the Libya venture is not all that new. It is similar to the one in Somalia in 1993 – initial success and then rather abrupt and unsentimental withdrawal as things begin to fall apart.

Although support for one tactic, direct military intervention, declined after Vietnam, the general policy of maintaining somewhat lesser exertions in dealing with the perceived Communist threat continued to be supported and a huge military continued to be extravagantly financed although it had little to do. And something like that seems likely in the case of today's monsters. There will be general support in principle for policies intended to deal with proliferation and international terrorism, but not so much for militarized ventures of invasion and particularly of occupation.[42]

The US military seems to be on much the same page. In its defense priority statement of January 2012, the Defense Department firmly emphasized (that is, rendered in italics) that "*U.S. forces will no longer be sized to conduct large-scale, prolonged stability operations.*" Later, when President Donald Trump suggested that "the military option" might be appropriate for dealing with the problems entailed by Venezuela (which had systematically destroyed itself but was occasionally belligerent and defiant), his defense secretary at the time, James Maddis, simply responded, "The Venezuelan crisis is not a military matter."[43] As David Sanger puts it, "America is out of the occupation business."[44] Although there was some backward creep after 2014 in response to the ISIS menace as discussed in Chapter 5, this basic policy perspective does not seem to have changed. Overall, as many military people have come increasingly to appreciate, many problems simply cannot be solved by military means.

The public also seems to be increasingly capable of containing the notion that it is the destiny of the United States to lead the world. The American record on this score, actually, is less than stellar. Out of sympathy over 9/11, NATO countries did more or less "follow" the United States into the invasion of Afghanistan. However, over time the "leader" lost its followers as the occupation increasingly became a debacle. And, when the United States tried to get support for its ill-destined invasion of Iraq in 2003, only the British and the Australians signed up to join its tiny "coalition of the willing." Most countries, including especially France, tried to dissuade the United States from the misguided venture – a true sign of friendship if not of blind followership. As noted earlier, for its prescient advice and its efforts to pacify the chief primate, France's effrontery was met with humorless derision in the United States Congress when a fat-laced accompaniment to hamburgers was relabeled "freedom fries." At that, Australia soon left the Iraq misadventure and so, later, did the United Kingdom where outraged parliamentarians from the party of invasion-supporting Prime Minister Tony Blair used the episode to destroy his political career. In the runup to Iraq, the United States, using not only "leadership" but bribery, also tried to get NATO ally Turkey to let it use its territory for bases for the invasion and failed. In an earlier decade, the United States had also tried to entice (aka "lead") some of its "followers" to help it out in the Vietnam War, with only modest success.

Although fully two-thirds of Americans continued to favor greater US involvement in the global economy in 2013, only 46 percent deemed it "very desirable" for the United States to exert strong leadership in world affairs – the lowest level ever registered by the poll question. In the same poll, only 11 percent of Europeans said they felt that way: the dominated, it would appear, do not seem to have gotten the message.[45] In a speech at West Point in 2014, President Barack Obama self-importantly contended that "the question we face is not whether America will lead but how we will lead."[46] Perhaps the American (and European) people can be forgiven for worrying about the results.

At the same time, the American military – despite its substantial record of failure – continues to receive high approval ratings in public opinion surveys. It's just that the public does not seem to want it actually to be used very much and then mainly (or only) when it espies a clear threat to the United States. And even where there was substantial public fear about a threat, as with ISIS, the military, anticipating that support even for popular ventures like that might well wane as American battle deaths were suffered, deemed it wise to configure troop deployments in a manner that minimized American casualties. If that happens, public support may not rise, but attention will wane. The ability to use drones and, as in Kosovo, to fight from distances like 40,000 feet fits this perspective.

Militarized interventionist internationalism above a very modest level, then, may well be dead – whether the inspiration for such interventions is liberal or neoconservative. However, it may never have actually been alive either – the public has never really bought the notion that American lives should be lost for humanitarian purposes, to spread democracy, or to make the world safe for others.

In the process, other notions may be declining in force. These include those holding that the United States can and should apply its military supremacy to straighten out lesser peoples even if a result of this policy becomes the establishment of something of a new American empire, that the United States should and can forcibly bring democracy to nations not now so blessed, that it has the duty to bring order to the Middle East, that it should embrace a mission to rid the world of evil, that international cooperation is of only very limited value, and that Europeans and other well-meaning foreigners are naive and decadent wimps. And, just possibly, a sense of humility may come to crowd out arrogance.

Aversion to International War as an Explanatory Variable

Despite some notable setbacks, there has been a substantial increase globally in economic development and political freedom since 1945. Moreover, not only has world war been avoided, but, as discussed throughout this book, international war, more generally, has increasingly been abandoned as a method for dealing with disputes between states.

Although the American military record during that time has been pretty unimpressive, both those who consider the United States to be "indispensable" and those who do not often give credit for these desirable results to the policies and efforts of the United States. It is argued, first, that the United States, aided perhaps by the attention-arresting fear of nuclear weapons, was necessary to provide worldwide security and thus to order the world. And, second, that the United States was instrumental, indeed vital, in constructing international institutions, conventions, and norms, in advancing economic development, and in expanding democracy - processes, it is contended, that in various ways have ordered the world and crucially helped to establish and maintain international peace.

Indeed, the United States has often been said to have presided over a condition grandly labeled "the American world order" or "the liberal world order" or "Pax Americana."

Christopher Fettweis supplies some vivid examples of this contention in operation. Neoconservatives Lawrence Kaplan and William Kristol argue that "In many instances, all that stands between civility and genocide, order and mayhem, is American power." For former national security advisor Zbigniew Brzezinski, a world without American stewardship would turn "violent and bloodthirsty" with "outright chaos" created by new attempts to build regional empires and redress old territorial claims. And British economic historian Niall Ferguson envisions it would be "a new Dark Age" in which "The wealthiest ports of the global economy ... would become the targets of plunderers and pirates. With ease, terrorists could disrupt the freedom of the seas . . . and limited nuclear wars could devastate numerous regions."[1] There is also Robert Kagan, who insists that the United States has supplied a "reliable security guarantee" which "has sustained the general peace" and that, were the Americans to retreat from their ordering responsibilities, "the jungle will grow back."[2] Unburdened by cluttering nuance or further explanation, Jake Sullivan, a foreign policy advisor in the Obama White House and a senior policy advisor to Hillary Clinton's 2016 campaign, assures us that "The fact that the major powers have not returned to war with one another since 1945 is a remarkable achievement of American statecraft." And, if US forces had been withdrawn from Europe and Asia, those regions "would look far different, and possibly far darker, today."[3] Bradley Thayer considers US power to be a "force for stability" that "causes many positive outcomes for the world" and that "Pax Americana" reduces the likelihood of war, particularly great power war.[4] Other analysts voice concern that, without the United States in charge, Europe might become incapable of securing itself from various threats materializing from somewhere or other, and that this could be destabilizing within the region and beyond while making the Europeans potentially vulnerable to the "influence" of outside rising powers. They also worry that Israel, Egypt, and/or Saudi Arabia might do something nutty in the Middle East and that Japan and South Korea might get nuclear weapons.[5] The United States, it is said, is the "guarantor of the world order."[6]

This line of thinking essentially rests on a counterfactual, although one rarely carefully assessed by its advocates: if, contrary to fact, the United States had (complacently) withdrawn from the world after 1945, things would have turned out much differently and, most likely, far worse.

I question that counterfactual. To do so, I draw on the discussion in this book to examine a competing counterfactual in which the United States substantially withdraws from providing military security in the postwar world, but remains an active international citizen otherwise. I conclude that the positive developments of the post-World War II era would likely mostly have happened even without much American security participation, and I contend that, for the most part, it was not the machinations of the reigning superpower that was instrumental, but the aversion to international war that was embraced after World War II especially by developed countries.

It was primarily this phenomenon, not nuclear fears or American efforts at security provision, that led to the remarkable condition of international peace that has risen since 1945. And it seems to me, in addition, that the establishment of norms and institutions, economic advance, and the progress of democratization are not so much the cause of international peace and aversion to international war as their consequence. That is, the aversion to international war should be seen as an explanatory or facilitating variable.[7]

We are thus into dueling counterfactuals here, a dicey condition in which proof is difficult and the best one can usually hope for is to establish a degree of shaky plausibility for a proposition. But the bold counterfactual assertions of the Pax Americanists as relayed above have only rarely been scrutinized, and to do so could be valuable on multiple levels. Thus, Thayer argues that US leadership "reduced friction among many states that were historical antagonists – most notably France and West Germany," while Bruce Russett and John Oneal credit a US-supported European security community for making armed conflict between France and Germany "unthinkable."[8] However, others might look at the condition differently. They would note, first, that there are quite a few clever people in France and Germany, and that over the centuries this quality has been used to discover a considerable number of ways to get into wars with each other. However, they might continue, there does not seem to be anyone in either country, even standing on a soapbox, who, since 1945, has advocated resuming the venerable tradition. This is a rather profound change and one, it might be plausibly suspected, that has not come about because the French and Germans have become less clever or because they needed cues from afar to appreciate the value of peace and the stupidities of war.

EXAMINING A COUNTERFACTUAL: AMERICA WITHDRAWS
IN THE SECURITY FIELD

Suppose, then, that the United States had retreated in 1945 to a sort of truculent isolationism in which it remained engaged economically and as a world citizen, continued to maintain a limited military force (including some nuclear weapons), but was not willing to provide military security abroad. It seems likely – entirely plausible – under that condition that the world would not look all that much different. That is, given the growth of aversion to international war and of an appreciation of its stupidity, it seems unlikely that the United States, with or without nuclear weapons, was necessary for the international security that emerged after World War II, particularly in the developed world.[9]

The United States does have a few specific security achievements. It can take credit for keeping South Korea independent – no other country at the time would have been able to do that.[10] However, as discussed in Chapter 1, it went to war there in 1950 for other reasons, and it badly botched the effort and massively increased the costs by a futile quest to liberate North Korea as well. The American military also forcefully pushed thuggish rulers out of tiny

Panama and even tinier Grenada – rather minor developments that would not have happened (as quickly at least) without the efforts of the United States. It also led a lengthy bombing campaign that resulted in the secession of Serbia's Kosovo province, and it productively used airpower to contribute to the downfall of ISIS in the 2010s as discussed in Chapter 5.

Beyond this, its specific contributions to world security are difficult to find.

The emergence of peace in Western Europe and Japan after World War II does likely owe something to American policy, and it can certainly take credit for being important in helping to establish a condition in which the losers of the Second World War came to view the world in much the same way as those who had bombed Dresden and Hiroshima, emerging as key contributors to an orderly world in the process. The United States was certainly strongly supportive of such developments and, in agreement with other war victors such as the United Kingdom and France, it wisely did not institute a vindictive policy against the war's losers. This was one of the most impressive instances of enlightened self-interest in history.

However, the United States hardly *forced* that to happen due to its "hegemonic" status. It may have nudged, persuaded, and encouraged the process to move along, but it had a highly responsive audience in devastated peoples who were most ready to embrace the message. That is, as discussed in Chapter 1, the war-exhausted people in those areas scarcely needed the United States to decide that war among them was a really stupid idea.

There was understandable concern (on all sides) about the potential rise of Germany in Europe. But it seems unlikely that the United States (or NATO) was required to keep Germany "down," as it is frequently put. As discussed in the Prologue, there had been no popular or political drive for war in Germany in the 1930s and, absent Hitler, it is likely the war in Europe would never have come about. Such an absolutely necessary ingredient for war (another Hitler) did not emerge on the scene after 1945, and, with the vivid memory of the disastrous war close at hand, it would likely have been quenched if it had.

It is conceivable that, without the American military presence, the Soviets would have been a bit more militarily assertive in Europe after World War II, particularly over the status of Berlin. But, given their bone-deep wariness about again getting into another war, the Soviets were far more likely to rely on the ideologically preferred methods of subversion and licit and illicit support for like-minded comrades in such places as Italy and France. They were often brutally dominant in the areas of Europe that were under the control of their military forces. But they couldn't even project this to such nominally friendly turf as Yugoslavia, which successfully broke with Moscow at the end of the 1940s, carving out a separate existence for itself – the Soviet Union was hardly a "hegemon" outside its direct area, or sphere, of control.

Indeed, it seems likely that, not only was the United States unnecessary to these developments, but that it was more nearly the follower than the leader in the process. Geir Lundestad has memorably argued that, although the United States established something of what might be called an "empire," in Western Europe after World War II, it was an "empire by invitation."[11] However, Lundestad may have chosen his words with an excessive amount of graciousness. To a considerable degree, the United States was not "invited" to become a major presence in Europe, but snookered into doing so. Concerned about what appeared to be a hostile military colossus to the east, Western Europeans wanted the United States, at its own expense, to provide additional military protection. As Michael Mastanduno points out, "Western European states gained security protection by pulling an initially reluctant, but eventually willing, United States into the NATO alliance."[12]

The Cold War would likely have come out the same no matter what policy the Americans followed.

To begin with, it certainly seems clear, as detailed in Chapter 1, that the Soviet Union had no interest whatever in getting into any sort of major war with or without nuclear weapons no matter how the United States happened to choose to array its nuclear (or nonnuclear) arsenal. Insofar as the Soviets wanted to "take over" other countries, they anticipated that this could come about through revolutionary or civil war processes within those countries, ones that, assisted and encouraged by the Communist states, would bring into control congenial, like-minded people and groups that would willingly join the Communist camp. Military measures designed to deter direct, Hitler-style military aggression simply had no relevance in that case.

This proposition would have held even if the United States had backed into a form of security isolationism. In the singularly unlikely event that the Soviet Union ever came seriously to contemplate military expansion to the west under that condition, it would in all probability still have been deterred from attacking Western Europe by the enormous potential of the American war machine. The problem for the USSR was that, even if it had the ability and the desire to blitz Western Europe (and even if there were no nuclear weapons to worry about), it could not have stopped the United States from repeating what it did after 1941: mobilizing with deliberate speed, putting its economy onto a wartime footing, and wearing the enemy down in a protracted conventional major war of attrition massively supplied from an unapproachable distance.

International Communism's real threat, or challenge, was not in the prospect for direct military action, but in its application of subversion and in its support, with varying degrees of subtlety, of congenial forces in other areas. It presented – or seemed to present – an ideology with some appeal: its model of class warfare and revolution often seemed to some to promise to right the wrongs of the capitalist world. Although the United States did ardently seek to oppose the ideology and its appeals, Communism ultimately self-destructed as suggested in Chapter 2: it collapsed mostly because of its own systemic inadequacies and misplaced spending priorities, not because of American policy machinations. The failed American war in Vietnam, designed to reverse Communist advances, was tragically misguided and unnecessary. Moreover, Communist expansionary ventures proved to be impotent, ineffective, and often counter-productive, and the biggest disaster for the advance of international Communism – the violent overthrow of internal Communism in Indonesia in 1965 – came as a complete surprise to American policymakers. Various lunatic Communist enterprises, such as Mao's Great Leap Forward and Great Proletarian Cultural Revolution in China, were wildly self-destructive, but they were scarcely generated by anything the United States did.

The settlement of outstanding issues concerning arrangements in central and eastern Europe became the first major task of the post-Cold War era as noted in Chapter 3. The United States certainly contributed to this remarkable process, but if it had instead simply been wistfully observing developments from across the Atlantic, the process would surely have taken place anyway – it was primarily set in motion and consummated by a permissive environment in Gorbachev's Moscow.

Turning to other developments in the first post-Cold War decade, the United States did very much take the lead in pushing Saddam Hussein's invading forces out of neighboring Kuwait in 1991. However, American hege-monic mastery in this case consisted mainly of begging the international community, which already agreed that Iraq's invasion of Kuwait was unaccept-able, to please, please, please let it launch a war to repel the invaders while taking all the casualties itself. That the bemused observers allowed themselves to be persuaded scarcely constitutes a supreme exercise in domination. Moreover, the military achievement was less than monumental. As pointed out in Chapter 3, Saddam's army, outgunned, outmanned, and bereft of strategy, tactics, training, defenses, morale, and leadership, scarcely presented much of a challenge. Moreover, the American war, and the tens of thousands of deaths that emerged in its execution and particularly in its aftermath, could probably have been avoided entirely: serious negotiations (with some con-cessions) might well have liberated Kuwait.

Other post-Cold War ventures in the 1990s included a pacifying mission in Somalia that became a military fiasco, while a subsequent genocide in Rwanda was met simply with wary and anxious watchfulness. The United States did provide a forum for contesting sides in the Bosnian war to settle their differences, but this happened only after the Serb side had been substantially routed by comparatively disciplined Croatian and Muslim armies and after the desperate Serbs had enlisted a man to lead the negotiations who for years had been strongly in favor of just such a settlement. At the end of the decade, NATO, with the US in the lead, bombed Serbia to withdraw thuggish forces from its Kosovo province. Although the bombing triggered deprivations by thugs and went on for months, it did eventually result in the secession of the province.

In the new century, as discussed in Chapter 4, American military policy, far from creating and preserving order, has mainly created and preserved disorder. In some perverse sense it may at least have actually achieved something that might be considered to be a degree of "indispensability" in that it carried out its aggressive wars in the Middle East essentially alone. It did have some material support at the start from NATO allies in Afghanistan, but this faded over time, and most of its friends tried to dissuade it from its ill-destined adventure in Iraq. But, far from visiting peace and contentment on lesser peoples, its military policy during the period has mostly been an abject failure. In conducting this policy, which has led to the deaths of hundreds of thousands of people, the United States has applied military muscularity primarily to deal with two perceived threats to world and US security that, as argued in Chapters 4, 5, and 6, have been massively exaggerated: international terrorism and nuclear proliferation.

The American military contribution was more restrained in two other failed military ventures in the new century as discussed in Chapter 5. Egged on by NATO allies, particularly Britain and France, it was instrumental (and perhaps even indispensable) in creating chaos in Libya by helping to topple the regime there. And when disorder broke out in a civil war in Syria, the United States, like many other outside states, stepped in to preserve it by variously supporting one group or another in an especially chaotic civil war that might have ended early but for the diverse supporting cast of interveners.

FABRICATING RULES AND INSTITUTIONS, PROMOTING ECONOMIC DEVELOPMENT, AND EXPANDING DEMOCRACY

The United States may have been helpful after World War II in fabricating international rules and institutions, promoting economic development, and expanding democracy. But, as with security arrangements, it was scarcely necessary. The impelling, or facilitating, cause in the process was the aversion toward international war.

That is, the establishment and maintenance of a culture of peace, or freedom from international war, may cause, or at least productively facilitate, other developments.[13] And, insofar as there is a causal relationship between international peace, institutions, capitalism, and democracy, it may be best to see peace as the independent variable – a condition that causes, or facilitates, the others. As Richard Betts puts it for institutions of collective security, "peace is the premise of the system, not the product."[14]

If international peace is the general expectation, it becomes much easier to create institutions and to fabricate rules and conventions that are intended to be supportive and reinforcing. But it is primarily the deep desire for peace that causes the conventions and rules, not the other way around – rather in the way that the rule about driving on one side of the street has been the result, not the cause, of a rather widespread desire to avoid being killed by oncoming traffic. Included in this was the establishment of a norm about territorial integrity.

The general response to World War II, none too surprisingly, was "let's not do that again." To carry out this deeply impelling desire, it was necessary to determine what that conflagration had, after all, been about. The general conclusion was that it had been about territory: Hitler sought living space to the east, Mussolini domination in Africa and the Balkans, the Japanese glorious empire in east and southeast Asia. This was not a new or unique discovery or conclusion. Wars may have been immediately motivated by ideology, religion, pique, aggressive impulse, military rivalry, nationalism, revenge, economic deprivation or exuberance, or the lust for battle, but such impelling motives and passions have generally been expressed in a quest to conquer and to possess territory for as far back as history has been recorded – and probably long before. Thus, observes John Vasquez, territory is "a general underlying cause of war," and "few interstate wars are fought without any territorial issue being involved in one way or another."[15]

Therefore, it would appear that a potential cure for most war – at least international war – would be to disallow territorial expansion by states. And, after a certain amount of shuffling around, that is what the peacemakers of 1945 set out to do. The League of Nations (which the United States never joined) had set up a system, or device, in which the world would be divided up into various chunks whose representatives would agree not to change borders by force.[16] Following the same logic after World War II, international boundaries were again declared essentially to be sacrosanct – that is, unalterable by the use or threat of military force – no matter how illogical or unjust some of them might seem to interested parties. And the peoples residing in the chunks of territory contained within them would be expected to establish governments which, no matter how disgusting or reprehensible, would then be dutifully admitted to a special club of "sovereign" states known as the United Nations. Efforts to change international frontiers by force or the threat of force were pejoratively labeled "aggression" and sternly declared to be unacceptable.

Rather amazingly, this process has, for various reasons and for the most part, worked. Although many international frontiers were in dispute, although there remained vast colonial empires in which certain countries possessed certain other countries or proto-countries, and although some of the largest states quickly became increasingly enmeshed in a profound ideological and military rivalry known as the Cold War, the prohibition against territorial aggression has been remarkably successful. In the decades since 1945, there have been many cases in which countries split through internal armed rebellion (including anti-colonial wars). However, reversing the experience and patterns of all recorded history, the only time one United Nations member tried to conquer another to incorporate it into its own territory was when Iraq "anachronistically" (to apply Michael Howard's characterization) invaded Kuwait in 1990, an act that inspired almost total condemnation in the world and one that was reversed in 1991 by military force.[17] The United States took the lead in this enterprise, but, as discussed earlier, it likely could have been accomplished by negotiation.

There are, however, a couple of problematic elements to the territorial integrity norm. In principle, it pretty much requires restraint when a country establishes a regime that is monumentally corrupt or incompetent or vicious to its own people. As discussed in Chapter 3, however, norms have evolved allowing international intervention in such cases if the UN's Security Council approves, but this process has not been invoked very often. Additionally, it essentially allows other countries to intervene on one side or the other in another country's civil war as long as they don't actually seek to take over the country. Figure 0.1 suggests that this has become increasingly common as seen recently, in particular, in the enormously destructive Syrian civil war that began in 2011. Moreover, despite the norm, there have continued to be small numbers of border conflicts between states which sometimes result in land seizures. For the most part, however, these have been over small pieces of territory with the "conquerors" working very hard to keep their ventures from escalating to war.[18] More generally, historian John Gaddis notes that during the Cold War there were "many occasions … in relations between Washington and Moscow that in almost any other age, and among almost any other antagonists, would sooner or later have produced war." Yet, he observes, the statesmen of the era "have, compared to their predecessors, been exceedingly cautious in risking war with one another."[9]

The United States played an important role in these developments, but it is scarcely obvious that it was a necessary one. The process was simply an updating of an idea that had first been put into effect some 25 years earlier, and it was impelled primarily by a desire to find a gimmick that would make international war rare or even expunge the idea entirely, not by the peculiar wishes of a single player. Moreover, in a condition in which there is a strong aversion to international war, it is not clear that a norm specifically banning military conquest is necessary.[20] It is, in fact, redundant. The only way to gain substantial territory by force is, obviously, to go to war. If war is no longer an acceptable method for resolving such issues, conquest will no longer happen.

As the first country to shrug off colonial overlordship, the United States often took the lead in the remarkable demise of colonialism. Its efforts may have helped speed the process, but, as Neta Crawford documents, it was one that had been underway for a considerable period of time.[21] That is, the institution was already waning, importantly impelled by the gathering realization among exhausted, war-torn colonial powers that colonies were scarcely worth maintaining, especially when local rebellions began to increase the costs of the upkeep.

The second half of the twentieth century saw a great expansion of international trade as well as of interdependence and communication, but this is more likely to be the consequence of peace than the cause of it.

If Europeans hardly needed the United States to decide that war among them was a really stupid idea, they did not need it to instill in them the notion that economic development and the quest for its ensuing prosperity was a smart one. In particular, the Germans and the Japanese were fully ready for a return to the comparative liberalism of the 1920s. American efforts may have speeded economic growth, but they were not essential. Its efforts probably did improve business and investor confidence somewhat in postwar Europe – an atmospheric contribution that is difficult to quantify – but it is difficult to imagine that European businesses would have failed to generate that on their own as peace continued to reign. And, although Michael Beckley and his associates argue that security-induced US subsidies helped Japanese economic growth in the 1960s, they concede that, otherwise, growth would still likely have been "solid."[22] In the process, misguided advice from the United States was corrected. In Japan, for example, the vision of the foreign overlords was of a country that would produce trinkets and cocktail napkins; the Japanese had other ideas.[23]

Moreover, any "leadership" in the process from the United States was substantially due to the huge size of its economy – all it had to do was allow access. The role of the United States in the reconstruction of international economic order may have been "central" after World War II, as Mastanduno argues.[24] But, however facilitating, it was not essentially necessary – Melvyn Leffler characterizes American help as "wise" and "prudent," but "marginal."[25] And, of course, Europeans and others were always quite pleased to accept bailout money like the Marshall Plan.[26] More generally, whatever the United States was doing, the world would need to settle such issues as fishing rights, territorial disputes, and the regulation of international trade. Actually, the United States has sometimes been more of a laggard than a leader in the process. For example, it is among the handful of countries yet to agree to the regulations embodied in the Law of the Sea Convention.[27]

The quest for international peace specifically affected trade and economic development in two ways.

The first derives from the fact that international tensions and the prospect of international war have a strong dampening effect on trade because each threatened nation has an incentive to cut itself off from the rest of the world economically in order to ensure that it can survive if international exchange is severed by military conflict.[28] By contrast, if countries that have previously been in a conflictual relationship lapse into a comfortable peace and become extremely unlikely to get into war, businesses in both places are likely to explore the possibilities for mutually beneficial exchange. But it is the peace that causes – or facilitates – the trade and consequent economic development, not the other way around.[29] Adam Smith once observed that "Little else is requisite to carry a state to the highest degree of opulence from the lowest barbarism, but peace, easy taxes, and a tolerable administration of justice."[30] Much the same can be said for the international order. Businesses tend to hate the uncertainty which inevitably accompanies war and the prospect of war. As Dwight Eisenhower once put it, "Every war is going to astonish you." In general, business people do not like to be astonished.

However, a culture of international peace is not sufficient for trade expansion to come about. It is necessary as well that free international trade be accepted as a good thing. If people think that wealth and wellbeing develop best when government isolates the country from foreign completion and investment, international trade, however facilitated by peace, will have no effect. Over the decades, the idea, long supported by most economists, that international trade should be more free and open has gradually became accepted, a process that was often halting and incoherent.[31] In fact, as Patrick Porter notes, it took until the 1990s before the notion reached general acceptance.[32] The United States was often, if not always, in support of the process, but it was a worldwide phenomenon, and American coaching and direction were scarcely required for other countries to appreciate the blessings of enhanced prosperity and eventually come to accept the notion that free trade was the best way to achieve it.

Second, the quest for peace has often led to the self-conscious development of economic arrangements as a device to promote peace even if the impact might not be particularly helpful economically. For example, it was the deep desire for international peace, not American machinations or simple economic considerations, that was the impelling force for the creation of the coal and steel community between France and Germany, an arrangement that eventually evolved into the European Union. The "original impetus" for this, notes Michael Mandelbaum, came "from the belief in the pacifying impact of international economic interconnections."[33] Or as its chief author, Robert Schuman, put it in 1950, the aim was to make war "not only unthinkable, but materially impossible."[34] That is, the motivating force was clearly the desire for peace: its inventors believed that if France and Germany more or less combined their economies they would be less likely to get into war with each other. However, the Germans and the French scarcely needed the gimmick, and its premise is challenged by the fact that countries with fully integrated economies have often still somehow managed to get into civil wars. But it was the desire for peace that caused the gimmick, not the other way around. If you could have convinced its authors that it was bad economics (labor unions tried at the time), they would still have gone ahead: they were primarily motivated by the pursuit of peace, not economic betterment. And it was a European idea, not an American one, one that would have been pursued even if the United States had withdrawn from the European scene.

Thus, since many of the institutions that have been fabricated in Europe have been specifically designed to reduce the danger of war between erstwhile enemies, it is difficult to see why the institutions should get the credit for the peace that has flourished there for the last three-quarters of a century, but they frequently do.[35] They are among the consequences of the remarkable international peace that has enveloped Western Europe since 1945, not its cause.

The process is also seen in the fabrication of the Bretton Woods agreement of 1944 to govern international monetary relations. This was impelled primarily by alarm over the mismanagement of currency exchange rates which, it was supposed, importantly helped cause World War II. According to its chief architect, the absence of such economic collaboration would "inevitably result in economic warfare that will be but the prelude and instigator of military warfare."[36] Possessed with by far the largest economy in the world at the time, the United States was instrumental in reaching the agreement and in carrying it out. But a repeat of World War II was scarcely in the cards in its aftermath no matter how currency exchange rates fluttered, and the world seems to have survived quite well even when the Americans abruptly and unilaterally abandoned the scheme in 1971.

The desire for international peace impelled American foreign economic policy as well. Thus, Mastanduno notes that

> For U.S. officials, economics and security were inextricably linked. Depression had led to war; enemies in the marketplace became enemies on the battlefield. Officials in the Truman administration believed that the restoration of economic prosperity would encourage peaceful relations among the world's powers.[37]

The connection is made specific in President Harry Truman's 1947 speech announcing the Truman Doctrine when he concludes that poor economic development leads to totalitarianism which leads in turn to war:

> The seeds of totalitarian regimes are nurtured by misery and want. They spread and grow in the evil soil of poverty and strife. They reach their full growth when the hope of a people for a better life has died. We must keep that hope alive. . . . If we falter in our leadership, we may endanger the peace of the world – and we shall surely endanger the welfare of our own nation.[38]

That is, it is the quest for international peace that was taken to make worldwide economic growth especially desirable, not the reverse.

Something like that may hold as well for the connection between peace and democracy: peace causes – or, more likely, facilitates – democracy.[39] Countries often restrict or even abandon democracy when domestic instability or external military threat seems to loom. By the same token, when they are comfortably at peace, people may come to realize that they no longer require a strongman to provide order and can afford to embrace the comparative benefits of democracy even if those might come with somewhat heightened uncertainty and disorderliness and possibly with the potential for less reliable leadership. That is, peace may furnish countries with the security and space in which to explore and develop democracy because democracy and democratic idea entrepreneurs are more likely to flourish when the trials, distortions, and disruptions of war – whether international or civil – are absent.

There were important advancements for democracy in the aftermath of World War II, a development that was certainly encouraged by the United

States. However, that encouragement was probably not necessary. Most of Western Europe had already accepted the system by then, and Germany, Italy, and Japan had had experience with democracy earlier and had seen the ruin that resulted when democracy was abandoned for regimes favoring militaristic expansion.

There was also a remarkable expansion of democracy after 1975, starting in Spain and Portugal and then spreading to almost all of Latin America as well as to South Korea, to Taiwan, and to some countries in southeast Asia, most notably Indonesia. Early in the twentieth century, the putatively "hegemonic" United States had tried to impose democracy by military means upon some countries in Latin America, with results that were dismal. This time. it mostly stood back, watching and encouraging, and perhaps leading by example – though it did, as noted, use force successfully to reimpose democracy when it lapsed in Grenada and Panama, and it also did some apt poking in the Philippines. Samuel Huntington supplies a considerable number of reasons for the phenomenon in what he calls "the third wave" of democratization, and he argues that American efforts were important in several cases. In these, the United States variously applied measures that had earlier failed in such episodes as the invasions of Nicaragua early in the century and in the strenuous and urgent efforts of the Alliance for Progress in the 1960s.[40] This time, they worked, But it seems more reasonable to suggest that this time the efforts struck a responsive chord rather than that they created one. Thus, American-armed efforts to install, or re-install, democracy in Grenada and Panama lasted, while similar ventures earlier had failed to do so after the American troops left. However, its somewhat similar efforts in Haiti did not work out so well, and the United States eventually gave up in disgust. It might be added that, although a culture of international peace may have helped facilitate democratic development in Latin America, it is not at all clear that democracy was necessary for the ensuing international peace there. The area has been free of international war since 1975, but that was mostly true as well for the 100 years before that during which only a few countries in the area were democratic.

The impressive advance in democracy (and capitalism) in countries in East Central Europe that escaped the Soviet embrace after 1989 was discussed in Chapter 3. This advance did not require much participation by the United States. The chief role model, as had been the case for Spain and Portugal in the mid-1970s, was that supplied by the open, productive, and prosperous countries in Western Europe, not by the United States. The newly liberated countries were attracted to the European Union and NATO – two clubs they could join if they came up to standards. For the most part, they were quite willing to try.

How much worse, then, would the world have turned out if the United States had adopted an isolationist perspective on security matters after World War II? A plausible answer, it appears, is "not much." The demands arising from war aversion and the ardent quest for international peace after the conflagration of World War II would have sufficed, and peace itself can often facilitate trade, the establishment of effective international rules, economic progress, and democratization. For the most part, the United States has not only failed to be indispensable, but, to a substantial degree, even to be necessary. The United States certainly contributed, but the process is aptly summarized by Stephen Walt: "Although the United States was almost always acting in its own self-interest, the fact that others had similar interests made it easier to persuade them to go along."[41]

And it should be stressed that, insofar as the United States has been indispensable in the twenty-first century, it has been in the dispensing of war and disorder, not peace and order. It remains to be seen whether it will continue the process in dealing with the threats it seems to want to believe are presented by China and Russia as well as by North Korea, Iran, and cyber.[42]

It must be said, however, that in one important respect, the achievement of the United States in this century is really quite amazing, even monumental.

It has expended multiple trillions of dollars in waging, or participating in, a series of unnecessary and hugely destructive wars and military errands abroad in which hundreds of thousands of people have perished. It has also expended more than a trillion dollars on a much-overwrought campaign against terrorists at home as discussed, and lamented, in Chapter 4. At the same time it has undergone, and endured, a decade-long, and therefore great, economic recession. And, rationalized by a truly creative ability to espy threat on (and well over) the horizon, it also continues extravagantly and wastefully to maintain, and even to expand, a much-adored, if bloated and unnecessary, military force that is by far the largest and most expensive in the world.

Yet, it has survived quite nicely. It still remains vigorous and quite desirable, even admirable, in many respects, and it sports an economy that, although potentially dangerously debt-ridden, continued to churn along rather impressively. That is, even following policies that were foolish, wantonly destructive, and absurdly costly, it emerged prosperous, productive, whole, and, of course, arrogant. The country is so strong, it can't even be destroyed by itself. In 2020, its often-muddled response to a new challenge by a global pandemic did not win the United States accolades for competence, but it will likely survive even that.

ANARCHY AS A DESIRABLE CONDITION?

In the immediate aftermath of World War II, Albert Einstein, along with fellow scientists and many others, fancied with a confidence bordering on intellectual arrogance that he had managed to discover the single device that could solve the problem of world peace: "*Only* the creation of a world government can prevent the impending self-destruction of mankind." Or, as Edward Teller, a physicist who was later to be instrumental in the development of the hydrogen bomb, put it in 1946, world government "*alone* can give us freedom and peace." Philosopher Bertrand Russell was equally certain: "It is entirely clear," he declared, "that there is *only one way* in which great wars can be permanently prevented and that is the establishment of an international government with a monopoly of serious armed force." And Robert Oppenheimer proclaimed with a similarly unclouded clarity of vision that "without world government, there could be no permanent peace," while Hans J. Morgenthau forcefully concluded, "There is no shirking the conclusion that international peace cannot be permanent without a world state."[43]

Without concerning himself with the fact that even states with well-armed and capable governments have nonetheless often managed to devolve into catastrophic civil war, Einstein insisted that world government was both an "absolute" and an "immediate" necessity, and suggested that it might emerge naturally out of the United Nations.[44] As it happens, peace between major countries has been maintained – there have been, to use Russell's term, no "great wars" – and international war more generally has notably declined. However, the United Nations deserves little credit for this remarkable development, and world government none at all.

In fact, if the nearly 200 states that constitute, or inhabit, the world order come substantially to abandon the idea that international war is a sensible method for solving problems among themselves, the notion that they live in a condition of "anarchy" becomes misleading and could encourage undesirable policy developments.

Technically, of course, the concept is accurate: there exists no international government that effectively polices the behavior of the nations of the world. It is, as Kenneth Waltz puts it, a condition of "self help."[45] The problem with the word lies in its inescapable connotations: it implies chaos, lawlessness, disorder, confusion, and both random and focused violence.[46] Waltz argues that under anarchy states "must experience conflict and will occasionally fall into violence."[47] And realist scholar John Mearsheimer argues that in a condition of anarchy, "there is little room for trust among states" and "security will often be scarce."[48]

Insofar as this perspective is a useful way to look at international politics, it holds only where the idea is generally accepted that violence is a suitable and useful method for doing business, as was standard throughout almost all of history during what Oona Hathaway and Scott Shapiro call "the Old World Order."[49] If that idea is abandoned – that is, if a culture of peace between nations is accepted – "anarchy" could become a desirable state. It would be equally accurate to characterize the international situation as "unregulated," a word with connotations that are far different, and perhaps far more helpful. What would emerge is what Hanns Maull calls a "system of cooperation and conflict among highly interdependent partners."[50]

The perspective also suggests that, as argued throughout this book, a huge military force-in-being is scarcely required and challenges by such countries as China and Russia are highly unlikely to lead to direct warfare. In addition, if it is the case that the United States has not been crucial for establishing and maintaining the world order, that order can survive, or work around to accommodate or undercut, various challenges that might be thrown at it by the United States – by the administration of Donald J. Trump, for example.[51] However deflating such conclusions might be to American triumphalists, it is good news more generally: maintenance of the "world order" is based on a general aversion to international war and does not depend on the United States. Moreover, if an aversion to international war caused the decline of such wars, occasional offensive behavior by one state or another will not change that regularity any more that the norm about everybody driving on the same side of the road can be undermined by the occasional misdirected drunk.

The constituent states of the world order might still harbor a great number of problems and disputes to work out. And with the United States firmly in the lead, they may continue to espy and inflate theat and to bloat their military budgets in mindless response to such imaginings – propensities lamented at length in this book.

But if, reversing the course of several millennia, they come to accept the idea that war is a decidedly stupid method for resolving their disputes, they would scarcely require an effective world government to avoid that once-venerable institution. Nor would they need a "hegemonic" United States.

APPENDIX:

A Sardonic Litany

At various points over the last three-quarters of a century, important people in the United States and elsewhere have seriously maintained, or have effectively maintained, a considerable number of assertions and propositions that have proven, this book suggests, to be wanting.

THE COLD WAR AND DETERRENCE

Although those running world affairs after World War II were the same people or the intellectual heirs of the people who had tried desperately to prevent that cataclysm, they were so incompetent, risk acceptant, or stupid that it was *only* visions of mushroom clouds that kept them from stumbling into a repeat performance.

In recent Western history, war has followed war in an ascending order of intensity, and it is clear that the War of 1939–45 was not the climax of this crescendo movement.

Although the Soviet Union had suffered enormously from a war imposed on it by an attacking army and could scarcely want to undergo anything resembling a repetition (with or without nuclear weapons), and, although its guiding ideology was built around subversion, class warfare, and civil war as methods for expansion, it was necessary to spend between $5 and $10 trillion on a nuclear arsenal to deter it from starting a global war that it did not want to wage.

It is only due to luck that the United States and the Soviet Union could rather unexpectedly go 50 years without engaging in direct war with each other and that they could have tens of thousands of thermonuclear weapons pointed at one another and never use any of them.

If the United States had not been essentially running things after World War II, the Western European countries would scarcely have been able to figure out that war in the area was a really stupid idea and that open trade among them was a good one.

If the United States had not been essentially running things after World War II, the war-ravaged Japanese would scarcely been able to figure out that war was a really stupid idea and that democracy, trade, and capitalist development were good ones.

If North Korea had been successful in taking over South Korea by military force in 1950, this, as President Harry Truman concluded, would have led, with certainty, to World War III.

The fact that Nikita Khrushchev was wary about having arms control inspectors running around his country meant that he had a huge arsenal to hide, not that he was afraid they would find out how militarily weak the Soviet Union was.

Although both sides in the Cuban missile crisis were led by men determined to keep the crisis from escalating to any sort of war, the world was at the brink of nuclear oblivion and would have helplessly toppled over it if one nuclear weapon had been detonated under water somewhere in the Atlantic Ocean.

If the Soviets had been able to implant nuclear-tipped missiles in Cuba, marginally increasing their nuclear capacity, there was a severe danger that they would suicidally use them to attack the United States rather than let them gather cobwebs (like other nuclear weapons around the world) until the Cubans eventually polished them up as tourist attractions for visiting Americans.

If one nuclear bomb or device goes off someplace in the world, total destruction of the human race is the likely eventual consequence.

THE COLD WAR AND CONTAINMENT

During the Cold War, the tiny Communist Party in the United States was filled with masters of deceit who were working insidiously and invisibly to take over the government and might well have been able to do so despite the fact that they seem to have had difficulty even infiltrating the occasional schoolboard in, for example, suburban Boston.

President John F. Kennedy was certainly correct to very seriously consider bombing Chinese nuclear facilities and to declare that "A Chinese nuclear test is likely to be historically the most significant and worst event of the 1960s," but it is incorrect to suggest that "historically the most significant and worst event of the 1960s" actually stemmed from his decision to begin to send American troops in substantial numbers to Vietnam largely to confront the Chinese threat that he came to believe lurked there.

If North Vietnam had been successful in taking over South Vietnam by military force in 1965, this, as President Lyndon Baines Johnson concluded, would have led, with certainty, to World War III.

If the Communists had been able to take over South Vietnam at some time other than the one they actually *did* do so, a huge number of other countries would have fallen into the Communist orbit and this would have precipitated World War III.

Despite the fact that the Communists in Vietnam were willing to accept battle deaths at a rate higher than had been borne by almost any combatant force in any international or colonial war in the previous 150 years, there was some US military policy that could have caused them to break.

President Richard Milhous Nixon said in 1970 that the United States would be seen as a "pitiful, helpless giant" if it lost its war in Vietnam, but that was no longer true in 1975.

The Vietnam debacle of 1975 came up almost not at all in the election campaign of 1976, but this does not refute the concern, repeatedly voiced during the war, that a Communist victory in Vietnam would lead to a new round of McCarthyism and political instability in the United States.

Although Gibbon was correct to conclude that "there is nothing more contrary to nature than the attempt to hold in obedience distant provinces," the best way to confront the challenge presented by the Soviet Union during the Cold War was to keep it from gathering distant provinces to hold in obedience.

Although it may have seemed that the Soviet Union sent troops to Afghanistan in 1979 in a desperate effort to replace an incompetent Communist client regime that was losing a civil war there, the venture, as President Jimmy Carter concluded, was actually part of a master plan in which the Soviets were attempting to dominate the entire Middle East.

In 1983, the civil war in Lebanon, which lasted until the 1990s, constituted, as President Ronald Reagan insisted, a threat to all the people of the world, not just to the Middle East itself.

Although the Cold War ended when the Soviet Union mellowed its ideology about the need to aggressively export class conflict, the Cold War was not really about ideology but about the distribution of military capabilities, something that did not change at the time at all.

THE POST-COLD WAR DECADE

If the Cold War was characterized as a jungle with a large dragon and many poisonous snakes, the elimination of the dragon means the jungle became not only more dangerous, but far, far more complex.

Because economics is war by other means, the peaceful development of Japan, once it became excessively prosperous, represented a threat to the United States.

Without the United States, the world might never have discovered that open markets and free trade were good ideas.

Chemical weapons, responsible for less than seven-tenths of 1 percent of the battle fatalities in World War I where they were extensively used, should be placed in the same category of destruction as nuclear ones.

It is sensible to enlarge the definition of "weapons of mass destruction" even to the point where it includes potato guns.

Panama's drug dealing dictator (formerly a US ally and CIA operative) threatened American lives and the safety of the Panama Canal in 1989.

The military coup against democracy in Haiti in 1991 (but not the one in Algeria in 1992 which was focused on Islamists) was a special outrage, and President George Herbert Walker Bush, in sentiments later echoed by President Bill Clinton, was correct to consider it to be an unusual and extraordinary threat to the national security, foreign policy, and economy of the United States.

When Saddam Hussein proclaimed that his military's defense of his invasion of Kuwait would lead to "the mother of all battles," his troops were willing to die to the last man to defend his expansionary whims and fantasies.

Although the Iraqi foe was greatly outnumbered and even more greatly outgunned in the Gulf War of 1991, and although it lacked strategy, tactics, training, defenses, morale, or leadership, the lopsided outcome of that war was due to modern technology, excellent training, high troop quality, fantastic host nation support, the revolutionary potential of emerging technologies, and the power of coherence and simultaneity.

Although Saddam Hussein had a considerable record of cutting deals particularly when he was backed into a corner, it was utterly impossible for him to accept a deal to back out of his rather whimsical invasion of Kuwait.

Although it may be difficult to find the Biblical reference, George Herbert Walker Bush was on sound theological ground when he revealed that Christ had ordained the United States to be a light unto the world.

NATO's bombing of Serb positions in Bosnia ended the war there even though the Bosnian Serbs were already in full retreat from attacks by Croatian and

Muslim forces and had asked a man to negotiate for them who had previously strongly supported a settlement to the war like the one eventually accepted.

The fact that for more than 20 years there have been no episodes (even small ones) of ethnic violence in Bosnia does not negate the convenient notion that the war there had been the product of ancient and immutable ethnic hatreds.

THE TWENTY-FIRST CENTURY

The United States is the one indispensable nation (as part of this, the United States stands taller and can see farther into the future), and this quality is not undermined or even seen to lapse a bit simply because its foreign and military policy in the Middle East in this century has been almost entirely misguided and has resulted in the deaths of hundreds of thousands people there.

The challenge of the 9/11 Commission that there was a "failure of imagination" before the attacks was overwhelmingly reversed when officials imaginatively disclosed in 2002 that there were between 2,000 and 5,000 al-Qaeda operatives loose in the United States (embedded in most US cities usually in the run-down sections talking to each other), and when American leaders and the public determined in 2015 that ISIS, a small band of mostly teenage fanatics in the Middle East who had disgustingly beheaded a few defenseless prisoners, presented a serious threat to the existence or survival of the United States.

Saddam Hussein, who trusted his army so little that he would not issue it many bullets or allow it into Iraq's capital with heavy equipment, was dangerous because he was planning to use this military force to dominate the Middle East.

Because al-Qaeda operatives used box cutters effectively on 9/11, they will, although under siege, soon apply equal, if previously undisclosed, talents in science and engineering to fabricate nuclear weapons and then detonate them on American cities.

Al-Qaeda, a group of perhaps 100 or 200 scrambling around under siege in Pakistan, could commit so much destruction in the United States that the country of 330 million would cease to exist.

Although the underwear bomber's explosive device was far too small to take down the airplane he was riding in and relied on a detonation process that would have been difficult to carry out even in a laboratory, it is perfectly appropriate to say that the scheme was almost successful and to designate the guy who constructed the bomb in Yemen as a master bomb builder.

While it may be true that the vehicle bomb a would-be terrorist tried to detonate at Times Square was almost comically inept in its construction, the venture can still be deemed to be nearly successful because, after all, he did manage to drive the car with the dud to the intended place and then park it.

Terrorist groups in the Middle East, consisting substantially of demented teenage fanatics, should be taken seriously when they divulge online that they have plans to behead the president in the White House and then to forcibly transform America into a Muslim province.

Although Islamist terrorists within the United States and abroad overwhelmingly justify their actions by insisting that their motivating force is hostility to American military policy and to what they see as its concerted war upon Islam in the Middle East, they are actually the prisoners of an ideology that seeks as its primary goal to expunge democracy and its associated values in the West.

There is something plausible about a policy that asks the regime in Syria to coordinate efforts to oppose Islamic State in the civil war there even while suggesting that, after Islamic State is defeated, the United States will seek to violently depose the Syrian regime.

Despite the fact that the Taliban had nothing to do with 9/11 and had been at considerable odds with their al-Qaeda guests who had repeatedly promised not to engage in terrorist activities or even oratory, and despite the fact that the two countries with the best connections to the Taliban, Saudi Arabia and Pakistan, were fully cooperative with the United States after 9/11, there was no method other than military force that could possibly have ousted al-Qaeda from Afghanistan.

When allies like France attempted to dissuade the United States from committing a major debacle by attacking Iraq in 2003, it was entirely fitting to respond to such effrontery by relabeling a fat-laced accompaniment to hamburgers as "freedom fries" while leaving the duly chastised French in a condition of relief that the righteous response had not been extended to include freedom dressing, freedom kissing, and "pardon my freedom."

Although most of the planning for 9/11 was carried out in apartments in Hamburg, Germany, al-Qaeda needs a safe haven to plan a repetition, and that safe haven must be in Afghanistan.

It was entirely fitting and sensible for President George W. Bush to proclaim in the aftermath of 9/11 that America's goal was now to "rid the world of evil,"

even though this would outclass God, who tried, and failed, some time ago
to do the same thing with that flood of His.

The people formulating the NATO charter may have had different scenarios
in mind when, in the wake of World War II, they put together Article 5 in
which an attack on one member is considered to be an attack on all, but they
would have approved activating the clause in 2001 when one member was
attacked by 19 suicidal men armed with box cutters.

Although Islamist terrorists in the United States have been able to kill but six
people per year since 9/11, they present a significant existential threat to the
country that requires the expenditure of trillions of dollars for countermeasures without bothering to evaluate whether those measures remotely
reduce the threat enough to justify their cost.

Although when arrested in the United States Islamist terrorists might overwhelmingly seem to be incompetent, ineffective, ignorant, inadequate,
unorganized, misguided, muddled, amateurish, dopey, unrealistic, moronic,
irrational, foolish, and gullible, they are actually relentless, patient, opportunistic, and flexible, show an understanding of the potential consequence of
carefully planned attacks on economic, transportation, and symbolic targets,
seriously threaten national security, and could inflict mass casualties, weaken
the economy, and damage public morale and confidence.

That Islamist terrorists have been able to kill but six people a year since 9/11 in
the United States is due to the effectiveness of counterterrorism measures
and not to the fact that their numbers are small, their determination limp,
and their competence poor and that they are inclined to announce their
agonies and hostilities over social media, often with pictures to prove it.

PRESENT CONCERNS

Although the major countries of the developed world have now remained at
peace with each other for a long period of time that is utterly without
precedent, this remarkable development has no consequence and should
not be taken to suggest there has been a fundamental change in attitudes
about the desirability of major war.

Coercive measures by the United States and its European allies to facilitate
Kosovo's secession from Serbia in 1999 are utterly irrelevant to Russian
efforts in the secession of Crimea from Ukraine in 2014, and the comparison
should never be brought up in polite company.

Because economics is war by other means, China's peaceful economic development threatens to make it hegemonic in the East Asian area the way the

United States is hegemonic in the Western Hemisphere (where it has magisterially worked to halt the flow of drugs and refugees and is in the process of forcing Mexico to pay for a border wall), and therefore the United States must act to stop or contain China's threatening development and it must use military force to do so should that (regrettably) become necessary.

Although scarcely impressive except in its possession of large numbers of nuclear weapons, Russia's desire to play a larger role on the international stage, and particularly in its geographic area, presents a dire threat.

China's desire to build a road for commerce across Asia and to lease and manage money-losing ports in various places represents a dire threat to the United States as do its efforts to fortify the South China Sea apparently to establish something of a hedge against the possible harassment of vital sea lanes by the US Navy which, at some time or other and without consulting anybody, appointed itself to police what it grandly chooses to call "the global commons."

As part of its role as the ultimate hegemon, the United States should seriously plan for going to war over territorial disputes by other countries over semi-submerged rocks in the South China Sea.

Although the United States has failed to ratify the Law of the Sea and is therefore not bound by it, it has a duty to make sure others do follow the Law's dictates.

Although the Taliban have every reason to distrust and revile al-Qaeda, they will, if successful in Afghanistan (population 35 million and declining), invite the tiny terrorist group back and combine forces not simply to consolidate their hold in that country, but to destabilize the entire area and quite possibly to take over Pakistan (population 200 million and growing).

Large terrorist attacks like 9/11 have become less likely, but, because small ones remain possible, we have become less safe.

The last four words of "The Star-Spangled Banner" accurately characterize Americans' response to the terrorism challenge.

President Barack Hussein Obama's applause line in a West Point speech proclaiming the United States to be "the one indispensable nation" (thereby suggesting that all other nations are, well, dispensable) was an unexceptional observation and was true, as he noted, not only for the entirety of twentieth century but will continue to be true for the entirety of the twenty-first, and the line should not be taken to suggest he was simply trying to raise the bar for authoritative bloviating to the point where even his successor would be humbled.

Since the United States is clearly the one indispensable nation, it is singularly inappropriate for other nations to emit similar inconsequential rattlings and to wallow in such self-important, childish, essentially meaningless, and decidedly fatuous rhetoric.

Although limited military ventures by the United States and others have at low cost sometimes been successful in removing criminal or criminalized regimes or insurgent movements as in Grenada in 1983, Panama in 1989, Rwanda in 1994, Croatia and Bosnia in 1995, East Timor in 1999, Liberia in 2003, Sierra Leone in 2000, Ivory Coast in 2002 and 2011, Mali in 2013, and Central African Republic in 2013, the experience has no relevance to future policy in part because some such interventions have failed.

It was more important to prolong the disastrous civil war in Syria than to bring it to an end even as it became clear that the incoherent anti-Assad rebellion, consisting of 1,200 separately identifiable entities, sustained for years by aid from the outside, was doomed to defeat.

Terrorism experts and counterterrorism officials who have repeatedly and erroneously proclaimed for years that al-Qaeda is on the rise should never be reminded of this and should instead be treated with due deference and asked for their current headline-grabbing, and predictably alarmist, prognostications.

The United State military bears little or no responsibility for the abject military failures in Iraq and Afghanistan, and it should be revered, venerated, repeatedly thanked for its service at keeping America free, and rewarded by having its budget increased so that it can carry out similar missions in the future even better.

Although cyberattacks have yet to kill a single person anywhere in the world, such efforts constitute not only a new and especially insidious form of warfare, but the greatest threat to American security.

No country since 1945 has "used" nuclear weapons for anything other than stoking the national ego or seeking to deter real or imagined threats, and the repeatedly promised cascades, waves, avalanches, and/or epidemics of nuclear proliferation have failed to materialize, but we still need to obsess about the problem.

While the anti-proliferation war against Iraq resulted in more deaths than the bombings of Hiroshima and Nagasaki combined, similar military measures must be used, if necessary, to deal with the potential or actual development of nuclear weapons by such countries as Iran and North Korea no matter how many lives are extinguished in the process.

The fact that America's allies spend proportionately far less than the United States on the military means that they are free riding on American largesse, not that they have been less inclined to inflate any threats that may exist.

Although the United States has meddled in scores, probably hundreds, of elections abroad over the last decades (or maybe centuries), such interference is unjustified and indeed diabolical if it is directed at American elections in part because American voters, in their blissful and heart-warming innocence, can readily be manipulated by the occasional spurious social media post.

The fact that the American military has been unable to train local troops to be effective in Vietnam, Iraq, and Afghanistan should not be taken to suggest the trainers don't know how to do it.

What might be called "fake news" has been a characteristic of political campaigns ever since they were invented as incumbents and challengers mislead, invent, and distort, but it is singularly inappropriate for foreigners, even marginally, to add to the cumulative heap of distorted information.

It is sensible for the United States to perpetuate failed wars indefinitely and at ever greater cost (particularly if the main victims are foreigners) because the alternative would be that the country's credibility would be besmirched.

Although American foreign and military policy in the current century has brought disastrous results to the Middle East leading to the deaths of hundreds of thousands (and hasn't done much better elsewhere), it is vital that the United States lead the world, and suggestions that the role be given over to some other country (Costa Rica comes to mind) on the ground that it could hardly do worse must be met with the airy contempt they so richly deserve.

It can validly be said that we have now entered a new Cold War, but it would be wrong to suggest that this is because the earlier one was, like today's version, characterized by an obsession with threats that did not exist or were destined to self-destruct.

Words and phrases like hegemony, primacy, spheres of influence, balance of power, anarchy, and power actually have some tangible meaning and improve understanding.

Insidious evil forces abroad are capable of undermining faith in American democracy and respect for American values by planting strange stuff on social media.

When a typhoon hits the Philippines, or schoolgirls are kidnapped in Nigeria, or masked men occupy a building in Ukraine, the world looks to America for help, though of course it may from time to time exercise its option not to respond.

Today more people live under elected governments than at any time in history, and this development is entirely due to American diplomacy, foreign assistance, and the sacrifices of its military.

The American invasions in Iraq and Afghanistan may have led to the deaths of hundreds of thousands, but the American military did become the strongest advocate for diplomacy and development in the process.

Although the United States has not only created disorder in the Middle East but preserved it, the question today is not whether the United States will lead, but how it will lead.

We live in a world that is more dangerous than it has ever has been.

The world today is far, far more complicated than it has ever been.

A world where America leads is a world where everybody ends up better off.

Notes

PROLOGUE THE RISE OF WAR AVERSION AND THE DECLINE OF INTERNATIONAL WAR

[1] *Troilus and Cressida*, Act IV, scene 2.

[2] Schroeder 1985, 88; de Long 2004. There are a few potential exceptions. The most likely prospect is the Soviet suppression of a rebellion in its satellite, Hungary, in 1956, although in many respects this seems more like a colonial war. There are some aspects of the Croatian offensive in neighboring Bosnia in 1993–94 during the chaotic civil war that are sometimes seen to be essentially international in scope. And NATO's rather bizarre "war" over Kosovo in 1999 might also be considered an exception as might the brief conflict between Russia and Georgia in 2008 and some aspects of the one involving Russia and Ukraine in 2014. See also Luard 1986, 395–99; Pinker 2011, 249–51; Sheehan 2008.

[3] Jefferson 1939, 262–63. Howard 2000, 13. Tilly 1990, 184. Luard 1986, 77.

[4] Howard 1989, 14.

[5] Howard 1991, 176; Keegan 1993, 59; Kaldor 1999, 5; Jervis 2002, 1; Record 2002, 6; Gaddis 2005, 262. See also Luard 1986; Mandelbaum 2002; Mack 2005, 523; Gleditsch 2008; Fettweis 2010; Lebow 2010; Pinker 2011 and 2018; Goldstein 2011; Horgan 2012; Gat 2012; Gat 2017; Cohen and Zenko 2019, 83; Allison 2014. For contrary views, see Braumoeller 2019; Gray 2005.

[6] Jervis 2011, 412. Johnson 1995.

[7] In addition, there were border skirmishes and conflicts in the 1970s between China and Vietnam and between Ethiopia and Somalia; regime-changing invasions by Tanzania of Uganda in 1978–79 and by the United States of tiny Grenada in 1983 and of Panama in 1989; and a brief armed disputation between Britain and Argentina in 1982 over some remote and nearly barren islands in the South Atlantic.

[8] See also Fettweis 2010; Hathaway and Shapiro 2017.

[9] See also Mueller 1989, 265. On the distinction between "negative" and "positive" peace, see Braumoeller 2019, 44–45.

[10] On this development, see Mueller 1989, 9–11.

[11] The data in Figure 0.1 are for "wars," defined, as noted in the figure, as violent armed conflicts which result in at least 1,000 military and civilian battle-related deaths in the year indicated. This is a fairly conventional definition. However, some consider the 1,000 battle death threshold to be absurdly low. Kenneth Waltz, for example, contends that "By historical standards, that casualty rate constitutes little more than a skirmish." Waltz 2012a, 162. Bear Braumoeller, on the other hand, considers international conflicts in which more than 1,000 battle or battle-related deaths were suffered in a year to be "all-out wars," and he concentrates instead almost entirely on international conflicts that are recorded in a dataset of "militarized interstate disputes." These are international applications or threats of military force that are specifically deemed to be "short of war." From this array, Braumoeller extracts "uses of force that were reciprocated by the target country," arguing that any of these could have escalated to "all-out wars" although scarcely any actually did so. He finds that such instances do not seem to have declined and concludes that "looking only at all-out war might fool us into believing that wars have become less common when in fact they have simply become more limited." Braumoeller 2019, 78, 81–82. Designating an international conflict in which no one is killed as a "war," as opposed to an incident (or perhaps kerfuffle), which would conform to common parlance, scarcely seems convincing. However, his conclusions do seem broadly to comply with the argument in the text here: while the incidence of international war as conventionally defined does seem to be in decline, limited international conflicts that are "short of war" do not show evidence of the same decline. Nonetheless, some might consider the fact that international conflicts have become more limited (generally to the point of being completely bloodless) rather than less common, to be a notable improvement.

[12] Woodward 1991, 313.

[13] Brodie 1973, ch. 6. Stromberg 1982. Luard 1986, ch. 6; Mueller 1989, ch. 2; MacMillan 2013, 266, 274–84, 328.

[14] Toynbee 1969, 214. Luard 1986, 365. Brodie 1973, 30. Hobsbawm 1987, 326. Holsti 1991, 175.

[15] For a more extensive discussion, see Mueller 1995a, 135–37; Mueller 2004a, 40–42.

[16] Kellet 1982, 292–93. The sentiment may be sound sadism, but it is foolish strategy: if that is the known intention of the attackers, the defenders would be likely to fight desperately, inflicting maximum harm on the attackers. For wartime Khan-like threats by Shakespeare's comparatively mild-mannered Henry V to mow fresh-fair virgins, violate pure maidens, defile shrill-shrieking daughters, and impale naked infants upon pikes, see Act III, scene 3.

[17] Luard 1986, 51.
[18] Small and Singer 1982, 82–99.
[19] Holsti 1991, 313.
[20] Wedgwood 1938, 516.
[21] Kaeuper 1988, 77–117. See also Friedrichs 1979.
[22] Overy 1982, 16.
[23] Gat 2017, ch. 6.
[24] For a survey, see Brodie 1973, 223–70.
[25] Hamann 1996, 73.
[26] von Suttner 1906.
[27] Hamann 1996, 183.
[28] Angell 1914.
[29] For discussions, see Mueller 1989, ch. 1; MacMillan 2013, ch. 10; Sheehan 2008, ch. 2.
[30] Mueller 1989, ch. 2.
[31] Brodie 1973, 31n.
[32] See John Mueller, "Preaching to the Masses: Strike Up the Band and War," essay in the liner notes for the 1991 recording of the Gershwin-Kaufman Strike Up the Band aln2.albumlinernotes.com/Preaching_To_The_Masses.html. Actually, Troilus and Cressida may not be a true exception. Although it clearly has a strong anti-war theme, the play was performed only a few times (if at all) in Shakespeare's lifetime, and it only achieved theatrical recognition after it was embraced by war opponents in the twentieth century.
[33] Taleb 2010. The characterization is my own, but it is certainly in the spirit of Taleb's rather confusing definition. In fact, Taleb is guilty of selection bias – all of his Black Swans have extreme impacts because that is how a Black Swan is defined. To avoid this, it is important to consider not only important events and episodes that lie "outside the realm of ordinary expectations" and have had an "extreme impact," thus becoming Black Swans, but also ones that have failed to do so even though they were as unexpected and as popularly embraced when they occurred. If one does this, it seems that when unexpected and emotion-engaging events become Black Swans, their "extreme impact" has derived not so much those qualities or from the intrinsic size or importance of the event, as from reaction, or overreaction, it generates, one that is often as extreme and unpredictable as the event itself. Moreover, although Taleb argues that "almost everything in social life is produced by rare but consequential shocks and jumps," it seems rather that most consequential developments in human history – if not the attitude change about war – stem not from dramatic events, but from changes in thinking and behavior that are gradual and often little-noticed as they occur. For a discussion, see Mueller and Stewart 2016c.
[34] Pinker 2011.
[35] Mueller 2011a, 172–75, 194–95. For his discussion of the abortion issue, see Pinker 2011, 426–28.

[36] On these developments in more detail, see Mueller 1989, 18–23; Mueller 2004a, 30–32.

[37] Luard 1986, 330–31, 354, 349, 361.

[38] Quoted, Mueller 2004a, 30.

[39] Rosecrance 1986. See also Luard 1986, 62–63.

[40] Luard 1986, 64.

[41] On this issue in more detail, see Mueller 2004a, 48–49.

[42] Mueller 2004a, 49.

[43] Mueller 1995a, 189.

[44] Mueller 1989, 30.

[45] Mueller 1989, 38.

[46] Luard 1986, 64.

[47] Vagts 1959, 451. See also Brodie 1973, 30, 272. On militarism in Europe before World War I, see MacMillan 2013, 274–84; Sheehan 2008, 35–41.

[48] Luard 1986, 368.

[49] Keegan 1989, V–1.

[50] Weinberg 1980, 664. The over-confident Hitler was hoping to avoid a long, multi-front war by conducting a series of separate and isolated wars that would be quickly successful. Mueller 1989, 67, 67n30; Luard 1986, 261.

[51] For example, to carry out his deeds, Hitler needed to rise in a country like Germany, not, say, Albania. For further comment on this, see Mueller 1989, 25. For a contrasting view, see Braumoeller 2019, 64.

[52] Jervis 2013, 35. Hinsley 1987, 71–72. Manchester 1988, 197. Lukacs 1997, xi. See also Record 2007, 70; Record 2011, 234; Brodie 1973, 271; Bouverie 2019, 412; Sheehan 2008, 111. For a more extended discussion and many more references, see Mueller 2004a, 54–65; Mueller 2018d. A few historians, perhaps two, have taken exception to this conclusion. One is A. J. P. Taylor, whose highly controversial book is deftly rebutted in Hinsley 1963, ch. 15. The other is Henry Ashby Turner, who argues that, even without Hitler, German generals would have embraced a limited revisionist military expansion against Poland. For a rebuttal, see Mueller 2004a, 60–62.

[53] Record 2007, 70. Kennedy 2010. May 2000, 453. Emphases in the original. See also Record 2011, 234. For a compilation of the statements against war in Hitler's foreign policy speeches during the 1930s, see "Hitler on Peace," April 17, 2005, available at politicalscience.osu.edu/faculty/jmueller/ hitpeace.

[54] On this comparison, see Mueller 1989, 11–12; Ray 1989.

[55] Mead 1964. Mueller 1989, 1995, ch. 8, 2010, ch. 4. Horgan 2012.

[56] Pinker 2011, xxiii, 278.

[57] Gat 2017, 142.

[58] Levy and Thompson 2011, 204–5.

[59] Gellner 1988; Fukuyama 1989. See also Mueller 1999, 2011a.

60 Luard 1986, 231–33. See also Mueller 1989, 2004.

61 Dahl 1971, 181, 188.

62 On slavery, see Mueller 1999, 196–97.

63 Dahl 1971, 181–82.

64 Tolstoy 1966 [1862–69], 1145.

65 See also Glaser 2018.

66 Lebow 2010; Maull 1990.

67 Morgenthau 1948, 13.

68 Huntington 1993a, 72

69 Morgenthau 1948, 183.

70 Art and Waltz 1983, 7.

71 Realist scholar Christopher Layne has dismissed any acceptance of the notion, promulgated at the time by Hanns Maull, of "global civilian powers" as a "popular intellectual fashion." Layne 1993, 9n12. Maull 1990; see also Rosecrance 1986. Increasingly, however, status, like beauty, lies in the eye of the beholder. China's quest to host the Olympics in the year 2000 stemmed in part from the belief that it would be a "mark of entry into the big league of world powers," while some Koreans apparently once came to believe that status is achieved when a country has many entries in the *Guinness Book of World Records*: says one, "The more records we have leads to world power." Mueller 1995a, 38n.

72 Will 1994, 62. It appears Coolidge actually put it this way: "Never go out to meet trouble. If you will just sit still, nine cases out of ten someone will intercept it before it reaches you." Quoted, Sinclair 1962, 252.

73 Kennedy 1987, 338, emphasis in the original. See also Fettweis 2010, 194; Kennedy 2010; Record 2007, 67.

74 Record 2007, 116.

75 Cooper 1978, 26.

76 Manchester 1988, 307. On public opinion in Germany in the 1930s confirming this judgment, see Kershaw 1987, 2, 143; Steinert 1977, 50.

77 Record 2007, 117.

78 Peter F. Langrock, Middlebury, Vermont.

79 On this issue more generally, see Mueller 1999. A summary of the argument is available at politicalscience.osu.edu/faculty/jmueller/ BUSVIRT15.pdf

80 Mueller 2006, 10. See also Cramer and Thrall 2009; Preble and Mueller 2014; Walt 2018a, 147–63. Cohen and Zenko 2019.

81 Worst case: Brodie 1978, 68. Cult: Brodie 1966, 93.

82 Gaddis 2011, 403. Mueller 2012. On the "blob," see Rhodes 2018.

83 On these issues, and especially on the essential irrelevance of nuclear weapons to the process, see Mueller 1985b; Mueller 1988; Mueller 1989; Mueller 1995a, ch. 5; Mueller 2004a, 164–65; Mueller 2010, ch. 3. For a different perspective, see Gaddis 1987, 230–31.

[84] Morell 2015, 266–67. On (erroneous) reports about an imminent atomic attack on New York City, see Allison 2004, 1–6. On that "avalanche" of intelligence reports, often generated more by panic than anything else, see Coll 2018, 77–78.

[85] Mayer 2008, 3. Coll 2018, 78. Giuliani: CNN, July 22, 2005.

[86] Thomas 2001a.

[87] Mueller 2002a, 2002b, and, most extensively, 2003. On the Pearl Harbor comparison, see Mueller 2011a, 192–93. See also Seitz 2004; Diab 2015.

[88] For a discussion of its (very) few attempts, all of which failed, see Mueller and Stewart 2016a, 103, 122.

[89] Schilling 1965, 389.

[90] Jervis 2001, 36.

[91] Mueller 2011a, x–xii.

[92] PBS NewsHour, January 26, 2012.

[93] A recent example: Gingrich 2019. See also Mueller 2011i.

[94] For a provocative assessment about an earlier threat, see Russett 1972.

[95] Finkel 2013, 11.

[96] Mueller 1989, 290n19.

[97] In a spirited book, Harlan Ullman argues that over the last half century "America has lost every war it has started" and, to explain the phenomenon, he focuses almost entirely on the inadequacy of civilian leaders, not on those of the military. He rather unhelpfully credits consistent failure to "a lack of sound strategic thinking" and proposes the full application of "brains and intellect" as the remedy. Ullman 2017, 1, 211, 228.

[98] Brodie 1978, 81. Also Brodie 1973, 126.

1 KOREA, MASSIVE EXTRAPOLATION, DETERRENCE, AND THE CRISIS CIRCUS

[1] On Japan, see Dower 1999, 29, 58–61.

[2] Historicus 1949, 198. See also Mueller 1989, 99–102; Jervis 2001, 59.

[3] Historicus 1949, 191, 212.

[4] Rich 1973. See also Mueller 2004a, 55–60.

[5] For a discussion of the Soviet view of international war, see, in particular, Burin 1963, 337–41. See also Mueller 1989, 99–102. On Stalin's caution, see also Leffler 1992, 102, 510.

[6] Quoted in Gaddis 1982, 35; see also 366–67. See also Leffler 1992, 499.

[7] Hogan 1987, 444.

[8] Millett 2005.

[9] Khrushchev 1970, 367–68.

[10] Stueck 2002, 70–75.

11 Stueck 2002, 73.
12 Ulam 1968, 525. See also Jervis 2001, 40.
13 Shulman 1963, 150.
14 Truman 1956, 333. Taubman 1982, 201–2.
15 Trachtenberg 1991, 112–13.
16 Gallup 1972, 933.
17 Acheson 1969, 375–76, 752–53. See also Thompson 2009, 141; Leffler 1992, 511.
18 Callahan 1990, 136–37. Thompson 2009, 141. For a fuller discussion, see Mueller 2006, 72–75. See also Pillar 2011a, 97–98; Bowie and Immerman 1998, 29–32. None of the interpretations of the reasons for the attack assessed in a classic article by Alexander George really quite embraces Bohlen's interpretation fully, though the one George calls the "soft-spot" probing interpretation comes closest. George 1955, 212–13.
19 Brodie 1973, 63–64, 79. See also Kaplan 1983, 39, 81; Paige 1968, 166, 171, 173; Taubman 1982, 201–2.
20 See Mueller 1973, 44.
21 Horne 2015, 311.
22 For an evaluation of the depths of the Soviet setback, see Zubok and Pleshakov 69–72.
23 On Korea as an important turning point, see also Gaddis 1974; May 1984; Trachtenberg 1991, 107–15; and especially Jervis 1980.
24 Callahan 1990, 120–23. See also Paige 1968, 137, 174; Taubman 1982, 214; Jervis 2001, 48; Stueck 2002, 82.
25 Brodie 1966, 71–72; see also Kaplan 1983, 339.
26 Brodie 1966, 71 72; see also Kaplan 1983, 339. Kennan 1977, 200. Never believed: Kennan 1987, 888–89.
27 Jervis 2001, 59. Mastny 2006, 3, 27. Danilevich: Thompson 2009, 262. See also Ambrose 1990; Khrushchev 1974, 533; Burr and Savranskaya 2009; Talbott 1990. For an extended discussion, see Mueller 2010, ch. 3.
28 Leffler 2007, 254.
29 Rhodes 2007, 306; see also Leffler 1992, 511.
30 Estimate (by Bruce Russett): Rhodes 2007, 307.
31 See also Mueller 2011b, 127–29.
32 Kaplan 1983, 135.
33 President's Commission on National Goals 1960, 1–2. CIA: Reeves 1993, 54. On the Soviet Union's apparent economic strength at the time, see Yergin and Stanislaw 1998, 22, 272.
34 Callahan 1990, 169.
35 Halperin 1961, 367.
36 Kaplan 1983, 165–67, 267, 288–89. See also Preble 2004, 82, 94; Talbott 1990.
37 Kaplan 1983, 124, 225, 302.

[38] Quoted admiringly in Boyle 1985, 73. See also Trachtenberg 2012, 25. On such predictions, see Gardner 2011. On the development of Morgenthau's apocalyptic alarmism, see McQueen 2018, ch. 5.

[39] Mueller 2010, 76. Thomas 2012, 285.

[40] Johnson 1997, 78.

[41] Kaplan 1983, 390, emphasis in the original.

[42] On this issue, see Mueller 2010, 65 and 252n24.

[43] As Huth and Russett point out, "Inclusion of positive inducements as a means to deter is not standard practice in academic writing or policy debates, but the lack of theoretical or practical attention cannot be justified on grounds of strict logic." And they label such considerations "a long-neglected and therefore underdeveloped component of deterrence theory" (1990, 471). For a fuller discussion, see Mueller 1995a, ch. 4.

[44] For a critique of the concept of "anarchy" in international politics, see Mueller 1995a, ch. 2, and the Afterword of this book. See also Wilson 2008.

[45] Johnson 1997, 29. Talbott 1990. On exaggerations of Soviet military capabilities, see Rhodes 2007. Many argued that any stability was "delicate," easily upset by technological or economic shifts. This view was prominently advanced in the late 1950s by strategist Albert Wohlstetter, who alarmingly argued that the United States existed in a "world of persistent danger" and that deterring general war over the next decade would be "hard at best." For a critique, see Mueller 2010, 66.

[46] Brodie 1966, 59.

[47] Brodie 1978, 68, 83.

[48] Kennan 1977, 170, 172.

[49] Rhodes 2007, 99.

[50] Hagerty 1983, 134.

[51] Eisenhower, 1948, 469. See also Bowie and Immerman 1998, 46.

[52] Callahan 1990, 174; Preble 2004, 77–78, 95.

[53] Eisenhower was also one of the few people who did not go into hysterics, programmed or otherwise, over the Soviet Union's Sputnik satellite launch of 1957 and over Soviet economic progress at the time. In major part, however, his reaction seems to have stemmed not so much from substance as from his hostility to the substantial defense expenditure increases it suggested or implied: he felt, incorrectly as it turned out, that either the American economy or the American people could not tolerate the bill. Kaplan 1983, 146–52; Callahan 1990, 172; Halperin 1961, 368, 371; Preble 2004, 77–78. In addition, in response to the Gaither Report, he (correctly) found it implausible that the Soviets would embark on a crash program to build liquid fuel missiles which were already in the process of being made obsolete by ones powered by solid fuel. Preble 2004, 80.

[54] Bowie and Immerman 1998, 47; see also 48–49, 153–54, 247–48, 251, 268n33. The absurdity of the situation in Eisenhower's eyes is poignantly captured

in his exasperated comment at a 1956 National Security Council meeting: "We are piling up armaments because we do not know what else to do to provide for our security." Gaddis 1997, 221. See also Mueller 2006, 77–78.

55 Eisenhower 1954, 71–72.

56 Bundy 1988, 341–42. See also Thomas 2012, 361. However, Eisenhower was willing in public to characterize war as "completely stupid," "futile," "dreadful," and "the greatest cancer." Bowie and Immerman 1998, 48.

57 www.c-span.org/video/?15026–1/president-dwight-eisenhower-farewell-address. A parallel with President Barack Obama's position on terrorism is discussed on page 180 of this volume.

58 Halperin 1961, 364, 369, 384.

59 See also Preble 2004, 16–17.

60 Hudson et al. 1961, 211.

61 Hudson et al. 1961, 181–82.

62 Shevchenko 1985, 103. See also Snyder 1987/88, 108.

63 Hudson et al. 1961, 138, 212.

64 On this issue, see, in particular, Frankel 2004, 176–81.

65 Medvedev 1983, 190; Allison 1971, 221.

66 Shevchenko 1985, 118. See also Lebow and Stein 1994, 110; Luard 1986, 233. A report from a "reliable, well-placed" Soviet source says that the leadership issued a formalized secret directive that it had decided not to go to war even if the United States invaded Cuba: Garthoff 1987, 51. On Khrushchev's mindset during the crisis, see Taubman 2003, 563, 566–67, 573.

67 Kennedy 1971, 40, 105. See also Kaplan 2020, 56–75.

68 Welch and Blight 1987/88, 27–28; Blight, Nye, and Welch 1987, 178–79; Lebow and Stein 1994, 127–28. Frankel 2004, 178–79.

69 Welch and Blight 1987/88, 27; see also Blight, Nye, and Welch 1987, 184; Brodie 1973, 426; Bundy 1988, 453–57, 461–62; Gaddis 1997, 269–72; Lebow and Stein 1994, ch. 6; Garthoff 2001, 181–82; Mueller 1989, 152–55; Mueller 2004a, 72–75; Mueller 2010; Jervis 2001, 57. On the political incentive for both leaders to exaggerate in retrospect the degree to which war was near, see Frankel 2004, 177.

70 Luard 1986, 232. Blainey 1973, 141. Kissinger 1979, 885. Tertrais 2017, 61. See also Brodie 1966, 53–57. A possible instance, however, is the almost breathtakingly unimportant "football war" between Honduras and El Salvador in 1969 in which it has been held that several days of hostilities were unintended and undesired. Luard 1986, 227n. However, the fighting seems to have been much more purposeful and was related to immigration issues, not to a set of soccer matches that were taking place at the same time: McKnight 2019. My thanks to an anonymous reviewer for this reference.

71 Brodie 1966, 57.

72 Hilsman 1967, 220. Kaplan 2020, 72.

[73] Frankel 2004, 179.

[74] Savranskaya 2005, 241, 246. There are some contradictions in this account; email enquiries to the author have gone unanswered.

[75] Huchthausen 2002, 169.

[76] Although the Americans take great credit for causing the subs to surface (after surfacing, they were politely pointed east and wished bon voyage), the captains all say that they surfaced only out of necessity (in particular to recharge their batteries), not because of US action. Savranskaya 2005, 243. See also Huchthausen 2002, 169. However, they had a substantial reason to say this because being forced to surface was against orders and the consequences of disobedience were severe. Savranskaya 2005, 242, but see also 250. When the offending Soviet submarine surfaced, it was greeted by the sailors on the destroyer with band music (including "Yankee Doodle"), hand waving, and playful mockery when someone on the ship's loudspeaker yelled, "Russians, go home!" In English, of course. Huchthausen 2002, 172–73.

[77] Savranskaya 2005, 247.

[78] Savranskaya 2005, 239.

[79] Savranskaya 2005, 247.

[80] Savranskaya 2005, 247. On this event, see also Tertrais 2017, 59–60.

[81] Savranskaya 2005, 251, 252.

[82] Frankel 2004, 125, 179.

[83] Comrades abroad: Werth 1964, xii. Fart: Lebow and Stein 1994, 110. Such comparative gentility was to last. The United States got around to normalizing relations with Cuba a half century later under the Obama administration. In celebration, a well-attended and lively exhibit of Cuban music and art was put on at the Kennedy Center in Washington in 2018. Although there were many maps of the island on display around the hall, all of them graciously neglected to label the Bay of Pigs.

[84] Frankel 2004, 175–76.

2 CONTAINMENT, VIETNAM, AND THE CURIOUS END OF THE COLD WAR

[1] Freeman 2018. Drezner 2019, 11. Sagan 2017, 82.

[2] On these issues, see also May 1984, 213; Gaddis 1974, 390.

[3] Kennan 1947, 566–67.

[4] Kennan 1947, 575, 581.

[5] Gaddis 1982, 43; Taubman 1982, 170.

[6] Kennan 1947, 580.

[7] Kennan 1947, 576. See also Gaddis 2011, 246.

[8] Gaddis 1982, 49.

9 For a discussion, see Weinstein 1978.
10 Holloway 1994, 138–44, 222, 283, 366. Mueller 2010, 49–50.
11 Radosh and Milton 1983, 284, 344.
12 O'Connor 2007, 278–79.
13 Hoover 1958, 81.
14 Philbrick 1952. Nevertheless, violence became a central element when his story was transmuted into a popular television series. All 117 episodes were reportedly approved in advance by the FBI. en.wikipedia.org/wiki/I_Led_3_Lives
15 Stephan 2000, xii. See Mueller 2007, 39–45.
16 Bialer 1986, 188–89.
17 For a discussion, see Mueller 1969, 10.
18 McNamara: Pentagon Papers 1971, Vol. 3, 500; see also 50–51. North Vietnam: Vo Nguyen Giap quoted by Maxwell Taylor in Fulbright 1966, 169. Le Duan: Asselin 2018, 136. Lin Piao 1965, 396, 398, 402, 410–11.
19 Mueller 1980.
20 Halberstam 1965, 315, 319. On this issue, see also Pillar 2011a, 86–87.
21 Goodwin 1991, 253. See also the map with threatening arrows from Lyndon Johnson's autobiography as reprinted in Mueller 1989, 172.
22 For more detail on this process, see Mueller 1989, 177–78. See also Kennan in Fulbright 1966, 109, 121, 133, 135, 140.
23 For data sources and further discussion of this issue, see Mueller 1973, 164–67; Mueller 1984a.
24 McGovern managed to do the seemingly impossible: he gained a lower percentage of the popular vote than Barry Goldwater had in 1964 even though McGovern represented the majority party and even though he was up against a candidate who, though formidable, was far less popular and far more vulnerable than Goldwater's opponent, Lyndon Johnson, had been in 1964.
25 Mueller 1973, ch. 6.
26 Pentagon Papers 1971, Vol. 3, 482–83. On this issue, see also Mueller 1980.
27 Pentagon Papers 1971, Vol. 4, 624.
28 Gelb and Betts 1979, 343, emphasis in the original.
29 Pentagon Papers 1971, Vol. 3, 484; Vol. 4, 624. Westmoreland: Pentagon Papers 1971, Vol. 3, 482; Westmoreland argues that this common reading of his 1965 timetable is inaccurate. Westmoreland 1976, 142–43. See Janis 1982, ch. 5; Gelb and Betts 1979, 126, 318–22.
30 Pentagon Papers 1971, Vol. 4, 624. "invariably pessimistic": Janis 1982, 106. On similar CIA estimates, see Epstein 1975, 95–110; Pentagon Papers 1971, Vol. 4, 26.
31 Interview on NBC-TV, July 2, 1971.

[32] For a full discussion, see Mueller 1980. This analysis estimates that the Communist suffered some 500,000 to 600,000 battle deaths in the war. However, Communist estimates are much higher than that: some 1.3 or 1.4 million in total with perhaps 981,000 combat deaths. In his recent, lengthy book on the war, Max Hastings evaluates such statistics and says that the Communist number seems to him to be "of the right order of magnitude." Hastings 2018, 739; also Asselin 2018, 252. On this issue, see also Spector 1993, 71–91, 314–15.

[33] For discussions of the disciplinary and organizational efforts required to achieve this remarkable resilience, see Asselin 2018, 121–25, 129–33; Spector 1993, ch. 4.

[34] Hastings 2018, 572.

[35] Westmoreland 1976, 251–52. Also: Hastings 2018, 633. On this issue, see also Berman 1974; Karnow 1991, 19–23; and especially Kellen 1972.

[36] Kinnard 1977, 67.

[37] Mueller 1980, 505, 509; Khrushchev 1970, 482.

[38] Nguyen 2012, 109, 148, 233–34, 242, 309–11; Asselin 2018, 139–40, 161, 167, 171, 191, 194, 291; Hastings 2018, 435, 601, 633, 635. For (futile) efforts during the war to see if the Communists might be weakening – to be reaching a breaking point – see Mueller 1980, 502n7. Most impressively, the rate of defection by Communist soldiers was very low: only 2,200 defected during course of the long war. Asselin 2018, 123. On measures designed to chart military progress in the war, see Daddis 2011.

[39] Asselin 2018, 251.

[40] On these decisions, see Schandler 1977.

[41] On polling on this issue, see Mueller 1989, 180–81.

[42] Sorley 1999, 380–81.

[43] Westmoreland: Race 1976, 393. For an array of such assertions, see Mueller 1980, 515–17.

[44] McMaster 1997, 328. See also Sorley 1999, and, for a rebuttal, Daddis 2017.

[45] Kellen 1972, 106. See also Mueller 1980, 512–15.

[46] Breslauer 1987, 436–37. Jervis 2001, 50. See also Hosmer and Wolfe 1983, ch. 12; Andrew and Mitrokhin 2003, 15–24.

[47] Mueller 1989, 197.

[48] Porter 1984, 240.

[49] Garthoff 1994, 1070, emphasis in the original. Johnson 1997, 166–69. See also Jervis 2001, 58; Halperin 1987, 45; Pillar 2011a, 112–14; Fettweis 2018, 39–40.

[50] On the rising costs of the Soviet overseas empire at the time, see Wolf et al. 1983.

[51] Gaddis 1982, 47.

⁵² Kennedy 1987, 488–98, 502. Bialer 1986. Pipes 1984, chs. 3–4. Beckley 2018, 28–31. Talbott 1990.
⁵³ Defense burden: Kennedy 1987, 498–504. East Europe: Bunce 1985, 1–46.
⁵⁴ Kennan 1947. In 1994, Kennan professed dismay at the "success" of the containment policy because it had taken so long, because the costs had been so high, and because the United States and its allies had demanded "unconditional surrender." Gaddis 2011, 249.
⁵⁵ On this phenomenon, see also Craig and Logevall 2009, 355. As it happens, the outcome of such a competition was presaged in the premise for a 1939 Hollywood comedy, *Ninotchka* (and a later musical, *Silk Stockings*): "Russian girl saturated with Bolshevist ideals goes to fearful, capitalistic, monopolistic Paris. She meets romance and has an uproarious good time. Capitalism not so bad, after all." Mueller 1985c, 387.
⁵⁶ Rush 1993, 19–25.
⁵⁷ There is a very substantial literature on the origins and development of this important ideological change and on Gorbachev's internal struggles. See, for example, Snyder 1987/88; Garthoff 1994, 255–65, 358–68, 753–57, 769–78; Zelikow and Rice 1995, ch. 1; Checkel 1997; Matlock 1995; Gaddis 1997; Vasquez 1998, ch. 13; English 2000; Suri 2002; Kramer 1999; Alexseev 1997, ch. 8. For analysis in 1986 concluding that the decline in fervor in the Soviet Union for its ideological commitment to the international Communist revolutionary movement could eventually result in the end of the Cold War and thus that "we may be coming to the end of the world as we know it," see Mueller 1986; see also Mueller 1989, chs. 5–9.
⁵⁸ Colton 1986, 191.
⁵⁹ Oberdorfer 1992, 158–64, see also 141–42.
⁶⁰ Inadequacy: Binder 1988. Ideologist: Keller 1988.
⁶¹ *New York Times*, December 9, 1988, A18.
⁶² Shultz 1993, 1107. See also Zelikow and Rice 1995, 16. Matlock 1995, 154, 192.
⁶³ On this process, see Mueller 2011a, ch. 5 and also Gould-Davies 1999; Jervis 2001, 60.
⁶⁴ Wohlforth 1996, 91.
⁶⁵ For a detailed discussion, see Mueller 2011a, ch. 5.
⁶⁶ Matlock 1995, 565–66.
⁶⁷ See Waltz 1979, 98, 170.
⁶⁸ As suggested in Morgenthau 1948, 327. See also Ray and Russett 1996. 457.
⁶⁹ Talbott 1990.
⁷⁰ See also Gould-Davies 1999; Macdonald 1995/96.
⁷¹ Matlock 1995, 649.
⁷² Waltz 1979, 98, 131, 170. Waltz 1988, 628. For an agile refutation of this perspective, see Kirshner 2010.

[73] Waltz 1988, 628.
[74] See also Mueller 1995a, ch. 2.

3 MILITARY INTERVENTION AND THE CONTINUED QUEST FOR THREAT AFTER THE COLD WAR

[1] On the Asian issue, see Choi 2006.
[2] Kennan 1989. Kissinger: Gordon 1989.
[3] Summers 1992, 12.
[4] For an extended discussion, see Mueller 2004b.
[5] See Mueller 1999.
[6] Mandelbaum 2016, 68–69, 123.
[7] Kennedy 1987, 461–67. Emphasis in the original.
[8] For data, see Mueller 2011a, 85.
[9] Huntington 1991, 8, 10.
[10] Professorships: Huntington 1993a, 77, 80. War: Friedman and LeBard 1991. Yearn: Layne 1993, 37.
[11] Woolsey 1993.
[12] For more on this phenomenon in the aftermath of the Cold War, see Mueller 1995a, ch. 1.
[13] Gates 1993. Brzezinski 1993, ix.
[14] Hoffmann 1992, 37.
[15] Woolsey 1993. See also Friedman 1992; Greenfield 1993.
[16] On this issue, see Mueller 2010, 11–15. On the history of "WMD" and for data on the use of the term, see Carus 2006. See also Mueller and Mueller 2009.
[17] Valentino 2003, ch. 1. For some qualification, see Pinker 2011, 713n15.
[18] Gray 2002, 3–7. See also Mueller 2006, ch. 7; Rawls 1999, 81, 93n; O'Connell 2003, 446–56. Hathaway and Shapiro 2017.
[19] Mearsheimer 2018. Walt 2018a.
[20] Preble 2009, 28.
[21] This construction, which, for better or worse, will reappear again later in this book, was first used in a short comment published in *New York Times* about the prospective American adventure in Libya in 2011. In the dark of night, however, a concerned editor bowlderized "half-vast" to the more dignified "limited." Mueller 2011c.
[22] DiPrizio 2016, ch. 4. Menon 2016.
[23] Woodward 1991, 116. Bush was also concerned, it appears, by lingering accusations that he was an indecisive, hesitant wimp. Woodward 1991, 129. On the wimp issue, see also Kinzer 2006, 250, 253.
[24] Woodward 1991, 164.

[25] On Grenada, see Mueller 1989, 195. In some respects another precedent might have been a military intervention in the Dominican Republic under the Johnson administration.

[26] This discussion draws on Mueller 1995b and Mueller 1994. For more detail and many more references, see those sources.

[27] Simpson 1991, 20, 107–8. See also Aburish 2000, 282. As Saddam put it later, "Law? What law? Law that puts Saddam to trial because the Kuwaitis said that we would make out of every Iraqi woman a prostitute for ten dinars in the street. And I have defended the honor of Iraq and revived the historical rights of Iraqis against these dogs." Transcript of Saddam in Court, nbcnews.com, July 1, 2004. www.nbcnews.com/id/5345118/ns/msnbc-about_msnbc_tv/t/transcript-saddam-court/#.XMWj7TBKgdU It was commented at the time that Saddam was out of touch with current prices.

[28] Woodward 1991, 215–22.

[29] Freedman and Karsh 1993, 462n.

[30] Simpson 1991, 227.

[31] Mueller 1994, 29–34.

[32] Emotionally absorbed: Woodward 1991, 255, 260; Barnes 1991. Yearn: Tucker and Hendrickson 1992, 91; Simpson 1991, 215–16; Aburish 2000, 296. See also Mueller 1994, 49–53.

[33] Freedman and Karsh 1993, 431, 9n; see also Simpson 1991, 17, 228, 231, 274.

[34] Mueller 1994, 56–58.

[35] Mueller 1994, 28.

[36] Mueller 1995b, 105.

[37] Dunnigan and Bay 1992, 386.

[38] Schwarzkopf 1991; see also Keaney and Cohen 1993, 237–38.

[39] For an extended discussion, see Mueller 1995b. See also Davis 2016.

[40] Hallion 1992, 231. The remnants of an entire Iraqi company surrendered to a female newspaper reporter from suburban Virginia who was armed, presumably, only with a pencil. Weil 1991.

[41] Moore 1991.

[42] Heidenrich 1993, 124.

[43] See Freedman and Karsh 1993, 417.

[44] Daponte 1993, 65.

[45] Tucker and Hendrickson 1992, 91.

[46] Barnes 1991, 8.

[47] Tucker and Hendrickson 1992, 86.

[48] On the possibility that Saddam was open to a face-saving deal, see Aburish 2000, 293, 301, also 303–4. Simpson concludes that "the survival of his régime was more important to him than the outcome of the war," and characterizes Saddam Hussein's condition as "malignant narcissism": "a paranoid approach to those around him; and almost total self-absorption; a lack of interest in or awareness of the suffering of others; the absence of

anything that might be called conscience in the pursuit of his own drives and impulsions." Simpson 1991, 17, 20.

[49] Tucker and Hendrickson 1992, 95; Brzezinski 1990, 4–19; Mueller 1990.

[50] Mueller 1973, 208–13.

[51] On comparisons with the Super Bowl, see Mueller 1994, ch. 9.

[52] For more on this issue, see Mueller 2011a, 179.

[53] For sources, see Mueller 2010, 133–34.

[54] Spagat 2010.

[55] Bush and Albright: Cockburn and Cockburn 1999, 43, 263; also 98. British: Aburish 2000, 342.

[56] Cockburn and Cockburn 1999, 43.

[57] Middle East: Cockburn and Cockburn 1999, 263. Bin Laden: Wright 2006, 259–60. The benign public acceptance of the sanctions, despite their human costs, is quite impressive, because the American public was strongly disinclined to blame the Iraqi people – unlike, say, the Japanese in World War II – for the policies of the country's leadership. Mueller 1994, 79; 2011a, 174.

[58] Memory of 1991: Cockburn and Cockburn 1999, ch. 1. Opposition: Cockburn and Cockburn 1999, ch. 7.

[59] For more detail and references on this venture, see Mueller 2004a, 105, 126–28.

[60] Bowden 1999.

[61] Mueller 2011a, 177.

[62] Bush 1991. Bush saw God working elsewhere as well. In 1992 he proclaimed that "Christ ordained" that the United States be "a light unto the world." Mueller 1994, 143.

[63] Mandelbaum 2016, 93n–94n. Because of the speed with which the genocide was conducted, however, it is not at all clear from a logistical standpoint that armed rescuers could have been deployed there in time to save the majority of the victims. See Kuperman 2001.

[64] On the 90 percent calculation, see Mueller 2004a, 99–100. For similar conclusions, see Straus 2006, 118. For more detail and references on the venture, see Mueller 2004a, 97–100, 139.

[65] For a fuller discussion of this conflict and for many additional sources, see Mueller 2004a, 88–95, 112–14, 130–32.

[66] Mandelbaum 2016, 97.

[67] Kaplan 1993, 1, 30 32. For a devastating critique of the argument, see Malcolm 1993, 83–88.

[68] Huntington 1993b, 1993c, 1996.

[69] Huntington 1993b, 37–38. For similar or related propositions from other analysts at the time, see Mueller 2004a, 195n2. For an able critique of this literature, see Kalyvas 2001.

[70] For an extended development of this argument, see Mueller 2004a.

[71] Doder and Branson 1999, 97–98.

[72] Burg and Shoup 1999, 84, 130.

[73] Burg and Shoup 1999, 137. More generally, see Andreas 2008.

[74] Mueller 2004a, 112–14.

[75] Included in this was the slaughter of thousands of Muslim men by Serbs after they successfully invaded the "safe area" of Srebrenica in 1995. Although in no way excusing the massacre, it may be relevant to point out that the Serbs were deeply bitter about the situation because they had accepted the city as a UN safe area in 1993 under the understanding that it would not be used for attacks against Serbs. Silber and Little 1997, 345. Nonetheless, the forces of Srebrenica defender Orić, regarded by some Muslims as "dangerous primitives," had repeatedly forayed out from the city to attack and kill Serb civilians. Rohde 1997, 109, 215–16, 409.

[76] Holbrooke 1998, 73.

[77] Milošević's affection for his Bosnian co-negotiators is indicated by his angry assertions to Holbrooke: "They are not my friends. They are not my colleagues. It is awful just to be in the same room with them for so long. They are shit." Holbrooke 1998, 105–6. Milošević on previous peace plans: Silber and Little 1997, chs. 21, 27. Final agreement: Burg and Shoup 1999, 356.

[78] Chege 2002, 147–60.

[79] Dorman 2009, 4.

[80] For a fuller discussion and sources on this episode, see Mueller 2004a, 95–97, 132–34.

[81] Harden 1999.

[82] Huntington 1996, 291, 294.

[83] Clapp 2017, 53–61.

[84] For a study that applies higher standards, see Mandelbaum 2016.

[85] Mackey 1989, 175, 204. The invasion did succeed in forcing most Palestinian fighters to flee the country, but within a year over 5,000 had filtered back. Mackey 1989, 250.

4 AL-QAEDA AND THE 9/11 WARS IN AFGHANISTAN, IRAQ, PAKISTAN

[1] For a discussion with multiple examples, see Mueller 2006, 45–47.

[2] Mearsheimer 2018. Walt 2018a.

[3] On al-Qaeda as a fringe group of the jihadist movement, see especially Gerges 2005, 2011.

[4] Fallows 2006, 142. On this issue, see also Abrahms 2006, 2018, 20–29, 64–65, 199–200; Sageman 2017a, ch. 1; Mueller and Stewart 2016a, 119–21; Betts 2012, 110.

A similar conclusion holds for the concept of "radicalization" of domestic terrorists. In almost all cases, the overwhelming driving force was simmering, and more commonly boiling, outrage at American foreign policy – the wars in Iraq and Afghanistan in particular, and also the country's support for Israel in the Palestinian conflict. Mueller and Stewart 2016a, 35–37; Gerges 2011, 153–67; Betts 2012, 110; Sageman 2008, 72–82; Mearsheimer 2011; Brooks 2011, 12–14.

[5] Smith 2007. See also Mueller and Stewart 2016a, 117–19.

[6] McDermott and Meyer 2012, 154, 311. U.S. v. Moussaoui, para. 76–89.

[7] U.S. v. Moussaoui, para. 89.

[8] Kenney 2010, 916–17.

[9] Wright 2006, 174, 200. Gerges 2011, 85, 90–91; Record 2007, 107–08.

[10] Gerges 2005, 27, 228, 233, also 270. See also Bergen and Cruickshank 2008; Wright 2006.

[11] Gerges 2005, 153; Sageman 2004, 47.

[12] Gerges 2011, 92.

[13] McDermott and Meyer 2012, 183. U.S. v. Moussaoui, para. 79.

[14] Full transcript of bin Laden's speech, October 30, 2004, www.aljazeera.net.

[15] See Mueller and Stewart 2016a, 121.

[16] Miller 2011. Shane 2011. See also Mueller 2011d; Ignatius 2012; Mueller and Stewart 2016a, ch. 4; Sageman 2008; Gerges 2011.

[17] Its record before 9/11 wasn't all that impressive either. See Mueller and Stewart 2016a, 121.

[18] For an array of examples, see Mueller and Stewart 2011, 36.

[19] Mueller and Stewart 2016a, ch. 4. See also Mueller 2006, ch. 8; Sageman 2008.

[20] Mueller and Stewart 2016a, 14.

[21] Sageman 2017a, 170. Sageman 2017b, 373.

[22] For rare, perhaps unique, questionings of this tendency in the early years after 9/11, see Mueller 2002a; Mueller 2002b; Mueller 2003a; Seitz 2004. See also Gerges 2005.

[23] Dr. Condoleezza Rice Discusses President's National Security Strategy. Washington, DC: Office of the Press Secretary, White House, October 1, 2002.

[24] Scheuer 2007, 160, 177, 226, 241, 242, 250, 252, 263; Scheuer 2006, 20.

[25] Morell 2015.

[26] Mueller 2019a.

[27] Jenkins 2011, 1. See also Mueller and Stewart 2016a, ch. 3; Brooks 2011; Friedman, Harper, and Preble 2010; LaFree et al. 2015, 99, 173.

[28] Mueller and Stewart 2016a, 33. Mueller 2019a, case 34.

[29] Allison 2004, 15.

[30] For extended discussions, see Mueller 2010, chs. 12–15; Jenkins 2008. See also Frost 2005; Lieber and Press 2013.

[31] Mueller and Stewart 2016a, 2.

[32] 10 million: derived from Graff 2011, 399. 20 million: derived from Bergen 2016, 63. See also Mueller and Stewart 2016a, 2.

[33] Mueller and Stewart 2016a, 1.

[34] Leinwand 2008.

[35] Mueller and Stewart 2011,

[36] Bergen 2016, 218. See also Liepman and Mudd 2016, 12.

[37] Miller 2009.

[38] For a more extensive development of this argument, see Mueller and Stewart 2016a, 106–12; Stewart and Mueller 2018, 10–13; Mueller and Stewart 2019.

[39] Jenkins 2011; see also Brooks 2011; Mueller 2019a; Mueller and Stewart 2012, 2016a; Stewart and Mueller 2018; Jenkins 2017.

[40] On aviation as a target, see in particular Stewart and Mueller 2018.

[41] Fortna 2015.

[42] Abrahms 2006, 42–78, and 2018.

[43] Schneier 2015a.

[44] Carle 2008.

[45] Wright 2006, 230–31, 287–88; Burke 2003, 150, 164–65; Brown 2010.

[46] Atran 2010b.

[47] Brown 2010, 1.

[48] Burke 2003, 167–68.

[49] For a more extended discussion with more references, see Mueller 2004a, 134–36. Popular support for chasing down the terrorists in Afghanistan, even though there was a prospect for considerable American losses, was exceedingly high – considerably higher than at the beginnings of the wars in Vietnam, Korea, or Iraq. Mueller 2011a, 200. NATO declared that, although the 9/11 attack had been perpetrated by only 19 people all of whom were now dead, that attack on one of its members would be taken to constitute an attack on all of them – the first, and thus far only, time the relevant provision in the NATO charter has been invoked.

[50] Woodward 2002, 253 (rent Afghans), 235 (suitcases). Additional information from a briefing by Enduring Freedom Special Forces veterans, Mershon Center, Ohio State University, November 19, 2002.

[51] Rubin 2013, 401. Coll 2018, 60.

[52] Van Linschoten and Kuehn 2012. See also Wright 2006.

[53] McCarthy 2001. See also Zenko 2014b; Horton 2017, 51–52. There was a parallel here with his father's decided unwillingness to negotiate with Saddam Hussein about the Iraq takeover of Kuwait in 1991: see Chapter 3.

[54] Feaver 2003.

[55] On Pearl Harbor, see Mueller 1995a, ch. 7.

[56] Tork Faradi on *The NewsHour with Jim Lehrer* (PBS television), January 14, 2003.

[57] In the first months and years after the defeat, it seems likely that many Taliban members could have been persuaded to rejoin Afghan society if they had not been pursued and arrested. If handled skillfully, some of their leaders could have been used to bring the bulk of the Taliban movement to a negotiated peace. Gall 2014, 75.

[58] Coll 2018.

[59] Pew Research Center, Pakistani Public Opinion Ever More Critical of U.S.: 74% Call America an Enemy, PewResearch Global Attitudes Study, June 27, 2012.

[60] Smith 2015, xvi.

[61] Fairweather 2014, 246.

[62] Coll 2018, 336.

[63] Coll 2018, 488. See also Davis 2012. On military dissembling on the war, see Glaser and Mueller 2019, 5–6, and more generally Mueller 2019b.

[64] Fairweather 2014, 305.

[65] Jaffe and Ryan 2016.

[66] Coll 2018, 496. The sentence is in mid-paragraph. For a somewhat wider discussion, see Coll 2018, 494–96.

[67] Fairweather 2014, 237–38.

[68] Bandow 2016b. See also Chopra 2017.

[69] Chopra 2017. Nordland 2018.

[70] Jackson 2018, 43–49. Tellis and Eggers 2017, 6.

[71] Mandelbaum 2016, 166–67. Coll 2018, 664.

[72] Woodward 2010, 376.

[73] See also Glaser and Mueller 2019.

[74] Quoted, Kennedy 2010.

[75] Mueller 2009. Crenshaw 2010. Glaser and Mueller 2019, 6–9.

[76] Kaminski 2009.

[77] Fairweather 2014, 246.

[78] Petraeus and O'Hanlon 2017.

[79] "Full text: Trump's Speech on Afghanistan," *Politico*, August 21, 2017.

[80] Blake 2018. On "experts," see Walt 2018a.

[81] See also Crenshaw 2010, 7.

[82] No foreign fighters: Williams 2008, 22–25. American commander: Whitlock 2010. Panetta: Drezner 2010. Extensive study: Jones 2008.

[83] "To the Point," Public Radio International, May 14, 2009.

[84] For detail and description, see Rashid 2000, chs. 1–2

[85] Rahim and Mashal 2018. Kapur 2018.

[86] For example, see Coll 2018, ch. 31.

[87] For more detail, see Glaser and Mueller 2019, 14–16.

[88] Osman 2018. See also Glaser and Mueller 2019.

89 Coll 2018.

90 For the argument that, as in Vietnam, "victory" in Afghanistan is "inconsequential" – that is, "it simply doesn't matter whether the United States wins or loses" – see Mearsheimer 2009. For the argument that it would be "a disaster for the prestige, influence, and self-image of America if Kabul fell in a manner similar to Saigon in 1975," see West 2018. On the remarkable equanimity with which the American public accepted foreign policy debacle in Vietnam, see Mueller 1984a. For concerns about an ISIS branch in Afghanistan, see Glaser and Mueller 2019, 13.

91 Osman 2018. See also Canadian Security Intelligence Service, 2019.

92 Perle 2000, 108–9.

93 Tenet 2007, 305–06.

94 georgewbush-whitehouse.archives.gov/news/releases/2002/01/20020129–11. html. See also Preble 2009, 35.

95 Mearsheimer 2018, 155.

96 Hymans 2006.

97 For assessments of Iraq's rather pathetic efforts to create nuclear weapons, see Hymans 2012.

98 Jervis 2006, 44.

99 Reports: Mueller 2006, 132n42.

100 For ammunition, see Fallows 2005, 72. For heavy weapons, see O'Kane 1998. Even war advocate Richard Perle had written a few years earlier that "Saddam's grip on the regular army ... has always been tenuous." Perle 2000, 109. For an extended discussion of Saddam's obsessive worries about a military coup, see Gordon and Trainor 2006, 55–66, 505. For critical prewar examinations of the assumption that Iraq, however armed, posed much of a threat, see Mearsheimer and Walt 2003, 50–59; Mueller 2003b.

101 Mueller 1995a, 114.

102 See also Walt 2000.

103 Position: The White House, "President Bush Outlines Iraqi Threat," October 7, 2002, www.whitehouse.gov. McCain: Congressional Record, October 10, 2002. Later Bush: Brookes 2007. Kenneth M. Pollack strenuously advocated in an influential book for a war whose "whole point" would be to "prevent Saddam from acquiring nuclear weapons." 2003, 418.

104 Rice 2000. Rice, 2002: transcripts.cnn.com/ TRANSCRIPTS/0209/08/ le.oo.html. Bush: Address to the Nation, October 7, 2002.

105 Tannenhaus 2003.

106 For their part, Democrats and liberals have derided the war as "unnecessary," but the bulk of them only came to that conclusion after

the United States was unable to find either nuclear weapons or weapons programs in Iraq. Many of them have made it clear they would support putatively preemptive (actually, preventive) military action and its attendant bloodshed if the intelligence about Saddam's programs had been accurate. Thus, five years into the bloody war, the disillusioned war-supporting liberal columnist Jacob Weisberg glumly confessed, "I thought he had WMD, and I thought there was a strong chance he'd use them against the United States or one of our allies.... Had I known Iraq had no active nuclear program, I wouldn't have supported an invasion." "How Did I Get Iraq Wrong?" Slate.com. 2008 www.slate.com/id/ 2187105/ By that time some 100,000 had perished as a result of the American invasion. A high price to keep Iraq from getting weapons that they would likely use, at most, as a deterrent. See also H. Clinton 2014, 136–37.

[107] Stein 2008. Some still consider it "open to debate," however, "that the war was fought primarily as a nonproliferation campaign." Sokolski 2014, 4n7.

[108] Perle 2009, 42–43. Russett 2005, 396. In contrast, John Mearsheimer seems to consider the war to be an exercise in "liberal hegemony" from the start. Mearsheimer 2018, 156. Paul Pillar stresses that notions about democratic transformation had been there from the beginning, and the initial emphasis on WMD and terrorism was a matter of "salesmanship, not sincerity." Pillar 2011a, 18.

[109] Fukuyama 2005.

[110] Mueller 2011a, 251.

[111] Mueller 2011a, 148.

[112] Mueller 2011a, 148.

[113] Kaplan and Kristol 2003, 98–99; Frum and Perle 2003, 163.

[114] Russett 2005, 398–400.

[115] Woodward 2004, 428.

[116] Kaplan and Kristol 2003, 104–5

[117] Krauthammer 2004, 23, 17.

[118] Kaplan and Kristol 2003, 124–25

[119] Russett 2005. On this issue, see also Porter 2015, 109; Mueller 2011a, ch. 7.

[120] Frum and Perle 2003, 162–63.

[121] Podhoretz 2002, 28. Emphasis in the original.

[122] Mearsheimer and Walt 2007.

[123] On the impact of the intifada, see Winter 2015.

[124] Larson and Savych 2005, 132–8. See also Mueller 1994, 88–89, 140–41.

[125] Mueller 2011a, ch. 9.

[126] Preston and Sobchak 2019, Vol. 1, 69.

[127] Gerges 2005.

[128] Pillar 2011a, 13. See also Mandelbaum 2016, 201.

[129] Wilson 2003. On the monumental inadequacy and incompetence of the Iraq military and its leadership during the 2003 war, see also

Zucchino 2003; Shanker 2004; Gordon and Trainor 2006; Mueller 2004a, 138.

[130] Pillar 2011a, 52. Walt 2018a, 171. Preston and Sobchak 2019, Vol. 1, 68.

[131] Mearsheimer and Walt 2007, 274.

[132] Preston and Sobchak 2019, Vol. 2, 639.

[133] Preston and Sobchak 2019, Vol. 2, 615, 620. For some early commentary on the incentives for Syria and Iran, see Mueller 2003c.

[134] Gerges 2005, 252–53, 256–59. Bergen and Cruickshank 2007. Warrick 2015, chs. 4–10.

[135] Mack 2008, 15.

[136] Mindless brutalities: Woodward 2008. Iraq polls: Mack 2008, 15–17. Grenier: Warrick 2008. See also Bergen and Cruickshank 2007; Jenkins 2008, 191; Mueller and Stewart 2016a, 124; Abrahms 2018, 78, 89.

[137] Mansoor 2013, 268, 322n23. Warrick 2015, chs. 12–14.

[138] Mueller 1973, 59–62. The process is almost uncannily illustrated in tables in Mueller 2011a, 201–2.

[139] Mueller 2005. Mueller 2011a, 200.

[140] Overseas, meanwhile, Bush's exuberant British ally, Prime Minister Tony Blair, arguably the most successful and effective politician in British history, was utterly destroyed politically by the war.

[141] On some (quiet) opposition, see Chapman 2020.

[142] Gause 2006.

[143] Pew Research Center, Pew Global Attitudes Project 2012 Spring Survey Topline Results, July 10, 2012 Release. In Lebanon, however, it came near 50/50.

[144] See also Denison 2020.

5 CHASING TERRORISTS AROUND THE GLOBE AND OTHER POST-9/11 VENTURES

[1] For a somewhat more extended discussion of the phenomenon with additional references, see Mueller and Stewart 2017b. See also Mueller and Stewart 2016d.

[2] For additional data on annual fatality risks, see Mueller and Stewart 2016a, 138

[3] Institute for Economics and Peace, Global Terrorism Index 2015, 4. See also LaFree et al. 2015, 54, and, more generally, chs. 3 and 4; Smith and Zeigler 2017.

[4] LaFree et al. 2015, 13; but see also 22–23. See also Stohl 1988, 14–15.

[5] Stohl 1988, 3.

[6] Von Clausewitz 1976, 87, 231.

[7] Pérez-Peña, Healy, and Medina 2016.
[8] On these distinctions, see also Mueller 2004a, 18–20.
[9] Karnow 1991, 254–55.
[10] Sageman 2017a, 91. See also Sageman 2017b, 12.
[11] The process is discussed in detail in Warrick 2015, 115–22. It is also seen in Daniel Byman's discussion of the rise and fall of the Zarqawi organization in Iraq. It "began as a small terrorist group" using "high-profile attacks" to "undermine the Iraqi government and make a name for itself." Then, "it came to embrace insurgency, destabilizing and eventually replacing local governments." But when its efforts to rule in Iraq failed, "it returned to insurgency and then survived using terrorism." Byman 2016, 146.
[12] "An Hour with Syrian President Bashar Al-Assad," charlierose.com, March 29, 2015.
[13] On this issue, see also Cronin 2015; Byman 2016, 144.
[14] In her analysis of civil wars, Virginia Page Fortna pointedly notes that many definitions of terrorism "are so broad as arguably to encompass all rebel groups in all civil wars." Indeed, she continues, "much of the terrorism literature could substitute *rebellion* or *insurgency* for *terrorism*." In civil wars, "civilian targeting is ubiquitous; almost all rebel groups (and almost all governments involved in civil wars) target individuals as a form of 'control' to force cooperation and deter civilians from providing aid to the opponent." For her approach she contrasts insurgencies that use terrorism as a tactic – which she differentiates as the employment of "a systematic campaign of indiscriminate violence against public civilian targets to influence a wider audience" – from those that do not. Fortna 2015, 522, 522n16.
[15] Stohl 2012.
[16] Burke 2003, 238.
[17] Quoted, Watts 2015, 157.
[18] For example, Dixon and Sahi 2016.
[19] In its present form, the Global Terrorism Database, for example, seems to severely undercount the number of "terrorist" deaths during civil wars in Algerian, Liberia, and Bosnia in the 1990s. And it finds that there were no terrorist deaths in Vietnam at all during the tumultuous war years of 1970–75. Similarly, before 2003, the State Department count of terrorist events included only international ones. After that year, however, the definition was changed so that much domestic terrorism – including much of what was happening in the war in Iraq – was included in its terrorism count. Later numbers, therefore, are not comparable to earlier ones. See National Counterterrorism Center 2006, ii–iii. After taking into account various problems with their dataset including those concerning what they call "data collection artifacts," LaFree and his colleagues come

up with a rough trend pattern for terrorism worldwide: a persistent rise from the 1970s to the early 1990s, a somewhat abrupt decline thereafter (which they say has yet to be "adequately explained"), and then a rise again a few years into the new century. LaFree et al. 2015, 28–34. But that pattern rather closely mirrors trends for the amount of civil warfare going on in the world as can be seen in Figure 0.1. See also Mueller 2004a, 87; Pinker 2011, 303.

[20] For an extended discussion, see Mueller 2011e, 112–22.

[21] Mueller and Stewart 2014.

[22] See K. Mueller 2015.

[23] Dandeker 2013, 119–20.

[24] For a provocative critique of the Libya operation, see Kuperman 2013; Kuperman 2015.

[25] The interveners in Libya showed little willingness to do much of anything about the conflict spawned by the Libyan venture in neighboring Mali in which democracy was toppled. Friedman 2012.

[26] Takeyh 2001, 62–72.

[27] On this issue, see, in particular, Pillar 2011b.

[28] Ashford 2015.

[29] Byman 2016, 134. This rather resembles the Cold War phenomenon in which Third World potentates found it very much to their advantage to portray local insurgents as Communists.

[30] Statement by Mr. Paulo Sérgio Pinheiro Chair of the Independent International Commission of Inquiry on the Syrian Arab Republic, United Nations Human Rights Council, Geneva, March 17, 2015.

[31] Rhodes 2018, 223–24.

[32] Rhodes 2018, 237.

[33] Pew Research Center 2013. See also Mueller 2013.

[34] Rhodes 2018, 237, 240.

[35] Coats 2018, 20.

[36] Dobbins et al. 2015.

[37] On this issue, see Kinzer 2016a.

[38] Fuller 2014.

[39] Sullivan 2019a.

[40] Jones 2012.

[41] Bergen 2013.

[42] Hawley and Means 2012, 234. Mueller 2019a, 514 and case 33.

[43] On these plots, see Mueller 2019a, case 36.

[44] For an extended discussion, see Mueller and Stewart 2011, ch. 2; Mueller and Stewart 2016a, 306n4.

[45] For similar disputes between al-Qaeda central and the previous group in Iraq from which ISIS emerged, see Sageman 2008, 53–64; Gerges 2011, 108–112.

[46] Byman 2016, 133–34. Mansoor 2013, ch. 10. Preston and Sobchak 2019, Vol. 2, ch. 15.

[47] Mardini 2014. See also Giglio 2019, 105, 184; Tamimi 2016; Mueller 2014c; Gerges 2016, 284–89; Byman 2016, 138–39, 150–53; Mueller and Stewart 2016; Mueller and Stewart 2016b; Abrahms 2018.

[48] Byman 2016, 160, 152. See also Gerges 2016, 165–69, 233, 264.

[49] Filkins 2014. Parker et al. 2014. Taub 2018, 58.

[50] Parker et al. 2014; Warrick 2015, 302–3; Taub 2018, 58. Outnumbered: Byman 2017, 72. See also Giglio 2019, 64–65; Mueller and Stewart 2016b; Mueller and Stewart 2017a.

[51] Morris and Ryan 2016.

[52] Cockburn 2015. Preston and Sobchak 2019, Vol. 2, 596. See also Giglio 2019, 114.

[53] For data, see Mueller and Stewart 2020. A poll in relatively war-approving Alabama as early as 2005 asked whether the United States should be prepared to send back troops to established order if full-scale civil war erupted after an American withdrawal. Only one-third approved doing so. Reilly 2005.

[54] For data, see Mueller and Stewart 2020. Obama arrestingly commented in an interview in 2014 that ISIS had made a major strategic error by killing the hostages because the anger it generated resulted in the American public's quickly backing military action. If he had been "an adviser to ISIS," Obama added, he would not have killed the hostages but released them and pinned notes on their chests saying, "Stay out of here; this is none of your business." Such a move, he speculated, might have undercut support for military intervention. Baker 2014; see also Giglio 2019, 73–77. On the general stupidity of the strategy and tactics of ISIS and on the media's persistent inability to note this, see Mueller and Stewart 2017b and Abrahms 2018, especially 78–80.

[55] Froomkin 2014. See also Zenko 2014b.

[56] Cross 2014.

[57] Zenko 2014b.

[58] Mueller and Stewart 2020. In 2015 and 2016, Obama repeatedly insisted that ISIS did not present a threat that was existential. Mueller and Stewart 2016a, 24–25; Schneier 2015b; see also Goldberg 2016. However, he clearly lost the debate.

[59] Kropp 2015.

[60] There was a rare contrarian report in the *New York Times* a few months after the fall of Mosul. It found that American and foreign intelligence people considered the Islamic State to pose no immediate threat to the United States. Some told the paper that they believe the actual danger posed by ISIS has been distorted in hours of television punditry and alarmist statements by politicians. Daniel Benjamin, a top counter-terrorism adviser during Obama's first term, characterized the public discussion

about the Islamic State as a "farce," with "members of the cabinet and top military officers all over the place describing the threat in lurid terms that are not justified." Mazzetti, Schmitt, and Landler 2014.

[61] For sources, Mueller and Stewart 2016b, 41n56–57.

[62] Morello and Warrick 2016. For a critique, see Mueller 2016a.

[63] Zalkind 2015.

[64] Susman 2015.

[65] For more detail and extensive references on this process, see Mueller and Stewart 2016b.

[66] Hansen-Lewis and Shapiro 2015, 152. See also Watts 2015; Shapiro 2013.

[67] Gordon 2015. The editors of the *New York Times* placed this uncharacteristically upbeat item on page A16.

[68] Dagher and Kaltenthaler 2016. See also Tessler, Robbins, and Jamal 2016; Giglio 2019, 242.

[69] Gerges 2016, 279–84.

[70] Mueller and Stewart 2016b, 37. Some analysts remained unconvinced that its overall effectiveness was waning even as the group went into decline. Thus, in July 2016, the *New York Times* published a column acknowledging that the appeal of Islamic State as "the promise of living in an Islamist utopia" and as a victorious military force was in severe decline, and that the group had suffered many defections in the ranks as well. But the group's shift in focus from dealing with territorial degradation to slaughtering civilians in random attacks was taken not to be a sign of its "desperation and weakness," but one that demonstrates its "strength and long-term survival skills." Hassan 2016.

[71] Taub 2018, 60. Giglio 2019, 139, 214, 223–24.

[72] Taub 2018, 60–61. Giglio 2019, 140, 268–69.

[73] For discussions of strategies that stress patient containment and harassment rather than direct confrontation while waiting for ISIS to implode, see Watts 2015; Hansen-Lewis and Shapiro 2015; Posen 2015; Biddle and Shapiro 2016.

[74] Mueller and Stewart 2016b, 36.

[75] Friedman 2016. See also Wood 2015. On the reaction to the killing of the Jordanian pilot, see Warrick 2015, 311–16.

[76] Byman and Shapiro 2014a. See also Byman and Shapiro 2014b; Brooks 2011; Benson 2014; Bailey 2014; Gerges 2011, 192; Byman 2016, 158. In the United States there have been many cases in which the would-be perpetrator used chat rooms or Facebook or Twitter to seek out like-minded souls and potential collaborators – and usually simply got connected to the FBI. Mueller and Stewart 2016a, 97–100.

[77] Callimachi 2017. Hughes and Meleagrou-Hitchens 2017, 1–8.

[78] Mueller 2017b. One of those coached shot himself in leg, another was supposed to drive over people but attacked with an ax instead because

he did not have a driving permit, a third detonated a bomb prematurely killing only himself, and an explosive in a suicide vest proved not lethal enough to smash a nearby flowerpot. About the only "success" for the "cybercoaches" seems to have been the slitting of the throat of an 85–year-old priest in northern France – perhaps the most disgusting, pointless, and thoroughly counterproductive act of terrorism in history.

[79] Mueller 2019a.

[80] Lichtblau 2016.

[81] Callimachi 2016. One top official in Belgium at the time was willing to go on the record to estimate that 200 ISIS fighters had returned to his country and that perhaps 100 of these might well be plotting to attack. Winter 2016.

[82] Two years later, the *New York Times* published another article on the issue: Callimachi 2018. However, it entirely ignores the issue of the returnees. Instead there is a catalogue, from sources exclusively deep within the terrorism industry, about "Islamic State attacks" overwhelmingly perpetrated or planned by people who had no connection to ISIS except perhaps inspirational. The article does acknowledge that the number of terrorist attacks in Europe is down, but it alarmingly adds that the number of terrorism arrests (which it calls "attempted attacks") there was up. In contrast, it seems much more likely that the number of arrests was up because the police were trying far harder than before to dig such conspirators up. As the article points out, "Facing intense public pressure to stop the attacks, Western law enforcement agencies have raised their game." On this issue, see Mueller 2018b.

[83] Byman and Shapiro 2014. For a broad consideration, see Hegghammer 2013.

[84] York 2015. Byman 2017, 67. See also Smith and Zeigler 2017.

[85] Ignatius 2017.

[86] Robinson 2017.

[87] See also Giglio 2019, 179, 181. Peter Mansoor has pointed out that the successful surge in Iraq in the previous decade required not only American effort, but dedicated locals. Mansoor 2013, 262–63. In a comparative study, Stephen Biddle and his colleagues conclude that security force assistance works best, and perhaps only, if the locals are convinced they face a mind-concentratingly existential challenge. Otherwise their interests are likely to depart considerably from those assisting them. Biddle, Macdonald, and Baker 2018, 89–142.

[88] This suggests that there would have been public support even for a greater troop involvement by the United States. However, there was an understandable wariness that, after a decade and a half of war in the area,

public support might soften considerably if American casualty rates were to rise. The "by, with, and through" approach avoided that problem.

6 THE RISE OF CHINA, THE ASSERTIVENESS OF RUSSIA, AND THE ANTICS OF IRAN

[1] Mueller and Stewart 2016a, 262; Fettweis 2018, 96. See also Betts 2012, 83.

[2] Jaffe 2012.

[3] Friedman 2008, 35. On the dynamics of balancing threat, see Walt 1987.

[4] Daddis 2015, 48.

[5] Defense Department, United States 2018.

[6] For early examinations of this proposition, see Mueller 1989; Ray 1989. For a more recent extended consideration, see Fettweis 2010.

[7] Jaffe 2012.

[8] On this issue, see Kenny 2013.

[9] Mearsheimer 2014, 12, 26, 30.

[10] Mearsheimer 2018, 228.

[11] For example, Beckley 2018; Brooks and Wohlforth 2008.

[12] Mearsheimer and Walt 2016.

[13] Bell 2016, 41.

[14] Zakaria 2019.

[15] See Mearsheimer 2011, 33. Walt 2011b.

[16] Mearsheimer and Walt 2016.

[17] Walt 2018a, 267.

[18] Friedberg 2011, 7–8, 275, 279. See also L. Goldstein 2015, 6–7.

[19] Friedberg 1993/4, 7. Also: Friedberg 2000, 147–59.

[20] Choi 2006, 2015.

[21] See also Bandow 2015.

[22] Walt 2019. See also Ross 2011. See also Shirk 2007, 190; Johnson 2013, 7–48; Scobell, Ratner, and Beckley 2014.

[23] Bell 2016, 37. See also Kenny 2020, ch. 4.

[24] Freeman 2018. See also Kang 2017.

[25] Shirk 2007, 255, 261. See also Friedman and Logan 2012, 181–82; Lebow and Valentino 2009.

[26] Betts 2012, 181. See also Kirshner 2010.

[27] Christianson 2015, 298.

[28] L. Goldstein 2015, 355.

[29] Freeman 2018.

[30] For example, Ignatius 2017. In contrast, see Beckley 2018, 89–97; Kang 2019.

[31] For a discussion, see Higgins-Bloom 2018. Quynh et al. 2019.

[32] Kastner 2015/16, 54–92.

33 Preble 2009, 69.
34 Freeman 2018. See also Beckley 2018, ch. 3.
35 See Samuel 2018.
36 Pei 2016, 260, 266–67.
37 Allison 2017, 124.
38 Allison 2017, 123.
39 Allison 2017, 130, 121.
40 Mandelbaum 2019b.
41 Lindsay 2014/15, 14.
42 Green 2018. Beckley 2018, 48.
43 Freeman 2018.
44 "Experts: Russia, the U.S. and China will determine the future of the world," rbth.com, October 26, 2018.
45 For a discussion, see Bacchus, Lester, and Zhu 2018; Zhou 2019.
46 L. Goldstein 2015, 337–38.
47 Grabow 2017. See also Zakaria 2019; Fravel et al. 2019; Brautigam 2019; Khanna 2019.
48 As observed in Betts 2012, 188.
49 Kennedy 2010.
50 Applebaum 2018.
51 Kiely, Gore, and Farley 2018.
52 Shifrinson 2016.
53 Sakwa 2015, 46. See also Mandelbaum 2016, 68–73.
54 Sakwa 2015, 47.
55 Fettweis 2018, 41–42.
56 Sakwa 2015.
57 Åslund 2019b, 211–12.
58 Kupchan 2002, 14.
59 Charap and Colton 2017, 169. See also Sakwa 2015, 72–73.
60 Gwartney and Montesinos 2018, Table 2.
61 Åslund 2019a.
62 Charap and Colton 2017, 167. In Ukraine, for example, more than half of the loans in the bank system are non-performing – the funds are simply stolen by bank mangers or given to cronies such as members of parliament who enjoy legal immunity from prosecution. Åslund 2019a.
63 On this issue, see especially Charap and Colton 2017, 113–23, 133, 172, 174–75.
64 Sakwa 2015, 73.
65 Charap and Colton 2017, 125. Sakwa 2015, 96.
66 Sakwa 2015, 89–90.
67 Charap and Colton 2017, 122. Sakwa 2015, 84.
68 Charap and Colton 2017, 156.

69 See Person 2015, and especially Treisman 2016.

70 Sakwa 2015, 49.

71 Charap and Colton 2017, 127. Sakwa 2015, 103–4.

72 Sakwa 2015, 109.

73 Charap and Colton 2017, 132. On the woeful condition of the Ukrainian military, see Sakwa 2015, 159; Clapp 2016.

74 Charap and Colton 2017, 152.

75 Horton 2018.

76 Person 2015.

77 Quoted, Sakwa 2015, 113.

78 Treisman 2016.

79 Charap and Colton 2017, 158–59.

80 Charap and Colton 2017, 161.

81 Jonathan Eyal as cited in Sakwa 2015, 117.

82 Åslund 2009.

83 Sakwa 2015, 149.

84 Charap and Colton 2017, 135–36. Hathaway and Shapiro 2017, 391–93. Åslund 2019b, ch. 7.

85 Assessment by Daniel Ahn, talk at the Mershon Center, Ohio State University, November 1, 2018.

86 Åslund 2019b, 242.

87 Greene 2017, 115.

88 See also Greene 2017.

89 Pinker 2015. More broadly on this issue, see Gaddis 1987, 230.

90 Goldberg 2016.

91 Charap and Colton 2017, 138. Sakwa 2015, 115.

92 Person 2015.

93 On this issue, see Sakwa 2015, 108.

94 As observed by Henry Gaffney in conversation, 2018.

95 Treisman 2016.

96 "Russia Beyond Putin," *Daedalus*, Spring 2017, edited by George W. Breslauer and Timothy Colton.

97 Trenin 2018, 3.

98 The White House, Office of the Press Secretary, Press Conference by the President, December 16, 2016. See also Åslund 2019b.

99 Åslund 2019b, 172, 226–29. In one year, 37 times more money went into bribery than the government spent on health, education, and agriculture combined. Dawisha 2014, 1.

100 See also Bandow 2016a; Kinzer 2016b.

101 Trenin 2018, 1, 4.

102 See also Sakwa 2015, 248–49.

103 Trenin 2018, 6.

[104] Kramer 2016.

[105] Charap and Colton 2017, 166. See also Trenin 2018, 1.

[106] See also Charap and Colton 2017, 179.

[107] Kramer 2012.

[108] On this situation, see Kinzer 2016a. See also Mueller 2015; Mueller 2018c.

[109] Sanger 2018, 175–77.

[110] See also Mueller 2017a; Carpenter 2017; Trachtenberg 2017; Shane 2018; Porter 2018 12–13; Beinhart 2018; Zenko 2018.

[111] https://en.wikipedia.org/wiki/Italian_general_election,_1948.

[112] Martinez and Suchman 1950.

[113] Beckley et al. 2018, 6.

[114] Interview with John Mueller, Belgrade, Serbia, 2001.

[115] Levin 2016.

[116] Jamieson 2018, 67.

[117] Mutz 2012, 5. See also Kalla and Broockman 2018. Even the efficacy of the bully pulpit has often been found to be much overrated. Edwards 2003; see also Mueller 2018a.

[118] Jamieson 2018, 208, 205–6. See also Nyhan 2018, 2019.

[119] Gessen 2017.

[120] Chapman 2018.

[121] Gessen 2017.

[122] Sanger 2018, 213.

[123] Sanger 2018, 233.

[124] On some of these issues, see also Walt 2018b.

[125] See also Mueller 1984b.

[126] See also Zakaria 2006.

[127] Mandelbaum 2019, 113.

[128] Rosecrance 1986.

[129] Charap and Colton 2017, 179. For a different perspective, see Blackwill and Gordon 2018, 15–17.

[130] Beckley 2018/19, 196–97. See also Beckley 2018, 78–83.

[131] Shlapak and Johnson 2016. Heginbotham et al. 2015.

[132] That such a strategy might have been used against the Japanese after Pearl Harbor, see Mueller 1995a, ch. 7.

[133] For example: Blackwill and Gordon 2018.

[134] For an agile discussion of the nostalgia-inspiring return of Cold War-like nuclear metaphysics, see Oliker 2018. For a proposed set of mostly military measures to deal with Russian election interference, see Blackwill and Gordon 2018, 18–27.

[135] Reich and Lebow 2014, 2.

[136] See also Walt 2013; Zenko 2014a.

[137] Reich and Lebow 2014, 16.

[138] Reich and Lebow 2014, 183.

[139] National Intelligence Council 2017, 44. Or, as Reuters summarizes the notion, "While hot war may be avoided, differences in values and interests among states and drives for regional dominance are leading to a spheres of influence world." Landay 2017.

[140] Milne 1935, 222–23.

7 PROLIFERATION, TERRORISM, HUMANITARIAN INTERVENTION, AND OTHER PROBLEMS

[1] Much of this discussion draws from Mueller 2010.

[2] See in particular Sagan and Waltz 2002.

[3] Brodie 1966, 93.

[4] Allison 2004, ch. 7. Cirincione 2007, 15.

[5] For example, Waltz 2012. It is impressive how casually the sanguinist perspective of Waltz – a plausible line of argument, whatever the reservations might be – has been commonly dismissed without even much analysis or effort at refutation. As Richard Betts notes, the argument cannot simply be "brushed off," yet that is exactly what has happened; "surprisingly few academic strategists" have tried to refute it in detail." Betts 2000, 64. Thus the generally careful and thoughtful Mitchell Reiss worries (or did in 2004) that we are nearing a nuclear "tipping point" that could trigger a "proliferation epidemic." Should this occur, he assures us, "few would take comfort in the assurances of some academic theorists [a double putdown if there ever was one] that 'more may be better,'" directly quoting Waltz, but not even affording him a footnote. Reiss 2004, 4. If academics have substantially ignored the argument, policymakers have been at least as oblivious. For example, James Kurth simply dismisses the Waltz argument out of hand: "There probably has not been a single foreign policy professional in the U.S. government," he noted in 1998, "that has found this notion to be helpful." Kurth 1998. But not, one strongly suspects, because any has spent any time thinking about it.

[6] On Stalin's mental condition, see Mueller 1989, 123. On Mao, see Dikötter 2010.

[7] See also Zakaria 2006.

[8] For an extended discussion, see Mueller 2010, especially chs. 4 and 5.

[9] On this issue, see the discussion in Chapter 4 and in particular the article noted there: Walt 2000. For a study concluding that nuclear weapons do not help countries achieve better results in coercive diplomacy, see Sechser and Fuhrmann 2017.

[10] de Gaulle 1968, 103; Gilpin 1981, 215.

[11] Christopher Layne contended in 1993 that Japan by natural impulse must soon come to yearn for nuclear weapons. And three years earlier, John Mearsheimer argued that "Germany will feel insecure without nuclear weapons." Mearsheimer 1990.

[12] Jervis 1989, 4. For an assessment of this issue, see Hymans 2006, 211–12.

[13] Mackby and Slocombe 2004, 210. See also Maull 1990.

[14] Hymans 2006, 5.

[15] Arkin 2006, 45. Reiss 1995; Paul 2000. For a discussion of the relevance of the Canadian case, concluding from it that the issue of nuclear proliferation – then often known as the "Nth country problem" – was approaching "a finite solution," see Mueller 1967. For some early commentary suggesting that alarm about nuclear proliferation was unjustified, see Rosecrance 1964, 293–314.

[16] Meyer 1984. See also Hymans 2006, 2–12. On the very limited impact of the Non-Proliferation Treaty on this process, see Mueller 2010, ch. 9.

[17] Hymans 2012a, 2012b.

[18] Barack Obama, Remarks at the American Israel Public Affairs Committee's Annual Policy Conference, Washington, DC, June 4, 2008. McCain: Reid and Baldwin 2006.

[19] For a more extended discussion, see Mueller 2010, 137–41.

[20] As Leonard Weiss notes, "restrictions on nuclear trade and development are important elements of a nonproliferation regime." Weiss 2017.

[21] Pinker 2018, 146–50.

[22] For an analysis of the major difficulties it would have had to overcome, see Hymans 2012a, 2012b.

[23] For more detail on this issue, see Mueller 2020.

[24] Oberdorfer 2001, 314.

[25] Oberdorfer 2001, 307–308, 316. Harrison 2002, 213. On this issue, see also Fallows 1994/95.

[26] Oberdorfer 2001, 308, 316, 324. See also Harrison 2002, 117–18.

[27] Oberdorfer 2001, 318.

[28] Oberdorfer 2001, 399. Natsios 2001, 215.

[29] Oberdorfer 2001, 147–48, 318.

[30] See page 107.

[31] Reiss 2004, 12.

[32] Burr and Richelson 2000/01, 61.

[33] Burr and Richelson 2000/01, 76–78. For Johnson's perspective more broadly, see his brilliant book *Improbable Dangers*.

[34] On this process, see Mueller 1989, 184–86. See also Bundy 1988, 531; Walt 2000, 198; Zakaria 2006.

[35] Bowden 2017.

[36] Bowden 2017.

[37] See, for example, Lee 2019.

38 Pillar 2011a. Bandow 2020.
39 Knight 2012. Lajka 2018.
40 Eberstadt 2019.
41 Lee 2019, 64, 69,
42 Sagan 2018, 36.
43 Lee 2019, 64.
44 Cha and Collins 2018.
45 Haggard and Noland 2017, 227, 234–39. See also Hastings 2016, 178–83.
46 Lee 2019, 64.
47 See also Bandow 2019. For a critique of sanctions more broadly, see Hanania 2020.
48 On this issue, see Mueller 2006; Mueller and Stewart 2016a, especially chs. 1, 3, and 4.
49 Sageman 2017a, 170. Sageman 2017b, 373.
50 At the same time, however, Americans may have become decidedly wary about getting involved in extended ground wars in the quest to counter terrorism, and public opinion seems to be poised to accept debacle in the Middle East if there are no direct attacks on Americans. For a discussion, see Mueller and Stewart 2016a, 57–66.
51 For data and a more extensive discussion, see Mueller and Stewart 2018. See also Mueller and Stewart 2020; Mueller and Stewart 2016a, ch. 2.
52 Brooks and Manza 2013, 40.
53 For more on this comparison, see Mueller and Stewart 2018, 19.
54 Atran 2010a, xiv.
55 Schneier 2015b. On this issue, see also Mueller and Stewart 2016a, 24–25, 254; Healy 2011; Diab 2015.
56 Goldberg 2016.
57 Jaffe 2015. See also Mueller 2016b.
58 Easterly and Geltzer 2017. On this general issue, see also Finer and Malley 2017; Malley and Finer 2018. On the bathtub comparison, see Mueller and Stewart 2019.
59 Simon 2001, 233–34.
60 National Research Council of the National Academies 2010. See also Mueller and Stewart 2011; Mueller and Stewart 2016a; Stewart and Mueller 2018; Cordesman 2015; Government Accountability Office 2017.
61 Woodward 2010, 363.
62 Luxenberg 2010.
63 Mueller 2011a, 192–93.
64 Sageman 2008, 153–54. See also Sageman 2017a, 2017b; Mueller and Stewart 2016a, 130.
65 Anderson 2017.

[66] Mueller 2010, 100–11. On the much overwrought anxieties in the early 1960s that envisioned China as the ultimate rogue, see Mueller 2010, 95–97; Gavin 2012.

[67] Andreas 2013, 330.

[68] Fettweis 2018, 37.

[69] Friedman and Logan 2012, 183–84.

[70] Zenko 2013. On these issues, see also Rid 2012, Gartzke 2013.

[71] Lindsay 2014/15, 47.

[72] Schneier 2018, 76. Libicki 2014, 117–35. Rid 2013, 166.

[73] Schneier 2018, 3, 16. Schneier rather disarmingly refers to the title as "clickbait." Schneier 2018, 90.

[74] Lindsay 2013. Sanger 2018. Schneier 2018, 72.

[75] Sanger 2018, 273, 292. See also Schneier 2018, 72.

[76] Cohen and Zenko 2019, 125–26.

[77] Gellman 2002.

[78] Quoted, Stohl 2007.

[79] Kenney 2015, 112.

[80] Libicki 2014; Ackerman 2013.

[81] Giacomello 2004.

[82] Lindsay 2014/15, 19.

[83] Bill Keller, conversation with John Mueller, April 9, 2011, Berkeley, CA. See also Kenny 2020, ch. 6.

[84] Savage 2013.

[85] Kenney 2010. By contrast, see Weimann 2006.

[86] Benson 2014, 306–7.

[87] Sageman 2008, 114.

[88] See Sageman 2008, 71, 91, 138–39, 152, 157, 182. See also Morell 2015, 107.

[89] Jenkins 2011, 17.

[90] On this issue, see, in particular, Odlyzko 2019.

[91] Schneier 2018, 102.

[92] On this consideration in different context, see Mueller 1985a.

[93] On this issue, see Rosecrance 1986, 9–16. See also Friedman and Logan 2012, 184.

[94] Preble 2009, 107–14.

[95] Bender 2013.

[96] It should be kept in mind, however, that the Navy has a long and deeply impressive record of exaggerating threat. In the 1880s, for example, Naval leaders espied a threat coming from the Chilean navy: "Of all the nations most likely to plunder the American coast," notes one historian, "Chile, possessed of three [British-built] ironclads, was the most frequently cited." Thompson 1992, 24. See also Posen 2014, ch. 3.

[97] Stewart 2014.

[98] See also Friedman and Logan 2012, 180–81, 187; Preble 2009, 94–96.

99 Fettweis 2018, 147.
100 See also Cohen and Zenko 2019.
101 As Barack Obama mused, "In Libya, everything went right – we saved thousands of lives, we didn't have a single casualty, and we took out a dictator who had killed hundreds of Americans. And at home, it was a political negative." Rhodes 2018, 239. See also Mueller 1994, ch. 6; Mueller 2011f.
102 On this distinction, see Mueller 2004a, ch. 1.
103 For a concerned discussion, see J. Goldstein 2015.
104 For example: Urquhart 1993, 3–4; see also Mueller 2004a, 152–53.
105 The process has been interestingly explored by Fortna 2008. See also Goldstein 2011; Doyle and Sambanis 2006; Fearon 2004. For a discussion arguing that UN peacekeeping forces are far more efficient, see Kenny 2020, ch. 7. See also Straus 2012; Burbach and Fettweis 2014, 1–25.
106 Kenny 2020, ch. 7.
107 See, for example, the Defense Department 2010, 5. On this issue, see Zenko 2013; Fettweis 2013, ch. 1; Fettweis 2018.

8 HEDGING, RISK, ARROGANCE, AND THE IRAQ SYNDROME

1 Nordlinger 1995, 4. See also Posen 2014.
2 For example, Brooks et al. 2012/13, 17–19.
3 For a discussion, see Kenny 2020, chs. 5–6.
4 See also Mueller and Stewart 2016a, ch. 4.
5 For some efforts to do so in the costly quest to counter terrorism, see Mueller and Stewart 2016a.
6 Betts 2012, 277. See also Fettweis 2018, 155.
7 On America's (rather amazing) rebuilding capacities at the time, see Mueller 1995a, 67–68, 87–94.
8 Schroeder 2004, ch. 9. For a proposal that, following Schroeder's logic, Mikhail Gorbachev's USSR might have been brought into NATO, see Mueller 1989–90.
9 Brodie 1978, 81. Brodie 1973, 126.
10 Walt 2011a. See also Bacevich 2014; Mandelbaum 2016, 195.
11 Dyer 2006.
12 Thucydides, *The Peloponnesian War*, 5.89.
13 Presidential debate of October 11, 2000.
14 Brooks and Wohlforth 2002, 22, 30, 32. For a similar conclusion, see Beckley 2018.
15 Brooks and Wohlforth 2002, 32–33.
16 Speech at the National Cathedral, September 14, 2001.
17 Mueller 2006, 216n.

[18] See, for example, Drezner 2013, 52–79; Denison 2020.

[19] Bandow 2015. See also Walt 2018a; Fettweis 2018.

[20] Albright 1998. Compare Zenko 2014a.

[21] Obama 2014.

[22] Pew Research Center 2012.

[23] Keller 2013. Rubin 2013. See also Stephens 2014.

[24] Bacevich 2005. Kagan 2003. Mearsheimer 2011. Maddow 2012. Daddis 2015. Putin 2013.

[25] There is another variant on these questions: "Since the United States is the most powerful nation in the world, we should go our own way in international matters, not worrying too much about whether other countries agree with us or not." Responses to this formulation follow much the same trajectory as the "stay out" question, but it has been asked much less frequently. It is excluded from the figure to reduce clutter and to enhance readability, but it is available at Mueller and Stewart 2020.

[26] See also Smeltz and Daadler 2014, 154.

[27] Smeltz 2015. Smeltz and Kafura 2018. Smeltz, Daalder, Friedhoff, Kafura, Woytowicz 2018. Polls seem to suggest that support for international trade rose after Donald Trump became president. However, any Trump effect may be peculiar: Republicans likely see him as pro-trade and therefore support it, but Democrats likely see him to be anti-trade and therefore, in reaction, support it more greatly than before.

[28] Holsti 2004, 266–82. See also Smeltz and Daadler 2014, 7–9, 11–12, 28; but also 31.

[29] See also Mearsheimer 2014, 11; Logan and Preble 2011.

[30] Preble 2009, 168.

[31] See also Mearsheimer 2014, 29–30.

[32] Mueller 2011a, 177.

[33] On the tendency of the public to value American lives far more than the lives of foreigners, see Mueller 2011a, 172–75.

[34] For data, see Mueller and Stewart 2020. Republican politicians, who opposed the deployment in Bosnia, were ready to exploit any problems – as were Democratic ones in the Gulf War of 1991.

[35] Sobel 1998, 258–59. See also Western 2005, 264–65.

[36] On Cambodia, see Adams and Joblove 1982, 217–25.

[37] For data, see Mueller and Stewart 2020. See also Braumoeller 2019, 29-32. It is sometimes argued that support for war is determined by the prospects for success rather than by casualties – that Americans are "defeat phobic" rather than "casualty phobic" and therefore that "persuading the public that a military operation will be successful" is "the linchpin of public support." Gelpi, Feaver, and Reifler 2009, 236–37. Things *did* actually improve in Iraq at the time of the surge, and the public clearly got the message: between 2007 and 2008, the percentage of people who thought

US efforts were making things better rose from 30 to 46 while those believing they were having no impact dropped from 51 to 32. And the percentage holding that the US was making significant progress rose from 36 to 46 while the percentage concluding that it was winning the war rose from 21 to 37. Despite this change, however, support for the war did not increase – nor did it do so on measures tapping those who favored the war, those who felt it had been worth the effort or the right decision, or those who favored staying as long as it takes. For data, see Mueller and Stewart 2020. Successful prosecution of a war, it appears, is unlikely to convert people who have already decided it was not worth the costs. Mueller 2005, 49. American casualty rates also eventually declined both in Iraq and in Afghanistan, but this, too, had no effect on support for the war, although there had been studies predicting that decreased casualty rates would cause support to increase. Gartner 2008, 105.

38 Mueller 2013. Pew Research Center for the People and the Press 2013. In 2017 and 2018, Donald Trump got away with such bombings by doing them abruptly and then by not further escalating.

39 Mueller 2011a, 194–96. See also Western 2005. On these issues, see Mueller 2011h; Mueller 2018a.

40 Mueller 2005; Mueller 2011a, 209–10, 217–19; Mueller 2011g. Mueller 2014b.

41 Dandeker 2013, 116.

42 See also Mueller and Stewart 2016a, ch. 2.

43 Naím and Toro 2018, 136.

44 Sanger 2012, 419. For additional evidence of reticence in the military, see Martinez 2013.

45 German Marshall Fund of the United States 2013. On this issue, see also Carpenter 2020.

46 Obama 2014.

AFTERWORD AVERSION TO INTERNATIONAL WAR AS AN EXPLANATORY VARIABLE

1 Fettweis 2018, 26, 164.

2 Kagan 2018, 135.

3 Not returned: Sullivan 2019a. Far darker: Sullivan 2019b. In 2016, he told the *Yale Daily News*, rather remarkably, "I deeply believe that a world where America leads is a world where everybody ends up better off." ballotpedia. org/Jake_Sullivan. Everybody.

4 Thayer 2013, 409.

5 Brooks et al. 2012/13, 34–35.

6 Ikenberry 2017. See also Ikenberry 2011. Such contentions are central to hegemonic stability theory in many of its forms.

[7] As will be seen, the approach supplies an explanation for several elements that Charles Glaser (2019) considers crucial: cooperation under anarchy, NATO cohesion, the lack of balancing against the United States after the Cold War, and major country peace during and after the Cold War.

[8] Thayer 2013, 409. Russett and Oneal 2001, 158.

[9] See also Fettweis 2010, 172–76. Although cautious enough not to want to run the experiment, Jervis considers it "very unlikely that pulling off the American security blanket would lead to thoughts of war." Jervis 2011, 415. Michael Beckley is concerned, for the most part, about what would happen if the United States were to withdraw *economically*. Beckley 2018, 150–54. However, economic isolationism is not a premise of this counterfactual.

[10] In the counterfactual, it is assumed that the United States would have stood back from the invasion and let it happen. However, it is possible to argue that even in that situation, the Americans would have envisioned a direct, if eventual, threat against itself, and might therefore have intervened even from an isolationist perspective. As noted in Chapter 1, President Harry Truman says he "felt certain that if South Korea was allowed to fall Communist leaders would be emboldened to override nations closer to our own shores. . . . If this was allowed to go unchallenged it would mean a third world war." Truman 1956, 333.

[11] Lundestad 1999, 5–6, 186–89. See also Lundestad 1986; Hogan 1987, 444.

[12] Mastanduno 2009, 129. Leffler 1992, x–xi. For a discussion of British efforts to get the United States into World War I (on their side), see Squires 1935. For a splendid example of Winston Churchill in full form with the same general purpose in mind for World War II, see Daalder and Lindsay 2018, vii. Michael Mandelbaum argues that "favorable trends" in Western Europe were not directly caused by US foreign policy, but that the trends "could flourish" because the United States "successfully discouraged the Soviet Union from attempting to invade Western Europe." Mandelbaum 2020. But this suggests that, if the Soviets never had the slightest intention of conducting such an invasion, the discouragement was scarcely needed and that the "favorable trends" would have happened regardless.

[13] See also Walt 2018a, 276–78.

[14] Betts 1992, 23–24; see also Schweller 2001, 183. Interestingly, although he finds the cause of the general peace elsewhere, Robert Kagan contends that "prosperity and democratic progress" have "flowed from it." Kagan 2018, 135.

[15] Vasquez 1993, 151, 293. See also Goertz et al. 2016.

[16] Indeed, as Oona Hathaway and Scott Shapiro note, League signatories would be required to use force to counter such aggression: they could no longer simply stand by neutrally as others fought it out. In fact, as they further point out, this requirement was the chief reason why the Americans stayed out of the League. Hathaway and Shapiro 2017, 105–6, 111–12, 161. They were wary of automatically being dragged, or snookered, into another

of that continent's seemingly congenital armed disputes like the supreme exercise in sustained collective idiocy in which they had just participated.

[17] Howard 2000, 92. For a discussion of the process and a detailed enumeration of territorial changes since 1945, see Zacher 2001. See also Hathaway and Shapiro 2017, ch. 13; Porter 2018, 11.

[18] Altman 2020.

[19] Gaddis 1987, 230. Gaddis attributes the "unaccustomed caution" to the "nuclear deterrent." But it seems likely that the contestants had little interest in getting into anything like World War II again either, whatever the precise weaponry. See Mueller 2010, ch. 3.

[20] For a different perspective, see Hathaway and Shapiro 2017.

[21] Crawford 2002.

[22] Beckley et al. 2018, 16.

[23] Dower 1999, ch. 17. See also Hogan 1987, 444.

[24] Mastanduno 2009, 127.

[25] Leffler 1992, 506.

[26] Lundestad 1999, 5–6, 186–89.

[27] Porter 2018, 15. Fettweis 2018, 79.

[28] Pollins 1989a, 1989b, 465–80. Li and Sacko 2002. See also Mandelbaum 2019, 4–5; Barbieri 2002.

[29] In this respect, as Edward Yardeni points out, the Cold War could be seen in part as a huge trade barrier. 2000, 94. With the demise of such politically derived and economically foolish constructs, trade was liberated. But it was the rise of peace that facilitated the trade, not the opposite.

[30] Quoted, Jones 1987, 235.

[31] On this process, see Yergin and Stanislaw 1998; Mueller 1999, ch. 5.

[32] Porter 2018, 8. See also Kenny 2020, ch. 3.

[33] Mandelbaum 2019, 5. On the notion that economic interdependence under some circumstances can be a facilitator of war, see Mueller 2014a.

[34] Robert Schuman, The Schuman Declaration, May 9, 1950.

[35] Thus see Russett and Oneal 2001, 158; Ikenberry 2001, ch. 6; and Ikenberry 2011, 3. For the argument that effective business-regulating institutions tend to be put into place when the behavior they seek to foster has already become fairly common, see Mueller 1999, 95–98.

[36] Harry Dexter White quoted in Pollard 1985, 8.

[37] Mastanduno 2009, 127–28. See also Leffler 1992, 149, 499.

[38] Harry S. Truman, The Truman Doctrine, March 29, 1947.

[39] See also Pietrzyk 2002; Payne 2006; Thompson 1996.

[40] Huntington 1991a, ch. 2. For pessimism by Huntington (and others) about the prospects for democracy in 1984 in the middle of what he was later to label the Third Wave, see Mueller 1999, 201.

[41] Walt 2020.

[42] See also Reich and Lebow 2014, 2, 134, 168, xi, 133; Porter 2018.

[43] Einstein 1960, 566. Teller, Russell, Oppenheimer: Mueller 2010, 74. Morgenthau 1948, 402. Emphasis added.

[44] Einstein 1960, 382, 417, 482. On the civil war comparison, see Milner 1991, 78.

[45] Waltz 1979, 111.

[46] See also Ellickson 1991, 138; Bull 1977, 46-51; Milner 1991, 69, 74.

[47] Waltz 1979, 138. Or: "With many sovereign states, with no system of law enforceable among them, with each state judging its grievances and ambitions according to the dictates of its own, reason or desire-conflict, sometimes leading to war, is bound to occur." Waltz 1959, 159.

[48] Mearsheimer 1990, 12, 45. See also Art and Waltz 1983, 3–6.

[49] Hathaway and Shapiro 2017.

[50] Maull 1990, 101. See also Milner 1991, 81–85.

[51] See also Carpenter 2020. Compare Ikenberry 2017.

References

Abrahms, Max. 2006. "Al Qaeda's Scorecard: A Progress Report on Al Qaeda's Objectives," *Studies in Conflict & Terrorism*, 25(5), 509–29.

2006. "Why Terrorism Does Not Work," *International Security* 31(2) Fall, 42–78.

2018. *Rules for Rebels: The Science of Victory in Militant History*. New York: Oxford University Press.

Aburish, Saïd K. 2000. *Saddam Hussein: The Politics of Revenge*. New York: Bloomsbury.

Acheson, Dean. 1969. *Present at the Creation: My Years at the State Department*. New York: Norton.

Ackerman, Spencer. 2013. "NSA Goes on 60 Minutes: The Definitive Facts Behind CBS's Flawed Report," theguardian.com, December 16.

Adams, William C., and Michael Joblove. 1982. "The Unnewsworthy Holocaust: TV News and Terror in Cambodia," in William C. Adams, ed., *Television Coverage of International Affairs*. Norwood, NJ: Ablex, 217–25.

Albright, Madeleine K. 1998. *The Today Show* (NBC), February 19.

Alexseev, Mikhail A. 1997.*Without Warning: Threat Assessment, Intelligence, and Global Struggle*. New York: St. Martin's Press.

Allison, Graham T. 1971. *Essence of Decision Explaining the Cuban Missile Crisis*. Boston: Little, Brown.

2004. *Nuclear Terrorism: The Ultimate Preventable Catastrophe*. New York: Times Books.

2014. "Good Year for a Great War?" nationalintererest.org, January 1.

2017. *Destined for War: Can America and China Escape Thucydides's Trap?* Boston and New York: Houghton Mifflin Harcourt.

Altman, Dan. 2020. "The Evolution of Territorial Conquest after 1945 and the Limits of the Norm of Territorial Integrity," *International Organization* 74(3) Summer, 490–522.

Ambrose, Stephen E. 1990. "Secrets of the Cold War," *New York Times*, December 27.

Anderson, Kenneth. 2017. "The Bathtub Fallacy and Risks of Terrorism," lawfare.com, April 13.

Andreas, Peter. 2008. *Blue Helmets and Black Markets: The Business of Survival in the Siege of Sarajevo*. Ithaca, NY: Cornell University Press.

2013. *Smuggler Nation: How Illicit Trade Made America*. New York: Oxford University Press.

Andrew, Christopher, and Vasili Mitrokhin. 2003. *The World Was Going Our Way: The KGB and the Battle for the Third World.* New York: Basic Books.

Angell, Norman. 1914. *The Great Illusion: A Study of the Relation of Military Power to National Advantage.* London: Heinemann.

Applebaum, Anne. 2018. "NATO is Once Again Practicing for the Worst," washintonpost.com, June 8.

Arkin, William M. 2006. "The Continuing Misuses of Fear," *Bulletin of the Atomic Scientists*, 62(5) September–October.

Art, Robert J., and Kenneth N. Waltz. 1983. "Technology, Strategy, and the Uses of Force," in *The Use of Force*, ed. Robert J. Art and Kenneth N. Waltz, Lanham, MD: University Press of America.

Ashford, Emma. 2015. *Friends Like These: Why Petrostates Make Bad Allies.* Washington, DC: Cato Institute, Policy Analysis 770, March 31.

Åslund, Anders. 2009. *How Ukraine Became a Market Economy and Democracy.* Washington, DC: Peterson Institute for International Economics.

2019a. "What is Wrong with the Ukrainian Economy? UkraineAlert," atlanticcouncil .org/blogs, April 26.

2019b. *Russia's Crony Capitalism: The Path from Market Economy to Kleptocracy.* New Haven and London: Yale University Press.

Asselin, Pierre. 2018. *Vietnam's American War: A History.* Cambridge, and New York: Cambridge University Press.

Atran, Scott. 2010a. *Talking to the Enemy: Faith, Brotherhood, and the (Un)making of Terrorists.* New York: Ecco.

2010b. "Turning the Taliban against Al Qaeda," *New York Times*, October 26.

Bacchus, James, Simon Lester, and Huan Zhu. 2018. *Disciplining China's Trade Practice at the WTO: How WTO Complaints Can Help Make China More Market-Oriented*, Washington, DC: Cato Institute, Policy Analysis 856, November 15.

Bacevich, Andrew J. 2005.*The New American Militarism: How Americans are Seduced by War.* New York: Oxford University Press.

2014. "Do We Really Need a Large Army?" *Washington Post*, February 27.

Bailey, Ronald. 2014. "The Internet Does Not Increase Terrorism: Most Terrorism Takes Place in Internet-free Zones," reason.com, November 28.

Baker, Peter. 2014. "Paths to War, Then and Now, Haunt Obama," nytimes.com, September 13.

Bandow, Doug. 2015. "The Ultimate Irony: Is China the 'America' of Asia?" nationalinterest .org, May 27.

2016a. "Why on Earth Would Russia Attack the Baltics?" nationalinterest.org, February 7.

2016b. "The Case for a US Withdrawal from Afghanistan," *Business Insider*, June 20.

2019. "Trump's Remarkable Diplomatic Efforts in North Korea," nationalinterest.org.

Barbieri, Katherine. 2002. *The Liberal Illusion: Does Trade Promote Peace?* Ann Arbor, MI: University of Michigan Press.

Barnes, Fred. 1991. "The Hawk Factor," *New Republic*, January 28, 8–9.

Beckley, Michael. 2018. *Unrivaled: Why America Will Remain the World's Sole Superpower.* Ithaca, NY: Cornell University Press.

2018/19. "Reply," *International Security* 43(3) Winter, 196–97.

Beckley, Michael, Yusaku Horiuchi, and Jennifer M. Miller. 2018. "America's Role in the Making of Japan's Economic Miracle," *Journal of East Asian Studies* 17(3) November.

Beinhart, Peter. 2018. "The U.S. Needs to Face Up to Its Long History of Election Meddling," theatlantic.com, July 22.

Bell, David A. 2016. "The Sound of Munich," *National Interest*, May/June, 34–42.

Bender, Bryan. 2013. "Chief of US Pacific Forces Calls Climate Biggest Worry," *Boston Globe*, March 9.

Benson, David C. 2014. "Why the Internet Is Not Increasing Terrorism," *Security Studies* 23(2),293–328.

Bergen, Peter. 2013. "Hyping the Terror Threat," cnn.com, December 3.

    2016. *United States of Jihad: Investigating America's Homegrown Terrorists.* New York, Crown.

Bergen, Peter, and Paul Cruickshank. 2007. "Self-Fulfilling Prophecy," *Mother Jones*, November–December.

Bergen, Peter, and Paul Cruickshank. 2008. "The Unraveling: The Jihadist Revolt Against bin Laden." New Republic, June 11.

Berman, Paul. 1974. *Revolutionary Organization.* Lexington, MA: D.C. Heath, Lexington Books.

Betts, Richard K. 1992. "Systems for Peace or Causes of War? Collective Security, Arms Control, and the New Europe," *International Security* 17(1) Summer.

    2000. "Universal Deterrence or Conceptual Collapse? Liberal Pessimism and Utopian Realism," in Victor A. Utgoff, ed., *The Coming Crisis: Nuclear Proliferation, U.S. Interests, and World Order,* Cambridge, MA, MIT Press.

    2012. *American Force: Dangers, Delusions, and Dilemmas in National Security.* New York: Columbia University Press.

Bialer, Seweryn. 1986. *The Soviet Paradox: External Expansion, Internal Decline.* New York: Knopf.

Biddle, Stephen, and Jacob Shapiro. 2016. "America Can't Do Much About ISIS," theatlantic.com, April 20.

Biddle, Stephen, Julia Macdonald, and Ryan Baker. 2018. "Small Footprint, Small Payoff: The Military Effectiveness of Security Force Assistance," *Journal of Strategic Studies* 41(1–2), 89–142.

Binder, David. 1988. "Soviet and Allies Shift on Doctrine: Guiding Terminology Changes – 'Class Struggle' Is Out, 'Struggle for Peace' In," *New York Times*, May 25.

Blackwill, Robert D. and Philip H. Gordon. 2018. *Containing Russia: How to Respond to Moscow's Intervention in U.S. Democracy and Growing Geopolitical Challenge.* New York: Council on Foreign Relations, Special Report No. 80, January.

Blainey, Geoffrey. 1973. *The Causes of Wars.* New York: Free Press.

Blake, Aaron. 2018. "President Trump's Full Washington Post Interview Transcript," annotated,washingtonpost.com, November 27.

Blight, James G., Joseph S. Nye, Jr., and David A. Welch. 1987. "The Cuban Missile Crisis Revisited." *Foreign Affairs* 66(1) Fall, 170–88.

Bouverie, Tim. 2019. *Appeasement: Chamberlain, Hitler, Churchill, and the Road to War.* New York: Crown.

Bowden, Mark. 1999. *Black Hawk Down: A Story of Modern War.* New York: Atlantic Monthly Press.

    2017. "How to Deal with North Korea," *Atlantic*, July/August.

Bowie, Robert R., and Richard H. Immerman. 1998. *Waging Peace: How Eisenhower Shaped an Enduring Cold War Strategy.* New York: Oxford University Press.

Boyle, Francis Anthony. 1985. *World Politics and International Law*. Durham, NC: Duke University Press.

Braumoeller, Bear F. 2019. *Only the Dead: The Persistence of War in the Modern Age*. New York: Oxford University Press.

Brautigam, Deborah. 2019. "Misdiagnosing the Chinese Infrastructure Push," theamerican-interest.org, April 4.

Breslauer, George W. 1987. "Ideology and Learning in Soviet Third World Policy," *World Politics* 39(3) April.

Breslauer, George W., and Timothy Colton, eds. 2017. "Russia Beyond Putin," *Daedalus*, Spring.

Brodie, Bernard. 1966. *Escalation and the Nuclear Option*. Princeton, NJ: Princeton University Press.

———. 1973. *War and Politics*. New York: Macmillan.

———. 1978. "The Development of Nuclear Strategy," *International Security* 2(4) Spring, 65–83.

Brookes, Peter. 2007 "Iran Emboldened: Tehran Seeks to Dominate Middle East Politics," *Armed Forces Journal*, April 2.

Brooks, Clem, and Jeff Manza. 2013. *Whose Rights? Counterterrorism and the Dark Side of American Public Opinion*. New York: Russell Sage.

Brooks, Risa A. 2011. "Muslim 'Homegrown' Terrorism in the United States: How Serious is the Threat?" *International Security* 36(2) Fall, 7–47.

Brooks, Stephen G., John Ikenberry, and William C. Wohlforth. 2012/13. "Don't Come Home America: The Case against Retrenchment," *International Security* 37(3) Winter .

Brooks, Stephen G., and William C. Wohlforth. 2002. "American Primacy in Perspective," *Foreign Affairs* 81(4) July/ August, 20–33.

———. 2008. *World Out of Balance: International Relations and the Challenge of American Primacy*. Princeton, NJ: Princeton University Press.

Brown, Vahid. 2010. "The Façade of Allegiance: Bin Laden's Dubious Pledge to Mullah Omar," *CTC Sentinel*, 3(10) January, 1–6.

Brzezinski, Zbigniew. 1990. "Patience in the Persian Gulf, Not War," *New York Times*, October 7.

———. 1993. *Out of Control: Global Turmoil on the Eve of the 21st Century*. New York: Scribner's.

Bull, Hedley. 1977. *The Anarchical Society: A Study of Order in World Politics*. New York: Columbia University Press, 1977.

Bunce, Valerie. 1985. "The Empire Strikes Back: The Evolution of the Eastern Bloc from a Soviet Asset to a Soviet Liability," *International Organization* 39(1) Winter, 1–46.

Bundy, McGeorge. 1988. *Danger and Survival: Choices about the Bomb in the First Fifty Years*. New York: Random House.

Burbach, David T., and Christopher J. Fettweis. 2014. "The Coming Stability? The Decline of Warfare in Africa and Implications for International Security," *Contemporary Security Policy*, October 10, 1–25.

Burg, Steven L., and Paul S. Shoup. 1999. *The War in Bosnia Herzegovina: Ethnic Conflict and International Intervention*. Armonk, NY: Sharpe.

Burin, Frederic S. 1963. "The Communist Doctrine of the Inevitability of War," *American Political Science Review* 57(2) June: 334–54.

Burke, Jason. 2003. *Al-Qaeda: Casting a Shadow of Terror*. New York: Tauris.

2015. *The New Threat*. New York: New Press, 216.

Burr, William, and Jeffrey T. Richelson. 2000–01. "Whether to 'Strangle the Baby in the Cradle'," *International Security* 25(3) Winter

Burr, William, and Svetlana Savranskaya, eds. 2009. Previously Classified Interviews with Former Soviet Officials Reveal U.S. Strategic Intelligence Failure Over Decades: 1995 Contractor Study Finds that U.S. Analysts Exaggerated Soviet Aggressiveness and Understated Moscow's Fears of a U.S. First Strike. George Washington University: National Security Archive: The Nuclear Vault.

Bush, George. 1991. "Remarks to the American Legislative Exchange Council," March 1, www.presidency.ucsb.edu/ws/?pid=19351.

Byman, Daniel. 2016. "Understanding the Islamic State: A Review Essay," *International Security* 40(4) Spring, 127–65.

2017. "Trump and Counterterrorism," *National Interest*, January/February.

Byman, Daniel, and Jeremy Shapiro. 2014a. *Be a Little Afraid. The Threat of Terrorism from Foreign Fighters in Syria and Iraq*. Washington, DC: Brookings Institution, Policy Paper 34, November.

2014b. "We Shouldn't Stop Terrorists from Tweeting," washingtonpost.com, October 9.

Callahan, David. 1990. *Dangerous Capabilities: Paul Nitze and the Cold War*. New York: HarperCollins.

Callimachi, Rukmini. 2016. "A Global Network of Killers, Built by a Secretive Branch of ISIS," *New York Times*, August 4, A1.

Callimachi, Rukmini. 2017. "Not 'Lone Wolves' After All: How ISIS Guides World's Terror Plots from Afar," *New York Times*, February 4, A1.

2018. "ISIS Attacks in West Drop Sharply, but Threat Remains High," nytimes.com, September 12.

Canadian Security Intelligence Service. 2019. "The Precarious Struggle for Stability." Ottawa, May.

Carle, Glenn L. 2008. "Overstating Our Fears," *Washington Post*, July 13.

Carpenter, Ted Galen. 2017. "U.S. Hypocrisy On Election Meddling," huffingtonpost. com, January 31.

2020. "The Pied Piper with No Mice?" theamericanconservative.com, August 3.

Carus, W. Seth. 2006. *Defining "Weapons of Mass Destruction."* Washington, DC: National Defense University Press.

Cha, Victor, and Lisa Collins. 2018. "The Markets: Private Economy and Capitalism in North Korea?" csis.org, August 26.

Chapman, Steve. 2018. "A Polarized America? Not Quite," chicagotribune.com, September 23.

2020. "No, Susan Rice Did Not Support the Iraq War," *chicagotribune.com*, July 5.

Charap, Samuel, and Timothy J. Colton. 2017. *Everyone Loses: The Ukraine Crisis and the Ruinous Contest for Post-Soviet Eurasia*. London and New York: Routledge.

Checkel, Jeffrey T. 1997. *Ideas and International Political Change: Soviet/Russian Behavior and the End of the Cold War*. New Haven, CT: Yale University Press.

Chege, Michael. 2002. "Sierra Leone: The State that Came Back from the Dead," *Washington Quarterly* 25(3) Summer, 147–60.

Choi, Jong Kun. 2006. "Predictions of Tragedy vs. Tragedy of Predictions in Northeast Asian Security," *Korean Journal of Defense Analysis* 18(1) Spring, 7–33.

2015. "Crisis Stability or Geneneral Stability? Assessing Northeast Asia's Absence of War and Prospects for Liberal Transition," *Review of International Studies*, 1–23.

Chopra, Anuj. 2017. "Afghan Soldiers Are Using Boys as Sex Slaves, and the U.S. Is Looking the Other Way," washingtonpost.com, July 18.

Christianson, Thomas J. 2015.*The China Challenge: Shaping the Choices of a Rising Power*. New York: Norton.

Cirincione, Joseph. 2007. "Cassandra's Conundrum," *National Interest*, No. 92, November–December, 15.

Clapp, Alexander. 2016. "The Maidan Irregulars," *National Interest*, May/June, 26–33.

2017. "The Bosnia Myth," *National Interest*, September/October, 53–61.

Clinton, Hillary Rodham. 2014. *Hard Choices*. New York: Simon & Schuster.

CNN. 2003. "Wolfowitz: WMD Chosen as Reason for Iraq War for 'Bureaucratic Reasons,'" CNN.com, May 30.

Coats, Daniel R. 2018. Director of National Intelligence, Statement for the Record: Worldwide Threat Assessment of the US Intelligence Community, February 13.

Cockburn, Andrew, and Patrick Cockburn. 1999. *Out of the Ashes: The Resurrection of Saddam Hussein*. New York: HarperCollins.

Cockburn, Patrick. 2015. "Isis Mass Graves: Iraqi Forensic Teams Recover 1,700 Military Cadets Slaughtered by Militants near Tikrit," *Independent*, April 7.

Colton, Timothy J. 1986. *The Dilemma of Reform in the Soviet Union*. New York: Council on Foreign Relations 1986.

Cohen, Michael A., and Micah Zenko. 2019. *Clear and Present Safety: The World Has Never Been Better and Why That Matters To Americans*. New Haven, CT: Yale University Press.

Cohen, Roger. 2013. "An Anchorless World," *New York Times*, September 12.

Coll, Steve. 2018. *Directorate S: The C.I.A. and America's Secret Wars in Afghanistan and Pakistan*. New York: Penguin Press.

Commission on the National Defense Strategy for the United States. 2018. "Providing for the Common Defense," Washington, DC: United States Institute for Peace.

Congressional Record. 2002. October 10.

Cooper, Matthew. 1978. *The German Army, 1933–1945*. New York: Stein and Day.

Cordesman, Anthony H. 2015. "Fear Versus Fact: Getting the Facts on Terrorism," Washington, DC: Center for Strategic and International Studies, December 17.

Craig, Campbell, and Fredrik Logevall. 2009. *America's Cold War: The Politics of Insecurity*. Cambridge, MA: Harvard University Press.

Cramer, Jane K. and A. Trevor Thrall, eds. 2009. *Threat Inflation: The Theory, Politics, and Psychology of Fear Mongering in the United States*. London and New York: Routledge.

Crawford, Neta. 2002. *Argument and Change in World Politics: Ethics, Decolonization, and Humanitarian Intervention*. Cambridge: Cambridge University Press.

Crenshaw, Martha. 2010. "Assessing the Al-Qa'ida Threat to the United States," *CTC Sentinel* 3(10) January, 6–9.

Cronin, Audrey. 2015. "ISIS Is Not a Terrorist Group," *Foreign Affairs*, March/April.

Cross, Phil. 2014. "Senator Inhofe Warns of Potential Terrorist Attacks on U.S. Soil," okcfox.com, August 20.

Daalder, Ivo H. and James M. Lindsay. 2018. *The Empty Throne: America's Abdication of Global Leadership*. New York: Public Affairs.

Daddis, Gregory A. 2011. *No Sure Victory: Measuring U.S. Army Effectiveness and Progress in the Vietnam War*. New York: Oxford University Press.

2015. "Afraid of Peace," National Interest, July/August.

2017. *Withdrawal: Reassessing America's Final Years in Vietnam*. New York: Oxford University Press.

Dahl, Robert. 1971. *Polyarchy*. New Haven, CT: Yale University Press.

Dagher, Munqith al-, and Karl Kaltenthaler. 2016. "Why Iraqis Living Under the Islamic State Fear Their Liberators," washingtonpost.com, April 11.

Dandeker, Christopher. 2013. "What 'Success' Means in Afghanistan, Iraq, and Libya," in James Burk, ed., *How 9/11 Changed Our Ways of War*. Stanford, CA: Stanford University Press, 116–48.

Daponte, Beth Osborne. 1993. "A Case Study in Estimating Casualties from War and Its Aftermath: The 1991 Persian Gulf War," *PSR Quarterly* 3(2) June.

Davis, Daniel L. 2012. "Truth, Lies and Afghanistan: How Military Leaders Have Let Us Down," *Armed Forces Journal*, February 1.

2016. "Did America Really Lose the First Gulf War? How Desert Storm Taught Us All the Wrong Lessons," nationalinterest.org, December 17.

Dawisha, Karen. 2014. *Putin's Kleptocracy: Who Owns Russia?* New York: Simon & Schuster.

de Gaulle, Charles. 1968. "The Thoughts of Charles de Gaulle," *New York Times Magazine*, May 12.

de Long, Bradford. 2004. "Let Us Give Thanks (Wacht am Rhein Department)," November 12, 2004 www.j-bradford-delong.net/movable_type/2004-2_archives/00053 6.html.

Denison, Benjamin. 2020. *The More Things Change, the More They Stay the Same: The Failure of Regime-Change Operations*. Washington, DC: Cato Institute, Policy Analysis No. 883, January 6.

Defense Department, United States. 2010. *Quadrennial Defense Review Report*, February.

2018. *National Defense Strategy of The United States of America: Sharpening the American Military's Competitive Edge*.

Diab, Robert. 2015. *The Harbinger Theory: How the Post-9/11 Emergency Became Permanent and the Case for Reform*. New York: Oxford University Press.

Dikötter, Frank. 2010. *Mao's Great Famine: The History of China's Most Devastating Catastrophe, 1958–1962*. New York: Walker.

DiPrizio, Robert C. 2002. *Armed Humanitarians*. Baltimore, MD: Johns Hopkins University Press.

Dixon, Robyn, and Aoun Sahi. 2016. "Diary of Terror," latimes.com, June 24.

Dobbins, James, Jeffrey Martini, and Philip Gordon. 2015. "A Peace Plan for Syria," rand.org, PE-182-RC.

Doder, Dusko, and Louise Branson. 1999. *Milošević: Portrait of a Tyrant*. New York: Free Press.

Dorman, Andrew M. 2009. *Blair's Successful War: British Military Intervention in Sierra Leone*. Farnham: Ashgate.

Doyle, Michael W., and Nicholas Sambanis. 2006. *Making War and Building Peace: United Nations Peace Operations*. Princeton, NJ: Princeton University Press.

Dower, John. 1999. *Embracing Defeat: Japan in the Wake of World War II*. New York: Norton.

Drezner, Daniel W. 2010. "Why I'm Glad I'm Not a Counter-Terrorism Expert," foreignpolicy.com, June 28.

2013. "Military Primacy Doesn't Pay (Nearly As Much As You Think)," *International Security* 38(1) Summer, 52–79.

2019. "This Time is Different: Why U.S. Foreign Policy Will Never Recover," *Foreign Affairs* 98(3) May/June.

Dunnigan, James F., and Austin Bay. 1992. *From Shield to Storm: High-Tech Weapons, Military Strategy, and Coalition Warfare in the Persian Gulf*. New York: Morrow.

Dyer, Gwynne. 2006. "The International Terrorist Conspiracy," gwynnedyer.com, June 2.

Easterly, Jennie, and Joshua Geltzer. 2017. "More Die in Bathtubs Than in Terrorism. It's Still Worth Spending Billions to Fight It," cnn.com, May 22.

Eberstadt, Nicholas. 2019. "Kim Jong-un's Terrible, Horrible, No Good, Very Bad Year," *New York Times*, August 15.

Edwards III, George C. 2003. *On Deaf Ears: The Limits of the Bully Pulpit*. New Haven, CT: Yale University Press.

Eisenhower, Dwight D. 1948. *Crusade in Europe*. Garden City, NY: Doubleday, 469. 1954. Public Papers of the Presidents.

Einstein, Albert. 1960. *Einstein on Peace*, ed. Otto Nathan and Heinz Norden. New York: Simon & Schuster.

Ellickson, Robert C. 1991. *Order without Law: How Neighbors Settle Disputes*. Cambridge, MA: Harvard University Press.

English, Robert D. 2000. *Russia and the Idea of the West: Gorbachev, Intellectuals, and the End of the Cold War*. New York: Columbia University Press.

Epstein, Edward Jay. 1975. *Between Fact and Fiction: The Problem of Journalism*. New York: Vintage.

Fairweather, Jack. 2014. *The Good War: Why We Couldn't Win the War or the Peace in Afghanistan*. New York: Basic Books.

Fallows, James. 1994/95. "The Panic Gap: Reactions to North Korea's Bomb," *National Interest*, Winter, 40–45.

2005. "Why Iraq Has No Army," *Atlantic*, December.

2006. *Blind into Baghdad: America's War in Iraq*. New York: Vintage.

Fearon, James D. 2004. "Neotrusteeship and the Problem of Weak States," *International Security* 28(4) Spring, 5–43.

Feaver, Peter D. 2003. "The Clinton Mind-Set," *Washington Post*, March 24, A21.

Fettweis, Christopher J. 2010. *Dangerous Times? The International Politics of Great Power Peace*. Washington, DC: Georgetown University Press, 2010.

2013. *The Pathologies of Power: Fear, Honor, Glory, and Hubris in U.S. Foreign Policy*. New York: Cambridge University Press.

2018. *Psychology of a Superpower: Security and Dominance in U.S. Foreign Policy*. New York: Columbia University Press.

Filkins, Dexter. 2014. "On The Rise of ISIS," *Frontline* (PBS), October 28.

Finer, Jon, and Robert Malley. 2017. "How Our Strategy Against Terrorism Gave Us Trump," *New York Times*, March 4.

Finkel, David. 2013. *Thank You for Your Service*. New York: Farrar, Straus and Giroux.

Fortna, Virginia Page. 2008. *Does Peacekeeping Work? Shaping Belligerents' Choices After Civil Wars*. Princeton, NJ: Princeton University Press.

2015. "Do Terrorists Win? Rebels' Use of Terrorism and Civil War Outcomes," *International Organization*, Summer.

Frankel, Max. 2004. *High Noon in the Cold War: Kennedy, Khrushchev, and the Cuban Missile Crisis*. New York: Ballantine.

Fravel, M. Taylor, J. Stapleton Roy, Michael D. Swaine, Susan A. Thornton, and Ezra Vogel. 2019. "China Is Not an Enemy," washingtonpost.com, July 3.

Freeman, Chas W., Jr. 2018. *The United States and China: Game of Superpowers Remarks to the National War College Student Body*. Washington, DC: Middle East Policy Council, February 8. mepc.org/speeches/united-states-and-china-game-superpowers.

Freeman, Lawrence, and Efraim Karsh. 1993. *The Gulf Conflict, 1990–1991: Diplomacy and War in the New World Order*. Princeton, NJ: Princeton University Press.

Friedberg, Aaron. 1993/94. "Ripe for Rivalry: Prospects for Peace in a Multipolar Asia," *International Security* 18(3) Winter.

2000. "Will Europe's Past Be Asia's Future?" *Survival* 42(3) Autumn, 147–59.

2011. *A Contest for Supremacy: China, America, and the Struggle for Mastery in Asia*. New York: Norton.

Friedman, Benjamin H. 2008. "The Terrible 'Ifs'," *Regulation*, Winter. 32–40.

2012. "Intervention in Libya and Syria Isn't Humanitarian or Liberal: Assad's Fall, Like Qaddafi's, Is Likely to Produce Extended Illiberal Chaos or a New Set of Autocrats," nationalinterest.org, April 5.

2016. "Does ISIS Even Have a European Strategy?" nationalinterest.org, April 2.

Friedman, Benjamin H., Jim Harper, and Christopher A. Preble, eds. 2010. *Terrorizing Ourselves*. Washington, DC: Cato Institute.

Friedman, Benjamin H., and Justin Logan. 2012. "Why the U.S. Military Budget is 'Foolish and Sustainable'," *Orbis*, Spring., 177–91.

Friedman, George, and Meredith LeBard. 1991. *The Coming War with Japan*. New York: St. Martin's.

Friedman, Thomas L. 1992. "It's Harder Now to Figure Out Compelling National Interests," *New York Times*, May 31, E5.

Friedrichs, Christopher R. 1979. *Urban Society in an Age of War*. Princeton, NJ: Princeton University Press.

Froomkin, Dan. 2014. "The Congressional Hyperbole Caucus." firstlook.org/theintercept, September 10.

Frost, Robin M. 2005. *Nuclear Terrorism after 9/11*. London: International Institute for Strategic Studies.

Frum, David, and Richard Perle. 2003. *An End to Evil: How to Win the War on Terror*. New York: Random House.

Fulbright, J. William. 1966. *The Vietnam Hearings*. New York: Vintage.

Fukuyama, Francis. 1989. "The End of History?" *National Interest*, Summer.

2005. "America's Parties and Their Foreign Policy Masquerade," *Financial Times*, March 8, 21.

Fuller, Graham E. 2014. "Embracing Assad Is a Better Strategy for the U.S. Than Supporting the Least Bad Jihadis," huffingtonpost.com, September 29.

Gaddis, John Lewis. 1974. "Was the Truman Doctrine a Real Turning Point?" *Foreign Affairs* 52(2) January, 386–401.

1982. *Strategies of Containment.* New York: Oxford University Press.

1987. *The Long Peace: Inquiries Into the History of the Cold War.* New York: Oxford University Press.

1992. *The United States and the Cold War: Implications, Reconsiderations, Provocations.* New York: Oxford University Press.

1997. *We Now Know: Rethinking Cold War History.* New York: Oxford University Press.

2005. *The Cold War: A New History.* New York: Penguin.

2011. *George F. Kennan: An American Life.* New York: Penguin.

Gall, Carlotta. 2014. *The Wrong Enemy: America in Afghanistan 2001–2014.* Boston, New York: Houghton Mifflin Harcourt.

Gallup, George H., ed. 1972. *The Gallup Poll: Public Opinion 1935–1971.* New York: Random House.

Gardner, Dan. 2011. *Future Babble: Why Expert Predictions Fail – and Why We Believe Them Anyway.* New York: Dutton.

Garthoff, Raymond L. 1987. *Reflections on the Cuban Missile Crisis.* Washington, DC: Brookings.

1994. *The Great Transition: American-Soviet Relations and the End of the Cold War.* Washington, DC: Brookings.

2001. *A Journey Through the Cold War: A Memoir of Containment and Coexistence.* Washington, DC: Brookings Institution Press.

Gartner, Scott Sigmund. 2008. "The Multiple Effects of Casualties on Public Support for War: An Experimental Approach," *American Political Science Review* 102(1) February.

Gartzke, Erik. 2013. "The Myth of Cyberwar: Bringing War in Cyberspace Back Down to Earth," *International Security* 38(1) Fall, 41–73.

Gat, Azar. 2012. "Is War Declining – And Why?" *Journal of Peace Research* 50(2), 149–57.

2017. *The Causes of War and the Spread of Peace.* Oxford: Oxford University Press.

Gates, Robert M. 1993. "No Time to Disarm," *Wall Street Journal,* August 23, A10.

Gause, III, F. Gregory. 2006. "Beware of What You Wish For," www.foreignaffairs.org, February 8.

Gavin, Francis J. 2012. *Nuclear Statecraft: History and Strategy in America's Atomic Age.* Ithaca, NY: Cornell University Press.

Gelb, Leslie H., with Richard K. Betts. 1979. *The Irony of Vietnam: The System Worked.* Washington, DC: Brookings.

Gellman, Barton. 2002. "Cyber-Attacks by Al Qaeda Feared: Terrorists at Threshold of Using Internet as Tool of Bloodshed, Experts Say," *Washington Post,* June 27, A1.

Gellner, Ernest. 1988. "Introduction," in Jean Baechler, John A. Hall, and Michael Mann, eds., *Europe and the Rise of Capitalism.* London: Basil Blackwell.

Gelpi, Christopher, Peter D. Feaver, and Jason Reifler. 2009. *Paying the Human Costs of War: American Public Opinion and Casualties in Military Conflicts.* Princeton, NJ: Princeton University Press.

George, Alexander. 1955. "American Policy Making and the North Korean Aggression," *World Politics* 7(2) January.

Gerges, Fawaz A. 2005. *The Far Enemy: Why Jihad Went Global.* New York: Cambridge University Press.

2011. *The Rise and Fall of Al-Qaeda*. New York: Oxford University Press.

2016. *ISIS: A History*. Princeton, NJ: Princeton University Press.

German Marshall Fund of the United States. 2013. Transatlantic Trends Topline Data.

Gessen, Masha. 2017. "Russian Interference in the 2016 Election: A Cacophony, Not a Conspiracy," *New Yorker*, November 3.

Giacomello, Giampiero. 2004. "Bangs for the Buck: A Cost-Benefit Analysis of Cyberterrorism," *Studies in Conflict & Terrorism* 27, 387–408.

Giglio, Mike. 2019. *Shatter the Nations: ISIS and the War for the Caliphate*. New York: PublicAffairs.

Gilpin, Robert. 1981. *War and Change in World Politics*. New York: Cambridge University Press.

Gingrich, Newt. 2019.*Trump vs. China: Facing America's Greatest Threat*. New York: Center Street.

Glaser, Charles. 2019. "A Flawed Framework: The Rise and Fall of the Liberal World Order," *International Security* 43(4) Spring.

Glaser, John. 2018. "Status, Prestige, Activism and the Illusion of American Decline," *Washington Quarterly*, Spring.

Glaser, John, and John Mueller. 2019. *Overcoming Inertia: Why It's Time to End the War in Afghanistan*. Washinton, DC, Cato Institute, Policy Analysis No. 878, August 13.

Gleditsch, Nils Petter. 2008. "The Liberal Moment Fifteen Years On," *International Studies Quarterly* 52(4) December, 691–712.

Goertz, Gary, Paul F. Diehl, and Alexandru Balas. 2016. *The Puzzle of Peace: The Evolution of Peace in the International System*. New York: Oxford University Press.

Goldberg, Jeffrey. 2016. "The Obama Doctrine: The U.S. President Talks Through His Hardest Decisions about America's Role in the World," *Atlantic*, April.

Goldstein, Joshua. 2011. *Winning the War on War: The Decline of Armed Conflict Worldwide*. New York: Dutton.

2015. "World Backsliding on Peace," huffingtonpost.com, August 3.

Goldstein, Lyle J. 2015. *Meeting China Halfway: How to Defuse the Emerging US-China Rivalry*. Washington, DC: Georgetown University Press.

Goodwin, Doris Kearns. 1991. *Lyndon Johnson and the American Dream*. New York: St. Martins Griffin.

Gordon, Michael R. 1989. "Kissinger Expects a United Germany," *New York Times*, November 16, A21.

2015. "ISIS Carries Out First 'Serious' Attack in Northern Iraq in Months, U.S. Says," *New York Times*, December 18, A16.

Gordon, Michael R., and Bernard E. Trainor. 2006. *Cobra II: The Inside Story of the Invasion and Occupation of Iraq*. New York: Pantheon.

Government Accountability Office. 2017. *Aviation Security: Actions Needed to Systematically Evaluate Costs and Effectiveness Across Security Countermeasures*, Report to Congresssional Requesters, GAO-17-794, September.

Grabow, Colin. 2017. *Responsible Stakeholders: Why the United States Should Welcome China's Economic Leadership*. Washington, DC: Cato Institute, Policy Analysis 821, October 3.

Graff, Garrett. 2011. *The Threat Matrix: The FBI in the Age of Terror*. New York: Little, Brown.

Gray, Christine. 2002. "From Unity to Polarization: International Law and the Use of Force against Iraq," *European Journal of International Law* 13(1), 3–7.

Gray, Colin S. 2005. *Another Bloody Century: Future Warfare*. London: Weidenfeld & Nicolson.

Green, Samuel A. 2017. "From Boom to Bust: Hardship, Mobilization and Russia's Social Contract," *Daedalus*, Spring, 113–27.

Green, Tanner. 2018. "One Belt, One Road, One Big Mistake: China's Signature Foreign-Policy Project is a Failure that the U.S. Shouldn't Copy," foreignpolicy. com, December 6.

Greenfield, Meg. 1993. "Reinventing the World," *Newsweek*, December 20, 128.

Gould-Davies, Nigel. 1999. "Rethinking the Role of Ideology in International Politics During the Cold War," *Journal of Cold War Studies* 1, Winter, 90–109.

Gwartney, James D., and Hugo M. Montesinos. 2018. "Former Centrally Planned Economies 25 Years after the Fall of Communism," *Cato Journal*, 38(1) Winter, 285–309.

Hagerty, James C. 1983. *The Diary of James C. Hagerty: Eisenhower in Mid-Course, 1954–1955*, ed. Robert H. Ferrell. Bloomington, IN: Indiana University Press.

Haggard, Stephan, and Marcus Noland. 2017. *Hard Target: Sanctions, Inducements, and the Case of North Korea*. Stanford, CA: Stanford University Press, 227.

Halberstam, David. 1965. *The Making of a Quagmire*. New York: Random House.

Hallion, Richard P. 1992. *Storm Over Iraq: Air Power and the Gulf War*. Washington, DC: Smithsonian Institution Press.

Halperin, Morton H. 1961. "The Gaither Committee and the Policy Process," *World Politics* 13(3)April, 360–84.

  1987. *Nuclear Fallacy: Dispelling the Myth of Nuclear Strategy*. Cambridge, MA: Ballinger.

Hamann, Brigitte. 1996. *Bertha von Suttner: A Life for Peace*. Syracuse, NY: Syracuse University Press.

Hanania, Richard. 2020. *Ineffective, Immoral, Politically Convenient: America's Overreliance on Economic Sanctions and What to Do about It*. Washington, DC: Cato Institute, Policy Analysis no. 884, February 18.

Hansen-Lewis, Jamie, and Jacob N. Shapiro. 2015. "Understanding the Daesh Economy," *Perspectives on Terrorism*, August.

Harden, Blaine. 1999. "Reservists a Crucial Factor In Effort Against Milosevic," *New York Times* July 9, A1.

Harrison, Selig S. 2002. *Korean Endgame: A Strategy for Reunification and U.S. Disengagement*. Princeton, NJ: Princeton University Press.

Hassan, Hassan. 2016. "Is the Islamic State Unstoppable?" nytimes.com, July 10.

Hastings, Justin V. 2016. *A Most Enterprising Country: North Korea in the Global Economy*. Ithaca, NY, and London: Cornell University Press.

Hastings, Max. 2018. *Vietnam: An Epic Tragedy, 1945–1975*. New York: Harper-Collins.

Hathaway, Oona A., and Scott J. Shapiro. 2017. *The Internationalists: How a Radical Plan to Outlaw War Remade the World*. New York: Simon & Schuster.

Hawley, Kip, and Nathan Means. 2012. *Permanent Emergency: Inside the TSA and the Fight for the Future of American Security*. New York: Palgrave Macmillan.

Healy, Gene. 2011. "Al Qaeda: Never an 'Existential Threat'," cato-at-liberty, September 13.

Hegghammer, Thomas. 2013. "Should I Stay or Should I Go? Explaining Variation in Western Jihadists' Choice between Domestic and Foreign Fighting," *American Political Science Review*, February.

Heginbotham, Eric, et al.,2015. *The U.S.-China Military Scorecard: Forces, Geography, and the Evolving Balance of Power, 1996–2017*. Santa Monica, CA: RAND Corporation.

Heidenrich, John G. 1993. "The Gulf War: How Many Iraqis Died?" *Foreign Policy*, Spring.

Higgins-Bloom, Kate. 2018. "Food Fight: Why the Next Big Battle May Not be Fought Over Treasure or Territory – But For Fish," *Foreign Policy*, Fall, 26–29.

Hilsman, Roger. 1967. *To Move a Nation: The Politics of Foreign Policy in the Administration of John F. Kennedy*. New York: Delta.

Hinsley, F. H. 1963. *Power and the Pursuit of Peace: Theory and Practice in the History of Relations Between States*. London: Cambridge University Press.

1987. "Peace and War in Modern Times," in Raimo Väyrynen, ed., *The Quest for Peace*. Beverly Hills, CA: Sage, 1987.

Historicus [George Allen Morgan]. 1949. "Stalin on Revolution," *Foreign Affairs* 27(2) January, 175–214.

Hobsbawm, Eric J. 1987. *The Age of Empire 1875–1914*. New York: Vintage.

Hoffmann, Stanley. 1992. "Delusions of World Order," *New York Review of Books*, April 9.

Hogan, Michael J. 1987. *The Marshall Plan: America, Britain, and the Reconstruction of Western Europe, 1947–1952*. Cambridge: Cambridge University Press.

Holbrooke, Richard. 1998. *To End a War*. New York: Random House.

Holsti, Kalevi J. 1991. *Peace and War: Armed Conflicts and International Order 1648–1989*. Cambridge: Cambridge University Press.

Holsti, Ole R. 2004. *Public Opinion and American Foreign Policy*. Ann Arbor: University of Michigan Press.

Holloway, David. 1994. *Stalin and the Bomb: The Soviet Union and Atomic Energy, 1939–1956*. New Haven, CT: Yale University Press.

Hoover, J. Edgar. 1958. *Masters of Deceit: The Story of Communism in America and How to Fight It*. New York: Holt, Rinehart, and Winston.

Horgan, John. 2012. *The End of War*. San Francisco: McSweeney's.

Horne, Alistair. 2015. *Hubris: The Tragedy of War in the Twentieth Century*. New York: HarperCollins.

Horton, Alex. 2018. "Putin Made a Show of Crossing the New Crimea Bridge. But He Was Upstaged by a Cat," washingtonpost.com, May 16.

Horton, Scott. 2017. *Fool's Errand: Time to End the War in Afghanistan*. Chicago: Libertarian Institute.

Hosmer, Stephen T., and Thomas W. Wolfe. 1983. *Soviet Policy and Practice Toward Third World Countries*. Lexington, MA: Lexington.

Howard, Michael. 1989. "A Death Knell for War," *New York Times Book Review*, April 30, 14.

1991. *The Lessons of History*. New Haven, CT: Yale University Press.

2000. *The Invention of Peace: Reflections on War and International Order*. London: Profile Books.

Huchthausen, Peter A. 2002. *October Fury*. New York: Wiley.

Hudson, G. F., Richard Lowenthal, and Roderick MacFarquhar, eds. 1961. *The Sino-Soviet Dispute*. New York: Praeger.

Hughes, Seamus, and Alexander Meleagrou-Hitchens. 2017, "The Threat to the United States from the Islamic State's Virtual Entrepreneurs," *CTC Sentinel*, March, 1–8.

Huntington, Samuel P. 1991a. *The Third Wave: Democratization in the Late Twentieth Century*. Norman, OK: University of Oklahoma Press.

———. 1991b. "America's Changing Strategic Interests," *Survival*, January/February, 3–17.

———. 1993a. "Why International Primacy Matters," *International Security* 17(4) Spring, 68–83.

———. 1993b. "The Clash of Civilizations?" *Foreign Affairs* 72(3) Summer, 22–49.

———. 1993c. "If Not Civilizations, What? Paradigms of the Post-Cold War World," *Foreign Affairs* 72(5) November/December, 186–94.

———. 1996. *The Clash of Civilizations and the Remaking of the World Order*. New York: Touchstone.

Huth, Paul, and Bruce Russett. 1990. "Testing Deterrence Theory: Rigor Makes a Difference." *World Politics* 42(4) July, 466–501.

Hymans, Jacques E. C. 2006. *The Psychology of Nuclear Proliferation: Identity, Emotions, and Foreign Policy*. New York: Cambridge University Press.

———. 2012a "Crying Wolf about an Iranian Nuclear Bomb," *Bulletin of the Atomic Scientists*, January 17.

———. 2012b. *Achieving Nuclear Ambitions: Scientists, Politicians, and Proliferation*. New York: Cambridge University Press.

Ignatius, David. 2012. "The Bin Laden Plot to Kill President Obama," *Washington Post*, March 16.

———. 2017a. "America Can Succeed Militarily in the Mideast. ISIS's Defeat in Mosul Tells us How," washingtonpost.com, July 11.

———. 2017b. "China Has a Plan to Rule the World," washingtonpost.com, November 28.

Ikenberry, G. John. 2001. *After Victory: Institutions, Strategic Restraint, and the Rebuilding of Order After Major Wars*. Princeton, NJ: Princeton University Press.

———. 2011. *Liberal Leviathan: The Origins, Crisis, and Transformation of the American World Order*. Princeton, NJ: Princeton University Press.

———. 2017. "The Plot Against American Foreign Policy: Can the Liberal Order Survive?" *Foreign Affairs*, May/June.

Institute for Economics and Peace, Global Terrorism Index 2015: Measuring and Understanding the Impact of Terrorism. New York.

Jackson, Ashley. 2018. "The Taliban's Fight for Hearts and Minds," *Foreign Policy*, Fall, 43–49.

Jaffe, Greg. 2012. "The World is Safer. But No One in Washington Can Talk About It," *Washington Post*, November 2.

Jaffe, Greg, and Missy Ryan. 2016. "The U.S. Was Supposed to Leave Afghanistan by 2017. Now It Might Take Decades," *Washington Post*, January 26.

Jamieson, Kathleen Hall. 2018. *Cyberwar: How Russian Hackers and Trolls Helped Elect a President; What We Don't, Can't, and Do Know*. New York: Oxford University Press.

Janis, Irving. 1982. *Groupthink: Psychological Studies of Policy Decisions and Fiascos*. Boston: Houghton Mifflin.

Jefferson, Thomas. 1939. *Democracy*, ed. Saul K. Padover. New York: Appleton-Century.

Jenkins, Brian Michael. 2008. *Will Terrorists Go Nuclear?* Amherst, NY: Prometheus.

2011. *Stray Dogs and Virtual Armies: Radicalization and Recruitment to Jihadist Terrorism in the United States Since 9/11*. Santa Monica, CA: RAND.

2017. *The Origins of America's Jihadists* Santa Monica, CA: RAND Corporation.

Jervis, Robert. 1980. "The Impact of the Korean War on the Cold War," *Journal of Conflict Resolution* 24(4) December, 563–92.

1989. *The Meaning of the Nuclear Revolution*, Ithaca, NY: Cornell University Press.

2001. "Was the Cold War a Security Dilemma?" *Journal of Cold War Studies* 3(1) Winter, 36–60.

2002. "Theories of War in an Era of Leading-Power Peace," *American Political Science Review* 96(1) March.

2006. "Reports, Politics, and Intelligence Failures: The Case of Iraq," *Journal of Strategic Studies* 29(1) February.

2011. "Force in Our Times," *International Relations* 25(4) December, 403–25.

2013. "Explaining the War in Iraq," in Jane K. Cramer and A. Trevor Thrall, eds., *Why Did the United States Invade Iraq?* London and New York: Routledge, 25–48.

Johnson, Alastair Ian. 2013. "How New and Assertive is China's New Assertiveness?" *International Security* 37(4) Spring.

Johnson, Paul. 1995. "Another 50 Years of Peace?" *Wall Street Journal*, May 5.

Johnson, Robert H. 1997. *Improbable Dangers: U.S. Conceptions of Threat in the Cold War and After*. New York: St. Martin's.

Jones, E. L. 1987. *The European Miracle*, second edition. Cambridge: Cambridge University Press.

Jones, Seth G. 2008. "The Rise of Afghanistan's Insurgency: State Failure and Jihad," *International Security*, 32(4), 7–40.

2012. "Think Again: Al Qaeda," foreignpolicy.com, May/June.

Kaeuper, Richard W. 1988. *War, Justice, and Public Order: England and France in the Later Middle Ages*. New York: Oxford University Press.

Kagan, Robert. 2003. *Of Paradise and Power: America and Europe and the New World Order*. New York: Knopf.

2018. *The Jungle Grows Back: America and Our Imperiled World*. New York: Knopf.

Kaldor, Mary. Press. *New and Old Wars: Organized Violence in a Global Era*. Cambridge: Polity.

Kalla, Joshua L. and David E. Broockman. 2018. "The Minimal Persuasive Effects of Campaign Contact in General Elections: Evidence from 49 Field Experiments," *American Political Science Review* 112(1) February, 148–66.

Kalyvas, Stathis N. 2001. "'New' and 'Old' Civil Wars: A Valid Distinction?" *World Politics* 54(1) October, 99–118.

Kaminski, Matthew. 2009. "Holbrooke of South Asia: America's Regional Envoy Says Pakistan's Tribal Areas Are the Problem," *Wall Street Journal*, April 11.

Kang, David C. 2017. *American Grand Strategy and East Asian Security in the Twenty-First Century*. New York: Cambridge University Press.

2019. "When It Comes to China, America Doth Protest Too Much," warontherocks.com, April 19.

Kaplan, Fred. 1983. *The Wizards of Armageddon*. New York: Simon and Schuster.

2020. *The Bomb: Presidents, Generals, and the Secret History of Nuclear War.* New York: Simon & Schuster.

Kaplan, Lawrence F., and William Kristol. 2003. *The War Over Iraq: Saddam's Tyranny and America's Mission.* Francisco, CA: Encounter Books.

Kaplan, Robert D. 1993. "A Reader's Guide to the Balkans," *New York Times Book Review,* April 18.

Kapur, Roshni. 2018. "How Afghanistan's Peace Movement Is Winning Hearts and Minds," truthout.org, September 22.

Karnow, Stanley. 1991. *Vietnam: A History.* New York, Penguin.

Kastner, Scott L. 2015/16. "Is the Taiwan Strait Still a Flash Point? Rethinking the Prospects for Armed Conflict between China and Taiwan," *International Security* 40(3) Winter, 54–92.

Keaney, Thomas A., and Eliot A. Cohen. 1993. *Gulf War Air Power Survey Summary Report.* Washington, DC: Department of the Air Force.

Keegan, John. 1989. "Only One Man Wanted to Ignite World War II," *Los Angeles Times,* August 27, V–1.

1993. *A History of Warfare,* New York: Knopf.

Kellen, Konrad. 1972. "1971 and Beyond: The View from Hanoi," in J. J. Zasloff and A. E. Goodman, eds., *Indochina in Conflict.* Lexington, MA: D.C. Heath, 99–112.

Keller, Bill. 1988. "New Soviet Ideologist Rejects Idea Of World Struggle Against West," *New York Times,* October 6.

2013. "Our New Isolationism," *New York Times,* September 8.

Kellet, Anthony. 1982. *Combat Motivation.* Boston: Kluwer-NiJhoff.

Kennan, George F. 1947. "The Sources of Soviet Conduct," *Foreign Affairs* 25(4) July, 566–82.

1977. *The Cloud of Danger: Current Realities of American Foreign Policy.* Boston: Little, Brown.

1987. "Containment Then and Now," *Foreign Affairs* 65(4) Spring.

1989. "This Is No Time for Talk Of German Reunification," *Washington Post* November 12, D1.

Kennedy, Paul. 1987. *The Rise and Fall of the Great Powers.* New York: Random House.

2010. "A Time to Appease," *National Interest,* June 28.

Kennedy, Robert F. 1971. *Thirteen Days: A Memoir of the Cuban Missile Crisis.* New York: Norton.

Kenney, Michael. 2010a. "'Dumb' Yet Deadly: Local Knowledge and Poor Tradecraft Among Islamist Militants in Britain and Spain," *Studies in Conflict & Terrorism* 33 (10) October, 911–22.

2010b. "Beyond the Internet: Mētis, Techne, and the Limitations of Online Artifacts for Islamist Terrorists," *Terrorism and Political Violence* 22(2) April, 177–97.

2015. "Cyber-Terrorism in a Post-Stuxnet World," *Orbis,* 59(1) Winter.

Kenny, Charles. 2013. *The Upside of Down: Why the Rise of the Rest Is Good for the West.* New York: Basic Books.

2020. *Close the Pentagon: Rethinking National Security for a Positive-Sum World.* Washington, DC: Center for Global Development.

Kershaw, Ian. 1987. *The "Hitler Myth": Image and Reality in the Third Reich.* New York: Oxford University Press.

Khanna, Parag. 2019. "Washington Is Dismissing China's Belt and Road. That's a Huge Strategic Mistake. The Project Presents a Unique Opportunity for the U.S. to Ensure Eurasia Stays Multipolar," politico.com, April 30.

Khrushchev, Nikita. 1970. *Khrushchev Remembers*, ed. Edward Crankshaw and Strobe Talbott. Boston: Little, Brown.

1974. *Khrushchev Remembers: The Last Testament*, ed. Strobe Talbott. Boston: Little, Brown.

Kiely, Eugene, D'Angelo Gore, and Robert Farley. 2018. "Trump's False Claims at NATO," factcheck.org, July 12.

Kinnard, Douglas. 1977.*The War Managers*. Hanover, NH: University Press of New England.

Kinzer, Stephen. 2006. *Overthrow*. New York: Times Books.

2016a. "On Syria: Thank you, Russia!" *Boston Globe*, February 13.

2016b. "The Inestimable Importance of Strategic Depth," *Boston Globe*, March 5.

Kirshner, Jonathan. 2010. "The Tragedy of Offensive Realism: Classical Realism and the Rise of China," *European Journal of International Relations* 18(1), 53–75.

Kissinger, Henry A. 1979. *White House Years*. Boston: Little, Brown.

Knight, Richard. 2012. "Are North Koreans Really Three Inches Shorter than South Koreans?" *BBC News Magazine*, April 23.

Kramer, Andrew E. 2012. "Russian Naval Base on Syria's Coast Is Frayed, but Remains Strategic," *New York Times*, June 19, A6.

2016. "Spooked by Russia, Tiny Estonia Trains a Nation of Insurgents," nytimes.com, October 31.

Kramer, Mark. 1999. "Ideology and the Cold War," *Review of International Studies* 25 (4) October, 539–76.

Krauthammer, Charles. 2004. "In Defense of Democratic Realism," *National Interest*, Fall.

Kropp, Bruce. 2015. "ISIS Not Coming, But The Ice's Are." WJBradio.com/ LocalNews, February 23, Posted at politicalscience.osu.edu/faculty/jmueller/ ISISinIllinois.pdf.

Kupchan, Charles A. 2002. *The End of the American Era: U.S. Foreign Policy and the Geopolitics of the Twenty-First Century*. New York: Knopf.

Kuperman, Alan J. 2001. *The Limits of Humanitarian Intervention: Genocide in Rwanda*. Washington, DC: Brookings Institution.

2013. "A Model Humanitarian Intervention? Reassessing NATO's Libya Campaign," *International Security* 38(1) Summer, 105–36.

2015. "Obama's Libya Debacle: How a Well-Meaning Intervention Ended in Failure," *Foreign Affairs*, March/April.

Kurth, James. 1998. "Inside the Cave: The Banality of I.R. Studies," *National Interest*, Fall.

LaFree, Gary, Laura Dugan, and Erin Miller. 2015. *Putting Terrorism in Context: Lessons from the Global Terrorism Database*. London and New York: Routledge.

Lajka, Arijeta. 2018. "North Korean Food Shortages Leave Generations Stunted," CBS News, November 19.

Landay, Jonathan. 2017. "U.S. Intelligence Study Warns of Growing Conflict Risk," reuters.com, January 9.

Laqueur, Walter. 2003. *No End To War*. New York: Continuum.

Larson, Eric V., and Bodgan Savych. 2005. *American Public Support for US Military Operations from Mogadishu to Baghdad*. Santa Monica, CA: RAND Corporation, 132–38.

Layne, Christopher. 1993. "The Unipolar Illusion: Why New Great Powers Will Rise," *International Security* 17(4) Spring, 5–51.

Lebow, Richard Ned. 2010. *Why Nations Fight: Past and Future Motives for War*. Cambridge: Cambridge University Press.

Lebow, Richard Ned, and Janice Gross Stein. 1994. *We All Lost the Cold War*. Princeton, NJ: Princeton University Press.

Lebow, Richard Ned, and Benjamin Valentino. 2009. "Lost in Transition: A Critical Analysis of Power Transition Theory," *International Relations* 23(3) September, 389–410.

Lee, Chung Min. 2019. *The Hermit King: The Dangerous Game of Kim Jong Un*. New York: All Points Books.

Lee, Jean H. 2019. "Nuclear Weapons and Their Pride of Place in North Korea," wilsoncenter.org, August 6.

Leffler, Melvyn P. 1992. *A Preponderance of Power: National Security, the Truman Administration, and the Cold War*. Stanford, CA: Stanford University Press.

  2007. *For the Soul of Mankind: The United States, the Soviet Union, and the Cold War*. New York: Hill and Wang.

Leinwand, Donna. 2008. "Psst – Leads from Public to FBI Rise," *USA Today*, August 15.

Levin, Dov H. 2016. "Sure, The U.S. and Russia Often Meddle in Foreign Elections. Does it Matter?" washingtonpost.com, September 7.

Levy, Jack S. and William Thompson. 2011. *The Arc of War: Origins, Escalation, and Transformation*. Chicago: University of Chicago Press.

Li, Quan, and David Sacko. 2002. "The (Ir)Relevance of Militarized Interstate Disputes for International Trade," *International Studies Quarterly* 46(1), 11–34.

Libicki, Martin. 2013. "Dealing with Cyberattacks," in Christopher A. Preble and John Mueller, eds., *A Dangerous World? Threat Perception and U.S. National Security*. Washington, DC: Cato Institute, 117–35.

Lichtblau, Eric. 2016. "F.B.I. Steps Up Use of Stings in ISIS Cases," nytimes.com, June 7.

Lieber, Kier A., and Daryl G. Press. 2013. "Why States Won't Give Nuclear Weapons to Terrorists," *International Security*, 38(1) Summer, 80–104.

Liepman, Andrew, and Philip Mudd. 2016. "Lessons from the Fifteen-Year Counterterrorism Campaign, CTC Sentinel, October, 12–15.

Lin Piao. 1972. "Long Live the Victory of People's War! September 3, 1965," in K. Fan, ed., *Mao Tse-Tung and Lin Piao: Post Revolutionary Writings*. Garden City, NY: Anchor.

Lindsay, Jon R. 2013. "Stuxnet and the Limits of Cyber Warfare," *Security Studies* 22(3), 365–404.

  2014/15. "The Impact of China on Cybersecurity: Fiction and Friction." *International Security* 39 (3) Winter, 7–47.

Logan, Justin, and Christopher A. Preble. 2011. "For U.S. Interventionists, 'Isolationism' Is Just a Dirty Word," cato.org, June 22.

Luard, Evan. 1986. *War in International Society*. New Haven, CT: Yale University Press.

Lukacs, John. 1997. *The Hitler of History*. New York: Knopf, xi.

Lundestad, Geir. 1986. "Empire by Invitation? The United States and Western Europe, 1945–1952," *Journal of Peace Research* 23(3), 263–77.

——— 1999. *East, West, North, South: Major Developments in International Politics since 1945*, Fourth Edition. New York: Oxford University Press.

Luxenberg, Steve. 2010. "Bob Woodward Book Details Obama Battles with Advisers over Exit Plan for Afghan War," washingtonpost.com, September 22.

McCarthy, Rory. 2001. "New Offer on Bin Laden," *Guardian*, October 16.

McDermott, Terry, and Josh Meyer. 2012. *The Hunt for KSM: Inside the Pursuit and Takedown of the Real 9/11 Mastermind, Khalid Sheikh Mohammed*. New York: Little, Brown.

Macdonald, Douglas J. 1995/96. "Communist Bloc Expansion in the Early Cold War: Challenging Realism, Refuting Revisionism," *International Security* 20, Winter, 152–88.

McKnight, Michael. 2019. "Soccer. War. Nothing More," *Sports Illustrated*, June 3.

McMaster, H. R. 1997. *Dereliction of Duty: Lyndon Johnson, Robert McNamara, the Joint Chiefs of Staff, and the Lies That Led to Vietnam*. New York: HarperPerennial.

McQueen, Alison. 2018. *Political Realism in Apocalyptic Times*. New York: Cambridge University Press.

Mack, Andrew. 2005. *Human Security Report 2005*. New York: Oxford University Press.

——— 2008. "Dying to Lose: Explaining the Decline in Global Terrorism." In *Human Security Brief 2007*. Vancouver, BC: Human Security Report Project, School for International Studies, Simon Fraser University, 8–21.

Mackby, Jennifer, and Walter Slocombe. 2004. "Germany: A Model Case, A Historical Imperative," in Kurt M. Campbell, Robert J. Einhorn, and Mitchell B. Reiss, eds., *The Nuclear Tipping Point: Why States Reconsider Their Nuclear Choices*, Washington, DC: Brookings Institution Press.

Mackey, Sandra. 1989. *Lebanon: Death of a Nation*. New York: Congdon & Weed.

Maddow, Rachel. 2012. *Drift: The Unmooring of American Military Power*. New York: Crown.

Malley, Robert, and Jon Finer. 2018. "The Long Shadow of 9/11: How Counterterrorism Warps U.S. Foreign Policy," *Foreign Affairs*, July/August.

MacMillan, Margaret. 2013. *The War that Ended Peace: The Road to 1914*. New York: Random House.

Malcolm, Noel. 1993. "Seeing Ghosts," *National Interest*, Summer, 83–88.

Manchester, William. 1988. *The Last Lion, Winston Spencer Churchill: Alone, 1932–1940*. Boston: Little, Brown 1988.

Mandelbaum, Michael. 2002. *The Ideas That Conquered the World: Peace, Democracy, and Free Markets in the Twenty-First Century*. New York: Public Affairs.

——— 2016. *Mission Failure: America and the World in the Post-Cold War Era*. New York: Oxford University Press.

——— 2019a. *The Rise and Fall of Peace on Earth*. New York: Oxford University Press.

——— 2019b. "Xi's Power Play: Revolution China Again." the-american-interest.com, January 21.

——— 2020. "Painful Lessons," the-american-interest.com, June 8.

Mansoor, Peter R. 2013. *Surge: My Journey with General David Petraeus and the Remaking of the Iraq War*. New Haven, CT: Yale University Press.

Mardini, Ramzy. 2014. "The Islamic State Threat Is Overstated," washingtonpost.com, September 12.

Martinez, C. Edda, and Edward A. Suchman, 1950. "Letters From America and the 1948 Elections in Italy," *Public Opinion Quarterly* 14(1) March.

Martinez, Luis. 2013. "Gen. Martin Dempsey Lays Out US Military Options for Syria," abcnews.go.com, July 22.

Mastanduno, Michael. 2009, "System Maker and Privilege Taker: U.S. Power and the International Political Economy," *World Politics* 61(1) January, 121–54.

Mastny, Vojtech. 2006. "Introduction," and "Imagining War in Europe" in Vojtech Mastny, Sven G. Holtsmark, and Andreas Wenger, eds., *War Plans and Alliances in the Cold War: Threat Perceptions in the East and West.* London and New York: Routledge, 1–45.

Matlock, Jack F., Jr. 1995. *Autopsy on an Empire: The American Ambassador's Account of the Collapse of the Soviet Union.* New York: Random House.

Maull, Hanns W. 1990. "Germany and Japan: The New Civilian Powers," *Foreign Affairs* 69(5)Winter, 91–106.

May, Ernest R. 1984. "The Cold War," in *The Making of America's Soviet Policy*, ed. Joseph S. Nye, Jr. New Haven, CT: Yale University Press.

2000. *Strange Victory: Hitler's Conquest of France.* New York: Hill and Wang.

Mayer, Jane. 2008. *The Dark Side: The Inside Story on How the War on Terror Turned into a War on American Ideals.* New York: Doubleday.

Mazzetti, Mark, Eric Schmitt, and Mark Landler. 2014. "Struggling to Gauge ISIS Threat, Even as U.S. Prepares to Act," *New York Times*, September 10.

Mead, Margaret. 1964. "Warfare Is Only an Invention – Not a Biological Necessity," in Leon Bramson and George W. Goethals, eds., *War: Studies from Psychology, Sociology, Anthropology.* New York: Basic Books.

Mearsheimer, John J. 1990. "Back to the Future: Instability in Europe after the Cold War," *International Security* 15(1) Summer, 5–56.

2009. "Hollow Victory," foreignpolicy.com, November 2.

2011. "Imperial by Design," *National Interest*, January/February.

2014. "America Unhinged," *National Interest*, January/February,

2018. *The Great Delusion: Liberal Dreams and International Realities.* New Haven, CT: Yale University Press.

Mearsheimer, John J., and Stephen M. Walt. 2003. "Iraq: An Unnecessary War," *Foreign Policy* 82(1) January/February, 50–59.

2007. *The Israel Lobby and U.S. Foreign Policy.* New York: Farrar Straus Giroux.

2016. "The Case for Offshore Balancing A Superior U.S. Grand Strategy," *Foreign Affairs*, July/August, 70–83.

Medvedev, Roy. 1983. *Khrushchev.* Garden City, NY: Doubleday.

Menon, Rajan. 2016. *The Conceit of Humanitarian Intervention.* New York: Oxford University Press.

Meyer, Stephen M. 1984. *The Dynamics of Nuclear Proliferation.* Chicago: University of Chicago.

Miller, Greg. 2009. "Cheney Assertions of Lives Saved Hard to Support," latimes.com, May 23.

2011. "Bin Laden Documents Reveal Strain, Struggle in al-Qaida," *Washington Post*, July 1.

Millet, Allan R. 2005. *The War for Korea, 1945–1950: A House Burning*. Lawrence, KS: University Press of Kansas.

Milne, A. A. 1935. *Peace With Honour*. New York: Dutton.

Milner, Helen. 1991. "The Assumption of Anarchy in International Relations Theory: A Critique," *Review of International Studies* 17, 67–85.

Moore, Molly. 1991. "Porous Minefields, Dispirited Troops and a Dog Named Pow," *Washington Post*, March 17, A1.

Morell, Michael. 2015. *The Great War of Our Time: The CIA's Fight Against Terrorism from al Qa'ida to ISIS*. New York: Twelve.

Morello, Carol, and Joby Warrick. 2016. "Islamic State's Ambitions and allure Grow as Territory Shrinks," washingtonpost.com, July 4.

Morgenthau, Hans J. 1948. *Politics Among Nations: The Struggle for Power and Peace*. New York: Knopf.

Morris, Loveday, and Missy Ryan. 2016. "After More Than $1.6 Billion in U.S. Aid, Iraq's Army Still Struggles," washingtonpost.com, June 10,

Mueller, John. 1967. "Incentives for Restraint: Canada as a Nonnuclear Power," *Orbis* 11(3) Fall, 864–84.

1969. *Approaches to Measurement in International Relations: A Non-Evangelical Survey*. New York: Appleton-Century-Crofts.

1973. *War, Presidents and Public Opinion*. New York: Wiley.

1980. "The Search for the 'Breaking Point' in Vietnam: The Statistics of a Deadly Quarrel." *International Studies Quarterly* 24(4) December, 497–519.

1984a. "Reflections on the Vietnam Protest Movement and on the Curious Calm at the War's End," in Peter Braestrup, ed., *Vietnam as History*. Lanham, MD: University Press of America, 151–57, politicalscience.osu.edu/faculty/jmueller/BRAESTRU.pdf.

1984b. "Lessons Learned Five Years After the Hostage Nightmare," *Wall Street Journal*, November 6, politicalscience.osu.edu/faculty/jmueller/WSJhostage.pdf.

1985a. "Crime Is Caused by the Young and Reckless," *Wall Street Journal*, March 6, politicalscience.osu.edu/faculty/jmueller/WSJcrime.pdf.

1985b. "The Bomb's Pretense as Peacemaker," *Wall Street Journal*, June 4, politicalscience.osu.edu/faculty/jmueller/WSJbomb.pdf.

1985c. *Astaire Dancing: The Musical Films*. New York: Knopf.

1986. "Containment and the Decline of the Soviet Empire: Some Tentative Comments on the End of the World As We Know It." Paper delivered at the International Studies Association Convention, Anaheim, CA, March 28, politicalscience.osu.edu/faculty/jmueller/isa1986.pdf.

1988. "The Essential Irrelevance of Nuclear Weapons: Stability in the Postwar World," *International Security* 13(2) Fall, 55–79.

1989. *Retreat from Doomsday: The Obsolescence of Major War*. New York: Basic Books.

1989–90. "A New Concert of Europe," *Foreign Policy*, Winter, 3–16

1990. "The Art of a Deal: No Rewards for Iraqi Aggression," *Arizona Republic*, December 16.

1991. "Taking Peace Seriously: Two Proposals," in Robert Jervis and Seweryn Bialer, eds., *Soviet-American Relations After the Cold War*. Durham, NC: Duke University Press, 262–75.

1994. *Policy and Opinion in the Gulf War* Chicago: University of Chicago Press.

1995a. *Quiet Cataclysm: Reflections on the Recent Transformation of World Politics.* New York: HarperCollins, politicalscience.osu.edu/faculty/jmueller/qcfull.pdf.

1995b. "The Perfect Enemy: Assessing the Gulf War," *Security Studies* 5(1) Autumn, 77–117.

1999. *Capitalism, Democracy, and Ralph's Pretty Good Grocery.* Princeton, NJ: Princeton University Press.

2002a. "Harbinger or Aberration? A 9/11 Provocation," *National Interest,* Fall, 45–50.

2002b. "False Alarms," *Washington Post,* September 29.

2003a. "Blip or Step Function?" Paper presented at the Annual Convention of the International Studies Association, Portland, OR, February 27, politicalscience.osu.edu/faculty/jmueller/ISA2003.PDF.

2003b. "Should We Invade Iraq?" *Reason,* January; also on reason.com, October 28–November 1, 2002: reason.com/debate/ai-debate1.shtml.

2003c "Debacle?" An op-ed pitched to the *Washington Post* on July 16, 2003, that went awry because the editor addressed had apparently changed jobs: politicalscience.osu.edu/faculty/jmueller/debacle.pdf.

2004a. *The Remnants of War.* Ithaca, NY: Cornell University Press.

2004b. "The Role of Business Virtue in Economic Development: Six Propositions Provoked in Part by P. T. Barnum with an Extrapolation to the Post-Communist Experience," June 14, 2004, politicalscience.osu.edu/faculty/jmueller/BUSVRCEU.pdf.

2005. "The Iraq Syndrome," *Foreign Affairs,* November/December, 44–54.

2006. *Overblown: How Politicians and the Terrorism Industry Inflate National Security Threats, and Why We Believe Them.* New York: Free Press.

2007. "Extrapolations from a Book about Nothing." In Helen Fehervary and Bernd Fischer, eds., *Cultural Poltics and the Politics of Culture: Essays to Honor Alexander Stephan.* Bern: Peter Lang, 39–45.

2009. "The 'Safe Haven' Myth," thenation.com, October 21, 2009.

2010. *Atomic Obsession: Nuclear Alarmism from Hiroshima to Al-Qaeda,* New York: Oxford University Press. Improved index in the paperback version.

2011a. *War and Ideas: Selected Essays.* London and New York: Routledge.

2011b. "Questing for Monsters to Destroy," in Melvyn Leffler and Jeffrey W. Legro, eds., *In Uncertain Times: American Foreign Policy after the Berlin Wall and 9/11.* Ithaca, NY: Cornell University Press, 117–30.

2011c. "Room for Debate: Should the U.S. Move Against Qaddafi? What We Should Know by Now," nytimes.com, March 2.

2011d. "The Truth about Al-Qaeda: Bin Laden's Files Revealed the Terrorists in Dramatic Decline," foreignaffairs.com, August 2.

2011e. "Action and Reaction: Assessing the Historic Impact of Terrorism," in Jean E. Rosenfeld, ed., *Terrorism, Identity, and Legitimacy: The Four Waves Theory and Political Violence.* New York and London: Routledge, 112–22.

2011f. "Will Obama's Libya 'Victory' Aid Re-Election Bid?" nationalinterest.org, December 1.

2011g. "The Iraq Syndrome Revisited: U.S. Intervention, From Kosovo to Libya," foreignaffairs.com, March 28.

2011h. "Public Opinion, the Media, and War," in Robert Y. Shapiro and Lawrence R. Jacobs (eds.), *Oxford Handbook on American Public Opinion and the Media.* Oxford and New York: Oxford University Press, 675–89.

2001i "Newt Gingrich, and the EMP Threat," nationalinterest.org, December 13.

2012. "History and Nuclear Rationality," nationalinterest.org, November 19.

2013. "Syria: It Wasn't Isolationism," nationalinterest.org, October 14.

2014a. "Economic Interdependence as a Facilitator of War," The Duck of Minerva, www.whileoliphaunt.com, March 13.

2014b. "Iraq Syndrome Redux: Behind the Tough Talk," foreignaffairs.com, June 18.

2014c. "The Islamic State Will Probably Be Defeated, But It's Not Thanks to President Obama," washingtonpost.com, September 16.

2015. "To Fight ISIS, Leave Assad in Power," TIME.com, November 17.

2016a. "Tracing the Islamic State's 'Allure'," Cato At Liberty blog, cato.org, July 5.

2016b. "Why Obama Won't Tell the Truth about Terrorism," nationalinterest.org, December 12.

2017a. "Hypocrisy on Election Interference," cato.org/blog, January 4.

2017b. "The Cybercoaching of Terrorists: Cause for Alarm?" *CTC Sentinel*, October 29–35.

2018a. "Risk, Reaction, Elite Cues, and Perceived Threat in International Politics." Paper presented at the Annual Convention of the American Political Science Association, Boston, MA, August 30, politicalscience.osu.edu/faculty/jmueller/ APSA2018risk.pdf.

2018b. "What Happened to the Islamic State Foreign Fighters That Had Returned to Europe?" nationalinterest.org, November 5. Available with additional materials at politicalscience.osu.edu/faculty/jmueller/ISISreturneesNot.pdf.

2018c. "The Price for Peace in Syria is Cooperation with Assad," nationalinterest.org, May 17.

2018d. "A Determined Man: World War I, Hitler, and the Unlikely March to World War II," warontherocks.com, November 11, 2018.

ed. 2019a. *Terrorism Since 9/11: The American Cases*. Columbus: Mershon Center, Ohio State University, politicalscience.osu.edu/faculty/jmueller/since .html. This compilation is routinely expanded.

2019b. "The War in Afghanistan: Feeding Optimism on a Diet of Despair," Cato At Liberty blog, December 16.

2020. "Nuclear Anti-Proliferation Policy and the Korea Conundrum: Some Policy Proposals," Washington, DC: Cato Institute, Policy Analysis 893, June 22.

Mueller, John, and Karl Mueller. 2009. "The Rockets' Red Glare: Just What Are 'Weapons of Mass Destruction,' Anyway?" foreignpolicy.com, July 7.

Mueller, John, and Mark G. Stewart. 2011. *Terror, Security, and Money: Balancing the Risks, Costs, and Benefits of Homeland Security*. New York: Oxford University Press.

2014. *Responsible Counterterrorism Policy*. Washington, DC: Cato Institute, Policy Analysis No. 755, September 10.

2016a. *Chasing Ghosts: The Policing of Terrorism*. New York: Oxford University Press.

2016b. "Misoverestimating ISIS: Comparisons with Al-Qaeda," *Perspectives on Terrorism* 10(4) August, 32–41.

2016c. "The Curse of the Black Swan," *Journal of Risk Research* 19(9–10) October–November, 1319–30, politicalscience.osu.edu/faculty/jmueller/ICOSSARjrrfin.pdf.

2016d. "Conflating Terrorism and Insurgency," lawfare.com, February 28.

2016e. "ISIS Isn't an Existential Threat to America," reason.com, May 27.

2017a. "The Islamic State Phenomenon." Paper presented at the National Convention of the International Studies Association, Baltimore, MD, February 25, politicalscience.osu.edu/faculty/jmueller/ISISisa2017.pdf.

2017b. "Misoverestimating Terrorism," in Michael S. Stohl, Richard Burchill, and Scott Englund, eds., *Constructions of Terrorism: An Interdisciplinary Approach to Research and Policy*. Oakland, CA: University of California Press, 21–37.

2018. *Public Opinion and Counterterrorism Policy*. Washington, DC: Cato Institute White Paper, February 20.

2019. "Terrorism and Bathtubs: Comparing and Assessing the Risks," *Terrorism and Political Violence*, published online October 29, 2018.

2020. "Trends in Public Opinion on Terrorism," politicalscience.osu.edu/faculty/jmueller/terrorpolls.pdf. This website is regularly updated.

Mueller, Karl P. ed. 2015. *Precision and Purpose: Airpower in the Libyan Civil War*. Santa Monica, CA: RAND Corporation.

Mutz, Diana C. 2012. "The Great Divide: Campaign Media in the American Mind," *Daedalus*, Fall.

Naím, Moisés, and Francisco Toro. 2018. "Venezuela's Suicide: Lessons from a Failed State," *Foreign Affairs* 97(6) November/December.

National Intelligence Council. 2017. *Global Trends: Paradox of Progress*, Washington, DC, NIC 2017–001, January.

National Research Council of the National Academies. 2010. *Review of the Department of Homeland Security's Approach to Risk Analysis*. Washington, DC: National Academies Press.

Natsios, Andrew S. 2001. *The Great North Korean Famine*, Washington, DC: United States Institute of Peace Press.

Nguyen, Lien-Hang T. 2012. *Hanoi's War: An International History of the War for Peace in Vietnam*. Chapel Hill, NC: University of North Carolina Press.

Nordland, Ron. 2018. "Afghan Pedophiles Get Free Pass From U.S. Military, Report Says," nytimes.com, January 23.

Nordlinger, Eric A. 1995. *Isolationism Reconfigured: American Foreign Policy for a New Century*. Princeton, NJ: Princeton University Press.

Nyhan, Brendan. 2018. "Fake News and Bots May Be Worrisome, but Their Political Power Is Overblown," nytimes.com, February 13.

2019. "Why Fears of Fake News Are Overhyped," gen.medium.com, February 4.

Obama, Barack. 2014. *Remarks by the President at the United States Military Academy Commencement Ceremony*. Washington, DC: Office of the Press Secretary, The White House, May 28.

Oberdorfer, Don. 1992. *The Turn: From the Cold War to a New Era*. New York: Touchstone 1992

2001. *The Two Koreas: A Contemporary History*. New York: Basic Books.

O'Brien, Miles, and Carol Costello. 2005 "Giuliani: 'Have to Be Relentlessly Prepared,'" (interview) *CNN*, July 22.

O'Connell, Mary Ellen. 2003. "Re-Leashing the Dogs of War," *American Journal of International Law* 97(2) April, 446–56.

O'Connor, Mike. 2007. *Crisis, Pursued by Disaster, Followed Closely by Catastrophe: A Memoir of Life on the Run*. New York: Random House.

Odlyzko, Andrew. 2019. "Cybersecurity Is Not Very Important," ubiquity.acm.org, June.

O'Kane, Maggie. 1998. "Saddam Wields Terror – and Feigns Respect," *Guardian*, November 24.

Oliker, Olga. 2018. "Moscow's Nuclear Enigma: What is Russia's Arsenal Really For?" *Foreign Affairs* 97(6) November/December, 52–57.

Osman, Borham. 2018. "The U.S. Needs to Talk to the Taliban in Afghanistan," nytimes.com, March 19.

Overy, R. J. 1982. "Hitler's War and the German Economy: A Reinterpretation," *Economic History Review* 35(2) May 1982.

Paige, Glenn D. 1968. *The Korean Decision, June 24– 30,1950*. New York: Free Press.

Parker, Ned, Isabel Coles, and Raheem Salman, "How Mosul Fell." Special Report, Reuters, 2014. graphics.thomsonreuters.com/14/10/MIDEAST-CRISIS:GHARA WI.pdf.

Payne, James L. 2006. "Election Fraud: Democracy Is An Effect, Not a Cause, of Nonviolence," *American Conservative*, March 13, 11–12.

Pentagon Papers. 1971. Senator Gravel Edition, Boston: Beacon.

Pei, Minxin. 2016. *China's Crony Capitalism: The Dynamics of Regime Decay*. Cambridge, MA: Harvard University Press.

Pérez-Peña, Richard, Jack Healy, and Jennifer Medina. 2016. "Shooting Scares Show a Nation Quick to Fear the Worst," nytimes.com, August 29.

Perle, Richard N. 2000. "Iraq: Saddam Unbound," in Robert Kagan and William Kristol, eds., *Present Dangers: Crisis and Opportunity in American Foreign and Defense Policy*. San Francisco, CA: Encounter Books, 99–110.

2009. "Ambushed on the Potomac," *National Journal*, January/February.

Person, Robert, 2015. "6 Reasons Not to Worry about Russia Invading the Baltics," washingtonpost.com, November 12.

Petraeus, David, and Michael O'Hanlon. 2017. "Getting an Edge in the Long Afghan Struggle." Global Attitudes & Trends: Global Opinion of Obama Slips, International Policies Faulted. Pew Research Center, June 13.

Pew Research Center. 2012. Pew Global Attitudes Project Spring Survey Topline Results July 10.

2013. Public Opinion Runs Against Syrian Airstrikes, Washington, DC, September 3.

Philbrick, Herbert. 1952. *I Led Three Lives: Citizen, "Communist," Counterspy*. New York: Grosset & Dunlap.

Pietrzyk, Mark E. 2002. *International Order and Individual Liberty: Effects of War and Peace on the Development of Governments*. Lanham, MD: University Press of America.

Pillar, Paul R. 2009. "Who's Afraid of a Terrorism Haven?" washingtonpost.com, September 16.

2011a. *Intelligence and U.S. Foreign Policy: Iraq, 9/11, and Misguided Reform*. New York: Columbia University Press.

2011b. "The Terrorist Consequences of the Libyan Intervention," nationalinterest. org, March 23.

Pinker, Steven. 2011. *The Better Angels of Our Nature: Why Violence Has Declined*. New York: Viking.

2015. "Response to the Book Review Symposium: Steven Pinker, *The Better Angels of Our Nature*," *Sociology* 49(4).

2018. *Enlightenment Now: The Case for Reason, Science, Humanism, and Progress.* New York: Viking.

Pipes, Richard. 2002. *Survival Is Not Enough.* New York: Simon and Schuster, 1984.

Podhoretz, Norman. 2002. "In Praise of the Bush Doctrine," *Commentary* 114(2) September 28.

Pollack, Kenneth M. 2003. *The Threatening Storm: The Case for Invading Iraq.* New York: Random House.

Pollard, Robert A , ed., 1985. *Economic Security and the Origins of the Cold War, 1945–1950.* New York: Columbia University Press.

Pollins, Brian. 1989a. "Conflict, Cooperation, and Commerce: The Effect of International Political Interactions on Bilateral Trade Flows," *American Journal of Political Science* 33(3), 737–61.

1989b. "Does Trade Still Follow the Flag?" *American Political Science Review* 83(2), 465–80.

Porter, Bruce D. 1984. *The USSR in Third World Conflicts: Soviet Arms and Diplomacy in Local War 1945–1980.* New York: Cambridge University Press.

Porter, Patrick. 2015. *The Global Village Myth: Distance, War, and the Limits of Power.* Washington, DC: Georgetown University Press.

2018. *A World Imagined: Nostalgia and Liberal Order.* Washington, DC: Cato Institute, Policy Analysis No. 843, June 5.

Posen, Barry R. 2014. *Restraint: A New Foundation for U.S. Grand Strategy.* Ithaca, NY: Cornell University Press.

2015."Contain ISIS," theatlantic.com, November 20.

Paul, T. V. 2000. *Power versus Prudence: Why Nations Forgo Nuclear Weapons,* Montreal: McGill–Queen's University Press.

Preble, Christopher A. 2004. *John F. Kennedy and the Missile Gap.* DeKalb, IL: Northern Illinois Press.

2009. *The Power Problem: How American Military Dominance Makes Us Less Safe, Less Prosperous, and Less Free.* Ithaca, NY: Cornell University Press.

Preble, Christopher A., and John Mueller, eds. 2014. *A Dangerous World? Threat Perception and U.S. National Security.* Washington, DC: Cato Institute.

President's Commission on National Goals. 1960. *Goals for Americans.* New York: Prentice-Hall.

Preston, Joel D., and Frank K. Sobchak, eds. 2019. *The U.S. Army and the Iraq War.* Carlisle, PA: Strategic Studies Institute and U.S. Army War College Press.

Putin, Vladimir V. 2013. "A Plea for Caution From Russia," *New York Times,* September 11.

Quynh, Nguyen Xuan, Andreo Calonzo, Philip J. Heijmans, Hannah Dormido and Adrian Leung. 2019. "China Is Winning the Silent War to Dominate the South China Sea," bloomberg.com, July 10.

Race, Jeffrey. 1976. "Vietnam Intervention: Systematic Distortion in Policy-Making," *Armed Forces and Society,* Spring.

Radosh, Ronald, and Joyce Milton. 1983. *The Rosenberg File: A Search for the Truth.* New York: Holt, Reinhart and Winston.

Rahim, Najim, and Mujib Mashal. 2018. "As Afghan Cease-Fire Ends, Temporary Friends Hug, Then Return to War," *New York Times,* June 17.

Rashid, Ahmed. 2000. *Taliban.* New Haven, CT: Yale University Press.

Rawls, John. 1999. *The Law of Peoples*. Cambridge, MA: Harvard University Press, 81, 93n.

Ray, James Lee. 1989. "The Abolition of Slavery and the End of International War," *International Organization* 43(3) Summer, 405–39.

Ray, James Lee, and Bruce Russett. 1996. "The Future as Arbiter of Theoretical Controversies: Predictions, Explanations and the End of the Cold War," *British Journal of Political Science* 26, October.

Record, Jeffrey. 2002. "Collapsed Countries, Casualty Dread, and the New American Way of War," *Parameters*, Summer.

2007. *The Specter of Munich: Reconsidering the Lessons of Appeasing Hitler*. Washington, DC: Potomac Books.

2011. "Appeasement: A Critical Evaluation Seventy Years On," in Frank McDonagh, ed., *The Origins of the Second World War: An International Perspective*. London: Continuum, 223–37.

Reeves, Richard. 1993. *President Kennedy: Profile of Power*. New York: Simon & Schuster.

Reich, Simon F., and Richard Ned Lebow. 2014. *Good-Bye Hegemony! Power and Influence in the Global System*. Princeton, NJ: Princeton University Press.

Reid, Tim, and Tom Baldwin. 2006. "Nuclear Iran Must Be Stopped at All Costs, Says McCain," *Times* (London), January 26.

Reilly, Sean. 2005. "Poll Shows Alabamians Still Support President," *Mobile Register*, May 22.

Reiss, Mitchell. 1995. *Bridled Ambition: Why Countries Constrain Their Nuclear Capabilities*, Washington, DC: Woodrow Wilson Center Press.

2004. "The Nuclear Tipping Point: Prospects for a World of Many Nuclear Weapons States," in Kurt M. Campbell, Robert J. Einhorn, and Mitchell B. Reiss, eds., *The Nuclear Tipping Point: Why States Reconsider Their Nuclear Choices*. Washington, DC: Brookings Institution Press.

Rhodes, Ben. 2018. *The World as It Is: A Memoir of the Obama White House*. New York: Random House.

Rhodes, Richard. 2007. *Arsenals of Folly: The Making of the Nuclear Arms Race*. New York: Knopf.

Rice, Condoleezza. 2000. "Promoting the National Interest." *Foreign Affairs* 79(1) January/February, 45–62.

Rich, Norman. 1973. *Hitler's War Aims: Ideology, the Nazi State, and the Course of Expansion*. New York: Norton.

Rid, Thomas. 2012. "Think Again: Cyberwar," *Foreign Policy*, March/April.

2013. *Cyber War Will Not Take Place*. New York: Oxford University Press.

Robinson, Linda. 2017. "SOF's Evolving Role: Warfare 'By, With, and Through' Local Forces," theRANDblog, rand.org/blog, May 9.

Rohde, David. 1997. *Endgame: The Betrayal and Fall of Srebrenica, Europe's Worst Massacre Since World War II*. New York: Farrar, Straus and Giroux.

Rosecrance, Richard N. 1964. "International Stability and Nuclear Diffusion," in Richard N. Rosecrance, ed., *The Dispersion of Nuclear Weapons: Strategy and Politics*, New York: Columbia University Press, 293–314.

1986. *The Rise of the Trading State: Conquest and Commerce in the Modern World*. New York: Basic Books.

Ross, Robert S. 2011. "Chinese Nationalism and Its Discontents," *National Interest*, November–December.

Rubin, Barnett R. 2013. *Afghanistan from the Cold War through the War on Terror*. New York: Oxford University Press.

Rubin, Jennifer. 2013. "Rubio and Others Run From Internationalism When It Matters," washingtonpost.com, September 8.

Rush, Myron. 1993. "Fortune and Fate," *National Interest*, Spring 1993, 19–25.

Russett, Bruce M. 1972. *No Clear and Present Danger: A Skeptical View of the United States' Entry into World War II*. New York: Harper and Row.

   2005. "Bushwhacking the Democratic Peace," *International Studies Perspectives* 6(4) November, 395–408.

Russett, Bruce M., and John R. Oneal. 2001. *Triangulating Peace: Democracy, Interdependence, and International Organizations*. New York: Norton.

Sagan, Scott D. 2017. "The Korean Missile Crisis," *Foreign Affairs*, November/December.

   2018. "Armed and Dangerous: When Dictators Get the Bomb," *Foreign Affairs*, 97 (6), November/December.

Sagan, Scott D., and Kenneth N. Waltz. 2002. *The Spread of Nuclear Weapons: A Debate Renewed*, Second Edition. New York: Norton.

Sageman, Marc. 2004. *Understanding Terror Networks*. Philadelphia: University of Pennsylvania Press.

   2008. *Leaderless Jihad*. Philadelphia: University of Pennsylvania Press.

   2017a. *Misunderstanding Terrorism*. Philadelphia: University of Pennsylvania Press.

   2017b. *Turning to Political Violence: The Emergence of Terrorism*. Philadelphia, PA: University of Pennsylvania Press.

Sakwa, Richard. 2015. *Frontline Ukraine: Crisis in the Borderlands*. London: Tauris.

Samuel, Sigal. 2018. "China Is Treating Islam Like a Mental Illness: The Country is Putting Muslims in Internment Camps – And Causing Real Psychological Damage in the Process," theatlantic.com, August 28.

Sanger, David E. 2012. *Confront and Conceal: Obama's Secret Wars and Surprising Use of American Power*. New York: Crown.

   2018. *The Perfect Weapon: War, Sabotage, and Fear in the Cyber Age*. New York: Crown.

Savage, Charlie. 2013. "Manning is Acquitted of Aiding the Enemy," *New York Times*, July 30.

Savranskaya, Svetlana V. 2005. "New Sources on the Role of Soviet Submarines in the Cuban Missile Crisis," *Journal of Strategic Studies* 28(2) April, 233–59.

Scobell, Andrew, Ely Ratner, and Michael Beckley. 2014. "China's Strategy Toward South and Central Asia: An Empty Fortress." Santa Monica: RAND Corporation Research Report.

Seitz, Russell. 2004. "Weaker Than We Think," *American Conservative*, December 6.

Schandler, Herbert Y. 1977. *The Unmaking of a President: Lyndon Johnson and Vietnam*. Princeton, NJ: Princeton University Press.

Schilling, Warner R. 1965. "Surprise Attack, Death, and War," *Journal of Conflict Resolution* 9(3) September.

Schneier, Bruce. 2015a. "Why Are We Spending $7 Billion on TSA?" cnn.com, June 5.

   2015b. "Obama Says Terrorism Is Not an Existential Threat," schneier.com, February 3.

   2018. *Click Here to Kill Everybody: Security and Survival in a Hyper-connected World*. New York: Norton.

Schroeder, Paul W. 1985. "Does Murphy's Law Apply to History?" *Wilson Quarterly,* New Year's.

2004. *Systems, Stability, and Statecraft.* New York: Palgrave Macmillan.

Scheuer, Michael. 2004. *Imperial Hubris: Why the West Is Losing the War on Terror.* Dulles, VA: Brassey's.

2006. "Courting Catastrophe: America Five Years After 9/11," *National Interest,* September/October.

Schweller, Randall L. 2001. "The Problem of International Order Revisited: A Review Essay," *International Security* 26(1) Summer.

Sechser, Todd S., and Matthew Fuhrmann. 2017. *Nuclear Weapons and Coercive Diplomacy.* Cambridge: Cambridge University Press.

Shane, Scott. 2011. "Pornography Is Found in Bin Laden Compound Files, U.S. Officials Say," *New York Times,* May 13.

2018. "Russia Isn't the Only One Meddling in Elections. We Do It, Too," nytimes. com, Feburary 17.

Shanker, Thom. 2004. "Regime Thought War Unlikely Iraqis Tell U.S." *New York Times,* February 12.

Shapiro, Jacob B. 2013. *The Terrorist's Dilemma: Managing Violent Covert Organizations.* Princeton, NJ: Princeton University Press.

Sheehan, James J. 2008. *Where Have All the Soldiers Gone? The Transformation of Modern Europe.* Boston: Houghton Mifflin.

Sheehan, Neil. 1964. "Much Is At Stake in Southeast Asian Struggle," *New York Times,* August 16, E4.

Shevchenko, Arkady N. 1985. *Breaking with Moscow.* New York: Knopf.

Shifrinson, Joshua R. Itzkowitz. 2016. "Deal or No Deal? The End of the Cold War and the U.S. Offer to Limit NATO Expansion," *International Security* 40(4) Spring, 7–44.

Shirk, Susan L. 2007. *China: Fragile Superpower.* New York: Oxford University Press.

Shlapak, David A. and Michael Johnson. 2016. *Reinforcing Deterrence on NATO's Eastern Flank: Wargaming the Defense of the Baltics.* Santa Monica, CA: RAND Corporation.

Shulman, Marshall D. 1963. *Stalin's Foreign Policy Reappraised.* New York: Atheneum.

Shultz, George P. 1993. *Turmoil and Triumph: My Years as Secretary of State.* New York: Scribner's.

Silber, Laura, and Allan Little. 1997. *Yugoslavia: Death of a Nation.* New York: Penguin.

Simon, Jeffry D. 2001. *The Terrorist Trap: America's Experience with Terrorism,* 2nd ed. Bloomington: Indiana University Press.

Simpson, John. 1991. *From the House of War: John Simpson in the Gulf.* London: Arrow.

Sinclair, Andrew. 1962. *Prohibition: The Era of Excess.* Boston: Little, Brown.

Small, Melvin, and J. David Singer. 1982. *Resort to Arms: International Civil Wars, 1816–1980.* Beverly Hills, CA: Sage.

Smeltz, Dina. 2015. *United in Goals, Divided in Means.* Chicago: Chicago Council on Global Affairs.

Smeltz, Dina, and Ivo Daalder. 2014. *Foreign Policy in the Age of Retrenchment: Results of the 2014 Chicago Council Survey of American Public Opinion and U.S. Foreign Policy.* Chicago: Chicago Council on Global Affairs.

Smeltz, Dina, Ivo Daalder, Karl Friedhoff, Craig Kafura, Lili Woytowicz. 2018. *America Engaged: American Foreign Policy and US Foreign Policy*. Chicago: Chicago Council on Global Affairs.

Smeltz, Dina, and Craig Kafura. 2018. *Record Number of Americans Endorse Benefits of Trade*. Chicago: Chicago Council on Global Affairs, August.

Smith, Graeme. 2015. *The Dogs Are Eating Them Now*. Berkeley, CA: Counterpoint.

Smith, Patrick. 2007. "The Airport Security Follies," nytimes.com, December 28.

Smith, Meagan, and Sean M. Zeigler. 2017. "Terrorism Before and After 9/11 – A More Dangerous World?" *Research and Politics*, October–December, 1–8.

Snyder, Jack. 1987/88. "The Gorbachev Revolution: A Waning of Soviet Expansionism?" *International Security* 12(3) Winter, 93–131.

Sobel, Richard. 1998. "The Polls – Trends: United States Intervention in Bosnia," *Public Opinion Quarterly* 62(2) Summer.

Sokolski, Henry D. 2014. *Underestimated: Our Not So Peaceful Nuclear Future*, Washington, DC: Nonproliferation Policy Education Center.

Sorley, Lewis. 1999. *A Better War: The Unexamined Victories and Final Tragedy of America's Last Years in Vietnam*. New York: Harcourt Brace.

Spagat, Michael. 2010. "Truth and Death in Iraq Under Sanctions," *Significance* 7(3), September, 116–20.

Spector, Ronald H. 1993. *After Tet: The Bloodiest Year in Vietnam*. New York: Free Press.

Squires, James Duane. 1935. *British Propaganda at Home and in the United States From 1914 to 1917*. Cambridge, MA: Harvard University Press.

Stein, Sam. 2008. "Rove: We Wouldn't Have Invaded Iraq If We Knew the Truth about WMDs," Huffington Post, December 2.

Steinert, Marlis G. 1977. *Hitler's War and the Germans: Public Mood and Attitude during the Second World War*. Athens, OH: Ohio University Press.

Stephan, Alexander. 2000. *Communazis: FBI Surveillance of German Emigré Writers*. New Haven, CT: Yale University Press.

Stephens, Bret. 2014. *America in Retreat: The New Isolationism and the Coming Global Disorder*. New York: Sentinel.

Stewart, Mark G. 2014. "Climate Change and National Security: Balancing the Costs and Benefits," in Christopher A. Preble and John Mueller, eds., *A Dangerous World? Threat Perception and U.S. National Security*. Washington, DC: Cato Institute, 137–54.

Stewart, Mark G., and John Mueller. 2018. *Are We Safe Enough? Measuring and Assessing Aviation Security*. Amsterdam: Elsevier.

Stohl, Michael. 1988. "Demystifying Terrorism: The Myths and Realities of Contemporary Political Terrorism," in Michael Stoll, ed., *The Politics of Terrorism*. New York and Basel: Marcel Dekker, 1–28.

2007. "Cyber Terrorism: A Clear and Present Danger, The Sum of All Fears, Breaking Point or Patriot Games?" *Crime, Law, and Social Change*, December.

2012. "State Terror: The Theoretical and Practical Utilities and Implications of a Contested Concept," in Richard Jackson and Samuel Justin Sinclair, eds., *Contemporary Debates on Terrorism*. London and New York: Routledge, 43–50.

Straus, Scott. 2006. *The Order of Genocide: Race, Power, and War in Rwanda*. Ithaca, NY: Cornell University Press.

2012. "Wars Do End! Changing Patterns of Political Violence in Sub-Saharan Africa," *African Affairs* 111(443) April, 179–201.

Stromberg, Roland N. 1982. *Redemption by War: The Intellectuals and 1914*. Lawrence, KS: Regents Press of Kansas.

Stueck, William. 2002. *Rethinking the Korean War: A New Diplomatic and Strategic History*. Princeton, NJ: Princeton University Press.

Sullivan, Jake. 2019a. "What Donald Trump and Dick Cheney Got Wrong About America," *Atlantic*, January/February.

2019b. "More, Less, or Different? Where U.S. Foreign Policy Should – and Shouldn't – Go From Here," *Foreign Affairs*, January/February.

Summers, Lawrence H. 1992. "The Next Chapter," *International Economic Insights* May/June.

Suri, Jeremi. 2002. "Explaining the End of the Cold War: A New Historical Consensus?" *Journal of Cold War Studies* 4, Fall, 60–92.

Susman, Tina. 2015. "Islamic State Presence in the U.S. is 'The New Normal,' FBI director says," latimes.com, November 19.

Takeyh, Ray. 2001. "The Rogue Who Came in From the Cold," *Foreign Affairs*, May/June, 62–72.

Talbott, Strobe. 1990. "Remaking the Red Menace: Gorbachev Is Helping the West by Showing that the Soviet Threat Isn't What It Used to Be – and, What's More, That It Never Was," *Time*, January 1, 36–38.

Taleb, Nicholas N. 2010. *The Black Swan: The Impact the Highly Improbable*, 2nd ed. New York: Random House.

Tamimi, Aymenn al-. 2016. "A Caliphate under Strain: The Documentary Evidence," *CTC Sentinel*, April.

Tannenhaus, Sam. 2003. "Interview with Paul Wolfowitz," *Vanity Fair*, May 9, 2003.

Taub, Ben. 2018. "Shallow Graves: ISIS Has Been Destroyed, but Will Iraq's Campaign of Revenge Help Bring About its Resurgence?" *New Yorker*, December 24 and 31, 54–71.

Taubman, William. 1982. *Stalin's American Policy*. New York: Norton.

2003. *Khrushchev: The Man and His Era*. New York: Norton.

Tellis, Ashley J., and Jeff Eggers, 2017. *U.S. Policy in Afghanistan: Changing Strategies, Preserving Gains*. Washington, DC: Carnegie Endowment for International Peace.

Tenet, George. 2007. *At the Center of the Storm: My Years at the CIA*. New York: HarperCollins.

Tertrais, Bruno. 2017. "'On The Brink' – Really? Revisiting Nuclear Close Calls Since 1945," *Washington Quarterly* 40(2) Summer, 51–66.

Tessler, Mark, Michael Robbins, and Amaney Jamal. 2016. "What Do Ordinary Citizens in the Arab World Really Think About the Islamic State?" washingtonpost.com, July 27.

Thayer, Bradley A. 2013. "Humans, Not Angels: Reasons to Doubt the Decline of War Thesis," *International Studies Review* 15, 405–11.

Thomas, Alice. 2001. "Exercise Caution, Experts Say: Desire for Revenge Could Cause Even More Problems," *Columbus Dispatch*, September 16, 5A; available at politicalscience.osu.edu/faculty/jmueller/COLDISP.pdf.

Thomas, Evan. 2012. *Ike's Bluff: President Eisenhower's Secret Battle to Save the World*. New York: Little, Brown.

Thompson, John A. 1992. "The Exaggeration of American Vulnerability: The Anatomy of a Tradition," *Diplomatic History* 16(1) Winter.

Thompson, Nicholas. 2009. *The Hawk and the Dove: Paul Nitze, George Kennan, and the History of the Cold War*. New York: Henry Holt.

Tilly, Charles. 1990. *Coercion, Capital, and European States, AD 990–1990*. Cambridge, MA: Blackwell.

Tolstoy, Leo. 1996 [1862–69]. *War and Peace*. New York: Norton.

Toynbee, Arnold J. 1969. *Experiences*. New York: Oxford University Press.

Trachtenberg, Marc. 1991. *History and Strategy*. Princeton, NJ: Princeton University Press.

2012. *The Cold War and After: History, Theory, and the Logic of International Politics*. Princeton, NJ: Princeton University Press.

2017. "A Double Standard?" H-Diplo, ISSF Policy Series America and the World – 2017 and Beyond, July 19, issforum.org/roundtables/policy/1-5at-trachtenberg.

Treisman, Daniel. 2016. "Why Putin Took Crimea: The Gambler in the Kremlin," *Foreign Affairs*, May/July.

Trenin, Dmitri. 2018. "Avoiding U.S.-Russia Military Escalation During the Hybrid War," Carnegie Endowment for International Peace, January.

Truman, Harry S. 1947. The Truman Doctrine, March 29.

1956. *Years of Trial and Hope*. Garden City: Doubleday.

Tucker, Robert W., and David C. Hendrickson. 1992. *The Imperial Temptation: The New World Order and America's Purpose*. New York: Council on Foreign Relations Press.

Ulam, Adam S. 1968. *Expansion and Coexistence*. New York: Praeger, 525.

2007. *Expansion and Coexistence*. New York: Praeger 1968, 525.

Ullman, Harlan. 2017. *Anatomy of Failure: Why America Loses Every War It Starts*. Annapolis, MD: Naval Institute Press.

Urquhart, Brian. 1993. "For a UN Volunteer Military Force," *New York Review of Books*, June 10, 3–4.

U.S. v. Moussaoui. nd. Substitution for the Testimony of Khalid Sheikh Mohammed, nd. Defendant's exhibit 941, en.wikisource.org/wiki/Substitution_for_the_Testimony_o f_Khalid_Sheikh_Mohammed.

Vagts, Alfred. 1959. *A History of Militarism*. New York: Norton.

Valentino, Benjamin. 2003. *Final Solutions: Mass Killing and Genocide in the 20th Century*. Ithaca, NY: Cornell University Press.

Van Linschoten, Alex Strick, and Felix Kuehn. 2012. *An Enemy We Created: The Myth of the Taliban-Al Qaeda Merger in Afghanistan*. New York: Oxford University Press.

Vasquez, John A. 1993. *The War Puzzle*. Cambridge: Cambridge University Press.

1998. *The Power of Power Politics*. Cambridge: Cambridge University Press.

von Clausewitz, Carl. 1976. *On War*. Princeton, NJ: Princeton University Press.

von Suttner, Baroness Bertha. 1906. *Lay Down Your Arms*, Second edition New York: Longmans, Green, 1906.

Walt, Stephen M. 1987. *The Origins of Alliances*. Ithaca, NY: Cornell University Press.

2000. "Containing Rogues and Renegades: Coalition Strategies and Counterproliferation," in Victor A. Utgoff, ed., *The Coming Crisis: Nuclear Proliferation, U.S. Interests, and World Order*. Cambridge, MA: MIT Press, 191–226.

2011a. "Is America Addicted to War? The Top 5 Reasons We Keep Getting into Foolish Fights," foreignpolicy.com, April 4.

2011b. "Explaining Obama's Asia Policy," foreignpolicy.com, November 18.

2013. "What to Read on U.S. Grand Strategy," foreignpolicy.com, January 2.

2018a. *The Hell of Good Intentions: America's Foreign Policy Elite and the Decline of U.S. Primacy.* New York: Farrar, Straus and Giroux.

2018b. "The Islamic Republic of Hysteria: The Trump Administration's Middle East Strategy Revolves Around a Threat that Doesn't Exist," foreignpolicy.com, January 18.

2019. "Be Afraid of the World, Be Very Afraid," foreignpolicy.com, May 20.

2020. "The Death of American Competence," foreignpolicy.com, March 23.

Waltz, Kenneth N. 1959. *Man, the State and War.* New York: Columbia University Press.

1979. *Theory of International Politics.* Reading, MA: Addison-Wesley.

1988. "The Origins of War in Neorealist Theory," *Journal of Interdisciplinary History* 18(4) Spring, 615–28.

2012a. "Waltz Responds," *Foreign Affairs* 91(5) September/October 162.

2012b. "Why Iran Should Get the Bomb: Nuclear Balancing Would Mean More Stability," *Foreign Affairs*, 91(4) July/August.

Warrick, Joby. 2008. "U.S. Cites Big Gains Against Al-Qaeda," washingtonpost.com, May 30.

2015. *Black Flags: The Rise of ISIS.* New York: Doubleday.

Watts, Clint. 2015. "Let Them Rot: The Challenges and Opportunities of Containing Rather Than Countering the Islamic State," *Perspectives on Terrorism* 9(4), 156–64.

Wedgwood, C. V. 1938. *The Thirty Years War.* London: Jonathan Cape.

Weil, Martin. 1991. "Iraqis Surrender to Reporter: Loudoun County Woman Encounters Remnants of a Company," *Washington Post*, February 27, A32.

Weinberg, Gerhard L. 1980. *The Foreign Policy of Hitler's Germany: Starting World War II, 1937–1939.* Chicago: University of Chicago Press.

Weimann, Gabriel. 2006. *Terror on the Internet: The New Arena, the New Challenges.* Washington, DC: United States Institute of Peace.

Weinstein, Allen. 1978. *Perjury: The Hiss-Chambers Case.* New York: Knopf.

Weiss, Leonard. 2017. "Safeguards and the NPT: When Our Current Problems Began," in Henry D. Sokolski, ed., *Nuclear Rules, Not Just Rights: The NPT Reexamined.* Washington, DC: Nonproliferation Policy Education Center.

Welch, David A., and James G. Blight. 1987/88. "The Eleventh Hour of the Cuban Missile Crisis: An Introduction to the ExComm Transcripts," *International Security* 12(3) Winter, 5–29.

Werth, Alexander. 1964. *Russia at War, 1941–1945.* New York: Dutton.

West, Bing. 2018. "Afghanistan Options: Leave, Increase, Stand Pat, or Cut Back?" Strategika, hoover.org, February 26.

Western, Jon. 2005. *Selling Intervention and War: The Presidency, the Media, and the American Public.* Baltimore: Johns Hopkins University Press.

Westmoreland, William. 1976. *A Soldier Reports.* Garden City, NY: Doubleday.

Whitlock, Craig. 2010. "Facing Afghan Mistrust, al-Qaeda Fighters Take Limited Role in Insurgency," *Washington Post*, August 23.

Will, George R. 1994. "The Tenth Problem," *Newsweek*, June 27, 62.

Williams, Brian Glyn . 2008. "Return of the Arabs: Al-Qa'ida's Current Military Role in the Afghan Insurgency," *CTC Sentinel* 1(3), 22–25.

Wilson, George C. 2003. "Why Didn't Saddam Defend His Country?" *National Journal*, April 19.

Wilson, Ward. 2008. "The Myth of Nuclear Deterrence," *Nonproliferation Review* 15(3) November, 421–39.

Winter, Eyal. 2015. "How Not to Treat Terror Anxiety," *Los Angeles Times*, December 23, A13.

Winter, Tom. 2016. "100 ISIS Fighters May be Plotting in Belgium: Official," nbcnews.com, June 2.

Wohlforth,William C. ed., 1996. *Witnesses to the End of the Cold War*. Baltimore and London: Johns Hopkins University Press.

Wolf, Charles, Jr., K. C. Yeh, Edmund Brunner, Jr., Aaron Gurwitz, and Marilee Lawrence. 1983. *The Costs of Soviet Empire*. Santa Monica, CA: Rand Corporation.

Wood, Graeme. 2015. "ISIL: Who's Calling the Shots?" politico.com, November 14.

Woodward, Bob. 1991. *The Commanders*. New York: Simon & Schuster.

    2002. *Bush at War*. New York: Simon & Schuster, 253.

    2004. *Plan of Attack*. New York: Simon & Schuster, 428.

    2008. "Why Did Violence Plummet? It Wasn't Just the Surge," *Washington Post*, September 8.

    2010. *Obama's Wars*. New York: Simon & Schuster.

Woolsey, R. James, Jr. 1993. Testimony before the Senate Intelligence Committee, February 2.

Wright, Lawrence. 2006. *The Looming Tower: Al-Qaeda and the Road to 9/11*. New York: Knopf. Page references are to the hard cover edition.

Yardeni, Edward. 2000. "The Economic Consequences of the Peace," in *Peace, Prosperity, and Politics*, ed. John Mueller. New York: Westview.

Yergin, Daniel, and Joseph Stanislaw. 1998. *Commanding Heights: The Battle between the Government and the Marketplace that is Remaking the Modern World*. New York: Simon & Schuster, 1998.

York, Chris. 2015. "Islamic State Terrorism Is Serious But We've Faced Even Deadlier Threats In The Past," huffingtonpost.co.uk, November 29.

Zacher, Mark. 2001. "The Territorial Integrity Norm: International Boundaries and the Use of Force," *International Organization* 55(2) Spring, 215–50.

Zakaria, Fareed. 2006. "For Iran, A Policy of Patience," washingtonpost.com, September 25.

    2019. "The New China Scare: Why America Shouldn't Panic About Its Latest Challenger," foreignaffairs.com, December 6.

Zalkind, Susan. 2015. "How ISIS's 'Attack America' Plan Is Working," dailybeast.com, June 22.

Zelikow, Philip, and Condoleezza Rice, 1995. *Germany Unified and Europe Transformed*. Cambridge, MA: Harvard University Press.

Zenko, Micah. 2013. "Most. Dangerous. World. Ever. The Ridiculous Hyperbole About Government Budget Cuts," foreignpolicy.com, February 26.

2014a. "The Myth of the Indispensable Nation: The World Doesn't Need the United States Nearly as Much as We Like to Think it Does," foreignpolicy.com, November 6.

2014b. "Exaggeration Nation," foreignpolicy.com, November 12.

2018. "The Problem Isn't Fake News From Russia. It's Us. Propaganda Has Long Affected Elections Around the World Because Publics Have an Appetite For It," foreignpolicy.com, October 3.

Zhou, Weihuan. 2019. *China's Implementation of the Rulings of the World Trade Organization*. New York and London: Hart Publishing.

Zubok, Vladislav, and Constantine Pleshakov. 1996. *Inside the Kremlin's Cold War: From Stalin to Khrushchev*. Cambridge, MA: Harvard University Press.

Zucchino, David. 2003. "Iraq's Swift Defeat Blamed on Leaders," *Los Angeles Times*, August 11.

Index